WOMEN ENTREPRENEURSHIP IN INDIA

WOMEN ENTREPRENEURSHIP IN INDIA

ANIL KUMAR
Reader, Haryana School of Business,
Guru Jambheshwar University of Science and Technology, Hisar

Foreword by

Dr. H.L. VERMA
Professor of Management,
Former Pro Vice-Chancellor
Guru Jambheshwar University of Science and Technology, Hisar

REGAL PUBLICATIONS
New Delhi - 110 027

WOMEN ENTREPRENEURSHIP IN INDIA

ISBN 81-89915-83-5

Typeset by
SHRI GANESH COMPOSERS
R-3/120, Balaji Chowk, Mohan Garden, New Delhi - 110 046

Printed in India at
NEW ELEGANT PRINTERS
A-49/1, Mayapuri, Phase-I, New Delhi - 110 064

Published by
REGAL PUBLICATIONS
F-159, Rajouri Garden, New Delhi - 110 027 • Phone : 45546396
E-mail : regalbookspub@yahoo.com

Contents

Foreword

It is a matter of great satisfaction to write foreword for a book on Women Entrepreneurship in India. The book is outcome of research study conducted by the author on the subject. Women entrepreneurship is an important area of academic interest having far reaching implications on the socio-economic development of the country. The current economic scene demands for an effective utilization of human and other resources. The process of economic reforms that was initiated in 1991 made an enhanced role of private sector in economic progress. Employment opportunities in public sector are on the decline. Entrepreneurship is the only effective way to deal with the growing problem of unemployment in the country. That is why the Government has initiated various schemes for entrepreneurship development. Women population which constitutes nearly half of the total population has relatively low participation in entrepreneurial activities, whereas in developed nations it is not so. The low representation of women in business calls for some concerted efforts to promote their role so that they can also contribute in the growth process of the nation. The experience of developed nations have demonstrated that when an economy moves from command to a market driven situation, the gender inequalities are generally abridged over a period of time. This book analyses all these issues in the context of women entrepreneurship in India.

The book has been divided into nine chapters which include introduction, socio-economic profile of women entrepreneurs, entrepreneurial process, financial structure of enterprises run by women entrepreneurs, training issues among women entrepreneurs, obstacle faced by women in business, perception of women entrepreneurs towards various entrepreneurship related issues, role of different promotional agencies in entrepreneurship development and conclusions.

The book provides an in-depth analysis of the various issues indicated above. It gives an insight into the process of women entrepreneurship. The analysis is based on the primary data collected and some sophisticated but relevant statistical techniques have been used for this purpose. The findings of the study have great informational value for those who have interest in the subject. The students, researchers and professionals would find material quite useful and relevant to satisfy their divergent academic requirements on the subject. The author has nicely brought out the fact that for the growth of small scale sector women entrepreneurship is highly important in Indian context. I endorse the views of the author on the subject. Women entrepreneurship has a great role to play in the economic development of the country.

Dr. H.L. VERMA
Professor of Management
Former Pro Vice-Chancellor

Preface

The entrepreneurship development and economic development are closely interrelated subjects. Entrepreneurship development opens large number of opportunities to the people in the era of globalization, liberalization and privatization of the economy. The issue of concern for the developing economies these days is how to utilize potential of human and other resources of the economy in an effective manner. Entrepreneurship development also ameliorate the volley of socio-economic problems encountered by the society. At global level majority of small enterprises are managed by women. In our economy, women constitutes almost half of total population, but their participation in business is found to be very low. To tap the human resource potential of female, the government has initiated various schemes to inculcate the spirit of entrepreneurship among women. The study given in this book highlights all these in the context of current socio-economic conditions of the country. The study has been divided into nine chapters. The first chapter gives conceptual framework of subject, review of relevant literature and research methodology used in the conduct of the study. The second chapter deals with socio-economic profile of women entrepreneurs. The third chapter gives an extensive review of entrepreneurial process among women entrepreneurs. The fourth and fifth chapters highlight the financial structure and training needs of enterprises managed by women entrepreneurs. The sixth chapter discusses the practical problems encountered by women entrepreneurs while managing their business. Chapter seven discusses the perception of women entrepreneurs towards various entrepreneurship related issues. Eighth chapter throws light on the role of various supporting agencies in the growth of entrepreneurship among women. The last chapter recapitulates some of the important findings based on the analysis of the study. Simple percentages, chi-square test and factor analytical model have been used to analyze the various aspects related to women entrepreneurs. Socio-economic variables have been taken into consideration while arriving at meaningful inferences.

The study brings out very interesting results which may prove an eye-opener to the planners and policy makers in the field of small enterprises development. It is hoped that book would be of great use to the researchers, professionals, corporate consultants and NGOs interested in the field of entrepreneurship development in general and women in particular.

I am thankful to all those who helped me in completion of this project. The author is also thankful to UGC for providing financial assistance for this project. I am also grateful to Dr. H.L. Verma, Professor, Haryana School of Business, Guru Jambheshwar University of Science and Technology, Hisar for writing the foreword of this book.

Hisar   ANIL KUMAR

Introduction

Entrepreneurship is considered to be an important input for rapid economic development. In developing economies it could play an effective role in coping with various socio-economic problems. Many developing regions do not suffer from resource constrains, rather the required skill is missing to convert the physical resources into the useful enterprises. The economic development of advanced countries of the world, to a large extent, has been attributed to growth of entrepreneurship in small and medium enterprises. In advanced countries, majority of small enterprises have been managed by women. Women-owned firms represented nearly 40 per cent of all firms in the United States and employed approximately 27.5 million people (NFWBO, 2001). Further, women are starting business at faster rate than their male counterparts. It has been seen that women out number men by at least two times, particularly when it comes to starting business in China. There are over five million women entrepreneurs constituting one-fourth of all entrepreneurs in China (Workshop Proceedings, 2000). In Japan too a similar trend has been noticed. The percentage of women entrepreneurs increased from 2.4 per cent in 1980 to 5.2 per cent in 1995 (Shigeko, 2000).

Considering the experience of western economies, the government of India followed the policy for development of entrepreneurship among human resources of the country in general and women in particular during post-liberalisation regime. Government has set-up large number of institutions to provide financial and other supportive measures for the growth of entrepreneurship among women. Post-reform period has seen the increase in participation of even NGOs for the growth of entrepreneurship among human resources of the country.

Under new economic regime the women participation in business has shown considerable improvement. At present in India 9.5 per cent women entrepreneurs are engaged in small business (GOI, 2001). In this chapter, concept of entrepreneur, review of literature, need for study, objective and methodology of the study have been discussed.

DEFINING ENTREPRENEUR

The word 'entrepreneur' is derived from French word 'entrepreneur'. In earlier 16th century it was applied to those who were engaged in military expeditions. In 17th century the word 'entrepreneur' was used for civil engineering activities such as construction and fortification. It was applied to business for the first time in 18th century, to designate a dealer who buys and sells goods at uncertain prices.

Entrepreneurship started catching up in 1980s just as professionalism in management caught up during 1970s. However, confusion still prevails as to what exactly we mean by the term 'entrepreneur'. An attempt therefore, has been made here to define entrepreneur.

There is generally no accepted definition or model of what the entrepreneur is or does. Much of the literature on entrepreneur is fragmented and highly controversial. In the past decade, a number of trends have emerged which distinguish between individual entrepreneurship and corporate entrepreneurship and entrepreneurs and small business owners. The literature abounds with criteria ranging from creativity, innovation, risk taking, high need achievement, etc. to personal traits such as appearance and life style. Models of the entrepreneurial leaders are almost as plentiful as the number of authors who write about them.

The French economist Cantillon, the first to introduce the term entrepreneur, defined him as an agent who purchased the means of production for combination into marketable products. Furthermore, at the moment of the factor purchases, the entrepreneur was unaware of the eventual price, which he would receive for his product.

Entrepreneurs perform a vital function in economic development. They have been referred to as the human agents needed to 'mobilise capital, to explore natural resources, to explore natural resources, to create markets and to carry on trade'. It will be said that the entrepreneurial input spells the difference between prosperity and poverty among nations. ·

According to Say, the entrepreneur's function is to combine the productive factors, to bring them together. Carrying out of new combination of productive factors is called 'enterprise' which in fact is fundamental phenomenon of economic development. The individual whose function is to carry them out is what we call 'entrepreneur'.

Many economic theories emphasize the significant role played by individual entrepreneurs as they combine talents, abilities and drive to transform resources into profitable undertakings. Schumpeter, the first major writer to highlight the human agent in the process of economic development, believed that the economy was propelled by the activities of persons "who wanted to promote new goods and new methods of production, or to exploit new sources of materials or new market" not merely for profit but also for the purpose of creating.

Schumpeter played with the word innovation and emphasized innovation as the function of an entrepreneur. Schumpcter's entrepreneur is highly specialized concern. The profitable opportunities and exploits them. The entrepreneur's motivation for profit is based not merely on his desire to raise consumption standard but also on such non-hedomistic goals as the desire to find a private dynasty—the will to conquer in the competitive battle and the job of creating, i.e. he tries to maximize his profits by innovations. His unique characteristic is that he gets satisfaction from using his capabilities in attacking problem.

The entire change and development of the civilization to a large extent is the result of trade, commerce and industrialization. In this development the human resource in general and entrepreneur in particular plays a pivotal role. McClelland has rightly hypothesized that the need for achievement in individuals, i.e. the entrepreneurial potential is the psychological factor, which engenders economic growth and decline. The sense of high need achievement and motivation introduced by entrepreneurs bring about the required necessities in a class of society which transform the perception of the economic thinking, which is necessary to bring about the economic development. The importance of entrepreneurs to progress cannot be more succinctly expressed than Zinkin's statement, "No entrepreneur, no development."

According to Kilby (1971), the entrepreneur performs following four major tasks:

    (i) Exchange relationship,
    (ii) Practical administration,
    (iii) Management control, and
    (iv) Technology

These four tasks consists of:

    (i) Exchange relationship
        (a) Perceiving opportunities in market.
        (b) Gaining command over scarce resources.
        (c) Purchasing inputs.
        (d) Marketing of products and responding to competition.
    (ii) Practical administration
        (a) Dealing with public bureaucracy.
        (b) Management of human relations within the venture.
        (c) Management of customer and supplier relations.
    (iii) Management control
        (a) Financial Management
        (b) Production Management
    (iv) Technology
        (a) Acquiring and overseeing assembling of the factory.
        (b) Industrial engineering.
        (c) Upgrading process and product quality.
        (d) Introduction of new production techniques and products.

All above fields of activities involve entrepreneur in decision-making under conditions of uncertainty. Thus, entrepreneur within Kilby's proposed framework, would have: (i) a determination of the types and degrees of uncertainty confronting the performance of a particular operation, and (ii) the ability to make the appropriate decisions necessary for the goal attainment. By nature an entrepreneur is neither a technician nor a financier, but he is considered an 'innovator'. Entrepreneurship is neither a profession nor a permanent occupation and, there, it cannot formulate a social class like capitalists or wage earners.

According to Harbison, an entrepreneur is not an 'innovator' but an 'organization builder' or one who has the skill to build an organization and who must be able to harness the new ideas of different innovators to the best of the organization.

During early twentieth century, Dewing equated entrepreneur with business promoter and viewed the promoter as one who transformed ideas into a profitable business. In enumerating the characteristics of a successful entrepreneur, Dewing wrote of the qualities of imagination, initiative, judgement and restraint.

ILO (1982) describes that 'entrepreneurs are people who have the ability to see and evaluate business opportunities; to gather the necessary resources to take advantage of them; and to initiate appropriate action to ensure success'.

Casson (1982) in his work, having considered both functional definition and an indicative definition describes entrepreneurs as 'someone who specializes in taking judgemental decisions about the co-ordination of scarce resources'.

In Denhof's analysis an entrepreneur "is primarily concerned with changes in the formula of production over which he has full control. . . . He devotes correspondingly little time to the carrying out of a specific formula". Danhof divides the functions of the entrepreneur into three major roles: obtaining relevant information, evaluating the information with regard to profit, and setting the operation in motion. Major emphasis in Danhof's definition is decision-making, or judgement under alternative choices.

Cunningham and Lischerson (1991) in their recent work have described six possible schools of thought on entrepreneurship. The first school of thought, i.e. 'Great Person School' says that an entrepreneur is born with an intuitive ability—a sixth sense and this sense helps him in start up stage. The second school of thought, i.e. 'Psychological Characteristics School' explains that entrepreneurs have unique values attitudes, and needs which drive them and help them especially in start-up stage. The third school, i.e. 'Classic School of Thought' says that central characteristic helps the entrepreneur much in innovation. This characteristic helps the entrepreneur much in start-up and early growth. 'Management School' is the fourth school of thought and it says entrepreneurs.are organizers of economic venture and they organize, own, manage and assume its risk. Such functional orientation helps them in early growth and maturity. The fifth school of thought is the 'Leadership School'. According to this school entrepreneurs are leaders of people and they have the ability to adopt their style to the needs of people. Such leadership personality suits them most during early growth and maturity situations. 'Intrapreneurship School' is the sixth school of thought. Intrapreneurship is the act of developing independent units, to create, market and expand services within the organization. An entrepreneur needs intrapreneurship during the situation of maturity and change.

Whatever is the definition, across the world entrepreneurs have been considered instrumental in initiating and sustaining socio-economic development. There are evidences to believe that countries, which have proportionately higher percentage of entrepreneurs in their population, have developed much faster as compared to countries, which have lesser percentage of them in the society. They discover new sources of supply of materials and markets and establish new and more effective forms of organizations. Entrepreneurs perceive new opportunities and seize them with super normal will power and energy, essential to overcome the resistance that social environment offers.

Like other economic concepts, entrepreneurship has long been debated and discussed. It has been used in various ways and in various senses, while some call entrepreneurship as 'risk-bearing' others view it 'innovating and yet other consider it 'thrill-seeking'.

In common parlance, Entrepreneurship meant the function of seeking investment and production opportunity, organizing an enterprise to undertake a new production process, raising capital, hiring labour, arranging the supply of raw materials, finding site, introducing a new technique and commodities, discovering new sources of raw materials and selecting top entrepreneurship is described as the function of handling economic activity, undertaking risk, creating something new and organizing and coordinating resources.

According to Cole (1959), Entrepreneurship is the purposeful activity of an individual or a group of associated individuals, undertaken to initiate, maintain or aggrandize profit by production or distribution of economic goods and services.

In all above definitions, entrepreneurship refers to the functions performed by an entrepreneur in estabilishing an enterprise. Just a management is regarded as what managers do, entrepreneurship may be regarded as what entrepreneurs do. Entrepreneurship is a process involving various actions to be undertaken to establish an enterprise. It is thus, the process of giving birth to a new enterprise. Innovation and risk bearing are regarded as the two basic elements involved in entrepreneurship.

Many characteristics of small enterprises enhance their pivotal positions in accelerating economic growth in countries.

- Small enterprises have a better chance to carry out a number of innovations like combination of new products, new materials, new methods of production, new markets, new source of materials and even new forms of organizations, resulting in increased productivity.
- Being change-susceptible and highly reactive to socio-economic influences on the outside, small enterprises can easily adapt to and adopt measures that will ensure not only their own viability but also the growth of the economy in which they are situated.
- Being fairly labour intensive, they provide an economic solution by creating employment and income opportunities in urban and rural areas at relatively low cost of capital investment.
- Decentralization and dispersal of industries into rural areas prevent the influx of job-seekers in cities and urbanizing centers, thus allowing for a more balanced growth of economy in the whole country by reducing the ossification of established social institutions and the concentration of economic power.
- By using indigenous raw materials and the promotion

of intermediate and capital goods, small enterprises can contribute to faster economic growth in a transitional economy.

- Being set-up by individuals, they provide a productive outlet for expressing the entrepreneurial spirit of human resources.

The large number of studies have been conducted in this field.

Choudary (1980) in his study has examined successful characteristics of rural entrepreneurship by taking a sample of 73 units drawn from Wanaparthy Taluk in Mehboobnagar district of Andhra Pradesh. The analysis clearly highlighted that rural youth need proper education and training facilities alongwith conducive environment and better rapport and communication with government and other agencies meant for entrepreneurship development. He also drawn conclusion that better contact with NGOs and social organization can also be helpful to a considerable extent.

Suri and Surupria (1983) made a study of the role stress on women entrepreneurs, using data from a sample of 40 entrepreneurs with an experience of two years or more in Ahmedabad city. The finding showed that the married migrant women entrepreneurs coming from nuclear families experienced a greater role stress than the unmarried local entrepreneurs from joint families.

Naisbutt (1985) suggests that certain products and services present opportunities specifically suited for women. This thinking is based on the assumption that the distinctly 'female' or 'male' imagery associated with certain industries and business sectors continue to endure and influence who does what. Welsh and Falbe (1994) in a study examined whether women are especially suited to new child care centres and concludes that these franchise opportunities were not necessarily a good match for women. In a study of Nascent Entrepreneurs, Carter (1994) found women to be more active in 'downstream industries' such as service and retail more frequently than men. A National Study in UK regarding Women Business Owners indicated that the women-owned businesses were concentrated in services (Hisrich and Brush, 1984, 1987) and women typically owned businesses in retiling, business services such as accounting or word processing or personal services, like hair care.

Rani (1986) examined the characteristics of women entrepreneurs and the factors that motivate them to start a business. About 30 respondents were randomly contacted during their training in entrepreneurial skills in Hyderabad in October 1985. The study revealed that the majority of them were in the age group 21-30 years, and were prompted by the desire "to do something independently." Among the other factors that motivated the trainees to start new enterprises were: (a) the desire to keep busy, (b) to supplement family income, and (c) to gain business and technical knowledge and to earn money.

Azad (1988) in his study on 'Development of Entrepreneurship Among Rural Women—An Overview' laid emphasis that in order to develop entrepreneurship there is a need to provide training through various formal and informal institutions. Infrastructure facilities should be provided to entrepreneurs on priority basis. Socio-cultural barriers should be examined in detail and "these have been inherited from the society, effort should be made to increase the literacy and awareness among the people so that these barriers may be able overcome." Serious efforts should be made to develop entrepreneurship among rural women.

Masters and Meier (1988) examined the risk taking propensity among male and female entrepreneurs. A sample of 250 entrepreneurs has been taken by using stratified random sampling technique. The study highlighted that no significant difference was found among male and female entrepreneurs. The reason to this may assigned to the growth of women's movement and their impact of behaviour of women in the business environment. Other factors may also have influenced but it could not be identified in the study.

Thomas and Khan (1990) in their paper "Women and Development in Wayanad has examined the background the women beneficiaries and their participation in different development programmes. A sample of 200 respondent comprising of 94 female and 106 male has been taken from Wayanad district of Kerala. Analysis reveals that majority of male and female respondents were having low level of education. Their participation in socio-cultural and political affairs was found to be low. Awareness of women among various development programs was low as compared to their male counterparts. Awareness about various programs should be increased among women so that their participation in various activities may be increased.

Stoner *et al.* (1990) in their study has examined work home conflict in female owners of small business. The respondents from two states of USA, i.e. Illinois and California have been taken. A sample of 300 female business owners has been selected for this purpose. The results of study highlighted that these owners are likely to experience work-home conflict regardless of their family structure or absolute amount of time spent at work. The role conflict is more prevalent in those owners who have lower self-esteem. Overall findings further revealed that female business owners need to be prepared to cope with the ramifications of work-home role conflict—particularly in the lean initial years in the life of the firm.

Rao (1991) identified the factors that impede and slow down the entrepreneurial development of rural women based on the response of a random sample of 81 women from Anantapur District of Andra Pradesh collected in 1988-89. The findings showed that economic backwardness, lack of family and community support, ignorance of opportunities, lack of motivation, shyness and inhibition, preference for traditional occupations and for secure jobs were some of the factors that inhibit the promotion of grass roots entrepreneurship among rural women.

Natarajan and Thenmozhy (1991) has examined Entrepreneurial Development programme among women who participating in EDP organized by Canara Bank of Tamilnadu. A sample of 27 women entrepreneurs was selected. It was concluded that women possessed entrepreneurial skill to start business venture. Well planned and properly conducted EDP will help women to emerge as successful entrepreneurs. The study also observed that motivation campaigns should be conducted for students pursuing post-graduate, engineering and polytechnic courses during vacations. Bank should provide financial assistance by waiving of collateral security to women to setup industrial units. Proper monitoring and counseling can nurture healthy growth of industries.

Rathore and Chhabra (1991) in their paper on 'Promotion of Women Entrepreneurship: Training Strategies' state that Indian women find it increasingly difficult to adjust themselves to the dual role that they have to play as traditional housewives and compete with men in the field of business and industry. Working women are often tossed between home and work and experience mental conflicts as they are not able to devote the necessary amount of time and energy to their home and children and find it mostly difficult and sometimes impossible to pursue a career.

Nelson (1991) in his study on 'Small Business Opportunities for Women in Jamaica' revealed that women were concentrated in businesses which required the least capital outlay, or which were an extension of household activities, for example, small scale retail or dress making/garment manufacturing. Majority of the women had encountered sex-bias while establishing and developing their business and 26 per cent believed that they would be socially isolated if they exhibited the assertiveness and strength usually associated with the male entrepreneur. About 30 per cent of the women, however identified advantages to being female. They could negotiate preferential treatment and solicit cooperation from males. Household responsibility played a significant role in the choice of economical activity among women. The sample respondents stated that they depended on their business to maintain their homes and support their families. Need for specialized training programmes for women in small business we also echoed by the respondents.

Carter and Cannon (1992) in their study on 'Women as Entrepreneurs' conducted in Great Britain find out that the way women approach starting an enterprise is dominated by the stage they have reached in their life cycle, that is, their age and domestic relationships. Differentiation by personal life cycle is important as women start business at very different stages in their lives. This affects the types of business started and their individual approach to business ownership. Majority of the women respondents were equally motivated towards achievement and were represented within either the younger, achievement-oriented group, the aspirants, or within the high achievers group of older women who had often come out of successful careers to start a business. The career paths pursued by women were usually in a traditionally female employment sectors, such as retailing and within service industries. Only a minority has participated in non-traditional sectors before starting in business. Regardless of their educational and career backgrounds, all had experienced problems in starting and running enterprises. Many of those were operational problems, which affect male business owners as well as female. Many respondents were willing to exploit their feminity in group situations or in certain types of negotiation, turning the perceived disadvantages of gender into an advantage. Women respondents were skeptical about the initiatives of Government for promoting women entrepreneurship.

Kolvereid *et al.* (1993) in their study, "Is it equally difficult for female entrepreneurs to start business in all countries" collected data from venture initiators in Great Britain, Norway and New Zealand. The results show relatively few significant gender differences in perceptions of the influence of the environment on business formation.

Beegam and Sarngadharan (1994) in their study on "Female Entrepreneurship in Kerala" has observed that female literacy rate in Kerala is much higher than all India average. Department of Industries and Commerce has been providing help to women entrepreneurs to start their ventures. There has been shift in type of enterprises run by women. Women entrepreneurs have been entering in modern industrial units such as chemicals, engineering, computer services, etc. Entrepreneurship among women in Kerala has also been the outcome of encouragement by their parents. The study laid emphasis that success of women entrepreneurs calls for reduction in domestic load in favour of economic activities.

Klein, (1995) in her paper on 'Returning to Work: Challenge for Woman' states that problems of compatibility between professional and private life are usually resolved to the detriment of women. With few exceptions, it is women who interrupt their career, when family obligations require such a choice. Their reintegration into active life poses problems but it is necessary not only as a basic human right but also for economic efficiency.

Taylor and Brooksbank (1995) examined the marketing practices among small New Zealand organizations by taking a sample of 427 small business owners. Findings revealed that the small business firms looks the marketing practices differently from their larger counterparts.

Breen *et al.* (1995) examined financial and family issues by taking a sample of 211 female entrepreneurs from Australia. The study highlighted that female business owners faced the problem of getting finance and started business with low initial capital. On the family front women entrepreneurs faced the problem of supervision and care for sick children.

Srivastava and Chaudhary (1995) in their work on 'Women Entrepreneurs: Problems, Perspective and Role Expectations from Banks' find out that no single factor but a host of motivating factors act simultaneously on the individual creating dissonance in her, which in turn motivates her to take an action directed towards elimination or reduction of dissonance in the individual. Women faced problems mainly in the areas of marketing of their products and approaching the banks for getting loans. Personal problems like time constraint and family stress were also cited. The study concludes that joint family is not an obstacle for developing entrepreneurs. In fact, it is a facilitating factor. The entrepreneurial role enhances familial bonds and increases role satisfaction of women entrepreneurs as a wife, mother and maker of a 'home'.

Nair (1996) in her paper on 'Entrepreneurship Training for Women in the Indian Rural Sector: A Review of Approaches and Strategies', while admitting a perceptible increase in both the intellectual and physical resources devoted to the cause of research and action in the field of women's development, argues that initiatives in this realm are largely policy induced and devoid of any clear focus or strategy. The author advocates that a carefully drawn up training system has to address the strategic needs of women for survival and growth. More importantly, the training system has to link up organically with some kind of credit delivery mechanism, either formal or informal. It has been observed that the formal system, with its highly standardized approach and bureaucratic machinery, has not been able to appreciate the extra-economic dimensions of women's development.

Sugumar (1996) analyzed entrepreneurial competence among small entrepreneurs by taking a sample of 50 non-entrepreneurs and 50 small entrepreneurs. Author has drawn the conclusion that a successful entrepreneur requires intra-punitive, initiative and risk taking competences. The study suggested that entrepreneurship training should be focused on developing the three behavioural competences along with other related business inputs.

Poojary (1997) examined the motivating factors among entrepreneurs. A sample of 39 entrepreneurs of small-scale industries located in Mangalore taluk of Dakshina Kannada district has been taken. The analysis revealed that there are large numbers of factors, which motivate the entrepreneurs to set-up small-scale entrepreneurs. He has also drawn the inference that entrepreneurship is a complex phenomenon and is subject to socio-economic specification.

Prasin G.P. and Devi Sanchitra R.K. (1997) on their study, "Women Traders in Manipur" has made an attempt to identify the various trading activities performed by women alongwith their general profile. The study revealed that women traders participate in variety of activities right from economic to social. Keeping in view, the contribution of women traders in the state economy more financial assistance should be provided on easy terms and conditions. Welfare measures should also be initiated to look after the education of their children and counseling cells should be set-up to advise the women entrepreneurs in reducing the size of their families.

Dutta (1997) in his study on, "Women entrepreneurs in Assam, Problems and the role of the promoting organizations" has highlighted that state adopted model developed by NISIET for promotion and development of entrepreneurship among women. In Assam women faced large number of problems some of which are inherent and some are technical in nature. People coming from other states have been dominated in business. Attitude of financial institutions to provide financial assistance has been inadequate. Middle man are dominating in marketing of the products produced by women entrepreneurs to develop entrepreneurship among women and manage business on scientific lines, there is need to provide training to women.

Kamble (1997) has examined socio-economic background of women entrepreneurs of Belgaum Taluka by taking a sample of 27 entrepreneurs who availed financial assistance from KSFC, selected on random basis. Women of Belgaum taluka emerged from varied socio-economic, educational and cultural backgrounds is a significant feature. Brahmin women are better educated and more enterprising than their counterparts in other communities. The occupational background of father/husband provides an environment favourable to the growth of entrepreneurship among women. Housewives are a potential source of entrepreneurship. Overwhelming proportion of women entrepreneurs entered the business in the age-group of 30-40 at a time when they had attained self-confidence and decision-making capacity. Technically qualified women entrepreneurs opted area according to their specialization.

Mohanty and Patnaik (1997) on their study "Women Entrepreneurship in Orissa", has examined the economic performance of enterprises established by women entrepreneurs and their role in promotion of SSI in the economic development of Dhenkanal district of Orissa. A sample of 37 units has been taken for analysis purpose. Analysis of study highlighted that marketing was one of the major problems among all the selected units. Entrepreneurial skill is badly lacking in most of the Industrial units. Debt equity ratio is more on viable units which should not be expected. The study further made the suggestions that entrepreneurship development needs to be supplemented by other facilities and services like upgrading of skills of workers, training on management and marketing, quality control and assistance in research and development. Emphasis should be laid on technological upgradation.

Prasad and Rao (1997) has analyzed the "Socio-Economic Background of Women Entrepreneurs—A Case Study of Andhra Pradesh". A sample of 120 women entrepreneurs from the state of Andhra Pradesh were interviewed on the basis of purposive sampling technique. The author draw the inference that first generation entrepreneurs should go for non-technical industries. Workshops and refresher courses should be conducted by various institutions to overcome different types of problems faced by women entrepreneurs. Women entrepreneurs should go for joint ventures to run industry on scientific lines.

Caputo and Dolinsky (1998) has examined the role of financial and human capital of household member to pursue self-employment among females. The analysis revealed that business knowledge and cooperation of husband in family matters contribute a lot to pursue the business. Finding further suggested that government should provide necessary skill to women to ensure rapid growth of entrepreneurship.

Saxena and Tripathi (1998) has studied the entrepreneurship among milk producers in women dairy cooperative societies. In this study, entrepreneurial behaviour of rural women engaged in dairy industry has been evaluated by taking a sample of 150 women entrepreneurs from 10 villages of Bareilly district in U.P. It was observed in the study that family education, status has positive attitude towards income and self-employment. Better facilities if made available in villages can help a lot in improving entrepreneurial attributes among women.

Punitha *et al.* (1999) examined the problems and constraints faced by women entrepreneurs in the Pondicherry region. A sample of 120 females enterprises were personally interviewed during the period June to July 1999 out of which 42 belonged to rural and 78 to urban areas. The major problems faced by rural women entrepreneurs are competition from better quality products and marketing problems. The problems for urban entrepreneurs are, apart form the competition from better quality products, is the difficulty in getting loans. The least problems faced by both rural and urban women entrepreneurs are ignorance about schemes, distance from market and ignorance about agency and institutions.

Bliss and Garratt (2001) has examined the working of organization for women in Poland. The paper has examined the various activities performed by these associations to promote women entrepreneurs. Information was collected from 12 support organization for women. Data collected from these organizations highlighted that basic purpose of these organization has been to provide inputs to women entrepreneurs in the field of professional ethics, protection of rights of women entrepreneurs and their companies exchange of experience and other activities.

Mambula (2002) analysed major constrains faced by SMEs in Nigeria. A sample of 32 small business entrepreneurs was taken. Analysis of data revealed that majority of SMEs face the problem of finance and infrastructure while managing their businesses. The author recommended that small business entrepreneurs should collaborate with each other to sort out the various problems faced by them. There is need to form alliance of Government, Research Institutions and Financial Institutions to create appropriate training for prospective small business.

Watson (2003) has examined the failure rates among female

control business in Australia. The analysis of study highlighted that failure rate female control business is relatively higher than male controlled business. But the difference is not significant after controlling for the effects of industry.

Kumar (2004) paper examines the marketing practices used by women entrepreneurs. A sample of 120 women entrepreneurs has been taken from six districts of Haryana State. The analysis of data highlights that the women entrepreneurs are dependent mainly on the customers as a means to advertise their products. Women entrepreneurs having invested more money use pamphlets, hoardings and newspapers. Women entrepreneurs are facing the problem of advertisement of their products due to paucity of resources and strategies to be followed in this regard. Some kind of cooperative marketing through organized way need to be evolved. Proper guidance in marketing area would go a long way in handling the enterprise data. There is need to improve information system and guidance to women entrepreneurs in market survey.

Kumar (2004) in his study Women Entrepreneurs: Their Profile and Barriers in Business has examined the major obstacles faced by women. After analyzing the different problems, one may draw the inference that with the change in taste and preferences, expectations of the people and rapid change in technology, there is a need to increase awareness and availability of technology to women entrepreneurs. It will also help them in solving the problem of provision of quality of product. Utilizing modern communication media should solve problems relating to social and cultural barriers. Success stories of women entrepreneurs should be published in local and national newspapers and telecasted through television.

Even with the spread of education women entrepreneurs face the problem of law relating to management of business. This problem can be solved by introducing the paper relating to management of small business at graduate or +2 levels. Last but not least all the major actors (Government, women associations, banks, etc.) have to play an important role in ensuring that women entrepreneurs have full knowledge of technology, legal and innovative skills to meet the needs and requirements of emerging hew markets.

Kumar (2004) has analyzed the preference shown by women

entrepreneurs in locating their business by taking a sample of 120 respondents from the State of Haryana. The analysis of data reveals that almost 50 per cent of women entrepreneurs were managing their businesses from their homes and one third had rented shops Choice of location of enterprises by women entrepreneurs further reveals that most of them wanted to operate their businesses near the homes followed by near the market. However, due to stringent rules and regulations they appeared to face problems while managing businesses from homes. Relaxation of rules and regulations can help the women entrepreneurs to explore their potential. Suitable arrangements to locate their businesses near the market can also prove more helpful.

Kumar (2005) has investigated the various factors affecting women while choosing business line. A sample of 120 women entrepreneurs has been selected from the state of Haryana. The analysis of data highlights that there is shift in attitude of women entrepreneurs while choosing business line. Women entrepreneurs do not take profitability and complexities involved in business into considerations. Women entrepreneurs want to take up only those lines of businesses in which they possess adequate knowledge and skill and require less investment. Efforts should be made to inculcate the spirit of entrepreneurship among women. Starting various workshops relating to entrepreneurship development at college level can do this. Better training facilities should be set-up and awareness of these facilities should be enhanced. It will help in increasing the knowledge of availability of various opportunities in the market.

Kumar (2005) examined the perception of women entrepreneurs towards various family related issues. A sample of 120 women entrepreneurs has been taken from six districts of the State of Haryana. Analysis of data highlights that only one-fourth women entrepreneurs face problems relating to care of their children. More incentives should be given to women entrepreneurs who want to set-up childcare centers and playway schools. These enterprises are demanded more by those women who are involved in business. Majority of women entrepreneurs are doing business not out of compulsion but do not want to confine themselves into four walls of home. Women are becoming more career oriented and want to establish themselves before going for marriage. Attitude of women has undergone a sea change after introduction of new economic policies due to spread of education and availability of various job opportunities in the private sector. Suitable policies need to be formulated to provide more assistance to these achievement-oriented women entrepreneurs. Banking and training institutions should further strengthen their activities in this direction.

Kumar (2005) examined the factors, which are compelling the women to enter into business. A sample of 120 women entrepreneurs has been taken for this purpose. Analysis of data reveals that women have started participating in economic activities not due to family compulsions but to achieve something in life or to make use of free time. It is an indication of high growth in the economy and positive development in the society. In our sample proportion of women entrepreneurs investing money in business is not large. It may also be due to lack of awareness of various sources of finance available to women entrepreneurs. Efforts should be made to increase the level of awareness regarding various sources of finance available to women entrepreneurs. Banks through rigorous interviews try to find those women entrepreneurs who are possessing better traits and skills to do business. Terms and conditions for financial assistance in these cases may be relaxed. It will be help in developing entrepreneurship among women to a greater extent.

Kumar (2005) studied the various obstacles faced by women entrepreneurs. A sample of 120 women entrepreneurs has been taken for this purpose. The analysis of data after applying factor analysis technique has clubbed the different problems into three categories, i.e. Infrastructure, Socio-cultural and Economic problems. The problems relating to finance can be tackled by increasing the awareness of various sources of finance available to women entrepreneurs. The cumbersome procedure needs to be made cost effective. Problems relating to information and technology should be solved by following liberalization policies for this sector. Latest technological innovations should be made available to women entrepreneurs through various government agencies. There is need to change mindset of the people so that women can perform economic function in an effective manner. Workshops and seminars should be organised at the local level. It will be possible for the women entrepreneurs to participate easily in these seminars to enhance their skill and knowledge. Women organisations should also play an important role in this direction.

Kumar (2005) examined perceptions of women entrepreneurs managing small enterprises towards the support agencies. A sample of 120 women entrepreneurs has been taken. The analysis of data highlights that slightly more than one-third women entrepreneurs agree that availing financing assistance, is a problem and rest of the respondents were either undecided or disagreed on this issue. The reason to this may be assigned to non-utilisation of these resources or low level of awareness. There is a need to increase the level of awareness of various sources of finance to women entrepreneurs. Modem communication media should be utilized to enhance the level of awareness. Workshops and seminars should be organized at local level by financial institutions and NGOs, tree of cost to increase the level of awareness regarding various schemes and facilities available to women entrepreneurs. Procedure to avail assistance further needs to be made simple and cost-effective. More encouragement should be given to assistance in case of small and micro-level enterprises managed by women entrepreneurs. Majority of women entrepreneurs disagree with the statement that policy provisions for growth of women entrepreneurship are sufficient. There is a need to increase the level of awareness regarding various programmes and policies enunciated for the growth of women entrepreneurship. Requirement of separate support agencies can be tackled by creating special cells under the charge of women officials within different departments. It will help women entrepreneurs in presenting their cases better.

Kumar (2006) examined the labour related problem among women entrepreneurs in Northern India by taking a sample of 450 respondents from five states of Northern India, i.e. Haryana, Punjab, Rajasthan, Himachal Pradesh and Delhi. The analysis of data reveals that women entrepreneurs face the problem of labour absenteeism and labour turnover. Women entrepreneurs should manage their enterprises in a scientific manner. Worker should be trained as per requirements of business. Progressive wage structure and better leadership styles can act as effective tools to sort out these problems. These techniques will also solve the problem of negative attitude of the labour. Large business association should also provide training to the existing and potential women entrepreneurs so that they may be able to utilize modern human resource management practices in an efficient manner. Women entrepreneurs also face the problem of lack of availability of skilled labour. Government should lay more emphasis on vocational education to improve the skill and human capital base of the population. It will help in increasing supply of better quality of labour in the market, which is need of the free market economies.

The above studies have touched the various areas relating to women entrepreneurs. But none of the studies covered the studies relating to women entrepreneur at regional level. The present study proposes to fill the gap in existing literature. This book studies indepth the following:

1. To study the growth and profile of women entrepreneurs in the States of Northern India.
2. To analyze the entrepreneurial process among women entrepreneurs in Northern India.
3. To examine the financial structure of enterprises owned by women entrepreneurs.
4. To study the various issues relating to training.
5. To examine the obstacles faced by women entrepreneurs in Northern India.
6. To seek the opinion of women entrepreneurs regarding various issues related to women entrepreneurs.
7. To study the extent of fulfilment of expectations from various business organizations.
8. To give suggestions and recommendations for the growth of women entrepreneurs.

Information has been collected from respondents by using pre-tested well-designed questionnaire. Principal demographic characteristics like age, level of education, structure of family, level of investment, income, training and sources of finance have been taken into consideration while analyzing the data. Moreover, all these characteristics can be beneficial for drawing the meaningful inferences for policy implications. Two stage random sampling technique has been used to choose the respondents for the above study. The classification of women entrepreneurs in different industries has been shown in Table 1.1.

Most of these women entrepreneurs have established their business after post-reform period, i.e. after 1991. All these women entrepreneurs have employed at least 5 workers in their enterprises. Simple percentages and chi-square test have been used to find out the association if any between these various demographic characteristics and different variables taken into consideration in our objectives. Factor analysis technique has also been used in the study.

TABLE 1.1

Industry-wise Classification of Enterprises Selected in Study by Women Entrepreneurs

Type of Industry	No. of Women Entrepreneurs	Percentage
Manufacturing	191	42.44
Trading	72	16.00
Services	145	32.22
Others	42	9.33
Total	450	100

CHAPTER SCHEME

The whole book has been divided into following chapters:

1. Introduction,
2. Socio-Economic profile of women entrepreneurs,
3. Entrepreneurial process among women entrepreneurs,
4. Financial structure of enterprises owned by women entrepreneurs,
5. Investigation of training related issues,
6. Obstacles faced by women in business,
7. Perception of women towards various entrepreneurship related issues,
8. Extent of fulfilment of expectations of women entrepreneurs from supporting agencies, and
9. Summary and conclusions.

REFERENCES

Azad, G.S., Development of Entrepreneurship Among Rural Women—An Overview, *Sedme Journal,* Vol. 15, No. 2, 1988, pp. 41-50.

Beegam, S. Resia and Sarngadharan, M., Female Entrepreneurship in Kerala, *Yojana,* Vol. 38, 1994, pp. 29-30.

Bliss, R.T. and Garratt, N.L. (2001), Supporting Women Entrepreneurs in Transitioning Economies, *Journal of Small Business Management,* Vol. 39 (4), pp. 336-44.

Breen *et al.,* Female Entrepreneurs in Australia: An Investigation of Financial and Family Issues, *Journal of Enterprising Culture,* Vol. 3, No. 4, 1995, pp. 445-61.

Caputo, R.K. and Dolinsky Arthur (1998). Women's Choice of Pursue Self-Employment: The Role of Financial and Human Capital of Household Members, *Journal of Small Business Management,* Vol. 36 (2), pp. 8-18.

Carter, S. and Cannon, T., *Women as Entrepreneurs: A Study of Female Business Owners: Their Motivations, Experience and Strategies for Success,* Academic Press, 1991.

Casson, Mark, The Entrepreneur: An Economic Theory, *Martin Robertson,* Oxford, 1982, p. 23.

Cole, A.H., *Business Enterprise in its Social Setting,* Harward University Press, Cambridge, 1959, p. 44.

Choudary, K.V.R., Successful Characteristics of Rural Entrepreneurship, *Sedme Journal,* Vol. 7, No. 2, 1980, pp. 89-103.

Cunningham, J., Barton and Lischerssen, Joe, Defining Entrepreneurship, *The Journal of Small Business Management,* Vol. 29, No. 1, Jan. 1991, p. 49.

Dutta Umin, Women Entrepreneurs in Assam, Problems and The Role of Promoting Organizations, *Indian Journal of Commerce,* Vol. 1, No. 193, 1997, pp. 225-28.

Government of India (2001-02), Third All Indian Census of SSI, DC(SSI), Ministry of SSI, New Delhi.

Kamble, H.Y., A Study of the Socio-Economic Back-Ground of Women Entrepreneurs of Belgaum Taluka, *Indian Journal of Commerce,* Vol. 1, No. 193, 1997, pp. 229-42.

Kilby, Peter, Entrepreneurship and Economic Development, *The Free Press,* New York, 1971.

Klein, Uta, Returning to Work: A Challenge for Women, *World of Work* ILO, No. 12, May/June 1995.

Kolvereid, Lars *et al.,* Is it Equally Difficult for Female Entrepreneurs to Start Business in All Countries? *Journal of Small Business Management,* October 1993.

Kumar, Anil, Obstacles Faced by Women in Business: A Factor Analytical

Study, *Asian Economic Review*, Vol. 47 (3), Hyderabad, Dec. 2005, pp. 457-64.

————, Enterprise Location: Choice of Women entrepreneurs, *Sedme Journal*, Vol. 33, No. 3, Sept. 2004, Hyderabad, pp. 11-20.

————, Marketing Practices used by Women Entrepreneurs, *Indian Development Review*, Vol. 3, No. 1, Dec. 2004, pp. 113-25.

————, Women Entrepreneurs: An Investigation of Factors Affecting Business Choice, *Indian Development Review*, Vol. 3, No. 1, pp. 113-25, June 2005, New Delhi.

————, Women Entrepreneurs: Their Perception Towards Various Support Agencies, *Indian Management Studies Journal*, Vol. 9, No. 2, Oct. 2005, pp. 149-62, Vishakhapatnam.

————, Women Entrepreneurs: Their Profile and Factors Compelling Business Choice, *GITAM Journal of Management*, Vol. 3, No. 2, July-Dec. 2005, pp. 134-44, Vishakhapatnam.

————, Women Entrepreneurs in Northern India: An Investigation of Labour Related Problems, *Journal of Social and Economic Policy*, Vol. 3, No. 1, June 2006, New Delhi, pp. 135-46.

————, Women Entrepreneurs: Perception Towards Family Issues, *Indian Journal of Development Research and Social Action*, Vol. 1, No. 2, December 2005, New Delhi, pp. 165-77.

————, Women Entrepreneurs: Their Profile and Barriers in Business, *Indian Journal of Social Development*, Vol. 4, No. 2, Dec. 2004, pp. 297-311.

Mambula, Perceptions of SME Growth Constraints in Nigeria, *Journal of Small Business Management*, Vol. 40, No. 1, 2002, pp. 58-65.

Masters, R. and Meier, R. (1988). Sex Differences and Risk-taking Propensity of Entrepreneurs, *Journal of Small Business Management*, Vol. 26 (1), pp. 31-36.

Meredath *et al.*, *The Practice of Entrepreneurship*, International Labour Office, Geneva, 1982, p. 3.

Mohanty, K. Malay and Patnaik, K. Sushil, Women Entrepreneurs in Orissa: A Case Study of Dhenkanal District, *Indian Journal of Commerce*, Vol. 1, No. 193, 1997, pp. 276-85.

Nair, Tara S., Entrepreneurship Training for Women in the Indian Rural Sector: A Review of Approaches and Strategies, *The Journal of Entrepreneurship*, 5, 1996, p. 1.

Naisbutt, John, *The Future of Franchising: Looking 25 Years Ahead to the Year 2010*, Washington DC, International Franchise Association, 1985.

National Foundation for Women Business Owners (NFWBO, 2001). Entrepreneurial Vision in Action: Exploring Growth Among Women and Men-owned Firms, Washington DC.

Natrajan, K. and Thenmozhy, A., Entrepreneurial Development Programme for Women—A Case Study, *Yojana*, Vol. 35 (8), May 15, 1991, pp. 6-8.

Nelson, Blossom O' Meally, Small Business Opportunities for Women in Jamaica, *Sedme Journal*, 1991.

Poojary, M.C., Entrepreneurship: Push or Pull Effect, *Sedme Journal*, Vol. 24, No. 3, 1997, pp. 11-18.

Prasad, A.G. and Rao, T. Venkateswara, Socio-Economic Background of Women Entrepreneurs—A Case Study of Andhra Pradesh, *Indian Journal of Commerce*, Vol. 1, No. 193, 1997, pp. 261-69.

Prasin, G.P. and Devi Sancharita, R.K., Women Traders in Manipur—A Case Study, *Indian Journal of Commerce*, Vol. 1, No. 193, 1997, pp 213-17.

Punitha, M. Sangeetha, S., Padmavathi, Women Entrepreneurs: Their Problems and Constraints. *Indian Journal of Labour Economics* Vol. 42, No. 4, Oct.-Dec., 1999, pp. 701-06.

Rani, S. Swarupa, Potential Women Entrepreneurs—A Study, *Sedme Journal*, Vol. 13, No. 3, 1986, pp. 13-22.

Rao, C., Harinarayana, Promotion of Women Entrepreneurs, *Sedme Journal*, Vol. 1, No. 2, 1991, pp. 21-28.

Rathore, B.S. and Chabbra, Rama, Promotion of Women Entrepreneurship—Training Strategies, *SEDME Journal*, Vol. 18, No. 1, 1991.

Saxena Deepti and Tripathi Hema, Entrepreneurship Among Milk Producers in Women Dairy Cooperative Societies, *Productivity*, Vol. 38, No. 4, 1999, pp. 582-90.

Shigeko Mitusuhasi, Access to markets, OECD Conference on Women Entrepreneurs in SMEs 2000: A major force in innovation and job creation. Synthesis, OECD, 29 November-1 December, Paris, France, 2000.

Srivastava, A.K. and Chaudhary, Sanjay, *Women Entrepreneurs: Problems, Perspective and Role Expectations from Banks*, Panjab University, Chandigarh, 1991.

Stoner *et al.* (1990), Work-Home Role Conflict in Female Owners of Small Businesses: An Exploratory Study, *Journal of Small Business Management*, Vol. 28 (1), pp. 30-38.

Sugumar, M., Entrepreneurial Competence Among Small Entrepreneurs, *Sedme Journal*, Vol. 23, No.4, 1996, pp. 1-11.

Suri and Sarupria, Psychological Factors Affecting Women Entrepreneurs – Some Findings, *The Indian Journal of Social Work*, Vol. 44, No. 3, 1983, pp. 287-95.

Taylor and Brooksbank, Marketing Practices Among Small New Zealand Organizations, *Journal of Enterprising Culture*, Vol. 3, No. 2, 1995, pp. 149-60.

Thomas, M.E. and Khan, M.Z., Women and Development in Wayanad, *Social Change*, Vol. 20, No. 2, 1990, pp. 26-34.

Watson, J. (2003), Failure Rates for Female-Controlled Businesses: Are They Any Different? *Journal of Small Business Management*, Vol. 41 (3), pp. 262-77.

Workshop proceedings, 2000, Second OECD Conference on Women Entrepreneurs in SMEs: A major force in innovation and job relation, Synthesis, OECD, 29 November-1 December, Paris, France.

Socio-Economic Profile of Women Entrepreneurs

Entrepreneurship is regarded as one of the most crucial factors in the economic development of every region of the country. It widens the horizons of economic development even in the socially and industrially backward regions. Dynamic entrepreneurs are considered to be the agent of change in a society. Entrepreneurs play a very important role in generating of new employment and setting up of new business. The problem of poverty, inequality and regional imbalances can be tackled with the development of entrepreneurship. Entrepreneurship among women is more suitable because it is possible to do work when she has free time. A self-employed women is gaining better status. It enables her to pool the small capital resources and skill available with women. It paves the way for fuller utilization of capital and also mobilizes the female human potential. Entrepreneurship development among women offers, mental satisfaction and provides diversion to women from routine work. It gives psychological satisfaction to women and enhanced identity in the society. Further, emergence of women entrepreneurs in the economy is an indicator of women's economic independence.

The present chapter is based on the empirical study undertaken to analyze the socio-economic profile of women entrepreneurs in Northern India.

Table 2.1 shows that almost same proportion of women entrepreneurs in the age group of 30-40 and 40+ are participating in the business. On the other hand, slightly less than one-third women entrepreneurs in the age group of less than 30 are also doing business. It reveals that during post reform period women entrepreneurs irrespective of their age group are participating in self-employment activities. Education-wise information further shows that 36 per cent women entrepreneurs below the age of 30 years, possessing graduate and post-graduate level of education are doing business. On the other hand, more than 56 per cent women entrepreneurs in the age group of more than 40 years possessing low level of education upto matric, are participating in economic activities. Women entrepreneurs in the lower age group, are opting entrepreneurial activity after acquiring higher level of education. It clearly reveals that entrepreneurship among educated women entrepreneurs in lower age groups is increasing at rapid rate. The value of chi-square is statistically significant at 1 per cent level of significance. It shows that these two variables vary significantly. 69 per cent women entrepreneurs hailing from urban areas and 53 per cent from rural areas upto age group of 40 are participating in the business activities. The reason for higher level of participation in urban areas may be attributed to more facilities and services available in urban areas. Similarly, 47 per cent women entrepreneurs in the age group of more than 40 hailing from rural areas are participating relatively more in business activities as compared to women entrepreneurs coming from urban areas (32 per cent) in the same age group. The value of chi-square is statistically significant at 1 per cent level of significance. The type of family of women entrepreneurs show that 68 per cent women entrepreneurs in the age group of below 30, and 30-40 are coming from nuclear families, whereas this ratio is 63 per cent in case of women entrepreneurs coming from joint families. The value of chi-square is statistically insignificant. 67 per cent women entrepreneurs in the age group of less than 30 and 30-40 are opting for individual form of business organizations, whereas 60 per cent women entrepreneurs in the same age group are opting other than individual form of business organization to do the business. It highlights that preference of women entrepreneurs has been towards other than form of business organizations to do business. It may also be due to more risk

TABLE 2.1
Age of Women Entrepreneurs (in years)

Group	Less than 30	30-40	40+
All Data	141 (31.33)	153 (34.00)	156 (34.67)
Education			
Primary	4 (16.67)	4 (16.67)	16 (66.67)
Matric	12 (15.00)	23 (28.75)	45 (56.25)
Graduate	68 (36.17)	64 (34.04)	5 (29.79)
Post Graduate	57 (36.08)	62 (39.24)	39 (24.68)
Chi-square = 38.715; df = 6; Significant at 1 per cent level			
Place of Origin			
Rural	25 (28.74)	21 (24.14)	41 (47.13)
Urban	116 (31.96)	132 (36.36)	116 (31.68)
Chi-square = 8.147; df = 2; Significant at 1 per cent level			
Type of Family			
Joint	61 (29.19)	70 (33.49)	78 (37.32)
Nuclear	80 (33.20)	83 (34.44)	78 (32.37)
Chi-square = 1.396; df = 2; Insignificant			
Form of Business Organization			
Sole	108 (34.95)	101 (32.69)	100 (32.36)
Others	33 (23.40)	52 (36.88)	56 (39.72)
Chi-square = 6.131; df = 2; Significant at 5 per cent level			
Investment (Lacs)			
<1	51 (41.46)	52 (42.28)	20 (16.26)
1-2	40 (27.78)	39 (27.08)	65 (45.14)
2-3	20 (25.97)	28 (36.36)	29 (37.66)
3-5	19 (29.69)	20 (31.25)	25 (39.06)
5-10	9 (29.03)	10 (32.26)	12 (38.71)
Above 10	2 (18.18)	4 (36.36)	5 (45.45)
Chi-square = 28.497; df = 10; Significant at 1 per cent level			
Income (Rs.)			
<7500	15 (27.78)	25 (46.30)	14 (25.93)
7500-10000	49 (32.45)	43 (28.48)	59 (39.07)
10000-15000	28 (28.87)	28 (28.87)	41 (42.27)
15000-20000	37 (37.00)	33 (33.00)	30 (30.00)
20000+	12 (25.00)	24 (50.00)	12 (25.00)
Chi-square = 15.832; df = 8; Significant at 5 per cent level			

(Contd.)

Group	Less than 30	30-40	40+
Training			
Got Training	91 (38.72)	94 (40.00)	50 (21.28)
No Training	50 (23.26)	59 (27.44)	106 (49.30)
Chi-square = 39.220; df = 2; Significant at 1 per cent level			
Sources of Finance			
Formal	39 (32.50)	39 (32.50)	42 (35.00)
Informal	102 (30.91)	114 (34.55)	114 (34.55)
Chi-square = 0.185; df = 2; Insignificant			
Age of Enterprise			
Below 10 years	136 (45.48)	112 (37.46)	51 (17.06)
Above 10 years	5 (3.31)	41 (27.15)	105 (69.54)
Chi-square = 139.795; df = 2; Significant at 1 per cent level			

involved in individual form of business organizations. 41 per cent women entrepreneurs in the age group of less than 30 years have invested less than Rs. 1 lac in business and only 18 per cent women entrepreneurs in the same age group have invested more than Rs. 10 lacs in business. It reveals that women entrepreneurs don't want to take more risk at initial stages. On the other hand, women entrepreneurs in the higher age groups have invested more money in business. It may be due to more experience and skill acquired over the period of time by these women entrepreneurs. The value of chi-square is statistically significant at 1 per cent level of significance. It shows that these two variables are positively associated. 46 per cent women entrepreneurs in the age group of 30-40 years are earning less than Rs. 7500 per month in business and only one-fourth women entrepreneurs in the higher age groups are earning Rs. 7500 p.m. in business. Almost same proportion of women entrepreneurs in the age group of less than 30 and 30-40 are earning income in the range of Rs. 10,000-15,000 per month. Information further reveals that age increases the knowledge and skills to perform the business effectively and efficiently. The value of chi-square is statistically significant at 5 per cent level of significance. It shows that age and level of earnings vary significantly. 78 per cent women entrepreneurs in the age group of less than 30 and 30-40 have undergone training before start of their business. On the other hand, 51 per cent women entrepreneurs in the same age group have not taken any training. Similarly, 49 per cent women entrepreneurs in the age group of more than 40 have not taken any training. It shows that women entrepreneurs in the higher age group do not need training to start their business. It interprets that with increase in age, need for training also declines. Almost same proportion of women entrepreneurs in different age groups have used formal and informal sources of finance in their business. The value of chi-square is statistically insignificant. It shows that these two variables are independent. 83 per cent women entrepreneurs upto age of 40 are having enterprises 10 years old. On the other hand, 69 per cent women entrepreneurs in the age group of more than 40 possess enterprises older than 10 years. It shows that there is a surge of entrepreneurship among women in the lower age group. The value of chi-square is statistically significant at 1 per cent level of significance.

Table 2.2 shows that educated women entrepreneurs have started participating in the business activities. 42 per cent women entrepreneurs are possessing graduate level of education and another 35 per cent post-graduate level of education. It reveals that women entrepreneurs after attaining higher level of education are choosing business line in their career. It may be due to decline in job opportunities in formal sector of the economy and increase in business opportunities in the private sector after liberalization of economy under new economic policies. Age-wise information further shows that 40 per cent women entrepreneurs in the age group of below 30 and 30-40 possess post-graduate level of education. Information vividly shows that more than 80 per cent women entrepreneurs below age group of 40 years possess higher level of education. It indicates a positive development in the economy and utilization of female resources in the business sector. The value of chi-square is statistically significant at 1 per cent level of significance. Level of education is found to be higher among women entrepreneurs hailing from urban areas than rural areas. It shows that higher level of education is still out of reach of female entrepreneurs of rural areas. It may be due to low accessibility or establishment of institutions of higher learning at far off places. There is need to set-up more institutions imparting higher level of education in rural areas. The value of chi-square is statistically significant at 1 per cent level of significance. It shows that these two variables vary significantly. Proportion of women entrepreneurs possessing higher level of education is found to be more among women entrepreneurs coming from nuclear families than from joint families. It may be due to lack of tendency to provide higher education to female in joint families. The value of chi-square is statistically significant at 1 per cent level of significance. Almost 80 per cent women entrepreneurs possessing graduate and post-graduate level of education are managing business under individual form of business organizations, whereas 70 per cent women entrepreneurs having same level of education are managing their business under other forms of business organization. The value of chi-square is statistically insignificant. It highlights that these two variables are independent. More than 85 per cent women entrepreneurs possessing higher level of education have invested more than Rs. 3 lacs in business. It may be due to more awareness of various sources of finance available to women entrepreneurs or higher risk taking ability among educated women entrepreneurs. Women entrepreneurs possessing low level of education have invested less money in business. The value of chi-square is statistically significant at 1 per cent level of significance. Educated women entrepreneurs are earning higher level of income as compared to women entrepreneurs possessing lower level of education. It shows that education helps in earning higher level of income. It may also be due to better management practices adopted by these women entrepreneurs. The value of chi-square further shows that these two variables are statistically significant. It seems that training is no longer a prerequisite for educated women entrepreneurs to start any business activities. 73 per cent women entrepreneurs possessing graduate and post-graduate level of education are doing business without having any training. The value of chi-square is statistically insignificant. Similarly, sources of finance no longer act as a barrier for educated

WOMEN ENTREPRENEURS

Women entrepreneurs having higher level of education are using formal and informal sources of finance to meet their business requirements. Information also signifies that to be entrepreneur sources of finance is not considered as a hurdle. The value of chi-square is statistically insignificant. 85 per cent women entrepreneurs having higher level of education have been involved in the business for the last ten years. On the other hand, 60 per cent women entrepreneurs possessing same level of education have been in business for more than 10 years. It shows that majority of women enterprises are young and have been established during post-reform period. Information reveals that overwhelming proportion of enterprises has been established recently. Analysis done indicates that impact of reform has been observed after the gap of five years. The value of chi-square is statistically significant at 1 per cent level of significance.

TABLE 2.2

Level of Education of Women Entrepreneurs

Group	Primary	Matric	Graduate	Post-Graduate
All Data	24 (5.33)	80 (17.78)	188 (41.78)	158 (35.11)
Age (years)				
Below 30	4 (2.84)	12 (8.51)	68 (48.23)	57 (40.43)
30-40	4 (2.61)	23 (15.03)	64 (41.83)	62 (40.52)
Above 40	16 (10.26)	45 (28.85)	56 (35.90)	39 (25.00)
Chi-square = 38.715; df = 6; Significant at 1 per cent level				
Place of Origin				
Rural	9 (10.34)	30 (34.48)	28 (32.18)	20 (22.99)
Urban	15 (4.13)	50 (13.77)	160 (44.08)	138 (38.02)
Chi-square = 28.898; df = 3; Significant at 1 per cent level				
Type of Family				
Joint	11 (5.26)	53 (25.36)	82 (39.23)	63 (30.14)
Nuclear	13 (5.39)	27 (11.20)	160 (44.08)	95 (39.42)
Chi-square = 15.967; df = 3; Significant at 1 per cent level				
Form of Business Organization				
Sole	16 (5.18)	47 (15.21)	132 (42.72)	114 (36.89)
Others	8 (5.67)	33 (23.20)	56 (39.72)	44 (31.21)
Chi-square = 4.802; df = 3; Insignificant				
Investment (Lacs)				
<1	5 (4.07)	18 (14.63)	61 (49.59)	39 (31.71)
1-2	6 (4.17)	39 (27.08)	49 (34.03)	50 (34.72)
2-3	11 (14.29)	12 (15.58)	30 (38.96)	24 (31.17)
3-5	2 (3.12)	7 (10.94)	26 (40.62)	29 (45.31)
5-10	—	4 (12.90)	16 (51.61)	11 (35.48)

(Contd.)

Group	Primary	Matric	Graduate	Post-Graduate
Above 10	—	—	6 (54.55)	5 (45.45)

Chi-square = 35.264; df = 15; Significant at 1 per cent level

Income (Rs.)

	Primary	Matric	Graduate	Post-Graduate
<7500	—	7 (12.96)	26 (48.15)	21 (38.69)
7500-10000	7 (4.64)	40 (26.49)	61 (40.40)	43 (28.48)
10000-15000	12 (12.37)	18 (18.56)	35 (36.08)	32 (32.99)
15000-20000	2 (2.00)	10 (10.00)	46 (46.00)	42 (42.00)
20000+	3 (6.25)	5 (10.42)	20 (41.67)	20 (41.67)

Chi-square = 32.184; df = 12; Significant at 1 per cent level

Training

	Primary	Matric	Graduate	Post-Graduate
Got Training	7 (2.98)	41 (17.45)	102 (43.00)	85 (36.17)
No Training	17 (7.91)	39 (18.14)	86 (40.00)	73 (33.95)

Chi-square = 5.612; df = 3; Insignificant

Sources of Finance

	Primary	Matric	Graduate	Post-Graduate
Formal	6 (5.00)	15 (12.50)	46 (38.33)	53 (44.17)
Informal	18 (5.45)	65 (19.70)	142 (43.03)	105 (31.82)

Chi-square = 6.884; df = 3; Insignificant

Age of Enterprise

	Primary	Matric	Graduate	Post-Graduate
Below 10 years	6 (2.01)	39 (13.04)	127 (42.47)	127 (42.47)
Above 10 years	18 (11.92)	41 (27.15)	61 (40.40)	31 (20.53)

Chi-square = 43.589; df = 3; Significant at 1 per cent level.

Table 2.3 shows that 81 per cent women entrepreneurs are hailing from urban areas and 19 per cent from rural areas. It reveals that growth of entrepreneurs is found to be more among urban females. It may be due to lack of facilities and stringent socio-cultural environment prevailing in rural areas. It may also be due to lack of commercial activities in rural areas and these women entrepreneurs have to move to urban areas to set-up their enterprises. Education-wise information further shows that women entrepreneurs having lower level of education belong to rural areas and women entrepreneurs possessing higher level of education are from urban areas. The value of chi-square is statistically significant at 1 per cent level of significance. More than 82 per cent women entrepreneurs hailing from urban areas are in the age groups of below 30 and 30-40. On the other hand, slightly more than one-fourth of the women entrepreneurs beyond the age of 40 belong to rural areas. The value of chi-square is statistically significant at 1 per cent level of significance.

TABLE 2.3

Nativity of Women Entrepreneurs

Group	Rural	Urban
All Data	87 (19.33)	363 (80.67)
Education		
Primary	9 (37.50)	15 (62.50)
Matric	30 (37.50)	50 (62.50)
Graduate	28 (14.89)	160 (85.11)
Post Graduate	20 (12.66)	138 (87.34)
Chi-square = 28.898; df = 3; ; Significant at 1 per cent level		
Age (years)		
Below 30	25 (17.73)	116 (82.27)
30-40	21 (13.73)	132 (86.27)
Above 40	41 (26.28)	115 (73.72)
Chi-square = 8.147; df = 2; Significant at 1 per cent level		
Type of Family		
Joint Family	53 (25.36)	156 (74.64)
Nuclear	34 (14.11)	207 (85.89)
Chi-square = 9.085; df = 1; Significant at 1 per cent level		
Form of Business Organization		
Sole	49 (15.86)	260 (84.14)
Others	38 (26.95)	103 (73.05)
Chi-square = 7.639; df = 1; Significant at 1 per cent level		
Investment (Lacs)		
<1	23 (18.70)	100 (81.30)
1-2	34 (23.61)	110 (76.39)
2-3	15 (19.48)	62 (80.52)
3-5	9 (12.50)	56 (87.50)
5-10	2 (6.45)	29 (93.55)
Above 10	5 (45.45)	6 (54.55)
Chi-square = 11.750; df = 5; Significant at 5 per cent level		

(*Contd.*)

Group	Rural	Urban
Income (Rs.)		
<7500	5 (9.26)	49 (90.74)
7500-10000	34 (22.52)	117 (77.48)
10000-15000	19 (19.59)	78 (80.41)
15000-20000	22 (22.00)	78 (78.00)
20000+	7 (14.58)	41 (85.42)
Chi-square = 5.650; df = 4; Insignificant		
Training		
Got Training	41 (17.45)	194 (82.55)
No Training	46 (21.40)	169 (78.60)
Chi-square = 1.222; df = 1; Insignificant		
Sources of Finance		
Formal	20 (16.67)	100 (83.33)
Informal	67 (20.30)	263 (79.70)
Chi-square = 0.746; df = 1; Insignificant		
Age of Enterprise		
Below 10 years	45 (15.05)	254 (84.95)
Above 10 years	42 (27.81)	109 (72.19)
Chi-square = 10.482; df = 1; ; Significant at 1 per cent level		

Majority of women entrepreneurs hailing from rural areas belong to joint families. Information shows that joint family system is still prevalent in rural areas and it may be one of the factors responsible for slower growth of entrepreneurship among women. Moreover, elders do not prefer their daughter or daughters-in-law to do business. The value of chi-square is statistically significant at 1 per cent level of significance. More than 73 per cent women entrepreneurs doing business under individual and other form of business organizations belong to urban areas. On the other hand, one-fourth women entrepreneurs coming from rural areas are doing business under other form of business organizations. It may also be due to lack of experience in business activities. Information reveals that women entrepreneurs hailing from rural areas do not want to take more risk by managing business on individual basis. More than 76 per cent women entrepreneurs having invested upto Rs. 10 lacs in business hail from urban areas. On the other hand, 45 per cent of women entrepreneurs coming from rural areas have invested more than Rs. 10 lacs in business. The value of chi-square is statistically significant at 5 per cent level of significance. More than 77 per cent women entrepreneurs earning different levels of income belong to urban areas. 82 per cent trained and 78 per cent untrained women entrepreneurs belong to urban areas. Information shows that women entrepreneurs in rural areas are not much aware of entrepreneurial support organizations. The values of chi-square are statistically insignificant. Institutional sources of finance have been used relatively more by women entrepreneurs hailing from urban areas than from rural areas. The reason to this may be attributed to lack of awareness or difficulty in approaching financial institution by women entrepreneurs coming from rural areas and these women entrepreneurs have to depend on informal sources of finance or their own savings to start their business. 84 per cent enterprises established in urban areas are less than 10 years old, while 72 per cent enterprises more than 10 years old belong to urban areas. It shows that entrepreneurship has blossomed more in urban areas. The value of chi-square is statistically significant at 1 per cent level of significance.

Table 2.4 shows that 54 per cent women entrepreneurs belong to nuclear families and 46 per cent from joint families. It shows that type of family is no longer a constraint for women. Information further indicates that joint family system is still prevalent in our society. Education-wise analysis reveals that major proportion of women entrepreneurs possessing lower level of education hail from joint families and women entrepreneurs having higher level of education belong to nuclear families. The value of chi-square is statistically significant at 1 per cent level of significance. It shows that these two variables vary significantly. More than 50 per cent women entrepreneurs in the age group of less than 30 and 30-40 hail from nuclear families. Almost same proportion of women entrepreneurs (50 per cent each) in higher age groups belong to joint and nuclear families. The value chi-square is statistically insignificant. It shows that these two variables are independent. 60 per cent women entrepreneurs hailing from rural areas belong to joint families. Analysis shows that joint family system is more prevalent in rural areas. On the other hand, majority of women entrepreneurs from urban areas

TABLE 2.4

Structure of Family of Women Entrepreneurs

Group	Joint	Nuclear
All Data	209 (46.44)	241 (53.56)
Education		
Primary	11 (45.83)	13 (54.17)
Matric	53 (66.25)	27 (33.75)
Graduate	82 (43.62)	106 (56.38)
Post Graduate	63 (39.87)	95 (60.13)
Chi-square = 15.967; df = 3; Significant at 1 per cent level		
Age (years)		
Below 30	61 (43.26)	80 (56.74)
30-40	70 (45.75)	83 (54.25)
Above 40	78 (50.00)	78 (50.00)
Chi-square = 1.396; df = 2; Insignificant		
Place of Origin		
Rural	53 (60.92)	34 (39.08)
Urban	156 (42.98)	207 (57.02)
Chi-square = 9.085; df = 1; Significant at 1 per cent level		
Form of Business Organization		
Sole	140 (45.31)	69 (48.94)
Others	169 (54.69)	72 (51.06)
Chi-square = 0.513; df = 1; Insignificant		
Investment (Lacs)		
<1	65 (52.85)	58 (47.15)
1-2	63 (43.75)	81 (56.25)
2-3	39 (50.65)	38 (49.35)
3-5	22 (34.38)	42 (65.62)
5-10	16 (51.61)	15 (48.39)
Above 10	4 (36.36)	7 (63.64)
Chi-square = 7.524; df = 5; Insignificant		
Income (Rs.)		
<7500	23 (42.59)	31 (57.41)
7500-10000	82 (54.30)	69 (45.70)
10000-15000	37 (38.14)	60 (61.86)

Group	Joint	Nuclear
15000-20000	45 (45.00)	55 (55.00)
20000+	22 (45.83)	26 (54.17)
Chi-square = 6.850; df = 4; Insignificant		
Training		
Got Training	104 (44.26)	131 (55.74)
No Training	105 (48.84)	110 (51.16)
Chi-square = 0.948; df = 1; Insignificant		
Sources of Finance		
Formal	38 (31.67)	82 (68.33)
Informal	171 (51.82)	159 (48.18)
Chi-square = 14.367; df = 1; Significant at 1 per cent level		
Age of Enterprise		
Below .J years	131 (43.81)	168 (56.19)
Above 10 years	78 (51.66)	73 (48.34)
Chi-square = 2.481; df = 1; Insignificant.		

hail from nuclear families. It shows that there is a decline in joint family system in urban areas. It may be due to higher mobility among the people of urban areas. The value of chi-square is statistically significant at 1 per cent level of significance. More than 51 per cent women entrepreneurs hailing from nuclear families are opting both forms of business organizations to perform business. 48 per cent women entrepreneurs coming from joint families are managing business under other than individual form of business organizations. It may be due to availability of more persons in joint families and to manage business effectively, involvement of more persons is essential in present business scenario. The value of chi-square is statistically insignificant. It shows that these two variables are not influencing each other. Level of investment done by these women entrepreneurs further reveal that around 50 per cent women entrepreneurs hailing from joint families have invested less than Rs. 1 lac, Rs. 2-3 lacs and Rs. 5-10 lacs. On the other hand, more than 63 per cent women entrepreneurs hailing from nuclear families invest money in the range of Rs. 3-5 lacs and more than Rs. 10 lacs in business. It indicates that women entrepreneurs coming from nuclear families have made more investment in business. It shows that entrepreneurship is growing among women entrepreneurs of nuclear families. On the other hand, in case of joint families elders take major decisions and even these decisions have to be binding on family members. The value of chi-square is statistically insignificant. Level of income earned by women entrepreneurs further shows that higher level of income has been earned by women entrepreneurs hailing from nuclear families than joint families. It may be due to more exposure to education and dexterity possessed by women entrepreneurs coming from nuclear families and cooperation received from family members. The value of chi-square is statistically insignificant. More than 50 per cent trained and untrained women entrepreneur hail from nuclear families. The values of chi-square are statistically insignificant. 68 per cent of women entrepreneurs hailing from nuclear families have taken financial assistance from financial institutions. It may be due to more awareness and knowledge, which may have been acquired by them from training institutes and from other sources. On the other hand, women entrepreneurs hailing from joint families are dependent on informal and internal sources of finance to manage their businesses. The value of chi-square is statistically significant at 1 per cent level of significance. 56 per cent women entrepreneurs own enterprises less than 10 years old belong to nuclear families. On the other hand, 51 per cent women entrepreneurs own enterprises more than 10 years old hail from joint families. It shows that women entrepreneurs from joint families have been involved in business for longer period of time. Information further highlights that post-reform period has observed growth of entrepreneurship among nuclear families. The value of chi-square is statistically insignificant.

Table 2.5 shows that 69 per cent of women entrepreneurs are managing business on individual basis and 31 per cent under other than individual form of business organizations. It shows that majority of women entrepreneurs want to manage business on individual basis and they do not want to take more risk in business. Education-wise information further shows that more than 70 per cent of women entrepreneurs possessing higher level of education are managing business on individual basis. On the other hand, 33 per cent to 41 per cent of women entrepreneurs possessing lower level of education are managing business under

TABLE 2.5

Forms of Business Organizations

Group	Individual	Others
All Data	309 (68.67)	141 (31.33)
Education		
Primary	16 (66.67)	8 (33.33)
Matric	47 (58.75)	33 (41.25)
Graduate	132 (70.21)	56 (29.79)
Post Graduate	114 (72.15)	44 (27.85)
Chi-square = 4.802; df = 3; Insignificant		
Age (years)		
Below 30	108 (76.60)	33 (23.40)
30-4ᴺ	101 (66.01)	52 (33.99)
Above 40	100 (64.10)	56 (35.90)
Chi-square = 6.131; df = 2; Significant at 5 per cent level		
Place of Origin		
Rural	49 (56.32)	38 (43.68)
Urban	260 (71.63)	103 (28.37)
Chi-square = 7.639; df = 1; Significant at 1 per cent level		
Type of Family		
Joint	140 (66.99)	69 (33.01)
Nuclear	169 (70.12)	72 (29.88)
Chi-square = 0.513; df = 1; Insignificant		
Investment (Lacs)		
<1	102 (82.93)	21 (17.07)
1-2	98 (68.06)	46 (31.94)
2-3	42 (54.55)	35 (45.45)
3-5	45 (70.31)	19 (29.69)
5-10	16 (51.61)	15 (48.39)
Above 10	6 (54.55)	5 (45.45)
Chi-square = 24.077; df = 5; Significant at 1 per cent level		
Income (Rs.)		
<7500	46 (85.19)	8 (14.81)
7500-10000	126 (83.44)	25 (16.56)
10000-15000	66 (68.04)	31 (31.96)

(Contd.)

Group	Individual	Others
15000-20000	48 (48.00)	52 (52.00)
20000+	23 (47.92)	25 (52.08)
Chi-square = 51.648; df = 4; Significant at 1 per cent level		
Training		
Got Training	162 (68.94)	73 (31.06)
No Training	147 (68.37)	68 (31.63)
Chi-square = 0.017; df = 1; Insignificant		
Sources of Finance		
Formal	70 (58.33)	50 (41.67)
Informal	239 (72.42)	91 (27.58)
Chi-square = 8.121; df = 1; Significant at 1 per cent level		
Age of Enterprise		
Below 10 years	204 (68.23)	95 (31.77)
Above 10 years	105 (69.54)	46 (30.46)
Chi-square = 0.080; df = 1; Insignificant		

other than individual form of business organizations. It may be due to less experience and difficulty in managing business in free market economies. The value of chi-square is statistically insignificant. More than 64 per cent women entrepreneurs in different age groups are managing business on individual basis. Slightly more than one-third women entrepreneurs in the age group of 30-40 and above 40 years are managing business on joint basis. The value of chi-square is statistically significant at 5 per cent level of significance. It shows that these two variables are positively associated. 43 per cent women entrepreneurs hailing from rural areas are doing business under other than individual form of business organization. It may be due to lack of exposure of markets or low level of education. On the other hand, 71 per cent of women entrepreneurs coming from urban areas are managing business on individual basis. The value of chi-square is statistically significant at 1 per cent level of significance. 67 per cent to 70 per cent women entrepreneurs irrespective of type of family are managing business under individual form of business organizations. On the other hand, one-third women entrepreneurs hailing from joint families are managing business on joint basis.

It may be due to availability of more persons in joint families. The value of chi-square is statistically insignificant. It seems logical that large scale business needs services of various experts in different fields to manage business effectively. More than 45 per cent women entrepreneurs investing Rs. 2-3 lacs and more than Rs. 5 lacs in business are managing business on joint basis. On the other hand, more than 68 per cent women entrepreneurs investing upto Rs. 2 lacs and Rs. 3-5 lacs are managing business on individual basis. The value of chi-square is statistically significant at 1 per cent level of significance. It shows that these two variables vary significantly. More than 83 per cent women entrepreneurs managing business on individual basis are earning upto Rs. 10,000 per month. On the other hand, 52 per cent women entrepreneurs managing business under other forms of business organizations are earning more than Rs. 15,000 per month in business. The reason to this may be assigned to economies of scale accrued in large scale business and effective utilization of manpower and other resources. The value of chi-square is statistically significant at 1 per cent level of significance. It shows that level of income and form of business organizations vary significantly. 68 per cent untrained women entrepreneurs are managing business under individual form of business organizations. The value of chi-square is statistically insignificant. 41 per cent of women entrepreneurs using formal sources of finance are doing business on joint basis. It may be due to preference of financial institutions to provide financial assistance more easily to large entrepreneurs and less risk involved in large businesses. On the other hand, 72 per cent women entrepreneurs using informal sources of finance are managing business on individual basis. The value of chi-square is statistically significant at 1 per cent level of significance. Almost same proportion of women entrepreneurs (68 per cent each) irrespective of life of their enterprises are managing business on individual basis. The value of chi-square is statistically insignificant.

Table 2.6 highlights that 42 per cent women entrepreneurs are involved in manufacturing sector and one-third in service sector. Only 16 per cent women entrepreneurs are doing business in trading activities. It reveals that there has been shift in pattern of business from manufacturing sector to service sector under new economic regime. It may be due to more business opportunities

TABLE 2.6

Type of Industry Run by Women Entrepreneurs

Group	Manufacturing	Trading	Services	Others
All Data	191 (42.44)	72 (16.00)	145 (32.22)	42 (9.33)
Education				
Primary	13 (54.17)	4 (16.67)	5 (20.83)	2 (8.33)
Matric	48 (60.00)	10 (12.50)	12 (15.00)	10 (12.50)
Graduate	74 (39.36)	27 (14.36)	73 (38.83)	14 (7.45)
Post Graduate	56 (35.44)	31 (19.62)	55 (34.81)	16 (10.13)
Chi-square = 23.975; df = 9; Significant at 1 per cent level				
Age (years)				
Below 30	53 (37.59)	32 (22.70)	40 (28.37)	16 (11.35)
30-40	72 (47.06)	14 (9.15)	50 (32.68)	17 (11.11)
Above 40	66 (42.31)	26 (16.67)	55 (35.26)	9 (5.77)
Chi-square = 14.391; df = 6; Significant at 5 per cent level				
Place of Origin				
Rural	46 (52.87)	13 (14.94)	22 (25.29)	6 (6.90)
Urban	145 (39.94)	59 (16.25)	123 (33.88)	36 (9.92)
Chi-square = 5.135; df = 3; Insignificant				
Type of Family				
Joint	91 (43.54)	36 (17.22)	63 (30.14)	19 (9.09)
Nuclear	100 (41.49)	36 (14.94)	82 (34.02)	23 (9.54)
Chi-square = 1.024; df = 3; Insignificant				
Form of Business Organization				
Sole	122 (39.48)	52 (16.83)	107 (34.63)	28 (9.06)
Others	64 (48.94)	20 (14.18)	38 (26.95)	14 (9.93)
Chi-square = 4.31 ; df = 3; Insignificant				
Investment (Lacs)				
<1	62 (50.41)	6 (4.88)	37 (30.08)	18 (14.63)
1-2	66 (45.83)	19 (13.19)	47 (32.64)	12 (8.33)
2-3	30 (38.96)	18 (23.38)	21 (27.27)	8 (10.39)
3-5	19 (29.69)	15 (23.44)	28 (43.75)	2 (3.12)
5-10	10 (32.26)	12 (38.71)	7 (22.58)	2 (6.45)
Above 10	4 (36.36)	2 (18.18)	5 (45.45)	
Chi-square = 43.623; df = 15; Significant at 1 per cent level				

Group	Manufacturing	Trading	Services	Others
Income (Rs.)				
< 7500	30 (55.56)	2 (3.70)	14 (25.93)	8 (14.81)
7500-10000	66 (43.71)	17 (11.26)	55 (36.42)	13 (8.61)
10000-15000	33 (34.02)	18 (18.56)	33 (34.02)	13 (13.40)
15000-20000	37 (37.00)	29 (29.00)	31 (31.00)	3 (3.00)
20000+	25 (52.08)	6 (12.50)	12 (25.00)	5 (10.42)
Chi-square = 34.480; df = 12; Significant at 1 per cent level				
Training				
Got Training	118 (50.21)	24 (10.21)	69 (29.36)	24 (10.21)
No Training	73 (33.95)	48 (22.33)	76 (35.35)	18 (8.37)
Chi-square = 18.946; df = 3; Significant at 1 per cent level				
Sources of Finance				
Formal	58 (48.33)	13 (10.83)	44 (36.67)	5 (4.17)
Informal	133 (40.30)	59 (17.88)	101 (30.61)	37 (11.21)
Chi-square = 9.750; df = 3; Significant at 5 per cent level				
Age of Enterprise				
Below 10 years	119 (39.80)	42 (14.05)	103 (34.45)	35 (11.71)
Above 10 years	72 (47.68)	30 (19.87)	42 (27.81)	7 (4.64)
Chi-square = 10.734; df = 3; Significant at 1 per cent level				

available in service sector, change in lifestyle and income of the people. Education-wise information further shows that women entrepreneurs possessing lower level of education are involved in manufacturing sector and women entrepreneurs having higher level of education are doing business in service sector. It seems that service sector needs more professional approach and women entrepreneurs having higher level of education might be having edge as compared to their counterparts having low level of education. The value of chi-square is statistically significant at 1 per cent level of significance. It shows that these variables vary significantly. 42 per cent to 47 per cent women entrepreneurs in the age group of 30-40 and more than 40 are doing business in manufacturing sector. Slightly more than one-third women entrepreneurs are engaged in service sector. On the other hand, 22 per cent and 28 per cent women entrepreneurs in lower age groups are involved in trading and services sector. It seems that younger women entrepreneurs are more inclined to do business in new emerging areas. The value of chi-square is statistically significant at 5 per cent level of significance. 52 per cent women entrepreneurs hailing from rural areas are involved in manufacturing activities. On the other hand, 50 per cent women entrepreneurs hailing from urban areas are involved in trading and service sector. The reason to this may be attributed to easy availability of training in service sector, more scope and low complexity involved. The value of chi-square is statistically insignificant. Type of family of women entrepreneurs further shows that women entrepreneurs are involved in different types of industries. More than 40 per cent of women entrepreneurs are involved in manufacturing activities and their next preferences are services and trading sector. The value of chi-square is statistically insignificant. Women entrepreneurs managing business under individual form of business organizations are more involved in manufacturing and service sector than other women entrepreneurs. It seems that business under trading and service sector is more viable under individual form of business organizations and manufacturing sectors in other than individual form of business organizations. The value of chi-square is statistically insignificant. Level of investment made by women entrepreneurs show that 45 per cent to 50 per cent women entrepreneurs investing upto Rs. 1-2 lacs and more than 30 per cent women entrepreneurs investing more than Rs. 3 lacs in business are involved in manufacturing sector. It seems that women entrepreneurs are engaged in households and cottage industries. Slightly more than one-third women entrepreneurs involved in manufacturing sector have invested more than Rs. 2 lacs in business. Women entrepreneurs involved in service sector have also invested more money in business. More than 43 per cent women entrepreneurs doing business in service sector have invested Rs. 3-5 lacs and more than Rs. 10 lacs in business. The value of chi-square is statistically significant at 1 per cent level of significance. Women entrepreneurs involved in manufacturing sector are earning higher level of income as compared to women entrepreneurs in other sectors. It reveals that manufacturing sector is still fetching more money inspite of opening up of economy and availability of cheap foreign goods in the market. 52 per cent women entrepreneurs in manufacturing sector are earning more than Rs. 20,000 per month and only 25 per cent women entrepreneurs in service sector are earning same level of income. It may be due to increase in competition and easy to establish service sector enterprises. The value of chi-square is statistically significant at 1 per cent level of significance. 50 per cent trained women entrepreneurs are involved in manufacturing sector and one-third in service sector. The value of chi-square is statistically significant at 1 per cent level of significance. Women entrepreneurs who have taken assistance from financial institution are relatively more engaged in manufacturing and service sector as compared to women entrepreneurs utilizing informal sources of finance. It seems that financial institutions are giving more preference to these sectors. The value of chi-square is statistically significant at 1 per cent level of significance. Women entrepreneurs having enterprises less than 10 years old are more involved in service sector and other industries than other women entrepreneurs. It shows that preference of younger generation of women entrepreneurs is towards services and other sectors and information further reveals that new sectors are fast emerging in free market economies. The value of chi-square is statistically significant at 1 per cent level of significance.

Table 2.7 shows that majority of women entrepreneurs have been in the business for the last ten years. It shows that entrepreneurship has grown during the last 10 years. Education-wise information further shows that women entrepreneurs having higher level of education has started participated in business activities during last ten years. On the other hand, women entrepreneurs having lower level of education were participating in the business activities for more than last 10 years. It shows that new economic policies have been able to instill concept of entrepreneurship among educated women. The value of chi-square is statistically significant at 1 per cent level of significance. 51 per cent women entrepreneurs hailing from rural areas and 69 per cent from urban areas have enterprises 10 years old. It shows that majority of entrepreneurs in our sample are young. The value of chi-square is statistically significant at 1 per cent level of significance. 70 per cent enterprises belonging to nuclear families are ten years old, whereas, 62 per cent enterprises of same age belong to joint families. It reveals that social and cultural barriers tied with family systems are no longer acting as obstacles in

TABLE 2.7

Age of Enterprise

Group	Below 10 years	Above 10 years
All Data	299 (66.44)	151 (33.56)
Education		
Primary	6 (25.00)	18 (75.00)
Matric	39 (48.75)	41 (51.25)
Graduate	127 (67.55)	61 (32.45)
Post Graduate	127 (80.38)	31 (19.62)
Chi-square = 43.589; df = 3; Significant at 1 per cent level		
Age (years)		
Below 30	136 (96.45)	5 (3.55)
30-40	112 (73.20)	41 (26.80)
Above 40	51 (32.69)	105 (67.31)
Chi-square = 139.795; df = 2; Significant at 1 per cent level		
Place of Origin		
Rural	45 (51.72)	42 (48.28)
Urban	254 (69.97)	109 (30.03)
Chi-square = 10.482; df = 1; Significant at 1 per cent level		
Type of Family		
Joint	131 (62.68)	78 (37.32)
Nuclear	16 (69.71)	73 (30.29)
Chi-square = 2.481; df = 1; Insignificant		
Form of Business Organization		
Sole	204 (66.02)	105 (33.98)
Others	95 (67.38)	46 (32.62)
Chi-square = 0.080; df = 1; Insignificant		
Investment (Lacs)		
<1	99 (80.49)	24 (19.51)
1-2	87 (60.42)	57 (39.58)
2-3	52 (67.53)	25 (32.47)
3-5	39 (60.94)	25 (39.06)
5-10	20 (64.52)	11 (35.48)
Above 10	2 (18.18)	9 (81.82)
Chi-square = 25.682; df = 5; Significant at 1 per cent level		

Group	Below 10 years	Above 10 years
Income (Rs.)		
<7500	41 (75.93)	13 (24.07)
7500-10000	96 (63.58)	55 (36.42)
10000-15000	66 (68.04)	31 (31.96)
15000-20000	66 (66.00)	34 (34.00)
20000+	30 (62.50)	18 (37.50)
Chi-square = 3.189; df = 4; Insignificant		
Training		
Got Training	175 (74.47)	60 (25.53)
No Training	124 (57.67)	91 (42.33)
Chi-square = 14.202; df = 1; Significant at 1 per cent level		
Sources of Finance		
Formal	76 (63.33)	44 (36.67)
Informal	223 (67.58)	107 (32.42)
Chi-square = 0.710; df = 1; Insignificant		

business. The value of chi-square is statistically insignificant. Almost same proportion of enterprises (66 per cent each) owned by experienced and unexperienced women entrepreneurs are 10 years old. It shows that experience is no longer a hurdle for women to enter in business line. The value of chi-square is statistically insignificant. 60 per cent to 80 per cent enterprises with investment upto Rs. 10 lacs are 10 years old and 81 per cent enterprises beyond investment of Rs. 10 lacs are more than ten years old. It reveals that post-reform period has seen the fast growth of micro and small enterprises. There is a need to formulate more liberal policies in this sector. The value of chi-square is statistically significant at 1 per cent level of significance. As high as 62 per cent enterprises are fetching more than Rs. 20,000 p.m. are ten years old. Information further shows that enterprises less than 10 years old are working in a professional manner. The value of chi-square is statistically significant at 1 per cent level of significance. It shows that level of income and age of enterprise very significantly. 74 per cent enterprises less than 10 years old are managed by trained women entrepreneurs. The value of chi-square is statistically significant at 1 per cent level of significance. More than 63 per cent enterprises have been managed with the help of formal and informal sources of finance which are ten years old. On the other hand, only one-third enterprises using same sources of finance are more than 10 years old. It shows that during post-reform regime enterprises have been run by using various sources of finance. It may also be due to growth of private finance in the new economic regime. Information further throws light on the fact that informal sources of finance are playing a dominant role in small and micro level enterprises. The value of chi-square is statistically significant at 1 per cent level of significance.

SUGGESTIONS AND POLICY IMPLICATIONS

The foregoing analysis reveals that in our sample, overwhelming proportion of women entrepreneurs are possessing higher level of education. There is a need to introduce business related course curriculum at +2 or graduate level to improve their skill in business field. With the spread of technical education in Northern India, suitable incentives should be provided to technically and professionally qualified women. Entrepreneurship is found to be at very low ebb in rural areas. Existing policies for the growth of women entrepreneurship in rural areas need to be further strengthened. Institutions of higher learning should be established in rural areas so that, female participation in higher education may be increased. Spread of education in rural areas will help in changing the mindset of people and problem relating to women participation in business will be increased to a large extent. Women prefer to establish home-based enterprises. Efforts should be made to provide information on various business opportunities available to potential women entrepreneurs, which can be started at their home place. There has been shift in structure of enterprises owned by women entrepreneurs. Under new economic regime, women entrepreneurs are entering in trading and service sector. It shows that service sector has made considerable growth during post-reform period. Overwhelming proportion of women entrepreneurs are using five workers and managing business on individual basis. Enterprises managed on joint basis can be more beneficial to women entrepreneurs. It will help them in solving the various problems faced by them and ultimately fetch more economies of scale in their businesses.

3

Entrepreneurial Process Among Women Entrepreneurs

The quest for economic independence and better social status forced women into self-employment and entrepreneurship. In recent years entrepreneurship development among women has picked up momentum. Several factors contributed to this most welcome phenomenon. The policies of central and state governments have undergone sweeping change in the recent period, particularly in the post-liberalisation era. The Industrial Policy Resolution of 1991 highlights the necessity to provide special training programmes to develop women entrepreneurship. The resolution further adds that the objective of such programmes is to increase the representation of women in the field of business and to enhance their economic and social status. There is also greater awareness now among Indian women about entrepreneurship as a career. The growing awareness is mainly due to the fact that the profile of Indian women has undergone perceptible change during the recent past. The citadels of academic excellence are no longer the prerogatives of men in India. In fact women are gradually willing to accept challenges and assume responsibilities in various fields: economic, social and political. In the present chapter, an attempt has been made to analyze the entrepreneurial process among women entrepreneurs in Northern India.

Table 3.1 reveals that 44 per cent women entrepreneurs are motivated by their husband, 30 per cent by their parents and only small proportion of women entrepreneurs motivated by their relatives (11 per cent) and friends (13 per cent). It shows that husband and family members are main motivating sources for the female entrepreneurs to join business line. Education-wise information further shows that women entrepreneurs having higher level of education are less motivated by their husband or parents than women entrepreneurs having lower level of education. The reason to this may be assigned to more experience and knowledge among highly educated women entrepreneurs and in this process they are less dependent on their family members. On the other hand, 50 per cent women entrepreneurs having education upto matric level are motivated by their husband to choose business line. Women entrepreneurs having studied upto graduate and post-graduate level of education are motivated by their parents. Only small proportion of women entrepreneurs are motivated by their relatives and friends. More than 50 per cent women entrepreneurs below the age of 30 are motivated by their parents and almost same proportion of women entrepreneurs having age beyond 30 are motivated by their husbands. The value of chi-square is statistically significant at 1 per cent level of significance. Almost same proportion of women entrepreneurs hailing from rural and urban areas are motivated by their husbands while choosing business line. The role of parents in motivating women to enter in business line is found to be more in rural areas than in urban areas. It may be due to lack of exposure in business line and commercial activities in rural areas. Lack of mobility may also be one of the reasons. The value of chi-square is statistically significant at 5 per cent level of significance. Women entrepreneurs (49 per cent) coming from nuclear families are relatively more motivated by their husbands than women entrepreneurs (38 per cent) coming from joint families. It shows that role of husband is found to be more in nuclear families than in joint families. On the other hand, due to availability of elders in joint families, the role of other family members becomes significant. On the other hand, the role of parents irrespective of type of family in motivating women is found to be almost same. The value of chi-square further shows that these two variables vary significantly. Almost same proportion of women

TABLE 3.1

Women Entrepreneurs Motivated by

Group	Parents	Relatives	Husband	Friends
All Data	138 (30.67)	51 (11.33)	199 (44.22)	62 (13.78)
Education				
Primary	8 (33.33)	4 (16.67)	12 (50.00)	—
Matric	14 (17.50)	12 (15.00)	42 (52.50)	12 (15.00)
Graduate	64 (34.04)	14 (7.45)	89 (47.34)	21 (11.17)
Post Graduate	52 (32.91)	21 (13.29)	56 (35.44)	29 (18.35)
Chi-square = 21.439; df = 9; Significant at 1per cent level				
Age (years)				
Below 30	74 (52.48)	3 (2.13)	38 (26.95)	26 (18.44)
30-40	24 (15.69)	26 (16.99)	79 (51.63)	24 (15.69)
Above 40	40 (25.64)	22 (14.10)	82 (52.56)	12 (7.69)
Chi-square = 70.976; df = 6; Significant at 1per cent level				
Place of Origin				
Rural	30 (34.48)	13 (14.94)	40 (45.98)	4 (4.60)
Urban	108 (29.75)	38 (10.47)	159 (43.80)	58 (15.98)
Chi-square = 8.424; df = 3; Significant at 5 per cent level				
Type of Family				
Joint	67 (32.06)	32 (15.31)	80 (38.28)	30 (14.35)
Nuclear	71 (29.46)	19 (7.88)	119 (49.38)	32 (13.28)
Chi-square = 8.907; df = 3; Significant at 5 per cent level				
Form of Business Organization				
Sole	99 (32.04)	34 (11.00)	138 (44.66)	38 (12.30)
Others	39 (27.66)	17 (12.06)	61 (43.26)	24 (17.02)
Chi-square = 2.311; df = 3; Insignificant				
Investment (Lacs)				
<1	39 (31.71)	9 (7.32)	53 (43.09)	22 (17.89)
1-2	43 (29.86)	29 (20.14)	53 (36.81)	19 (13.19)
2-3	19 (24.68)	9 (11.69)	33 (42.86)	16 (20.78)
3-5	19 (29.69)	1 (1.56)	40 (62.50)	4 (6.25)
5-10	13 (41.94)	—	17 (54.54)	1 (3.23)
Above 10	5 (45.45)	3 (27.27)	3 (27.27)	—
Chi-square = 45.179; df = 15; Significant at 1per cent level				

(*Contd.*)

Group	Parents	Relatives	Husband	Friends
Income (Rs.)				
<7500	17 (31.48)	3 (5.56)	28 (51.85)	6 (11.11)
7500-10000	39 (25.83)	20 (13.25)	70 (46.36)	22 (14.57)
10000-15000	22 (22.68)	23 (23.71)	37 (38.14)	15 (15.46)
15000-20000	38 (38.00)	2 (2.00)	42 (42.00)	18 (18.00)
20000+	22 (45.83)	3 (6.25)	22 (45.83)	1 (2.08)
Chi-square = 40.930; df = 12; Significant at 1per cent level				
Training				
Got Training	91 (38.72)	12 (5.11)	89 (37.87)	43 (18.30)
No Training	47 (21.86)	39 (18.14)	110 (51.16)	19 (8.84)
Chi-square = 39.018; df = 3; Significant at 1per cent level				
Sources of Finance				
Formal	51 (42.50)	6 (5.00)	50 (41.67)	13 (10.83)
Informal	87 (26.36)	45 (13.64)	149 (45.15)	49 (14.85)
Chi-square = 14.535; df = 3; Significant at 1per cent level				
Age of Enterprise				
Below 10 years	94 (31.44)	34 (11.37)	124 (41.47)	47 (15.72)
Above 10 years	44 (29.14)	17 (11.26)	75 (49.67)	15 (9.93)
Chi-square = 4.136; df = 3; Insignificant				

entrepreneurs doing business under individual and other form of business organizations are motivated by their husbands to choose business line. On the other hand, 32 per cent and 27 per cent women entrepreneurs doing business under individual and other form of business organizations are motivated by their parents to enter in business line. The value of chi-square further shows that these two variables are independent. 24 per cent to 31 per cent women entrepreneurs investing money upto Rs. 5 lacs in business are motivated by their parents and more than 40 per cent investing money beyond Rs. 5 lacs are motivated by their parents. On the other hand, 62 per cent to 55 per cent women entrepreneurs investing money in the range of Rs. 3-10 lacs in business are motivated by their husbands. The value of chi-square is statistically significant at 1 per cent level of significance. More than 42 per cent women entrepreneurs earning income in all ranges except Rs. 10,000-15,000 per month are motivated by their husbands. The value of chi-square is statistically significant at 1 per cent level of significance. It shows that there exist variations between these two variables. 51 per cent women entrepreneurs who have not undergone training before start of their business are motivated by their husbands, whereas this ratio is 38 per cent in case of trained women entrepreneurs. It seems that untrained women entrepreneurs need more guidance and advise in business process. 39 per cent trained women entrepreneurs are motivated by their parents. The role of relatives is found to be more in case of untrained women entrepreneurs and friends in case of trained women entrepreneurs. It seems that people do not want to take risk in business and motivate their daughters/wives to take training before start of business. The value of chi-square is statistically significant at 1 per cent level of significance. 42 per cent of women entrepreneurs who have availed assistance from financial institutions are motivated by their parents. On the other hand, 45 per cent of women entrepreneurs who are dependent on informal sources of finance are motivated by their husbands. The value of chi-square is statistically significant at 1 per cent level of significance. 50 per cent of women entrepreneurs whose enterprises are more than 10 years old are motivated by their husbands whereas, this ratio is 42 per cent in case of women entrepreneurs having enterprises less than 10 years old. It seems that younger women entrepreneurs need less motivation from various sources. Almost same proportion of women entrepreneurs irrespective of their age of enterprises are motivated by their parents. The value of chi-square is statistically insignificant. It shows that these two variables are independent. The idea to start business is a very complicated process under changing economic scenario. Moreover, income, taste and preferences, standard of living and requirements of people are changing very rapidly. Business opportunities are also increasing tremendously under new economic regime and colossal amount of information is available from various sources such as internet, newspapers, magazines and various agencies imparting information in the field of business.

Table 3.2 shows the sources, from where business ideas have been taken by women entrepreneurs. Information vividly shows that under changing economic scenario individual cannot have business ideas independently. Information has to be taken from

TABLE 3.2

Who gave you Idea to Start Business

Group	Self	Relatives	Friends	Govt.	Family	Others
All Data	74 (16.44)	37 (8.22)	58 (12.89)	4 (0.89)	264 (58.67)	13 (2.89)
Education						
Primary	5 (20.83)	3 (12.50)	—	—	16 (66.67)	—
Matric	18 (22.50)	4 (5.00)	9 (11.25)	2 (2.50)	44 (55.00)	3 (3.75)
Graduate	19 (10.11)	9 (4.79)	29 (15.43)	—	127 (67.55)	4 (2.13)
Post Graduate	32 (20.25)	21 (13.29)	20 (12.66)	2 (1.27)	77 (48.73)	6 (3.80)
Chi-square = 33.269; df = 15; Significant at 1per cent level						
Age (years)						
Below 30	20 (14.18)	6 (4.26)	22 (15.60)	—	92 (65.5)	1 (0.71)
30-40	27 (17.65)	13 (8.50)	25 (16.34)	1 (0.65)	83 (54.25)	4 (2.61)
Above 40	27 (17.31)	18 (11.54)	11 (7.05)	3 (1.92)	89 (57.05)	8 (5.13)
Chi-square = 21.698; df = 10 ; Significant at 1per cent level						
Place of Origin						
Rural	19 (21.84)	8 (9.20)	11 (12.64)	—	46 (52.87)	3 (3.45)
Urban	55 (15.15)	29 (7.99)	47 (12.95)	4 (1.10)	218 (60.06)	10 (2.75)
Chi-square = 3.730; df = 5; Insignificant						
Type of Family						
Joint	38 (18.18)	20 (9.57)	21 (10.05)	1 (0.48)	117 (55.98)	12 (5.74)
Nuclear	36 (14.94)	17 (7.05)	37 (15.95)	3 (1.24)	147 (61.00)	1 (0.41)
Chi-square = 16.234; df = 5; Significant at 1per cent level						
Form of Business Organization						
Sole	58 (18.77)	23 (7.44)	34 (11.00)	—	184 (59.55)	10 (3.24)
Others	16 (11.35)	14 (9.93)	24 (17.02)	4 (2.84)	80 (56.74)	3 (2.13)
Chi-square = 16.000; df = 5; Significant at 1per cent level						
Investment (Lacs)						
<1	22 (17.89)	7 (5.69)	15 (12.00)	—	76 (61.79)	3 (2.44)
1-2	22 (15.28)	18 (12.50)	29 (20.14)	2 (1.39)	71 (49.31)	2 (1.39)
2-3	14 (18.18)	7 (9.09)	11 (14.29)	—	40 (51.95)	5 (6.49)
3-5	9 (14.06)	2 (3.2)	—	—	50 (78.12)	3 (4.69)
5-10	5 (16.13)	—	2 (6.45)	2 (6.45)	22 (70.97)	—
Above 10	2 (18.18)	3 (27.27)	1 (9.09)	—	5 (45.45)	—
Chi-square = 58.170; df = 25; Significant at 1per cent level						

Group	Self	Relatives	Friends	Govt.	Family	Others
Income (Rs.)						
<7500	10 (18.52)	1 (1.85)	4 (7.41)	—	37 (68.52)	2 (3.70)
7500-10000	17 (11.26)	16 (10.60)	23 (15.23)	—	89 (58.94)	6 (3.97)
10000-15000	18 (18.56)	15 (15.46)	19 (19.59)	—	45 (46.39)	—
15000-20000	25 (25.00)	—	10 (10.00)	2 (2.00)	58 (58.00)	5 (5.00)
20000+	4 (8.33)	5 (10.42)	2 (4.17)	2 (4.17)	35 (72.92)	—
Chi-square = 57.797; df = 20; Significant at 1per cent level						
Training						
Got Training	25 (10.64)	12 (5.11)	36 (15.32)	4 (1.70)	156 (66.38)	2 (0.85)
No Training	49 (22.79)	25 (11.63)	22 (10.23)	—	108 (50.23)	11 (5.12)
Chi-square = 33.867; df = 5; Significant at 1per cent level						
Sources of Finance						
Formal	12 (10.00)	5 (4.17)	13 (10.83)	4 (3.33)	86 (71.67)	—
Informal	62 (18.79)	32 (9.70)	45 (13.64)	—	178 (53.94)	13 (3.94)
Chi-square = 28.384; df = 5; Significant at 1per cent level						
Age of Enterprise						
Below 10years	51 (17.06)	25 (8.36)	48 (16.05)	—	171 (57.19)	4 (1.34)
Above 10years	23 (15.23)	12 (7.95)	10 (6.62)	4 (2.65)	93 (61.59)	9 (5.96)
Chi-square = 22.820; df = 5; Significant at 1per cent level						

various sources if one has to be successful in business. Information contained in Table highlights that only 16 per cent women entrepreneurs started business without taking assistance from other sources. 58 per cent women entrepreneurs took idea from family members, 13 per cent from friends and 8 per cent from relatives. Education-wise information reveals that only one-fifth women entrepreneurs do not take business idea from outside except women entrepreneurs possessing graduate level of education (10 per cent). It shows that education enhances the awareness of business opportunities. The proportion of women entrepreneurs who have taken idea from their family members vary from 49 per cent to 67 per cent. It shows that family members are playing a significant role in providing business ideas to female members. The role of relatives and friends in imparting business ideas has been found to be negligible. The idea to start business from various sources is found to be increasing with the level of education. The value of chi-square further justifies the argument given in this table. Level of education and business ideas from various sources differ significantly. Women entrepreneurs in lower age group have taken assistance from various sources to get business idea than women entrepreneurs in higher age group. 65 per cent women entrepreneurs in the age group of less than 30 have taken business idea from their family members, followed by friends and self. On the other hand, the role of individual in business is found to be low among all age groups of women entrepreneurs. The value of chi-square is statistically significant at 1 per cent level of significance. It shows that these two variables differ significantly. Almost same proportion of women entrepreneurs hailing from rural and urban areas took assistance from their relatives and friends while going for business. The role of family members (60 per cent) is found to be more among urban women entrepreneurs than rural women entrepreneurs (53 per cent). The value of chi-square is statistically significant at 1 per cent level of significance. Role of family members, relatives and friends are found to be slightly on higher side among women entrepreneurs coming from nuclear families than that of joint families. The value of chi-square is statistically significant at 1 per cent level of significance. Almost same proportion of women entrepreneurs managing business under individual and other form of business organization take the assistance of family members to have business idea. Women entrepreneurs managing business under other than individual forms of business organizations take assistance from friends and govt. agencies to start business. It shows that large business needs assistance from various sources to fulfil various requirements. Role of relatives is found to be almost same in both the cases. Similarly, individual role to start business without any external assistance is found to be more among sole proprietors (19 per cent) than other forms of business organizations (11 per cent). It may be due to small size of business, individual can think of taking risk. The value of chi-square is statistically significant at 1 per cent level of significance. Less than one-fifth women entrepreneurs investing different levels of money started their business without taking idea from external sources. More than 70 per cent women entrepreneurs investing money in the range of Rs. 3-10 lacs take assistance from family members in taking business ideas and in other investment ranges, this proportion varies from 45 per cent to 62 per cent. The role of relatives (27 per cent) is found to be more among women entrepreneurs having invested money in the range of Rs. 10 lacs and above. Assistance from relatives and friends is higher among women entrepreneurs investing money upto Rs. 3 lacs in business. The value of chi-square is statistically significant at 1 per cent level of significance. Less than one-fifth women entrepreneurs earning different levels of income start business without any assistance. 46 per cent to 72 per cent women entrepreneurs earning different levels of income take assistance from family members to start their business. The value of chi-square is statistically significant at 1 per cent level of significance. Untrained women entrepreneurs take assistance from various sources to start their business than trained women entrepreneurs. The reason to this may be attributed to lack of knowledge in business and failure to identify various business opportunities available in the market. On the other hand, trained women entrepreneurs get all this information from institutes imparting training in the field of entrepreneurship development. The value of chi-square is statistically significant at 1 per cent level of significance. Women entrepreneurs who have not taken financial assistance from financial institutions have taken idea from various sources to start their business ventures. The value of chi-square is statistically significant at 1 per cent level of significance. It shows that these two variables are positively associated. Women entrepreneurs whose enterprises are less than 10 years old take assistance from various sources. It highlights that new generation of entrepreneurs have broaden their outlook than old enterprise, which might be having conservative view. The value of chi-square is statistically significant at 1 per cent level of significance.

Table 3.3 shows that 37 per cent women entrepreneurs have completed their projects in less than three months, 43 per cent in 3-6 months period and 20 per cent women entrepreneurs complete their projects in more than 6 months. Information vividly reveals that 80 per cent projects have been completed by women entrepreneurs within the time period of 6 months. It corroborates the arguments of various researchers in the field of small business that small enterprises can be started in less time period. Slightly more than one-third women entrepreneurs possessing different level of education (except in case of matric level) completed their

TABLE 3.3

Time taken to Complete the Project (in months)

Group	Below 3	3-6	6-12	12-24	24+
All Data	165 (36.67)	195 (43.33)	66 (14.67)	18 (4.00)	6 (1.33)
Education					
Primary	9 (37.50)	11 (45.83)	1 (4.17)	3 (12.50)	—
Matric	34 (42.50)	31 (38.75)	12 (15.00)	2 (2.50)	1 (1.25)
Graduate	64 (34.04)	90 (47.87)	23 (12.23)	8 (4.26)	3 (1.60)
Post Graduate	58 (36.71)	63 (39.87)	30 (18.99)	5 (3.16)	2 (1.27)
Chi-square = 12.951; df = 12; Insignificant					
Age (years)					
Below 30	50 (35.46)	62 (43.97)	26 (18.44)	2 (1.42)	1 (0.71)
30-40	55 (35.95)	65 (42.48)	24 (15.69)	9 (5.88)	—
Above 40	60 (38.46)	68 (43.59)	16 (10.26)	7 (4.49)	5 (3.21)
Chi-square = 14.150; df = 8; Insignificant					
Place of Origin					
Rural	27 (31.03)	40 (45.98)	13 (14.94)	5 (5.75)	2 (2.30)
Urban	138 (38.02)	155 (42.70)	53 (14.60)	13 (3.58)	4 (1.10)
Chi-square = 2.690; df = 4; Insignificant					
Type of Family					
Joint	76 (36.36)	92 (44.02)	28 (13.40)	8 (3.83)	5 (2.39)
Nuclear	89 (36.93)	103 (42.74)	38 (15.77)	10 (4.15)	1 (0.41)
Chi-square = 3.792; df = 4; Insignificant					
Form of Business Organization					
Sole	131 (42.39)	130 (42.07)	40 (12.94)	3 (0.97)	5 (1.62)
Others	34 (24.11)	65 (46.10)	26 (18.44)	15 (10.64)	1 (0.71)
Chi-square = 34.402; df = 4; Significant at 1 per cent level					
Investment (Lacs)					
<1	70 (56.91)	43 (34.96)	9 (7.32)	—	1 (0.81)
1-2	52 (36.11)	62 (43.06)	26 (18.06)	4 (2.78)	—
2-3	25 (32.47)	36 (46.75)	9 (11.69)	6 (7.79)	1 (1.30)
3-5	16 (25.00)	31 (48.44)	10 (15.62)	3 (4.69)	4 (6.25)
5-10	2 (6.45)	19 (61.29)	8 (25.81)	2 (6.45)	—
Above 10	—	4 (36.36)	4 (36.36)	3 (27.27)	—
Chi-square = 83.586; df = 20; Significant at 1 per cent level					

Group	Below 3	3-6	6-12	12-24	24+
Income (Rs.)					
<7500	43 (79.63)	11 (20.37)	—	—	—
7500-10000	62 (41.06)	66 (43.71)	19 (12.58)	2 (1.32)	2 (1.32)
10000-15000	37 (38.14)	34 (35.05)	21 (21.65)	4 (4.12)	1 (1.03)
15000-20000	22 (22.00)	61 (61.00)	14 (14.00)	—	3 (3.00)
20000+	1 (2.08)	23 (47.92)	12 (25.00)	12 (25.00)	—
Chi-square = 145.519; df = 16; Significant at 1 per cent level					
Training					
Got Training	88 (37.45)	108 (45.96)	28 (11.91)	11 (4.68)	—
No Training	77 (35.81)	87 (40.47)	38 (17.67)	7 (3.26)	6 (2.79)
Chi-square = 10.531; df = 4; Significant at 5 per cent level					
Sources of Finance					
Formal	38 (31.67)	56 (46.67)	22 (18.33)	3 (2.50)	1 (0.83)
Informal	127 (38.48)	139 (42.12)	44 (13.33)	15 (4.55)	5 (1.52)
Chi-square = 4.263; df = 4; Insignificant					
Age of Enterprise					
Below 10 years	103 (34.45)	127 (42.47)	55 (18.39)	12 (4.01)	2 (0.67)
Above 10 years	62 (41.06)	68 (45.03)	11 (7.28)	6 (3.97)	4 (2.65)
Chi-square = 12.742; df = 4; Significant at 1 per cent level					

projects in less than three months. Similarly, 46 per cent to 48 per cent women entrepreneurs possessing low and higher level of education complete their projects in 3-6 months' period. It may be due to difference in type of business run by them. The value of chi-square is statistically insignificant. Age-wise information further shows that almost same proportion of women entrepreneurs in different age groups complete their projects in less than three months and 3-6 months' period respectively. 18 per cent women entrepreneurs in the age group of less than 30 took 6-12 months' period to complete their projects, whereas this ratio is 15 per cent to 10 per cent in case of women entrepreneurs in higher age groups. The value of chi-square is statistically insignificant. 38 per cent women entrepreneurs hailing from urban areas complete their projects in the period of less than 3 months, whereas this ratio is 31 per cent in case of women entrepreneurs coming from rural areas. On the other hand, almost same proportion of women entrepreneurs hailing from urban and rural areas have completed their projects in 6-12 months' period. The value of chi-square is statistically insignificant. Almost same proportion of women entrepreneurs irrespective of type of family have completed their projects in different time periods. The value of chi-square is statistically insignificant. Women entrepreneurs managing business under other than individual forms of business organizations have completed their projects in longer period of time than women entrepreneurs managing business under individual form of business organizations. The value of chi-square is statistically significant at 1 per cent level of significance. Projects involving more investment take longer time period in completion than other projects. 32 per cent to 36 per cent projects with investment upto Rs. 3 lacs have been completed in less than 3 months. On the other hand, projects involving more than investment (Rs. 3 lacs) were completed in more than three months period. The value of chi-square is statistically significant at 1 per cent level of significance. It shows that level of investment and time period in completion of project vary significantly. Women entrepreneurs earning lower level of income complete their project in shorter span of time than other women entrepreneurs. It shows that a large project fetches economies of scale although these projects take longer time in completion. The value of chi-square is statistically significant at 1 per cent level of significance. It shows that these two variables vary significantly. Trained women entrepreneurs have completed their projects in less time period than untrained women entrepreneurs. It shows that training helps women entrepreneurs in project formulation and implementation. The value of chi-square is statistically significant at 5 per cent level of significance. 39 per cent women entrepreneurs who have used informal sources of finance have completed their projects in less than 3 months as compared to other women entrepreneurs (32 per cent). It may be due to very small projects and requires less formalities. But women entrepreneurs using formal sources of finance have completed their projects in much earlier time periods (3-6 and 6-12 months) than other women entrepreneurs. The reason to this may be attributed to availability of finance and use of expertise during project implementation stage. The value of chi-square is statistically insignificant. Number of women entrepreneurs who have enterprises less than 10 years old have completed their project much earlier than women entrepreneurs possessing enterprises more than 10 years old. It shows that new economic regime has provided more facilities to women entrepreneurs as compared to earlier one. The value of chi-square is statistically significant at 1 per cent level of significance. Table 3.4 reveals that 28 per cent women entrepreneurs are managing their business from their home and purchase shops and 34 per cent from rental premises. Only 5 per cent women entrepreneurs are managing business on plots provided by government. Education-wise information reveals that only 20 per cent women entrepreneurs having post-graduate level of

TABLE 3.4

Location of Enterprise

Group	Home	Rented shops	Purchased	Govt.	Others
All Data	128 (28.44)	153 (34.00)	134 (29.78)	23 (5.11)	12 (2.67)
Education					
Primary	10 (41.67)	5 (20.83)	5 (20.83)	2 (8.33)	2 (8.33)
Matric	25 (31.25)	32 (40.00)	20 (25.00)	3 (3.75)	—
Graduate	61 (32.45)	66 (35.11)	51 (27.13)	6 (3.19)	4 (2.13)
Post Graduate	32 (20.25)	50 (31.65)	58 (36.71)	12 (7.59)	6 (3.80)
Chi-square = 23.155; df = 12; Significant at 5 per cent level					
Age (years)					
Below 30	37 (26.24)	49 (34.75)	47 (33.33)	4 (2.84)	4 (2.84)
30-40	46 (30.07)	60 (39.22)	41 (26.80)	6 (3.92)	—
Above 40	45 (28.85)	44 (28.21)	46 (29.49)	13 (8.33)	8 (5.13)
Chi-square = 16.898; df = 8; Significant at 5 per cent level					
Place of Origin					
Rural	30 (34.48)	29 (33.33)	20 (22.99)	5 (5.75)	3 (3.45)
Urban	98 (27.00)	124 (34.16)	114 (31.40)	18 (4.96)	9 (2.48)
Chi-square = 3.398; df = 4; Insignificant					
Type of Family					
Joint	69 (33.01)	72 (34.45)	57 (27.27)	8 (3.83)	3 (1.44)
Nuclear	59 (24.48)	81 (33.61)	77 (31.95)	15 (6.22)	9 (3.73)
Chi-square = 7.187; df = 4; Insignificant					

(Contd.)

Group	Home	Rented shops	Purchased	Govt.	Others
Form of Business Organization					
Sole	108 (34.95)	98 (31.72)	88 (28.48)	9 (2.91)	6 (1.94)
Others	20 (14.18)	55 (39.01)	46 (32.62)	14 (9.93)	6 (4.26)
Chi-square = 28.022; df = 4; Significant at 1 per cent level					
Investment (Lacs)					
<1	64 (52.03)	34 (27.64)	22 (17.89)	2 (1.63)	1 (0.81)
1-2	37 (25.69)	65 (45.14)	35 (24.31)	3 (2.08)	4 (2.78)
2-3	23 (29.87)	22 (28.57)	25 (32.47)	7 (9.09)	—
3-5	4 (6.25)	14 (21.88)	36 (56.25)	6 (9.38)	4 (6.25)
5-10	—	12 (38.71)	14 (45.16)	4 (12.90)	1 (3.23)
Above 10	—	6 (54.55)	2 (18.18)	1 (9.09)	2 (18.18)
Chi-square = 115.630; df = 20; Significant at 1 per cent level					
Income (Rs.)					
<7500	28 (51.85)	19 (35.19)	7 (12.96)	—	—
7500-10000	52 (34.44)	62 (41.06)	31 (20.53)	6 (3.97)	—
10000-15000	31 (31.96)	35 (36.08)	23 (23.71)	1 (1.03)	7 (7.22)
15000-20000	17 (17.00)	21 (21.00)	50 (50.00)	10 (10.00)	2 (2.00)
20000+	—	16 (33.33)	23 (47.92)	6 (12.50)	3 (6.25)
Chi-square = 99.603; df = 16; Significant at 1 per cent level					
Training					
Got Training	64 (27.23)	91 (38.72)	71 (30.21)	6 (2.55)	3 (1.28)
No Training	64 (29.77)	62 (28.84)	63 (29.30)	17 (7.91)	9 (4.19)
Chi-square = 13.373; df = 4; Significant at 1 per cent level					
Sources of Finance					
Formal	8 (6.67)	37 (30.83)	50 (41.67)	16 (13.33)	9 (7.50)
Informal	120 (36.36)	116 (35.15)	84 (25.45)	7 (2.12)	3 (0.91)
Chi-square = 71.514; df = 4; Significant at 1 per cent level					
Age of Enterprise					
Below 10 years	73 (24.41)	118 (39.46)	93 (31.10)	8 (2.68)	7 (2.34)
Above 10 years	55 (36.42)	35 (23.18)	41 (27.15)	15 (9.93)	5 (3.31)
Chi-square = 24.135; df = 4; Significant at 1 per cent level					

education are managing their business from their homes, whereas this ratio is 42 per cent in case of women entrepreneurs possessing primary level of education. It seems that educated women entrepreneurs want to avail benefits of nearness of market while doing business. On the other hand, women entrepreneurs possessing lower level of education due to scarcity of finance want to avoid the fixed cost of capital in business. 40 per cent of women entrepreneurs are managing their business from rental buildings. One-fourth women entrepreneurs having education upto graduate level are managing their business from purchased buildings. Only 7 per cent women entrepreneurs possessing post-graduate and primary level of education are managing their business from plots provided by government. The value of chi-square is statistically significant at 5 per cent level of significance. One-third women entrepreneurs in the age group of below 30 are operating their business either on the rental or purchased building. Almost same proportion of women entrepreneurs in the age group above 40 are operating their business from rental and purchased buildings. Only 8 per cent women entrepreneurs in the age group of above 40 are doing business on the plots provided by government. It seems that women entrepreneurs in the higher age group are able to avail basic infrastructural facilities from government. It may be due to experience and opportunities available to them. 39 per cent women entrepreneurs in the age group of 30-40 are managing their business from rental buildings. The value of chi-square is statistically significant at 5 per cent level of significance. One-third of women entrepreneurs hailing from rural areas are managing their business from their home, whereas, one-fourth women entrepreneurs from urban areas doing business from their home place. Almost same proportion of women entrepreneurs coming from rural and urban areas are managing their business from rental buildings and plots provided by government. It reveals that women entrepreneurs want to avail benefits of market while doing business. The value of chi-square is statistically insignificant. Only one-fourth of women entrepreneurs hailing from nuclear families are operating their business from their home places whereas this ratio is one-third in case of women entrepreneurs coming from joint families. It seems that women entrepreneurs of nuclear families are more aware of benefits of operating business other than their home place. The value of chi-square is statistically insignificant. 35 per cent women entrepreneurs managing business under individual form of business organizations are operating their business from their home and 31 per cent from rental buildings. On the other hand, 39 per cent women entrepreneurs managing business under other than individual forms of business organization are doing business from rental buildings and 33 per cent from purchased shops. 10 per cent women entrepreneurs are managing business on the plots provided by governments. It shows that women entrepreneurs managing business on large scale are able to get various benefits from government. The value of chi-square is statistically significant at 1 per cent level of significance. 52 per cent women entrepreneurs investing less than Rs. 1 lacs in business are managing business from their home. Only 27 per cent women entrepreneurs investing same level of money are doing business from rented buildings. On the other hand, 38 per cent to 54 per cent women entrepreneurs investing more than Rs. 5 lacs in business are operating their business from rental buildings. 56 per cent to 45 per cent women entrepreneurs invested money in the range of Rs. 3-10 lacs are managing their business from purchased shops. It shows that assistance from government on provision of fixed assets has been found to be low. The value of chi-square is statistically significant at 1 per cent level of significance. Level of income earned by women entrepreneurs further show that higher level of income has been earned by only those women entrepreneurs who have been operating their business from other than home place. It shows that location of business affects the earnings of women entrepreneurs. The value of chi-square is statistically significant at 1 per cent level of significance. Almost same proportion of trained and untrained women entrepreneurs are managing their business from their home and purchased buildings. On the other hand, trained women entrepreneurs (38 per cent) are managing their businesses from rented buildings, whereas this ratio is 28 per cent in case of untrained women entrepreneurs. But untrained women entrepreneurs are also managing their business on the plots provided by governments. The value of chi-square is statistically significant at 1 per cent level of significance. Overwhelming proportion of women entrepreneurs who have taken financial assistance from financial institutions are managing their business from purchased buildings and plots provided by government. On the other hand, women entrepreneurs using informal sources of finance are managing their business either from home or rented buildings. The value of chi-square is statistically significant at

1 per cent level of significance. 39 per cent to 31 per cent women entrepreneurs who have been in business for last 10 years are managing their business from rented and purchased buildings. On the other hand, women entrepreneurs having enterprises more than 10 years older are managing their business on the plots provided by government. It shows that these women entrepreneurs have been able to manage fixed assets from government during controlled regime. The value of chi-square is statistically significant at 1 per cent level of significance.

Table 3.5 highlights that 56 per cent women entrepreneurs are doing business to achieve something, whereas 25 per cent women entrepreneurs are entering in business line to make use of free time. Only 18 per cent women entrepreneurs are doing business due to the family compulsions. It reveals that majority of women entrepreneurs are doing business to achieve something. It is a true indicator of entrepreneurship development among women. Education-wise information further projects that women entrepreneurs possessing higher level of education are doing business to achieve something. On the other hand, women entrepreneurs educated upto matric level are doing business due to family compulsions. Only small proportion of women entrepreneurs are doing business just to make use of free time. The value of chi-square is statistically significant at 1 per cent level of significance. Age-wise information further shows that younger women entrepreneurs are more achievement oriented than women entrepreneurs having more age. More than 60 per cent women entrepreneurs upto the age group of 40 are doing business to achieve something and one-fourth women entrepreneurs are doing business to make use of free-time. 32 per cent women entrepreneurs beyond age of 40 are in business line due to family compulsion. The value of chi-square is statistically significant at 1 per cent level of significance. 57 per cent women entrepreneurs hailing from urban areas and 48 per cent from rural areas are doing business to achieve something. On the other hand, 32 per cent women entrepreneurs coming from rural areas are entering in business line due to family compulsions. The reason to this may be attributed to stagnation in agriculture and decline in employment opportunities in rural areas. Only small proportion of women entrepreneurs are doing business just to make use of

TABLE 3.5

Reasons for Entering in Business Line

Group	Achieve something	Make use of free time	Family compulsion
1	2	3	4
All Data	252 (56.00)	115 (25.56)	83 (18.44)
Education			
Primary	6 (25.00)	6 (25.00)	12 (50.00)
Matric	33 (41.25)	24 (30.00)	23 (28.75)
Graduate	109 (57.98)	51 (27.13)	28 (14.89)
Post Graduate	104 (65.82)	34 (21.52)	20 (12.66)
Chi-square = 33.607; df = 6; Significant at 1 per cent level			
Age (years)			
Below 30	90 (63.83)	40 (28.37)	11 (7.80)
30-40	92 (60.13)	40 (26.14)	21 (13.73)
Above 40	70 (44.87)	35 (22.44)	51 (32.69)
Chi-square = 34.187; df = 4; Significant at 1 per cent level			
Place of Origin			
Rural	42 (48.28)	17 (19.54)	28 (32.18)
Urban	210 (57.85)	98 (27.00)	55 (15.15)
Chi-square = 13.714; df = 2; Significant at 1 per cent level			
Type of Family			
Joint	108 (51.67)	51 (24.40)	50 (23.92)
Nuclear	144 (59.75)	64 (26.56)	33 (13.69)
Chi-square = 7.859; df = 2; Significant at 1 per cent level			
Form of Business Organization			
Sole	174 (56.31)	77 (24.92)	58 (18.77)
Others	78 (55.32)	38 (26.95)	25 (17.73)
Chi-square = 0.230; df = 2; Insignificant			
Investment (Lacs)			
<1	62 (50.41)	40 (32.52)	21 (17.07)
1-2	78 (54.17)	38 (26.39)	28 (19.44)
2-3	47 (61.04)	13 (16.88)	17 (22.08)
3-5	37 (57.81)	17 (26.56)	10 (15.62)

1	2	3	4
5-10	22 (70.97)	6 (19.35)	3 (9.68)
Above 10	6 (54.55)	1 (9.09)	4 (36.36)
Chi-square = 12.941; df = 10; Insignificant			
Income (Rs.)			
<7500	26 (48.15)	19 (35.19)	9 (16.67)
7500-10000	64 (42.38)	58 (38.41)	29 (19.21)
10000-15000	48 (49.48)	19 (19.59)	30 (30.93)
15000-20000	78 (78.00)	13 (13.00)	9 (9.00)
20000+	36 (75.00)	6 (12.50)	6 (12.50)
Chi-square = 54.602; df = 8; Significant at 1 per cent level			
Training			
Got Training	146 (62.13)	62 (26.38)	27 (11.49)
No Training	106 (49.30)	53 (24.65)	56 (26.05)
Chi-square = 16.329; df = 2; Significant at 1 per cent level			
Sources of Finance			
Formal	88 (73.33)	19 (15.83)	13 (10.83)
Informal	164 (49.70)	96 (29.09)	70 (21.21)
Chi-square = 19.971; df = 2; Significant at 1 per cent level			
Age of Enterprise			
Below 10 years	182 (60.87)	85 (28.43)	32 (10.70)
Above 10 years	70 (46.36)	30 (19.87)	51 (33.77)
Chi-square = 35.608; df = 2; Significant at 1 per cent level			

free time. Information throws light on the fact that to do business is not an easy job, it requires a lot of time, skill, money and manpower. It may be due to these reasons that women entrepreneurs have not given much preference to make use of free time variable. The value of chi-square is statistically significant at 1 per cent level of significance. It reveals that nativity and reasons for entering in business line vary significantly. Women entrepreneurs coming from nuclear families are more achievement-oriented than women entrepreneurs coming from joint families. 60 per cent women entrepreneurs coming from nuclear families are doing business to achieve something, whereas this proportion is 52 per cent in case of women entrepreneurs coming from joint families. The value of chi-square is statistically significant at 1 per cent level of significance. Almost same proportion of women entrepreneurs doing business under individual and other forms of business organizations are doing business to achieve something. Similarly, one-fourth of women entrepreneurs doing business under different forms of business organizations are doing business to make use of free time. Similar type of inferences have been observed in case of family compulsion preference of women entrepreneurs. The value of chi-square is statistically insignificant. It shows that there is no association between these two variables. More than 50 per cent women entrepreneurs investing upto Rs. 2 lacs, between Rs. 3-5 lacs and more than Rs. 10 lacs in business are doing business to achieve something, whereas this ratio is more than 60 per cent in case of women entrepreneurs investing money other than above mentioned ranges. Only small proportion of women entrepreneurs investing different levels of money are doing business to make use of free time and family compulsion. The value of chi-square is statistically insignificant. Higher achievement-oriented women entrepreneurs are earning higher level of income than women entrepreneurs doing business just to make use of free time of family compulsion. In this table, 75 per cent of women entrepreneurs are earning income above Rs. 15,000 per month are highly achievement oriented. 35 per cent to 38 per cent of women entrepreneurs doing business to make use of free time are earning upto Rs. 10,000 per month. The value of chi-square is statistically significant at 1 per cent level of significance. It shows that these two variables are statistically significant. Trained women entrepreneurs are more achievement-oriented than untrained women entrepreneurs. It shows that training enhances the skill and knowledge and in this process they are able to overcome the various obstacles faced by them in business and become achievement-oriented. In this table, 62 per cent trained and 49 per cent untrained women entrepreneurs are doing business to achieve something. Only one-fourth women entrepreneurs irrespective of their level of training are doing business to make use of free time. On the other hand, 26 per cent untrained women entrepreneurs are doing business due to family compulsions. The value of chi-square is statistically significant at 1 per cent level of significance. The women entrepreneurs having taken assistance from formal sources of finance are more achievement-oriented than women entrepreneurs who have taken financial assistance from informal sources. The value of chi-square is statistically significant at 1 per cent level of significance. Women entrepreneurs who have enterprises less than 10 years old are more achievement oriented than women entrepreneurs having enterprises more than 10 years old. 34 per cent women entrepreneurs having enterprises more than 10 years old are doing business due to family compulsion. It seems that women entrepreneurs having younger enterprises are more achievement-oriented. The value of chi-square is statistically insignificant.

Table 3.6 highlights that money and desire to be independent have been one of the main factors motivating the women entrepreneurs to be an entrepreneur. It seems that money is still a prime mover among women entrepreneurs while choosing business line. Education-wise information further shows that women entrepreneurs possessing lower level of education are relat'vely motivated by monetary factors than women entrepreneurs having higher level of education. Women entrepreneurs possessing higher level of education are influenced by their desire to be independent. The other factors like status and identity have been prime motivating factors among highly educated women entrepreneurs. The value of chi-square is statistically insignificant. It shows that these two variables do not vary significantly. Women entrepreneurs in the age group of above 40 are relatively more motivated by monetary factors than women entrepreneurs in lower age group. It vividly shows that younger women entrepreneurs are influenced by other than monetary factors. Analysis of data further reveals that younger generation of women entrepreneurs is having different missions while going for business. In this table women entrepreneurs in lower age group are influenced by independence, self-identity and status. The value of chi-square further corroborates our findings. Women entrepreneurs coming from rural areas are more motivated by monetary factors than women entrepreneurs coming from urban areas. It clearly depicts that motivating factors of rural and urban women entrepreneurs are entirely different. The value of chi-square is statistically significant at 1 per cent level of significance. Women entrepreneurs hailing from nuclear families are relatively more motivated by money, independence, self-identity and status than women entrepreneurs coming from joint families. On the other hand, women entrepreneurs belonging to joint families want to be independent followed by monetary, self-respect and family necessity while going for business. It also shows that women entrepreneurs in joint families want some identity and status in large families. The value of chi-square is statistically significant at 1 per cent level of significance. Almost same proportion of women entrepreneurs irrespective of forms of business organizations are motivated by their desire for independence, status, self-respect and self-identity factors. The value of chi-square is statistically insignificant. Women entrepreneurs investing less money are relatively more influenced by monetary factors. It seems that women entrepreneurs investing less money are more oriented towards monetary factors. It may be due to less risk-taking capacity and other problems such as family compulsions encountered by them. On the other hand, women entrepreneurs investing more money are influenced by status in society and self-respect. The value of chi-square is statistically significant at 1 per cent level of significance. It shows that level of investment and motivating factors vary significantly. Women entrepreneurs earning higher level of income are relatively more influenced by other than monetary factors. It depicts that higher earning capacity shifts the attitude of women entrepreneurs towards other factors. The value of chi-square is statistically significant at 1 per cent level of significance. Trained women entrepreneurs are more influenced by independent monetary factors followed by self-respect and employment generation factors. On the other hand, untrained women entrepreneurs are more concerned towards monetary and family necessity factors. The value of chi-square is statistically significant at 1 per cent level of significance. Proportion of women entrepreneurs, who have not taken financial assistance from financial institutions, are relatively more influenced by monetary factors alone. On the other hand, women entrepreneurs who have taken financial assistance from financial institutions are influenced by their desire to be independent, status and monetary factors. On the other hand, the attitude of women entrepreneurs on other factors is found to be almost same. The value of chi-square is statistically insignificant. Women entrepreneurs having enterprises below 10 years of age are also influenced by non-monetary factors than women entrepreneurs having enterprises more than 10 years old. It vividly shows that women entrepreneurs who have recently established their business are having different motivating factors.

TABLE 3.6
Factors that Motivated you to Become Entrepreneur

Group	Money	Independent	Status	Self-actualization	Identity	Necessity	Role model	Others
All Data	120 (26.67)	116 (25.78)	55 (12.22)	46 (10.22)	50 (11.11)	49 (10.89)	5 (1.11)	9 (2.00)
Education								
Primary	20 (83.33)	2 (8.33)	—	1 (4.17)	—	1 (4.17)	—	—
Matric	33 (41.25)	10 (12.50)	11 (13.75)	10 (12.50)	1 (1.25)	11 (13.75)	2 (2.50)	2 (2.50)
Graduate	49 (26.06)	49 (26.06)	20 (10.64)	24 (12.77)	17 (9.04)	21 (11.17)	3 (1.60)	5 (2.66)
Post Graduate	18 (11.39)	55 (34.81)	24 (15.19)	11 (6.96)	32 (20.25)	16 (10.13)	—	2 (1.27)
Chi-square = 100.346; df = 21; Insignificant								
Age (years)								
Below 30	20 (14.18)	39 (27.66)	14 (9.93)	15 (10.64)	32 (22.70)	16 (11.35)	—	5 (3.55)
30-40	36 (23.53)	50 (32.68)	19 (12.42)	14 (9.15)	13 (8.50)	15 (9.80)	4 (2.61)	2 (1.31)
Above 40	64 (41.03)	27 (17.31)	22 (14.10)	17 (10.90)	5 (3.21)	18 (11.54)	1 (0.64)	2 (1.28)
Chi-square = 63. 997; df = 14; Significant at 1 per cent level								
Place of Origin								
Rural	32 (36.78)	16 (18.39)	4 (4.60)	9 (10.34)	9 (10.34)	17 (19.54)	—	—
Urban	88 (24.24)	100 (27.55)	51 (14.05)	37 (10.19)	41 (11.29)	32 (8.82)	5 (1.38)	9 (2.48)
Chi-square = 22.378; df = 7; Significant at 1 per cent level								

(Contd.)

TABLE 3.6 (Contd.)

Group	Money	Independent	Status	Self-actualization	Identity	Necessity	Role model	Others
Type of Family								
Joint	52 (24.88)	44 (21.05)	24 (11.48)	34 (16.27)	20 (9.57)	29 (13.88)	2 (0.96)	4 (1.91)
Nuclear	68 (28.22)	72 (29.88)	32 (12.86)	12 (4.98)	30 (12.45)	20 (8.30)	3 (1.24)	5 (2.07)
Chi-square = 22.105; df = 7; Significant at 1 per cent level								
Form of Business Organization								
Sole	76 (24.60)	83 (26.86)	35 (11.33)	31 (10.03)	34 (11.00)	38 (12.30)	5 (1.62)	7 (2.27)
Others	44 (31.21)	33 (23.40)	20 (14.18)	15 (10.64)	16 (11.35)	11 (7.80)	—	2 (1.42)
Chi-square = 7.154; df = 7; Insignificant								
Investment (Lacs)								
<1	29 (23.58)	44 (35.77)	2 (1.63)	11 (8.94)	20 (16.26)	13 (10.57)	4 (3.25)	—
1-2	42 (29.17)	37 (25.69)	14 (9.72)	17 (11.81)	14 (9.72)	16 (11.11)	—	4 (2.78)
2-3	32 (41.56)	20 (25.97)	6 (7.79)	7 (9.09)	6 (7.79)	5 (6.49)	—	1 (1.30)
3-5	14 (21.88)	6 (9.38)	22 (34.38)	4 (6.25)	7 (10.94)	8 (12.50)	1 (1.56)	2 (3.12)
5-10	2 (6.45)	4 (12.90)	10 (32.26)	7 (22.58)	3 (9.68)	5 (16.13)	—	—
Above 10	1 (9.09)	5 (45.45)	1 (9.09)	—	—	2 (18.18)	—	2 (18.18)
Chi-square = 120.191; df = 35; Significant at 1 per cent level								
Income (Rs.)								
<7500	15 (27.78)	15 (27.78)	2 (3.70)	5 (9.26)	7 (12.96)	6 (11.11)	4 (7.41)	—
7500-10000	45 (29.80)	34 (22.52)	26 (17.22)	15 (9.93)	15 (9.93)	16 (10.60)	—	—

10000-15000	28 (28.87)	29 (29.90)	6 (6.19)	8 (8.25)	7 (7.22)	14 (14.43)	—	5 (5.15)
15000-20000	19 (19.00)	30 (30.00)	11 (11.00)	10 (10.00)	19 (19.00)	10 (10.00)	1 (1.00)	—
20000+	13 (27.08)	8 (16.67)	10 (20.83)	8 (16.67)	2 (4.17)	3 (6.25)	—	4 (8.33)

Chi-square = 75.788; df = 28; Significant at 1 per cent level

Training

Got Training	50 (21.28)	76 (32.34)	27 (11.49)	29 (12.34)	25 (10.64)	18 (7.66)	3 (1.28)	7 (2.98)
No Training	70 (32.56)	40 (18.60)	28 (13.02)	17 (7.91)	25 (11.63)	31 (14.42)	2 (0.93)	2 (0.93)

Chi-square = 23.238; df = 7; Significant at 1 per cent level

Sources of Finance

Formal	25 (20.83)	39 (32.50)	20 (16.67)	8 (6.67)	14 (11.67)	12 (10.00)	—	2 (1.67)
Informal	95 (28.79)	77 (23.33)	35 (10.61)	38 (11.52)	36 (10.91)	37 (11.21)	5 (1.52)	7 (2.12)

Chi-square = 11.698; df = 7; Insignificant

Age of Enterprise

Below 10 years	64 (21.40)	86 (28.76)	37 (12.37)	35 (11.71)	41 (13.71)	31 (10.37)	—	5 (1.67)
Above 10 years	56 (37.09)	30 (19.87)	18 (11.92)	11 (7.28)	9 (5.96)	18 (11.92)	5 (3.31)	4 (2.65)

Chi-square = 30.295; df = 7; Significant at 1 per cent level

It may be due to higher level of education and change in attitude of women towards business. The value of chi-square is statistically significant at 1 per cent level of significance.

Table 3.7 shows that majority of women entrepreneurs (80 per cent) take the help from family members in project formulations. Role of outside experts and other sources are found to be negligible. The reason being, women entrepreneurs want to avoid the consultancy cost while formulating the project. Education-wise

TABLE 3.7

Who Helped you in Project Formulation

Group	No one	Friends	Experts	Family	Others
All Data	9 (2.00)	47 (10.44)	20 (4.44)	358 (79.56)	16 (3.56)
Education					
Primary	—	—	2 (8.33)	22 (91.67)	—
Matric	—	7 (8.75)	—	68 (85.00)	5 (6.25)
Graduate	4 (2.13)	14 (7.45)	7 (3.72)	157 (83.51)	6 (3.19)
Post Graduate	5 (3.16)	26 (16.46)	11 (6.96)	111 (70.25)	5 (3.16)
Chi-square = 25.276; df = 12; Significant at 1 per cent level					
Age (years)					
Below 30	5 (3.55)	15 (10.64)	7 (4.96)	108 (76.60)	6 (4.26)
30-40	2 (1.31)	19 (12.42)	8 (5.23)	121 (79.08)	3 (1.96)
Above 40	2 (1.28)	13 (8.33)	5 (3.21)	129 (82.69)	7 (4.49)
Chi-square = 6.555; df = 8; Insignificant					
Place of Origin					
Rural	1 (1.15)	7 (8.05)	3 (3.45)	71 (81.61)	5 (5.75)
Urban	8 (2.20)	40 (11.02)	17 (4.68)	287 (79.06)	11 (3.03)
Chi-square = 2.739; df = 4; Insignificant					
Type of Family					
Joint	4 (1.91)	18 (8.61)	8 (3.83)	167 (79.90)	12 (5.74)
Nuclear	5 (2.07)	29 (12.03)	12 (4.98)	191 (79.25)	4 (1.66)
Chi-square = 6.854; df = 4; Insignificant					
Form of Business Organization					
Sole	8 (2.59)	30 (9.71)	12 (3.88)	245 (79.29)	14 (4.53)
Others	1 (0.71)	17 (12.06)	8 (5.67)	113 (80.14)	2 (1.42)
Chi-square = 34.402; df = 4; Insignificant					

Group	No one	Friends	Experts	Family	Others
Investment (Lacs)					
<1	4 (3.25)	15 (12.20)	3 (2.44)	98 (79.67)	3 (2.44)
1-2	—	19 (13.19)	13 (16.88)	123 (85.42)	2 (1.39)
2-3	2 (2.60)	8 (10.39)	—	49 (63.64)	5 (6.49)
3-5	—	4 (6.25)	4 (12.90)	54 (84.38)	6 (9.38)
5-10	—	—	—	27 (87.10)	—
Above 10	3 (27.27)	1 (9.09)	—	7 (63.64)	—
Chi-square = 105.017; df = 20; Significant at 1 per cent level					
Income (Rs.)					
<7500	4 (7.41)	2 (3.70)	—	48 (88.89)	—
7500-10000	—	20 (13.25)	—	125 (82.78)	6 (3.97)
10000-15000	2 (2.06)	13 (13.40)	2 (2.06)	77 (79.38)	3 (3.09)
15000-20000	—	9 (9.00)	14 (14.00)	70 (70.00)	7 (7.00)
20000+	3 (6.25)	3 (6.25)	4 (8.33)	38 (79.17)	—
Chi-square = 105.017; df = 16; Significant at 1 per cent level					
Training					
Got Training	5 (2.13)	29 (12.34)	12 (5.11)	183 (77.87)	6 (2.55)
No Training	4 (1.86)	18 (8.37)	8 (3.72)	175 (81.40)	10 (4.65)
Chi-square = 3.783; df = 4; Insignificant					
Sources of Finance					
Formal	3 (2.50)	10 (8.33)	5 (4.17)	98 (81.67)	4 (3.33)
Informal	6 (1.82)	37 (11.21)	15 (4.55)	260 (78.79)	12 (3.64)
Chi-square = 1.046; df = 4; Insignificant					
Age of Enterprise					
Below 10 years	6 (2.01)	35 (11.71)	16 (5.35)	234 (78.26)	8 (2.68)
Above 10 years	3 (1.99)	12 (7.95)	4 (2.65)	124 (82.12)	8 (5.30)
Chi-square = 5.134; df = 4; Insignificant					

information further highlights that women entrepreneurs having lower level of education formulate the project with the help of family members. It may be due to lack of experience and skill in project formulation. On the other hand, women entrepreneurs possessing higher level of education take assistance from various sources in project formulations. It shows that women entrepreneurs having higher level of education want to minimize various complexities involved in business over the period of time.

The value of chi-square is statistically significant at 1 per cent level of significance. Proportion of women entrepreneurs having age more than 40 take less help from other sources than women entrepreneurs in lower age groups. In this table, 83 per cent women entrepreneurs in the age group of more than 40 sought help of family members in project formulations. On the other hand, women entrepreneurs in the age group of 40 have taken assistance from friends, experts and other sources in project formulation. It seems that younger generation of women entrepreneurs understand the complexities of business under changing economic scenario and in this process they want to minimize the risk in business. The value of chi-square is statistically insignificant. Almost same proportion of women entrepreneurs hailing from rural and urban areas sought help of various agencies in project formulation. The value of chi-square is statistically insignificant. Women entrepreneurs coming from nuclear and joint families also take assistance in project formulation from various sources. Same variations are observed in case of assistance taken from friends in project formulations. The value of chi-square is statistically insignificant. Almost same proportion of women entrepreneurs managing business under various forms of business organizations take assistance from various sources in preparation of their project. The value of chi-square is statistically insignificant. 63 per cent to 87 per cent women entrepreneurs investing different levels of money sought assistance from family members in project formulations. 12 per cent to 16 per cent women entrepreneurs investing money in the range of Rs. 2-3 lacs and 5-10 lacs has taken assistance from outside experts in project formulations. It seems that big projects need help of highly specialized persons to remain competitive in free market economies in long-run. On the other hand, women entrepreneurs investing money upto Rs. 3 lacs in business sought the help of friends in project formulation. It seems that these women entrepreneurs want to save the cost of hiring of experts in project formulation. The value of chi-square is statistically significant at 1 per cent level of significance. Assistance of outside experts is found to be more among women entrepreneurs earning higher level of income. It shows that assistance of outside experts brings economies of scale in business. Women entrepreneurs earning lower and middle range of income take assistance of friends in project formulation. Contribution of self is found to be negligible in almost all the cases. The value of chi-square is statistically significant at 1 per cent level of significance. It depicts that these two variables vary significantly. Assistance taken by trained entrepreneurs from different sources is found to be slightly on higher side than untrained women entrepreneurs. The value of chi-square is statistically insignificant. Similar types of conclusions have been observed in case of women entrepreneurs availing assistance from formal and informal sources. Women entrepreneurs having enterprises less than 10 years old take more assistance from various sources than other women entrepreneurs. It seems that younger generation of women entrepreneurs in order to avoid various problems in the free market economies have to take assistance from outside experts. The value of chi-square is statistically insignificant.

SUGGESTIONS AND POLICY IMPLICATIONS

The role of different agencies in motivating women to enter in business line has been found to be negligible. Moreover, overwhelming proportion of women entrepreneurs in our study has higher level of education. Educational institutions should play an important role in this direction. EDP should be organized at colleges and universities level so that mindset of students may be changed during their study time period. These efforts will be beneficial to generate gainful employment opportunities in the economy and dependence on formal sector of the economy for employment generation will also decline. Similarly, majority of women entrepreneurs are achievement-oriented. Institutions should provide various types of assistance in a liberalized manner to these women entrepreneurs. Although majority of the projects were completed by women entrepreneurs well in time. There is a need to provide consultancy and guidance through various agencies in this direction. NGOs and women organisations should play a vital role in this direction. Similarly, large number of women entrepreneurs are operating their business from their home and rental places. It seems that location of enterprise at home is not suitable for business. Provision of fixed capital can be useful to these small enterprises.

Financial Structure of Enterprises Owned by Women Entrepreneurs

The small-scale sector has been playing an important role in the economic development of the country. It helps in utilization of otherwise dormant resources, balanced regional development, equitable distribution of income and widening the base of entrepreneurial supply. Moreover, these small enterprises provide breeding ground for innovations and enhanced the competitive advantage of domestic producers under rapid changing economic scenario. To set-up business, adequate finance is required. Finance has been rightly said to be life-blood of any business. Adequate finances are necessary to oil the wheels of business. The growth of any enterprises largely depends upon the availability of adequate finance in proper time. Individual entrepreneurs cannot provide all funds needed by their units. The entrepreneurs has to depend on the various sources of finance to establish and run their business.

Table 4.1 shows that 48 per cent women entrepreneurs have used family wealth to finance their business, one-fifth used personal wealth and institutional finance and only small proportion of women entrepreneurs has taken assistance from relatives and private agencies. Information lucidly highlights that

TABLE 4.1

Sources of Finance used by Women Entrepreneurs

Group	Personal	Bank	Relatives	Family	Private Finance
1	2	3	4	5	6
All Data	95 (21.11)	103 (22.89)	27 (6.00)	214 (47.56)	11 (2.44)
Education					
Primary	1 (4.17)	4 (16.67)	5 (20.83)	11 (45.83)	3 (12.50)
Matric	19 (23.75)	15 (18.75)	3 (3.75)	41 (51.25)	2 (2.50)
Graduate	44 (23.40)	39 (20.74)	9 (4.79)	96 (51.06)	—
Post Graduate	31 (19.62)	45 (28.48)	10 (6.33)	66 (41.77)	6 (3.80)
Chi-square = 35.219; df = 12; Significant at 1 per cent level					
Age (years)					
Below 30	31 (21.99)	30 (21.28)	3 (2.13)	72 (51.06)	5 (3.55)
30-40	31 (20.26)	33 (21.57)	14 (9.15)	75 (49.02)	—
Above 40	33 (21.15)	40 (25.64)	10 (6.41)	67 (42.95)	6 (3.85)
Chi-square = 13.819; df = 8; Insignificant					
Place of Origin					
Rural	13 (14.94)	21 (24.14)	4 (4.60)	48 (55.17)	1 (1.15)
Urban	82 (22.59)	82 (22.59)	23 (6.34)	166 (45.73)	10 (2.75)
Chi-square = 4.427; df = 4; Insignificant					
Type of Family					
Joint	41 (19.62)	37 (17.70)	8 (3.83)	120 (57.42)	3 (1.44)
Nuclear	54 (22.41)	66 (27.59)	19 (7.88)	94 (39.00)	8 (3.32)
Chi-square = 17.671; df = 3; Significant at 1 per cent level					
Form of Business Organization					
Sole	75 (24.27)	60 (19.42)	19 (6.15)	152 (49.19)	3 (0.97)
Others	20 (14.18)	43 (30.50)	8 (5.67)	62 (43.97)	8 (5.67)
Chi-square = 19.210; df = 3; Significant at 1 per cent level					
Investment (Lacs)					
<1	28 (22.76)	11 (8.94)	6 (4.88)	78 (63.41)	—
1-2	31 (21.53)	30 (20.83)	14 (9.72)	69 (47.92)	—
2-3	17 (22.08)	16 (20.78)	4 (5.19)	33 (42.86)	7 (9.09)
3-5	12 (18.75)	28 (43.75)	3 (4.69)	21 (32.81)	—

(Contd.)

1	2	3	4	5	6
5-10	7 (22.58)	12 (38.71)	—	10 (32.36)	2 (6.45)
Above 10	—	6 (54.55)	—	3 (27.27)	2 (18.18)

Chi-square = 87.796; df = 20; Significant at 1 per cent level

Income (Rs.)					
<7500	21 (38.89)	12 (22.22)	2 (3.70)	19 (35.19)	—
7500-10000	37 (24.50)	24 (15.89)	9 (5.96)	81 (53.64)	—
10000-15000	12 (12.37)	20 (20.62)	9 (9.28)	49 (50.52)	7 (7.22)
15000-20000	22 (22.00)	31 (31.00)	2 (2.00)	43 (43.00)	2 (2.00)
20000+	3 (6.25)	16 (33.33)	5 (10.42)	22 (45.83)	2 (4.17)

Chi-square = 50.804; df = 16; Significant at 1 per cent level

Training					
Got Training	45 (19.15)	56 (23.83)	13 (5.53)	119 (50.64)	2 (0.85)
No Training	50 (23.26)	47 (21.86)	14 (6.51)	95 (44.19)	9 (4.19)

Chi-square = 7.358; df = 4; Insignificant

Sources of Finance					
Formal	8 (6.67)	88 (73.33)	1 (0.83)	20 (16.67)	3 (2.50)
Informal	87 (26.36)	15 (4.55)	26 (7.88)	194 (58.79)	8 (2.42)

Chi-square = 238.206; df = 4; Significant at 1 per cent level

Age of Enterprise					
Below 10 years	64 (21.40)	60 (20.07)	17 (5.69)	151 (50.00)	7 (2.34)
Above 10 years	31 (20.53)	43 (28.48)	10 (6.62)	63 (41.72)	4 (2.65)

Chi-square = 4.949; df = 4; Insignificant

family and personal wealth is still playing a dominant role in financing of medium, small and micro-level enterprises. Education-wise information further shows that 41 per cent to 51 per cent women entrepreneurs irrespective of their level of education utilize family wealth to finance their business. 21 per cent women entrepreneurs having primary level of education have taken assistance from their relatives. Almost same proportion of women entrepreneurs (23 per cent each) possessing matric and graduate level of education use personal wealth in business. It also shows that women entrepreneurs also want to curtail the cost of credit in the initial stage of business. Proportion of women entrepreneurs utilizing assistance from financial institutions is found to be enhancing with the level of education. Data contained in table depicts that only 16 per cent of women entrepreneurs using primary level of education use institutional sources of finance, whereas 28 per cent women entrepreneurs having post-graduate level of education use institutional finance. It may be due to more awareness about various sources of finance available to small enterprises and process of getting assistance from other sources. The value of chi-square is statistically significant at 1 per cent level of significance. It shows that these two variables vary significantly. Almost same proportion of women entrepreneurs (21 per cent each) in different age groups have utilized personal wealth to finance their business. Almost same proportion of women entrepreneurs (21 per cent each) in the age group of less than 30 and 30-40 have used institutional finance, whereas only 25 per cent of women entrepreneurs in the age group of above 40 years use bank finance. Family wealth has been used relatively more by women entrepreneurs in lower age group (51 per cent) as compared to women entrepreneurs in higher age groups (43 per cent). It seems that younger women entrepreneurs are dependent on their family members to finance their business. Women entrepreneurs (55 per cent) hailing from rural areas use family wealth more than their urban counterparts (46 per cent). Similarly, proportion of women entrepreneurs (23 per cent) using personal wealth is also found to be more in urban areas than rural areas. The reason to this may be assigned to more dependence on internal sources of finance by women entrepreneurs hailing from rural areas. But almost same proportion of women entrepreneurs irrespective of their place of origin use bank loans to finance their enterprises. The values of chi-square are statistically insignificant. As high as 57 per cent women entrepreneurs belonging to joint families have used family wealth as compared to other women entrepreneurs (39 per cent). It may be due to easy availability of money from family members. Institutional sources of finance are used relatively more by women entrepreneurs hailing from nuclear families (27 per cent) than those from joint families (17 per cent). It may be due to scarcity of finance among women entrepreneurs coming from nuclear families. On the other hand, women entrepreneurs coming from joint families may have the desire to save the cost of credit by not taking assistance from outside. Proportion of women entrepreneurs (22 per cent) coming from nuclear families use personal wealth more than their counterparts in joint families (19 per cent). It seems that women entrepreneurs in nuclear families might be doing some job before entering into self-employment activities. Similarly, women entrepreneurs coming from nuclear families have also taken more assistance from their relatives and private agencies than other women entrepreneurs. Analysis of data vividly shows that women entrepreneurs hailing from joint families are dependent on internal sources of finance as compared to other women entrepreneurs. It may also be due to lack of awareness or mobility among women entrepreneurs of joint families. The value of chi-square further corroborates our findings. Women entrepreneurs managing business under individual forms of business organizations have used more family wealth and personal savings in their business than women entrepreneurs managing business under other than individual form of business organizations. On the other hand, institutional sources of finance have been used relatively more by large scale enterprises. The reason to this may be attributed to more awareness and willingness of financial institutions to provide assistance to enterprises managed on joint basis. The value of chi-square is statistically significant at 1 per cent level of significance. Almost same proportion of women entrepreneurs investing upto Rs. 10 lacs in business use personal savings in their business. Proportion of women entrepreneurs using bank finance is found to be increasing with increase in level of investment in business. It shows that requirement of institutional finance enhances with level of investment. In this table, 54 per cent of women entrepreneurs investing more than Rs. 10 lacs in business have taken assistance from financial institutions. Role of family wealth is also found to be on decline with increase in the level of investment. It further shows that large-scale business requirements cannot be fulfiled by internal sources alone. Women entrepreneurs investing more than Rs.10 lacs have also used private finance in their business. Information in this table further throws light on the fact that small and micro-level enterprises are still dependent on non-institutional sources of finance in their business. It may be due to reluctance of financial institutions to provide finance to these small enterprises due to higher risk and lack of proper project formulations, etc. There is need to further strengthen policies related to small and micro-level enterprises. The value of chi-square is statistically significant at 1 per cent level of significance. Women entrepreneurs earning lower level of income have used internal sources of finance as compared to women entrepreneurs earning higher level of income. In this table more than 70 per cent women entrepreneurs have used family wealth and personal savings. On the other hand, 33 per cent women entrepreneurs earning more than Rs. 20,000 per month in business use institutional finance. Similarly, private finance and assistance from relatives have also been taken by women entrepreneurs earning higher level of income. The value of chi-square is statistically significant at 1 per cent level of significance. Almost same proportion of women entrepreneurs irrespective of their training use institutional finance in their business. Proportion of women entrepreneurs using family wealth is found to be more among trained women entrepreneurs than other women entrepreneurs. Untrained women entrepreneurs have also used private finance more than their trained counterparts. The value of chi-square is statistically insignificant. Majority of women entrepreneurs have also taken assistance from informal sources of finance. The value of chi-square is statistically significant at 1 per cent level of significance. Women entrepreneurs possessing enterprises less than 10 years old have used relatively used internal sources of finance than other women entrepreneurs. 28 per cent women entrepreneurs having enterprises more than 10 years old have used bank finance in their business than other women entrepreneurs (20 per cent). The value of chi-square is statistically insignificant.

Table 4.2 shows that 49 per cent women entrepreneurs have good knowledge of various sources of finance available to women entrepreneurs, 26 per cent possess average level of awareness and another 24 per cent possess low level of awareness. Education-wise information further shows that 42 per cent to 58 per cent women entrepreneurs having different level of education are aware of various sources of finance. It may be due to increase in level of education. The value of chi-square is statistically insignificant. Proportion of women entrepreneurs in lower and upper age group are relatively more aware of various sources of finance as compared to women entrepreneurs in middle age groups. It may be due to lack of opportunity to get information or less necessity felt by them. The value of chi-square is statistically insignificant. It shows that these two variables are independent. Women entrepreneurs (52 per cent) hailing from urban areas are more aware of various sources of finance than women entrepreneurs (39 per cent) coming from rural areas. It may be due to lack of mobility among women entrepreneurs coming from rural areas. The value of chi-square is statistically

TABLE 4.2

Awareness of Sources of Finance

Group	Outstanding	Good	Average	Below Average	Poor
1	2	3	4	5	6
All Data	23 (5.11)	198 (44.00)	117 (26.00)	47 (10.44)	65 (14.44)
Education					
Primary	—	14 (58.33)	4 (16.67)	3 (12.50)	3 (12.50)
Matric	4 (5.00)	29 (36.25)	20 (25.00)	13 (16.25)	14 (17.50)
Graduate	9 (4.79)	79 (42.02)	46 (24.47)	23 (12.23)	31 (16.49)
Post Graduate	10 (6.33)	76 (48.10)	47 (29.75)	8 (5.06)	17 (10.76)
Chi-square = 16.813; df = 12; Insignificant					
Age (years)					
Below 30	11 (7.80)	59 (41.84)	40 (28.37)	11 (7.80)	20 (14.18)
30-40	9 (5.88)	62 (40.52)	40 (26.14)	16 (10.46)	26 (16.99)
Above 40	3 (1.92)	77 (49.36)	37 (23.72)	20 (12.82)	19 (12.18)
Chi-square = 10.518; df = 8; Insignificant					
Place of Origin					
Rural	4 (4.60)	30 (34.48)	35 (40.23)	10 (11.49)	8 (9.20)
Urban	19 (5.23)	168 (46.28)	82 (22.59)	37 (10.19)	57 (15.70)
Chi-square = 12.846; df = 4; Significant at 1 per cent level					
Type of Family					
Joint	9 (4.31)	88 (42.11)	63 (30.14)	22 (10.53)	27 (12.92)
Nuclear	14 (5.81)	110 (45.64)	54 (22.41)	25 (10.37)	38 (15.77)
Chi-square = 4.022; df = 4; Insignificant					
Form of Business Organization					
Sole	14 (4.53)	125 (40.45)	74 (23.95)	38 (12.30)	58 (18.77)
Others	9 (6.38)	73 (51.77)	43 (30.50)	9 (6.38)	7 (4.96)
Chi-square = 21.085; df = 4; Significant at 1 per cent level					

1	2	3	4	5	6
Investment (Lacs)					
<1	4 (3.25)	39 (31.71)	28 (22.76)	15 (12.20)	37 (30.08)
1-2	5 (3.47)	54 (37.50)	49 (34.03)	18 (12.50)	18 (12.50)
2-3	4 (5.19)	26 (33.77)	28 (36.36)	14 (18.18)	5 (6.49)
3-5	6 (9.38)	45 (70.31)	10 (15.62)	—	3 (4.69)
5-10	4 (12.90)	23 (74.19)	2 (6.45)	—	2 (6.45)
Above 10	—	11 (100.0)	—	—	—
Chi-square = 105.370; df = 20; Significant at 1 per cent level					
Income (Rs.)					
<7500	4 (7.41)	14 (25.93)	11 (20.37)	6 (11.11)	19 (35.19)
7500-10000	7 (4.64)	56 (37.09)	46 (30.46)	13 (8.61)	29 (19.21)
10000-15000	—	45 (46.39)	24 (24.74)	14 (14.43)	14 (14.43)
15000-20000	10 (10.00)	45 (45.00)	29 (29.00)	14 (14.00)	2 (2.00)
20000+	2 (4.17)	38 (79.17)	7 (14.58)	—	1 (2.08)
Chi-square = 76.720; df = 16; Significant at 1 per cent level					
Training					
Got Training	16 (6.81)	102 (43.40)	53 (22.55)	29 (12.34)	35 (14.89)
No Training	7 (3.26)	96 (44.65)	64 (29.77)	18 (8.37)	30 (13.95)
Chi-square = 6.821; df = 4; Insignificant					
Sources of Finance					
Formal	14 (11.67)	93 (77.50)	10 (8.33)	3 (2.50)	—
Informal	9 (2.73)	105 (31.82)	107 (32.42)	44 (13.33)	65 (19.70)
Chi-square = 108.663; df = 4; Significant at 1 per cent level					
Age of Enterprise					
Below 10 years	20 (6.69)	118 (39.46)	87 (29.10)	33 (11.04)	41 (13.71)
Above 10 years	3 (1.99)	80 (52.98)	30 (19.87)	14 (9.27)	24 (15.89)
Chi-square = 12.423; df = 4; Significant at 1 per cent level					

significant at 1 per cent level of significance. It shows that these two variables vary significantly. Women entrepreneurs (51 per cent) belonging to nuclear families are relatively more aware of various sources of finance as compared to women entrepreneurs (46 per cent) belonging to joint families. The value of chi-square is statistically significant at 1 per cent level of significance. Awareness related to various sources of finance is found to be more among women entrepreneurs (58 per cent) managing business under other than individual form of business organizations as compared to women entrepreneurs (45 per cent) doing business under individual form of business organizations. It may be due to involvement of more than one person in business. The value of chi-square is statistically significant at 1 per cent level of significance. It shows that awareness of various sources of finance and form of business organizations vary significantly. Women entrepreneurs investing more money in business are relatively more aware as compared to women entrepreneurs investing less money in business. It shows that requirement of money compels the entrepreneurs to find various sources of finance to fill the gap in investment. In this table all the women entrepreneurs investing more than Rs. 10 lacs in business are aware of sources of finance. Similarly, more than 80 per cent of women entrepreneurs having made investment between Rs. 3-10 lacs are aware of various sources of finance. The value of chi-square is statistically significant at 1 per cent level of significance. Women entrepreneurs (83 per cent) earning higher level of income are found to be more aware of various sources of finance than women entrepreneurs (32 per cent) earning low level of income. The value of chi-square further justifies our findings that these two variables are positively associated. Women entrepreneurs those who have undergone training before start of their business ventures are slightly more aware (50 per cent) of various sources of finance than other women entrepreneurs (48 per cent). It shows that women entrepreneurs irrespective of their level of training are becoming aware of various sources of finance over the period of time. The value of chi-square is statistically in significant. It seems logical that those women entrepreneurs who have used bank finance in their business are relatively more aware than other women entrepreneurs. In this table, only one-third women entrepreneurs who have used informal sources of finance are also aware of formal sources of finance. The value of chi-square is statistically significant at 1 per cent level of significance. Women entrepreneurs (54 per cent) having enterprises more than 10 years old are relatively more aware of various sources of finance than other women entrepreneurs (46 per cent). It shows that with the increase in the life of enterprises awareness, various sources of finance also enhance. The value of chi-square is statistically significant at 1 per cent level of significance.

Table 4.3 shows that only 26 per cent women entrepreneurs avail the assistance from financial institutions. Education-wise information further shows that 33 per cent women entrepreneurs possessing post-graduate level of education avail financial assistance. One-fourth women entrepreneurs possessing primary and graduate level of education have also availed financial assistance. It reveals that only small proportion of women entrepreneurs irrespective of their level of education have taken assistance from financial institutions. The value of chi-square is statistically insignificant. It highlights that education and availing of financial assistance have no association with each other. Almost same proportion of women entrepreneurs (one fourth) in different age groups have taken assistance from financial institutions. The value of chi-square is statistically insignificant. 23 per cent women entrepreneurs hailing from rural areas and 28 per cent from urban areas have taken assistance from financial institutions to start their business ventures. It highlights that access to financial institutions has been confined only to few selected women entrepreneurs. The value of chi-square is statistically insignificant. Women entrepreneurs (34 per cent) belonging to nuclear families have availed assistance from financial institutions relatively more than women entrepreneurs (18 per cent) coming from joint families. It may be due to less resources available to women entrepreneurs hailing from nuclear families. The value of chi-square is statistically significant at 1 per cent level of significance. It shows that these two variables are positively associated. 22 per cent women entrepreneurs managing business under individual forms of business organizations and 35 per cent managing business under other than individual form of business organizations have taken assistance from financial institutions. The value of chi-square is statistically significant at 5 per cent level of significance. It shows that these two variables vary significantly. 81 per cent women entrepreneurs having invested more than Rs. 10 lacs in business have availed assistance from financial institutions and 43 per cent to 54 per cent women entrepreneurs investing money in the range of Rs. 3-10 lacs have taken loans. On the other hand, only small proportion of women entrepreneurs investing upto Rs. 3 lacs have taken loans from financial institutions. It may be due to reluctance on the part of institutions to provide assistance to small enterprises due to involvement of more risk. The value of chi-square is statistically significant at 1 per cent level of significance. 52 per cent women entrepreneurs earning more than Rs. 20,000 per month and 36 per cent women entrepreneurs earning income in the range of Rs. 15,000-20,000 have taken assistance from financial institutions. On the other hand, less than one-fourth women entrepreneurs who have been earning lower level of income have taken assistance. The value of chi-square further shows that these two variables vary significantly. Trained women entrepreneurs (30 per cent) have availed assistance relatively more from financial institutions than untrained women entrepreneurs (23 per cent). It shows that training helps in increasing the knowledge of availing assistance from financial institutions. The value of chi-square is statistically significant at 1 per cent level of significance. Less than 29 per cent of women entrepreneurs irrespective of their life of enterprises have taken assistance from financial institutions. The value of chi-square is statistically insignificant. It shows that age of enterprise and availing of financial assistance are not associated with each other.

TABLE 4.3
Availed of Financial Assistance

Group	Yes	No
All Data	120 (26.67)	330 (73.33)
Education		
Primary	6 (25.00)	18 (75.00)
Matric	15 (18.75)	65 (81.25)
Graduate	46 (24.47)	142 (75.53)
Post Graduate	53 (33.54)	105 (66.46)
Chi-square = 6.884; df = 3; Insignificant		
Age (years)		
Below 30	39 (27.66)	102 (72.34)
30-40	39 (25.49)	114 (74.51)
Above 40	42 (26.92)	114 (73.08)
Chi-square = 0.185; df = 2; Insignificant		
Place of Origin		
Rural	20 (22.99)	67 (77.01)
Urban	100 (27.55)	263 (72.45)
Chi-square = 0.746; df = 1; Insignificant		

Group	Yes	No
Type of Family		
Joint	38 (18.18)	171 (81.82)
Nuclear	82 (34.02)	159 (65.98)
Chi-square = 14.367; df = 1; Significant at 1 per cent level		
Form of Business Organization		
Sole	70 (22.65)	239 (77.35)
Others	50 (35.46)	91 (64.54)
Chi-square = 8.121; df = 1; Insignificant		
Investment (Lacs)		
<1	20 (16.26)	103 (83.74)
1-2	35 (24.31)	109 (75.69)
2-3	11 (14.29)	66 (85.71)
3-5	28 (43.75)	36 (56.25)
5-10	17 (54.84)	14 (45.16)
Above 10	9 (81.82)	2 (18.18)
Chi-square = 52.500; df = 5; Significant at 1 per cent level		
Income (Rs.)		
<7500	14 (25.93)	40 (74.07)
7500-10000	23 (15.23)	128 (84.77)
10000-15000	22 (22.68)	75 (77.32)
15000-20000	36 (36.00)	64 (64.00)
20000+	25 (52.08)	23 (47.92)
Chi-square = 31.211; df = 4; Significant at 1 per cent level		
Training		
Got Training	70 (29.79)	165 (70.21)
No Training	50 (23.26)	165 (76.74)
Chi-square = 2.449; df = 1; Insignificant		
Age of Enterprise		
Below 10 years	76 (25.42)	223 (74.58)
Above 10 years	44 (29.14)	107 (70.86)
Chi-square = 0.710; df = 1; Insignificant		

Table 4.4 highlights that 59 per cent women entrepreneurs have invested upto Rs. 2 lacs in business, 17 per cent between Rs. 2-3 lacs and only 14 per cent invested between Rs. 3-5 lacs. Small proportion of women entrepreneurs (9 per cent) invest more than

TABLE 4.4

Level of Investment made by Women Entrepreneurs

(in lacs)

Group	Upto 1 lac	1 – 2	2 – 3	3 – 5	5 – 10	10+
All Data	123 (27.33)	144 (32.00)	77 (17.11)	64 (14.22)	31 (6.89)	11 (2.44)
Education						
Primary	5 (20.83)	6 (25.00)	11 (45.83)	2 (8.33)	—	—
Matric	18 (22.50)	39 (48.75)	12 (15.00)	7 (8.75)	4 (5.00)	—
Graduate	61 (32.45)	49 (26.06)	30 (15.96)	26 (13.83)	16 (8.51)	6 (3.19)
Post Graduate	39 (24.68)	50 (31.65)	24 (15.19)	29 (18.35)	11 (6.96)	5 (3.16)
Chi-square = 35.264; df = 15; Significant at 1 per cent level						
Age (years)						
Below 30	51 (36.17)	40 (28.37)	20 (14.18)	¹ ˙ (13.48)	9 (6.38)	2 (1.42)
30-40	52 (33.99)	39 (25.49)	28 (18.30)	20 (13.07)	10 (6.54)	4 (2.61)
Above 40	20 (12.82)	65 (41.67)	29 (18.59)	25 (16.03)	12 (7.69)	5 (3.21)
Chi-square = 28.497; df = 10; Significant at 1 per cent level						
Place of Origin						
Rural	23 (26.44)	34 (39.08)	15 (17.24)	8 (9.20)	2 (2.30)	5 (5.75)
Urban	100 (27.55)	110 (30.30)	62 (17.08)	56 (15.43)	29 (7.90)	6 (1.65)
Chi-square = 11.750; df = 5; Significant at 5 per cent level						
Type of Family						
Joint	65 (31.10)	63 (30.14)	39 (18.66)	22 (10.53)	16 (7.66)	4 (1.91)
Nuclear	58 (24.07)	81 (33.61)	38 (15.77)	42 (17.43)	15 (6.22)	7 (2.90)
Chi-square = 7.524; df = 5; Insignificant						
Form of Business Organization						
Sole	102 (33.01)	98 (31.72)	42 (13.59)	45 (14.56)	16 (5.18)	6 (1.94)
Others	21 (14.89)	46 (32.62)	35 (24.82)	19 (13.48)	15 (10.64)	5 (3.55)
Chi-square = 24.077; df = 5; Significant at 1 per cent level						
Income (Rs.)						
<7500	39 (72.22)	15 (27.78)	—	—	—	—
7500-10000	52 (34.44)	66 (43.71)	15 (9.93)	18 (11.92)	—	—
10000-15000	17 (17.53)	41 (42.27)	28 (28.87)	8 (8.25)	3 (3.09)	—
15000-20000	11 (11.00)	19 (19.00)	30 (30.00)	27 (27.00)	13 (13.00)	—
20000+	4 (8.33)	3 (6.25)	4 (8.33)	11 (22.92)	15 (31.25)	11 (22.92)
Chi-square = 300.549; df = 20; Significant at 1 per cent level						

Group	Upto 1 lac	1 – 2	2 – 3	3 – 5	5 – 10	10+
Training						
Got Training	82 (34.89)	70 (29.79)	38 (16.17)	24 (10.21)	13 (5.33)	8 (3.40)
No Training	41 (19.07)	74 (34.42)	39 (18.14)	40 (18.60)	18 (8.37)	3 (1.40)
Chi-square = 20.021; df = 5; Significant at 1 per cent level						
Sources of Finance						
Formal	20 (16.67)	35 (29.17)	11 (9.17)	28 (23.33)	17 (14.17)	9 (7.50)
Informal	103 (31.21)	109 (33.03)	66 (20.00)	36 (10.91)	14 (4.24)	2 (0.61)
Chi-square = 52.500; df = 5; Significant at 1 per cent level						
Age of Enterprise						
Below 10 years	99 (33.11)	87 (29.10)	52 (17.39)	39 (13.04)	20 (6.69)	2 (0.67)
Above 10 years	24 (15.89)	57 (37.75)	25 (16.56)	25 (16.56)	11 (7.28)	9 (5.96)
Chi-square = 25.682; df = 5; Significant at 1 per cent level						

Rs. 5 lacs in business. It shows that the majority of enterprises owned by women entrepreneurs are micro and small enterprises. Information further shows that women entrepreneurs have invested less money in the initial phase of business to avoid risk. Level of investment is found to be more with increase in level of education. In our sample 28 per cent women entrepreneurs having post-graduate level of education have invested more than Rs. 3 lacs in business. On the other hand, majority of women entrepreneurs possessing lower level of education have invested upto Rs. 3 lacs in business. It seems that risk taking capacity is found to be more among educated women entrepreneurs. More efforts should be made to increase the level of education among women entrepreneurs by formulating liberalized policies. The value of chi-square is statistically significant at 1 per cent level of significance. It shows that these two variables are positively associated. Age-wise information further shows that women entrepreneurs (27 per cent) in the higher age groups have invested more money in business than women entrepreneurs in lower age groups (21 per cent). It shows that with increase in age, confidence to manage business also increases. But more than 50 per cent women entrepreneurs irrespective of their age groups have invested upto Rs. 2 lacs in business. The value of chi-square is statistically significant at 1 per cent level of significance. Women entrepreneurs hailing from rural areas have invested less money in business than other women entrepreneurs. In this table, 24 per cent women entrepreneurs coming from urban areas have invested more than Rs. 3 lacs in business, whereas only 17 per cent women entrepreneurs hailing from rural areas invest same level of investment. The value of chi-square is statistically significant at 5 per cent level of significance. It shows that place of origin and levels of investment vary significantly. Proportion of women entrepreneurs (27 per cent) hailing from nuclear families have invested more than Rs. 3 lacs in business than other women entrepreneurs (21 per cent). It shows that entrepreneurship is more among women entrepreneurs of nuclear families. It may be due to more assistance from family members and more skill possessed by them. On the other hand, women entrepreneurs hailing from joint families cannot avail better opportunities in increasing their skills due to unfavourable conditions prevailing in their families. The value of chi-square is statistically insignificant. It seems logical that individual form of business organizations need less investment than other form of business organizations. 27 per cent women entrepreneurs managing business under other than individual form of business organizations have invested more than Rs. 3 lacs in business, whereas only 20 per cent women entrepreneurs have invested same money in individual form of business organizations. The value of chi-square is statistically significant at 1 per cent level of significance. It highlights that these two variables are positively correlated. It has been observed that large-scale business fetches more economies of scale and consequently increases the level of earnings. In this table, higher level of income earned by those women entrepreneurs who have invested more money in business. Efforts should be made to encourage women entrepreneurs to increase the level of investment in the business. Higher level of investment also increases competitiveness among entrepreneurs and in this process prices of the commodity also decline. The value of chi-square further justifies our findings that these two variables are positively associated. It seems that training increases the knowledge and skill among women entrepreneurs to perform the business in an effective manner. Women entrepreneurs who have taken training before start of their business have invested more money than untrained women entrepreneurs. The value of chi-square is statistically significant at 1 per cent level of significance. It has been observed that increase in financial facilities also sometimes encourage women entrepreneurs to invest more money in business. Information in this table shows that women entrepreneurs who have been able to take assistance from financial institutions have invested more money than women entrepreneurs who have taken assistance from informal sources of finance. The reason to this may be assigned to low cost of credit. The value of chi-square is statistically significant at 1 per cent level of significance. Established businesses have invested more money than new ones. Women entrepreneurs having enterprises more than 10 years old have invested more money in business than other women entrepreneurs possessing younger enterprises. It may be due to lower risk involved in older enterprises due to low level of competition prevailing at the start of new economic reforms. On the other hand, women entrepreneurs who have established their business less than 10 years ago don't want to take more risk in business. The value of chi-square is statistically significant at 1 per cent level of significance.

Table 4.5 reveals that 45 per cent of women entrepreneurs are earning income upto Rs. 10,000 per month and almost same proportion of women entrepreneurs (22 per cent each) are earning in the range of Rs. 10,000-15,000 and Rs. 15,000-20,000 per month. Only 10 per cent of women entrepreneurs are earning more than Rs. 20,000 per month in business. Education-wise information further shows that almost same proportion of women entrepreneurs (12 per cent each) possessing lower and higher level of education are earning more than Rs. 20,000 per month. Women entrepreneurs earning income in the range of Rs. 15,000- 20,000 per month is found to be increasing with increase in level of education. On the other hand, women entrepreneurs earning income in the range of Rs. 10,000-15,000 is on decline with increase in education. It shows that level of income shows variations with level of education. Information further reveals that to earn higher level of income, skill and knowledge in the form of formal education sometimes does not work. It shows the gap in theory and practice while doing business. The value of chi-square is statistically significant at 1 per cent level of significance. Age-wise information further shows that same proportion of women entrepreneurs in the lower age group are earning higher level of income than women entrepreneurs in the upper age group. It

TABLE 4.5

Level of Income Earned by Women Entrepreneurs

(in Rs.)

Group	Upto 7,500	7,500-10,000	10,000-15,000	15,000-20,000	20,000+
1	2	3	4	5	6
All Data	54 (12.00)	151 (33.56)	97 (21.56)	100 (22.22)	48 (10.67)
Education					
Primary	—	7 (29.17)	12 (50.00)	2 (8.33)	3 (12.50)
Matric	7 (8.75)	40 (50.00)	18 (22.50)	10 (12.50)	5 (6.25)
Graduate	26 (13.83)	61 (32.45)	35 (18.62)	46 (24.47)	20 (10.64)
Post Graduate	21 (13.29)	43 (27.22)	32 (20.25)	42 (26.58)	20 (12.66)

Chi-square = 32.184; df = 12; Significant at 1 per cent level

Group	Upto 7,500	7,500-10,000	10,000-15,000	15,000-20,000	20,000+
Age (years)					
Below 30	15 (10.64)	49 (34.75)	28 (19.86)	37 (26.24)	12 (8.51)
30-40	25 (16.34)	43 (28.10)	28 (18.30)	33 (21.57)	24 (15.69)
Above 40	14 (8.97)	59 (37.82)	41 (26.28)	30 (19.23)	12 (7.69)

Chi-square = 15.832 ; df = 8; Significant at 5 per cent level

Group	Upto 7,500	7,500-10,000	10,000-15,000	15,000-20,000	20,000+
Place of Origin					
Rural	5 (5.75)	34 (39.08)	19 (21.84)	22 (25.29)	7 (8.05)
Urban	49 (13.50)	117 (32.23)	78 (21.49)	78 (21.49)	41 (11.29)

Chi-square = 5.650; df = 4; Insignificant

Group	Upto 7,500	7,500-10,000	10,000-15,000	15,000-20,000	20,000+
Type of Family					
Joint	23 (11.00)	82 (39.23)	37 (17.70)	45 (21.53)	22 (10.53)
Nuclear	31 (12.86)	69 (28.63)	60 (24.90)	55 (22.82)	26 (10.79)

Chi-square = 6.850; df = 4; Insignificant

Group	Upto 7,500	7,500-10,000	10,000-15,000	15,000-20,000	20,000+
Form of Business Organization					
Sole	46 (14.89)	126 (40.78)	66 (21.36)	48 (15.53)	23 (7.44)
Others	8 (5.67)	25 (17.73)	31 (21.99)	52 (36.88)	25 (17.73)

Chi-square = 51.648; df = 4; Significant at 1 per cent level

Group	Upto 7,500	7,500-10,000	10,000-15,000	15,000-20,000	20,000+
Investment (Lacs)					
<1	39 (31.71)	52 (42.28)	17 (13.82)	11 (8.94)	4 (3.25)
1-2	15 (10.42)	66 (45.83)	41 (28.47)	19 (13.19)	3 (2.08)
2-3	—	15 (19.48)	28 (36.36)	30 (38.96)	4 (5.19)
3-5	—	18 (28.12)	8 (12.50)	27 (42.19)	11 (17.19)

1	2	3	4	5	6
5-10	—	—	3 (9.68)	13 (41.94)	15 (48.39)
Above 10	—	—	—	—	11 (100.0)

Chi-square = 300.549; df = 20; Significant at 1 per cent level

Training

Got Training	39 (16.60)	71 (30.21)	42 (17.87)	50 (21.28)	33 (14.04)
No Training	15 (6.98)	80 (37.21)	55 (25.58)	50 (23.26)	15 (6.98)

Chi-square = 18.844 ; df = 4; Significant at 1 per cent level

Sources of Finance

Formal	14 (11.67)	23 (19.17)	22 (18.33)	36 (30.00)	25 (20.83)
Informal	40 (12.12)	128 (38.79)	75 (22.73)	64 (19.39)	23 (6.97)

Chi-square = 31.211; df = 4; Significant at 1 per cent level

Age of Enterprise

Below 10 years	41 (13.71)	96 (32.11)	66 (22.07)	66 (22.07)	30 (10.03)
Above 10 years	13 (8.61)	55 (36.42)	31 (20.53)	34 (22.52)	18 (11.92)

Chi-square = 3.189; df = 4; Insignificant

shows that women entrepreneurs in the younger age group possess more dexterity to perform business in changing economic scenario than other women entrepreneurs. On the other hand, almost same proportion of women entrepreneurs in different age groups are earning income upto Rs. 10,000 per month. Information clearly reveals that to earn higher level of income certain level of skill is must in business. The value of chi-square is statistically significant at 1 per cent level of significance. Almost same proportion of women entrepreneurs hailing from rural and urban areas are earning higher and lower level of income. It shows that place of origin is not affecting the level of income earned by women entrepreneurs. The value of chi-square is statistically insignificant. 50 per cent of women entrepreneurs coming from joint families are earning income upto Rs. 10,000 per month in business, whereas 40 per cent of women entrepreneurs from nuclear families are earning same level of income. On the other hand, almost same proportion of women entrepreneurs (32 per cent each) are earning more than Rs. 15,000 per month. The value of chi-square is statistically insignificant. It shows that type of family and level of income earned by women entrepreneurs do not vary significantly. The level of investment made by women entrepreneurs further reveals that all the women entrepreneurs investing more than Rs. 10 lacs in business are earning more than Rs. 20,000 per month in business and 90 per cent of women entrepreneurs investing money in the range of Rs. 5-10 lacs are earning more than Rs. 15,000 per month in business. Only small proportion of women entrepreneurs having invested upto Rs. 2 lacs in business are earning more than Rs. 15,000 per month. It shows that higher level of investment brings economies of scale in business and cost of product also declines. Moreover, ability to hire experts in business also increases. The value of chi-square is statistically significant at 1 per cent level of significance. It shows that these two variables are positively associated with each other. Women entrepreneurs who have taken training before start of business ventures are earning higher level of income than other women entrepreneurs. It shows that training helps in increasing the level of income. Efforts should be made to provide more training facilities to women entrepreneurs so that, their skill and knowledge may be updated over the period of time. The value of chi-square is statistically significant at 1 per cent level of significance. 50 per cent of women entrepreneurs who have used formal sources of finance are earning more than Rs. 15,000 per month in business than other women entrepreneurs (26 per cent) who have used informal sources of finance. It shows that availability of formal sources of finance on the one handed reduces cost of credit and on the other hand, helps in removing various difficulties in business. The value of chi-square is statistically significant at 1 per cent level of significance. It shows that there exist variations between these two variables. Almost same proportion of women entrepreneurs irrespective of the life of their enterprises are earning lower and higher level of income. It shows that women entrepreneurs having younger enterprises have the capacity to compete with well established enterprises. It may be due to more knowledge and skill possessed by younger women entrepreneurs. The value of chi-square is statistically significant at 1 per cent level of significance.

SUGGESTIONS AND POLICY APPLICATIONS

Individual and family wealth constitute major sources of

finance among women entrepreneurs. The role of institutional finance in financing enterprises owned by women entrepreneurs has remained low. Awareness of various sources of finance has not been percolated down to paraxis level in the real sense. There is a need to intensify the efforts to increase the level of awareness of various sources of finance available to women entrepreneurs. Modern communication media should be utilized more effectively to enhance the level of awareness among women entrepreneurs. It will help them in reducing dependence on informal sources of finance and cost of credit will reduce further. Women entrepreneurs will be able to increase the level of investment in their business. EDP programmes should be conducted for existing and potential entrepreneurs to increase their knowledge and awareness of various sources of finance and business opportunities available to them.

Investigation of Training Related Issues

Micro and Small enterprises are playing an important role in the economic development of the country. These enterprises require less capital. Traditional skill and knowledge, local raw material can be utilized in these enterprises. Moreover, these enterprises can be set-up anywhere, thus helps in dispersal of industries geographically. Because of these advantages, efforts are being made to develop this sector for generating gainful employment opportunities.

In the era of globalization, liberalization and privatization of Indian economy, it becomes imperative to chalk out strategies for the further growth of small-scale sector in India and to make it more competitive in the free market economies. Micro and small-scale sector can be strengthened through various methods. One of the methods is to provide training to existing and new entrepreneurs. It has been observed that management of small firms is unique. It bears little or no resemblance to management processes found in large organizations. Moreover, these small enterprises cannot afford to hire experts in various fields of management. All the management functions are performed by individual. Training is considered is an useful instrument for the growth of entrepreneurship. Training will help entrepreneurs in refreshing their knowledge and skill in business. Latest information about business trends, challenges and opportunities available in the market can also be known by taking training. Training is also helpful in enhancing efficiency and effectiveness of entrepreneurs. It has been observed due to lack of proper training entrepreneurs in micro and small enterprises are unable to compete in free market economies and this led to closure of small and micro-enterprises. Experience from developed and developing countries all over the world observed that entrepreneurship can be developed through planned efforts. In the present chapter, an attempt has been made to analyze the various training related issues among women entrepreneurs in Northern India.

Table 5.1 shows that 52 per cent women entrepreneurs have undergone training before start of their business. Information vividly highlights the significance of training in the era of opening up of the economy and increase in competition in the market. Education-wise information further shows that more than 51 per cent of women entrepreneurs possessing education beyond matric level take training. It shows that women want to minimize risk in business and prefer to take training. On the other hand, 71 per cent women entrepreneurs having primary level of education have not taken training before start of their business. The value of chi-square is statistically insignificant. More than 61 per cent of women entrepreneurs in first two age groups have undergone training and only one-third women entrepreneurs in the age group of more than 40 years take training. It shows that as age increases the maturity to take decisions also improves or less necessity is felt by them. The value of chi-square is statistically significant at 1 per cent level of significance. It shows that these two variables are positively associated. Proportion of women entrepreneurs having taken training before start of their business is found to be more among urban women entrepreneurs than women entrepreneurs hailing from rural areas. The value of chi-square is statistically insignificant. 54 per cent women entrepreneurs coming from nuclear families take training before start of their business, whereas 50 per cent of women entrepreneurs from joint families take training. The reason to this may be attributed to availability of guidance in joint families. Almost same proportion of women entrepreneurs (51 per cent) managing business

TABLE 5.1

Have you taken Training

Group	Yes	No
All Data	235 (52.22)	215 (47.78)
Education		
Primary	7 (29.17)	17 (70.83)
Matric	41 (51.25)	39 (48.75)
Graduate	102 (54.26)	86 (45.74)
Post Graduate	85 (53.80)	73 (46.20)
Chi-square = 5.612; df = 3; Insignificant		
Age (years)		
Below 30	91 (64.54)	50 (35.46)
30-40	94 (61.44)	59 (38.56)
Above 40	50 (32.05)	106 (67.95)
Chi-square = 39.220 ; df = 2; Significant at 1per cent level		
Place of Origin		
Rural	41 (47.13)	46 (52.87)
Urban	194 (53.44)	169 (46.56)
Chi-square = 1.122; df = 1; Insignificant		
Type of Family		
Joint Family	104 (49.76)	105 (50.24)
Nuclear	131 (54.36)	110 (45.64)
Chi-square = 0.948; df = 1; Insignificant		
Form of Business Organization		
Sole	162 (52.43)	147 (47.57)
Others	73 (51.77)	68 (48.23)
Chi-square = 0.017; df = 1; Insignificant		
Investment (Lacs)		
<1	82 (66.67)	41 (33.33)
1-2	70 (48.61)	74 (51.39)
2-3	38 (49.35)	39 (50.65)
3-5	24 (37.50)	40 (62.50)
5-10	13 (41.94)	18 (58.06)
Above 10	8 (72.73)	3 (27.27)
Chi-square = 20.021; df = 5; Significant at 1 per cent level		

Group	Yes	No
Income (Rs.)		
<7500	39 (72.22)	15 (27.78)
7500-10000	71 (47.02)	80 (52.98)
10000-15000	42 (43.30)	55 (56.70)
15000-20000	50 (50.00)	50 (50.00)
20000+	33 (68.75)	15 (31.25)
Chi-square = 18.844; df = 4; Significant at 1 per cent level		
Sources of Finance		
Formal	70 (58.33)	50 (41.67)
Informal	165 (50.00)	165 (50.00)
Chi-square = 2.449; df = 1; Insignificant		
Age of Enterprise		
Below 10 years	175 (58.53)	124 (41.47)
Above 10 years	60 (39.74)	91 (60.66)
Chi-square = 14.202 ; df = 1; Significant at 1 per cent level		

under individual and other forms of business organizations take training before start of their enterprise. The value of chi-square is statistically insignificant. 66 per cent women entrepreneurs investing less than Rs. 1 lac in business take training. It seems that women entrepreneurs want to reduce risk in the initial stage of business. Similarly 72 per cent women entrepreneurs who have invested more than Rs. 10 lacs in business also take training before the start of business. It may be due to more complexities involved in large-scale businesses. The value of chi-square is statistically significant at 1 per cent level of significance. 72 per cent women entrepreneurs earning less than Rs. 7,500 per month and 68 per cent women entrepreneurs earning more than Rs. 20,000 per month have undergone training before the start of their business. The value of chi-square is statistically significant at 1 per cent level of significance. More than 50 per cent of women entrepreneurs using formal and informal sources of finance take training. The value of chi-square is statistically insignificant. 58 per cent women entrepreneurs who have been in business during last 10 years prefer to take training before the start of business. It may be due to increase in competition and desire of women entrepreneurs to understand new concepts in business. On the other hand, only 39 per cent of women entrepreneurs who have enterprises more than 10 years old take training. It may be due to less need felt by them during controlled regime. The value of chi-square is statistically significant at 1 per cent level of significance.

Table 5.2 reveals that 83 per cent women entrepreneurs have taken training from private institutes and only 17 per cent from government institutes. It reveals that post-reform period has observed the growth of private institutes imparting education in the field of entrepreneurship development. Education-wise information further shows that more than 71 per cent women entrepreneurs irrespective of their level of education have taken training from private institutes. The value of chi-square is statistically insignificant. 74 per cent to 91 per cent women entrepreneurs in the age group of more than 40 and below 30

TABLE 5.2

Got Training From

Group	Government	Private
All Data	39 (16.46)	196 (82.70)
Education		
Primary	2 (28.57)	5 (71.43)
Matric	9 (21.95)	32 (78.05)
Graduate	15 (14.42)	87 (83.65)
Post Graduate	13 (15.29)	72 (84.71)
Chi-square = 1.942; df = 3; Insignificant		
Age (years)		
Below 30	8 (8.79)	83 (91.21)
30-40	18 (18.75)	76 (79.17)
Above 40	13 (26.00)	37 (74.00)
Chi-square = 7.642; df = 2; Significant at 5 per cent level		
Place of Origin		
Rural	12 (29.27)	29 (70.73)
Urban	27 (13.78)	167 (85.20)
Chi-square = 5.762; df = 1; Significant at 1 per cent level		

Group	Government	Private
Type of Family		
Joint	18 (17.31)	86 (82.69)
Nuclear	21 (15.79)	110 (82.71)
Chi-square = 0.068; df = 1; Insignificant		
Form of Business Organization		
Sole	26 (16.05)	136 (83.95)
Others	13 (17.33)	60 (80.00)
Chi-square = 0.112; df = 1; Insignificant		
Investment (Lacs)		
<1	11 (13.10)	71 (84.52)
1-2	10 (14.29)	60 (85.71)
2-3	15 (39.47)	23 (60.53)
3-5	1 (4.17)	23 (95.83)
5-10	2 (15.38)	11 (84.62)
Above 10	—	8 (100.0)
Chi-square = 19.523; df = 5; Significant at 1 per cent level		
Income (Rs.)		
<7500	1 (2.44)	38 (92.68)
7500-10000	10 (14.08)	61 (85.92)
10000-15000	14 (33.33)	28 (66.67)
15000-20000	10 (20.00)	40 (80.00)
20000+	4 (12.12)	29 (87.88)
Chi-square = 15.268; df = 4; Significant at 1 per cent level		
Sources of Finance		
Formal	13 (18.06)	57 (79.17)
Informal	26 (15.76)	139 (84.24)
Chi-square = 0.118; df = 1; Insignificant		
Age of Enterprise		
Below 10 years	26 (14.69)	149 (84.18)
Above 10 years	13 (21.67)	47 (78.33)
Chi-square = 1.497; df = 1; Insignificant		

have undergone training from private institutes. It shows that women entrepreneurs are more inclined towards private institutes to fulfil their need for training. The value of chi-square is statistically significant at 5 per cent level of significance. 85 per cent women entrepreneurs from urban areas and 70 per cent from rural areas take training from private institutes. Only 29 per cent women entrepreneurs hailing from rural areas take training from government institutes. The value of chi-square is statistically significant at 1 per cent level of significance. Almost same proportion of women entrepreneurs coming from joint and nuclear families have undergone training from private institutes. The reason to this may be assigned to the spread of private institutes under new economic regime. The value of chi-square is statistically insignificant. Almost same proportion of women entrepreneurs managing business under individual and other forms of business organizations have taken training from private institutes. The value of chi-square is statistically insignificant. More than 80 per cent of women entrepreneurs investing different levels of money in business except in the range of Rs. 2-3 lacs have taken assistance from private institutes to learn business concepts. The value of chi-square is statistically significant at 1 per cent level of significance. Women entrepreneurs earning higher level of income have taken training from private institutes. The value of chi-square is statistically significant at 1 per cent level of significance. It shows that these two variables vary significantly 79 per cent to 84 per cent women entrepreneurs using formal and informal sources of finance have taken the assistance from private sector institutes to understand the basics of business. 84 per cent women entrepreneurs possessing enterprises less than 10 years old also sought training from private sector, whereas 78 per cent women entrepreneurs having enterprises more than 10 years old also had training from private institutes. The value of chi-square is statistically insignificant.

Table 5.3 shows that majority of women entrepreneurs (56 per cent) have not incurred expenditure on training. It seems that majority of women entrepreneurs have taken training informally from various sources like relatives and friends. Enterprises involved in various traditional and household enterprises are providing this training to their relatives and family members. Education-wise information further reveals that 70 per cent of women entrepreneurs possessing primary level of education do not spend much money on training. It seems that they might be having business family background and learned business process while doing business. Similarly, more than 52 per cent women entrepreneurs possessing higher level of education did not spend money on business. It shows that educated women entrepreneurs might have learnt business process while studying. 20 to 26 per cent women entrepreneurs irrespective of their level of education incurred more than Rs. 5,000 on training to learn various techniques of business. It shows that these women entrepreneurs want to reduce the risks involved in modern business. The value of chi-square is statistically insignificant. 44 per cent of women entrepreneurs in the age group of less than 30 and between 30-40 got training without incurring expenditure, whereas 78 per cent women entrepreneurs in the age group of more than 40 did not incur expenditure. On the other hand, one-fourth and one-third women entrepreneurs in the age group of less than 30 and 30-40 spent upto Rs. 5,000 and above Rs. 5,000 respectively in business. The value of chi-square is statistically significant at 1 per cent level of significance. It shows that these two variables are positively

TABLE 5.3
Expenditure Incurred on Training

Group	Nil	Upto Rs. 5,000	Above Rs. 5,000
All Data	252 (56.00)	89 (19.78)	109 (24.22)
Education			
Primary	17 (70.83)	1 (4.17)	6 (25.00)
Matric	51 (63.75)	13 (16.25)	16 (20.00)
Graduate	98 (52.13)	45 (23.94)	45 (23.94)
Post Graduate	86 (54.43)	30 (18.99)	42 (26.58)
Chi-square = 8.493; df = 6; Insignificant			
Age (years)			
Below 30	61 (43.26)	36 (25.53)	44 (31.21)
30-40	68 (44.44)	36 (23.53)	49 (32.03)
Above 40	123 (78.85)	17 (10.90)	16 (10.26)
Chi-square = 51.190; df = 4; Significant at 1 per cent level			
Place of Origin			
Rural	56 (64.37)	16 (18.39)	15 (17.24)
Urban	196 (53.99)	73 (20.11)	94 (25.90)
Chi-square = 3.623; df = 2; Insignificant			

Group	Nil	Upto Rs. 5,000	Above Rs. 5,000
Type of Family			
Joint Family	117 (55.98)	47 (22.49)	45 (21.53)
Nuclear	135 (56.02)	42 (17.43)	64 (26.56)
Chi-square = 2.616; df = 2; Insignificant			
Form of Business Organization			
Sole	174 (56.31)	59 (19.09)	76 (24.60)
Others	78 (55.32)	30 (21.28)	33 (23.40)
Chi-square = 0.307; df = 2; Insignificant			
Investment (Lacs)			
<1	48 (39.02)	36 (29.27)	39 (31.71)
1-2	90 (62.50)	26 (18.06)	28 (19.44)
2-3	40 (51.95)	15 (19.48)	22 (28.57)
3-5	52 (81.25)	6 (9.38)	6 (9.38)
5-10	19 (61.29)	4 (12.90)	8 (25.81)
Above 10	3 (27.27)	2 (18.18)	6 (54.55)
Chi-square = 41.617; df = 10; Significant at 1 per cent level			
Income (Rs.)			
<7500	18 (33.33)	17 (31.48)	19 (35.19)
7500-10000	100 (66.23)	30 (19.87)	21 (13.91)
10000-15000	60 (61.86)	15 (15.46)	22 (22.68)
15000-20000	59 (59.00)	23 (23.00)	18 (18.00)
20000+	15 (31.25)	4 (8.33)	29 (60.42)
Chi-square = 59.102; df = 8; Significant at 1 per cent level			
Training			
Got Training	41 (17.45)	85 (36.17)	109 (46.38)
No Training	211 (98.14)	4 (1.86)	—
Chi-square = 297.100; df = 2; Significant at 1 per cent level			
Sources of Finance			
Formal	58 (48.33)	26 (21.67)	36 (30.00)
Informal	194 (58.79)	63 (19.09)	73 (22.12)
Chi-square = 4.268; df = 2; Insignificant			
Age of Enterprise			
Below 10 years	144 (48.16)	70 (23.41)	85 (28.43)
Above 10 years	108 (71.52)	19 (12.58)	24 (15.89)
Chi-square = 22.235; df = 2; Significant at 1 per cent level			

associated. Proportion of women entrepreneurs who spent money on training is found to be less in rural areas than in urban areas. It may be due to strong social ties prevailing among the families of rural areas. On the other hand, proportion of women entrepreneurs spending more than Rs. 5,000 on training is found to be more in urban areas (26 per cent) than in rural areas (17 per cent). The reason to this may be attributed to more competition in urban markets. The value of chi-square is statistically insignificant. Almost same proportion of women entrepreneurs (55 per cent each) hailing from joint and nuclear families did not spend money on training. On the other hand, proportion of women entrepreneurs (26 per cent) spending more than Rs. 5,000 on training is found to be more among nuclear families than in joint families. The reason being in joint families, the knowledge of business is available from various sources within the family. The value of chi-square is statistically insignificant. Almost same proportion of women entrepreneurs doing business under different form of business organizations did not spend money on training. On the other hand, almost same proportion of women entrepreneurs under different forms of business organizations spend Rs. 5000 and more than Rs. 5000 on training to enhance their skill and knowledge. It shows that joint ventures need more skill and information to survive in the market. The value of chi-square is statistically insignificant. 54 per cent of women entrepreneurs investing more than Rs. 10 lacs in business spend more than Rs. 5,000 on training and another 18 per cent spend less than Rs. 5,000. It shows that these women entrepreneurs prefer to spend more money on training to avoid unnecessary risk. On the other hand 29 per cent women entrepreneurs investing less than Rs. 1 lac in business spend less than Rs. 5,000 on training. It shows that women entrepreneurs investing less money in business want to save the cost of training. The value of chi-square is statistically significant at 1 per cent level of significance. 60 per cent women entrepreneurs earning income more than Rs. 20,000 per month spend more than Rs. 5,000 on training. On the other hand, 31 per cent women entrepreneurs earning same level of income did not spend money on training. 59 per cent to 66 per cent women entrepreneurs who did not spend money on training are earning income in the range of Rs. 7,500-10,000, Rs. 10,000-15,000 and Rs. 15,000-20,000 per month. The value of chi-square is statistically significant at 1 per cent level of significance. It shows that these two variables vary significantly. Only 17 per cent women entrepreneurs have taken training without spending money and 46 per cent women entrepreneurs have spent more than Rs. 5,000 on training. The value of chi-square is statistically significant at 1 per cent level of significance. 48 per cent women entrepreneurs who have taken loans from financial institutions did not spend money on training. It seems that financial institutions might require experience in business before sanctioning loans to their clients. On the other hand, 58 per cent women entrepreneurs who have not taken assistance from financial institutions took training without spending money. Only 22 per cent women entrepreneurs using informal sources of finance spend more than Rs. 5,000 on training. It shows that women entrepreneurs using informal sources of finance want to minimize risk involved in business. The value of chi-square is statistically insignificant. 72 per cent women entrepreneurs possessing enterprises more than 10 years do not spend money on training. On the other hand, 23 to 28 per cent women entrepreneurs possessing enterprises less than 10 years old spend Rs. 5,000 and more than 5,000 on training. It shows significance of training expressed by these women entrepreneurs. It shows that women entrepreneurs possessing enterprises more than 10 years old do not require much training due to low level of competition prevailing in the market before the introduction of new economic reforms. On the other hand, competition has recently increased due to decline in job opportunities in the formal sector of economy. The value of chi-square is statistically significant at 1 per cent level of significance.

Table 5.4 shows that almost same proportion of women entrepreneurs take training for the period of six and more than six months before start of their business. Education-wise information further reveals that 71 percent women entrepreneurs possessing primary and 61 per cent graduate level of education spend more than six months to understand the various concepts of business. On the other hand, 46 per cent women entrepreneurs possessing matric and 38 per cent possessing post-graduate level of education take training for the period of more than six months. It reveals that women entrepreneurs spend various time periods to understand various processes of business. The value of chi-

TABLE 5.4

Duration of Training

Group	Upto 6 months	Above 6 months
All Data	116 (49.36)	119 (50.64)
Education		
Primary	2 (28.57)	5 (71.43)
Matric	22 (53.66)	19 (46.34)
Graduate	40 (39.22)	62 (60.78)
Post Graduate	52 (61.18)	33 (38.82)

Chi-square = 10.461; df = 3; Significant at 1 per cent level

Age (years)		
Below 30	49 (53.85)	42 (46.15)
30-40	37 (39.36)	57 (60.64)
Above 40	30 (60.00)	20 (40.00)

Chi-square = 6.757; df = 2; Significant at 5 per cent level

Place of Origin		
Rural	20 (48.78)	21 (51.22)
Urban	96 (49.48)	98 (50.52)

Chi-square = 0.007; df = 1; Insignificant

Type of Family		
Joint Family	53 (50.96)	51 (49.04)
Nuclear	63 (48.09)	68 (51.91)

Chi-square = 0.191; df = 1; Insignificant

Form of Business Organization		
Sole	85 (52.47)	77 (47.53)
Others	31 (42.47)	42 (57.53)

Chi-square = 2.015; df = 1; Insignificant

Investment (Lacs)		
<1	48 (58.54)	34 (41.46)
1-2	33 (47.14)	37 (52.86)
2-3	14 (36.84)	24 (63.16)
3-5	14 (58.33)	10 (41.67)
5-10	2 (15.38)	11 (84.62)
Above 10	5 (62.50)	3 (37.50)

Chi-square = 12.612; df = 5; Significant at 5 per cent level

(Contd.)

Group	Upto 6 months	Above 6 months
Income (Rs.)		
<7500	21 (53.85)	18(46.15)
7500-10000	46 (64.79)	25 (35.21)
10000-15000	15 (35.71)	27 (64.29)
15000-20000	25 (50.00)	25 (50.00)
20000+	9 (27.27)	24 (72.73)
Chi-square = 16.653; df = 4; Significant at 1 per cent level		
Sources of Finance		
Formal	26 (37.14)	44 (62.86)
Informal	90 (54.55)	75 (45.45)
Chi-square = 5.955; df = 1; Insignificant		
Age of Enterprise		
Below 10 years	84 (48.00)	91 (52.00)
Above 10 years	32 (33.33)	28 (46.67)
Chi-square = 14.202; df = 1; Insignificant		

square is statistically significant at 1 per cent level of significance. Women entrepreneurs in middle age groups spend more time to understand the various techniques of business than women entrepreneurs in lower and higher age groups. The value of chi-square is statistically significant at 5 per cent level of significance. Almost same proportion of women entrepreneurs hailing from urban and rural areas spend same time period in training. The value of chi-square is statistically insignificant. Similar type of conclusions have been observed in case of women entrepreneurs coming from joint and nuclear families. 57 per cent women entrepreneurs managing business under other than individual forms of business organizations spend more than six months to know the various concepts of business. It may be due to large scale operation of the plant and risk involved in business. The values of chi-square are statistically insignificant. 84 per cent women entrepreneurs investing Rs. 5-10 lacs in business take training for the period of more than six months and 63 per cent women entrepreneurs investing Rs. 2-3 lacs in business take training for the same time period. On the other hand, only 37 per cent women entrepreneurs investing more than Rs. 10 lacs in business spend more than six months in business. The reason to this may be attributed to easily availability of experts in business areas. The value of chi-square is statistically significant at 5 per cent level of significance. Women entrepreneurs earning higher level of income take training for longer duration than women entrepreneurs earning lower level of income. It reveals that longer period training has proven to be beneficial for women entrepreneurs. The value of chi-square is statistically significant at 1 per cent level of significance. 62 per cent women entrepreneurs who have used formal sources of finance take training for longer period of time than other women entrepreneurs. It shows that women entrepreneurs want to minimize the risk or it may be the preference of financial institutions. The value of chi-square is statistically insignificant. Number of women entrepreneurs (91) possessing enterprises less 10 years old spend more time in training than other women entrepreneurs. The reason to this may be assigned to change in economic scenario over a period of time and women entrepreneurs feel it necessary to survive in the free markets. The value of chi-square is statistically insignificant.

Table 5.5 highlights the type of training needed by women entrepreneurs. Information in the table signifies that women entrepreneurs have sought training in the field of management of small enterprises, marketing and quality control aspect. It seems that women entrepreneurs are fully aware of changing market conditions and change in attitude of consumers towards various aspects of product. Education-wise information further reveals that 22 per cent to 31 per cent women entrepreneurs having different level of education sought training on management of small enterprises. On the other hand, women entrepreneurs possessing higher level of education lay more emphasis on marketing aspect of the product. Need for training on quality control was also expressed by women entrepreneurs possessing lower level of education. It seems that women entrepreneurs having lower level of education face the problem of quality of product in the free market economies. It may also be due to increase in consumer awareness and expectations and competition in the market. The value of chi-square is statistically insignificant. Women entrepreneurs in higher age group need training on management of small enterprises than their counterparts in lower age groups. On the other hand, women entrepreneurs in lower age group lay more emphasis on marketing and quality control.

TABLE 5.5

Type of Training needed by Women Entrepreneurs

Group	Management of small enterprise	Technical	Financial	Marketing	Quality Control	Time Management	Production Management	Information Technology
All Data	115 (25.56)	61 (13.56)	10 (2.22)	103 (22.89)	103 (22.89)	28 (6.22)	19 (4.22)	11 (2.44)
Education								
Primary	6 (25.00)	2 (8.33)	—	5 (20.83)	7 (29.17)	1 (4.17)	2 (8.33)	1 (4.17)
Matric	25 (31.25)	15 (18.75)	5 (6.25)	10 (12.50)	16 (20.00)	7 (8.75)	—	2 (2.50)
Graduate	42 (22.34)	29 (15.43)	3 (1.60)	46 (24.47)	48 (25.53)	7 (3.72)	7 (3.72)	6 (3.19)
Post Graduate	42 (26.58)	15 (9.49)	2 (1.27)	42 (26.58)	32 (20.25)	13 (8.33)	10 (6.33)	2 (1.27)

Chi-square = 32.025; df = 21; Insignificant

Group	Management of small enterprise	Technical	Financial	Marketing	Quality Control	Time Management	Production Management	Information Technology
Age (years)								
Below 30	31 (21.99)	8 (5.67)	3 (2.13)	44 (31.21)	42 (29.79)	3 (2.13)	8 (5.67)	2 (1.42)
30-40	38 (24.84)	27 (17.65)	6 (3.92)	28 (18.30)	28 (18.30)	16 (10.46)	7 (4.58)	7 (4.58)
Above 40	46 (29.49)	26 (16.67)	1 (0.64)	35 (22.44)	33 (21.15)	9 (5.77)	4 (2.56)	2 (1.28)

Chi-square = 41.515; df = 14; Significant at 1 per cent level

Group	Management of small enterprise	Technical	Financial	Marketing	Quality Control	Time Management	Production Management	Information Technology
Place of Origin								
Rural	22 (25.29)	15 (17.24)	1 (1.15)	18 (20.69)	23 (26.44)	4 (4.60)	2 (2.30)	2 (2.30)
Urban	93 (25.62)	46 (12.67)	9 (2.48)	85 (23.42)	80 (22.04)	24 (6.61)	17 (4.68)	9 (2.48)

Chi-square = 3.875; df = 1; Insignificant

Type of Family

Joint	61 (29.19)	31 (14.83)	3 (1.44)	43 (20.57)	38 (18.18)	15 (7.18)	11 (5.26)	7 (3.35)
Nuclear	54 (22.41)	30 (12.45)	7 (2.90)	60 (24.90)	65 (26.97)	13 (5.39)	8 (3.32)	4 (1.66)

Chi-square = 11.141; df = 7; Insignificant

Form of Business Organization

Sole	67 (21.68)	46 (14.89)	6 (1.94)	69 (22.33)	78 (25.24)	20 (6.47)	12 (3.88)	11 (3.56)
Others	48 (34.04)	15 (10.64)	4 (2.84)	34 (24.11)	25 (17.73)	8 (5.67)	7 (4.96)	—

Chi-square = 15.334; df = 7; Significant at 5 per cent level

Investment (Lacs)

<1	21 (17.07)	19 (15.45)	10 (8.13)	19 (15.45)	36 (29.27)	9 (7.32)	3 (2.44)	6 (4.88)
1-2	37 (25.69)	22 (15.28)	—	28 (19.44)	32 (22.22)	14 (9.72)	11 (7.64)	—
2-3	35 (45.45)	9 (11.69)	—	17 (22.08)	11 (14.29)	2 (2.60)	2 (2.60)	1 (1.30)
3-5	12 (18.75)	9 (14.06)	—	23 (35.94)	14 (21.88)	3 (4.69)	2 (3.12)	1 (1.56)
5-10	8 (25.81)	2 (6.45)	—	9 (29.09)	8 (25.81)	—	1 (3.23)	3 (9.68)
Above 10	2 (18.18)	—	—	7 (63.64)	2 (18.18)	—	—	—

Chi-square = 96.504; df = 35; Significant at 1 per cent level

Income (Rs.)

<7500	6 (11.11)	11 (20.37)	7 (12.96)	8 (14.81)	15 (27.78)	1 (1.85)	5 (9.26)	1 (1.85)
7500-10000	31 (20.53)	21 (13.91)	1 (0.66)	34 (22.52)	38 (25.17)	17 (11.26)	3 (1.99)	6 (3.97)
10000-15000	29 (29.90)	17 (17.53)	—	21 (21.65)	23 (23.71)	3 (3.09)	3 (3.09)	1 (1.03)
15000-20000	35 (35.00)	12 (12.00)	2 (2.00)	27 (27.00)	16 (16.00)	2 (2.00)	3 (3.00)	3 (3.00)
20000+	14 (29.17)	—	—	13 (27.08)	11 (22.92)	5 (10.42)	5 (10.42)	—

Chi-square = 85.904; df = 28; Significant at 1 per cent level

(Contd.)

TABLE 5.5 (Contd.)

Group	Management of small enterprise	Technical	Financial	Marketing	Quality Control	Time Management	Production Management	Information Technology
Training								
Got Training	48 (20.43)	30 (12.77)	7 (2.98)	37 (15.74)	77 (32.77)	17 (7.23)	13 (5.53)	6 (2.55)
No Training	67 (31.16)	31 (14.42)	3 (1.40)	66 (30.70)	26 (12.09)	11 (5.12)	6 (2.79)	5 (2.33)
Chi-square = 41.321; df = 7; Significant at 1 per cent level								
Sources of Finance								
Formal	20 (16.67)	17 (14.17)	—	41 (34.17)	28 (23.33)	7 (5.83)	6 (5.00)	1 (0.83)
Informal	95 (28.79)	44 (13.33)	10 (3.03)	62 (18.79)	75 (22.73)	21 (6.36)	13 (3.94)	10 (3.03)
Chi-square = 19.860; df = 7; Significant at 1 per cent level								
Age of Enterprise								
Below 10 years	76 (25.42)	35 (11.71)	5 (1.67)	73 (24.41)	57 (25.08)	15 (5.02)	13 (4.35)	7 (2.34)
Above 10 years	39 (25.83)	26 (17.22)	5 (3.31)	30 (19.87)	28 (18.54)	13 (8.61)	6 (3.97)	4 (2.65)
Chi-square = 8.404; df = 7; Insignificant								

Training on technical aspect is also required by women entrepreneurs in the middle and higher age groups. The value of chi-square is statistically significant at 1 per cent level of significance. It shows that two variables vary significantly. Women entrepreneurs hailing from rural area lay more stress on technical and quality control. Training on marketing of products is sought more by women entrepreneurs coming from urban areas. It seems that women entrepreneurs from urban areas are more concerned with marketing aspect of business. The value of chi-square is statistically insignificant. Women entrepreneurs coming from joint families lay more emphasis on training on management of small enterprises. On the other hand, women entrepreneurs coming from nuclear families desire training on marketing and quality aspect. The value of chi-square is statistically insignificant. It seems that business process has become so complicated and cumbersome that women entrepreneurs managing business on other than individual forms of business organizations also need training on management of small enterprises. In this table 34 per cent women entrepreneurs sought training on management of small enterprises. On the other hand, women entrepreneurs managing business on individual basis express desire on quality control aspects. It seems that problem of provision of quality product is found to be more among household industries and micro-level enterprises. On the other hand, almost same proportion of women entrepreneurs express desire to take training on marketing of product. It may be due to increase in competition in the market and availability of large number of substitutes, marketing of the product is becoming complicated. The value of chi-square is statistically significant at 1 per cent level of significance. It shows that these two variables are positively associated. Level of investment made by women entrepreneurs highlights the interesting trends observed by relating to the area of training needed by women entrepreneurs. 63 per cent women entrepreneurs investing more than Rs. 10 lacs in business express desire to take training on marketing of the product followed by management of small enterprises (18 per cent each). Training on marketing of the product is also sought by women entrepreneurs investing money in the range of Rs. 2-10 lacs in business. Similarly, training on quality aspect is also sought by women entrepreneurs investing different levels of money. But proportion of women entrepreneurs requiring training on quality control is found to be more among small enterprises. The value of chi-square is statistically significant at 1 per cent level of significance. Women entrepreneurs earning higher level of income want training in the field of management of small enterprises and marketing. It seems that women entrepreneurs understand the changing expectations of the people under free market economies. The value of chi-square is statistically significant at 1 per cent level of significance. It shows that the level of income and training needed by women entrepreneurs in various fields vary significantly. 32 per cent trained women entrepreneurs lay more emphasis on quality aspect, whereas same proportion of untrained women entrepreneurs express desire to take training in the field of marketing of the product. One-third untrained women entrepreneurs also desire training in the field of management of small enterprises. The value of chi-square is statistically significant at 1 per cent level of significance. Women entrepreneurs who have used formal sources of finance lay more emphasis on marketing aspects than other women entrepreneurs. On the other hand, same proportion of women entrepreneurs using formal and informal sources of finance require training in the field of quality control. The value of chi-square is statistically significant at 1 per cent level of significance. Almost same proportion of women entrepreneurs irrespective of age of their enterprises express need to take training in the field of management of small enterprises. On the other hand, women entrepreneurs possessing enterprises less than 10 years old lay more emphasis on marketing and quality aspects. It reveals that new enterprises need more training in these areas due to liberalized policies followed by government and growth of enterprises managed by women. The value of chi-square is statistically insignificant. Analysis throws light on the fact that desire of women entrepreneurs to take training in specialized areas has increased tremendously. Women entrepreneurs have become more conscious about their survival in the market. NGOs and institutes providing training in the field of entrepreneurship development should lay more emphasis on specialized courses for existing and potential women entrepreneurs to sort out various problems in business.

SUGGESTIONS AND POLICY IMPLICATIONS

Overwhelming proportion of women entrepreneurs have undergone training before establishing their enterprises. The analysis of data further highlights that majority of women entrepreneurs have taken training from informal sources. It may be due to lack of finances and awareness of various institutes providing training in the field of entrepreneurship development. Effort should be made to increase the awareness of various institutes imparting training to new and existing entrepreneurs. To survive in the free-markets women entrepreneurs must have comprehensive understanding of various concepts of business and recent trends prevailing in the market. This information can only be provided through training programmes. A major proportion of women entrepreneurs have desired to take training in the field of marketing and quality control. Institutes providing training in specialized areas should be further strengthened and short-term courses should be conducted for those desires of taking training in these areas.

Obstacles Faced by Women in Business

Micro and small enterprises constitute an important segment of the Indian economy. This sector has potential to generate gainful employment opportunities. This sector can assure equitable distribution of income and wealth and balance regional development. This sector can also act as nursery for the growth of entrepreneurship among population in general and women in particular. The new economic regime has offered large number of opportunities and challenge to micro and small enterprises of our economy. As a result of this, micro and small-scale sector has engulfed by large number of problems. The present chapter examines various obstacles faced by women entrepreneurs in Northern India.

Table 6.1 shows that 36 per cent women entrepreneurs reveal that they face problem upto a great extent to get information relating to product and other 34 per cent to some extent. 12 per cent women entrepreneurs do not face problem of getting information. Education-wise information further reveals that 58 per cent women entrepreneurs possessing matric level of education face this problem to a great extent. One-fourth women entrepreneurs possessing graduate level of education and 36 per cent post-graduate level of education face the problem of getting information upto a great extent. Analysis of data vividly projects

TABLE 6.1

**Extent of Problem of Getting Information Relating to Product
Faced by Women Entrepreneurs**

Group	To great extent	To large extent	To some extent	To little extent	Not at all
1	2	3	4	5	6
All Data	49 (10.89)	116 (25.78)	153 (34.00)	76 (16.89)	56 (12.44)
Education					
Primary	5 (20.83)	8 (33.33)	8 (33.33)	2 (8.33)	1 (4.17)
Matric	16 (20.00)	31 (38.75)	23 (28.75)	6 (7.50)	4 (5.00)
Graduate	15 (7.98)	33 (17.55)	67 (35.64)	44 (23.40)	29 (15.43)
Post Graduate	13 (8.23)	44 (27.85)	55 (34.81)	24 (15.19)	22 (13.92)
Chi-square = 39.265; df = 12; Significant at 1 per cent level					
Age (years)					
Below 30	9 (6.38)	18 (12.77)	60 (42.55)	28 (19.86)	26 (18.44)
30-40	20 (13.07)	44 (28.76)	45 (29.41)	27 (17.65)	17 (11.11)
Above 40	20 (12.82)	54 (34.62)	48 (30.77)	21 (13.46)	13 (8.33)
Chi-square = 31.91; df = 8; Significant at 1 per cent level					
Place of Origin					
Rural	6 (6.90)	30 (34.48)	36 (41.38)	7 (8.05)	8 (9.20)
Urban	43 (11.85)	86 (23.69)	117 (32.23)	69 (19.01)	48 (13.22)
Chi-square = 12.385; df = 4; Significant at 1 per cent level					
Type of Family					
Joint	22 (10.53)	55 (26.32)	83 (39.71)	34 (16.27)	15 (7.18)
Nuclear	27 (11.20)	61 (25.31)	70 (29.05)	42 (17.43)	41 (17.01)
Chi-square = 12.627; df = 4; Significant at 1 per cent level					
Form of Business Organization					
Sole	32 (10.36)	76 (24.60)	106 (34.30)	51 (16.50)	44 (14.24)
Others	17 (12.06)	40 (28.37)	47 (33.33)	25 (17.73)	12 (8.51)
Chi-square = 3.458; df = 4; Insignificant					
Investment (Lacs)					
<1	10 (8.13)	22 (17.89)	40 (32.52)	31 (25.20)	20 (16.26)
1-2	28 (19.44)	33 (22.92)	51 (35.42)	21 (14.58)	11 (7.64)
2-3	7 (9.09)	29 (37.66)	30 (38.96)	7 (9.09)	4 (5.19)
3-5	4 (6.25)	18 (28.12)	21 (32.81)	8 (12.50)	13 (20.31)

(Contd.)

1	2	3	4	5	6
5-10	—	10 (32.26)	7 (22.58)	6 (19.35)	8 (25.81)
Above 10	—	4 (36.36)	4 (36.36)	3 (27.27)	—

Chi-square = 53.497; df = 20; Significant at 1 per cent level

Income (Rs.)

<7500	3 (5.56)	5 (9.26)	18 (33.33)	18 (33.33)	10 (18.52)
7500-10000	20 (13.25)	38 (25.17)	43 (28.48)	31 (20.53)	19 (12.58)
10000-15000	20 (20.62)	33 (34.02)	30 (30.93)	7 (7.22)	7 (7.22)
15000-20000	5 (5.00)	18 (18.00)	51 (51.00)	13 (13.00)	13 (13.00)
20000+	1 (2.08)	22 (45.83)	11 (22.92)	7 (14.58)	7 (14.58)

Chi-square = 67.399; df = 16; Significant at 1 per cent level

Training

Got Training	18 (7.66)	51 (21.70)	88 (37.45)	39 (16.60)	39 (16.60)
No Training	31 (14.42)	65 (30.23)	65 (30.23)	37 (17.21)	17 (7.91)

Chi-square = 16.435; df = 4; Significant at 1 per cent level

Sources of Finance

Formal	7 (5.83)	22 (18.33)	45 (37.50)	14 (11.67)	32 (26.65)
Informal	42 (12.73)	94 (28.48)	108 (32.73)	62 (18.79)	24 (7.27)

Chi-square = 37.185; df = 4; Significant at 1 per cent level

Age of Enterprise

Below 10 years	32 (10.70)	63 (21.07)	102 (34.11)	52 (17.39)	50 (16.72)
Above 10 years	17 (11.26)	53 (35.10)	51 (33.77)	24 (15.89)	6 (3.97)

Chi-square = 20.929; df = 4; Significant at 1 per cent level

that inspite of spread of information and technology, it is not easily available to small business sector. It may also be due to infrastructural constrains and lack of awareness regarding availability of technology. The value of chi-square is statistically significant at 1 per cent level of significance. It shows that these two variables are positively associated. Women entrepreneurs in the higher age groups (42 per cent and 46 per cent respectively) face this problem relatively more as compared to women entrepreneurs in lower age groups (19 per cent). It reveals that younger generation of women entrepreneurs might be aware of prevalence and accessibility of information. The value of chi-square is statistically significant at 1 per cent level of significance. 41 per cent to 35 per cent women entrepreneurs hailing from urban and rural face this problem upto a large extent in getting information related to product. The value of chi-square is statistically significant at 1 per cent level of significance. Almost same proportion of women entrepreneurs coming from nuclear and joint families face this problem. On the other hand, 17 per cent women entrepreneurs hailing from nuclear families do not face this problem, whereas this proportion is 7 per cent in case of other women entrepreneurs. The value of chi-square is statistically significant at 1 per cent level of significance. Forms of business organizations of women entrepreneurs further reveal that women entrepreneurs managing under other than individual forms of business organizations face the problem relatively more as compared to women entrepreneurs managing business in small scales. In our sample, 40 per cent women entrepreneurs managing business under other than individual forms of business organization face this problem to great extent. Efforts should be made to provide information to these enterprises. The value of chi-square is statistically insignificant. One-third women entrepreneurs investing money more than Rs. 3 lacs in business face this problem to a large extent than women entrepreneurs investing less money in business. On the other hand, more than 40 per cent women entrepreneurs having invested money in the range of Rs. 1-3 lacs face this problem to a large extent. It reveals that small business needs more information for its survival. The value of chi-square is statistically significant at 1 per cent level of significance. 54 per cent to 48 per cent women entrepreneurs earning income in the range of Rs. 10,000-15,000 per month and above Rs. 20,000 per month face this problem to a large extent. It highlights that information is not easily available even to women entrepreneurs earning higher level of income. Suitable policies need to be followed to transfer information to small enterprises at low prices. The value of chi-square is statistically significant at 1 per cent level of significance. Untrained women entrepreneurs (45 per cent) face this problem more intensively than trained women entrepreneurs (29 per cent). More efforts should be made to increase training facilities and awareness regarding these facilities should be enhanced by utilizing modern communication media. The value of chi-square is statistically significant at 1 per cent level of significance Women entrepreneurs who have availed financial assistance from informal sources face this problem more than other women entrepreneurs. In this table, 41 per cent women entrepreneurs who have not availed the financial facilities face this problem to a larger extent. The value of chi-square is statistically significant at 1 per cent level of significance. It shows that there exist variations between these two variables. Enterprises having more age confront with this problem relatively more than younger enterprises. It reveals that old enterprises are managing their business on traditional line than new enterprises and in this process, these enterprises face this problem to a large extent. Women entrepreneurs managing older enterprise need to adopt modern methods of management to overcome this problem. The value of chi-square is statistically significant at 1 per cent level of significance.

Table 6.2 highlights that 25 per cent women entrepreneurs feel that product or services rendered by them fetches low prices. Education-wise information further reveals that the women entrepreneurs possessing low level of education feel that product or service rendered by them fetches low price than women entrepreneurs possessing higher level of education. It seems that women entrepreneurs possessing lower level of education face the problem of selling of product. It may also be due to increase in competition and availability of substitutes in the market. In this table, 46 per cent to 33 per cent women entrepreneurs possessing upto matric level of education face the problem of selling the product at low price to a large extent. On the other hand, only 18 to 20 per cent women entrepreneurs having education beyond graduate level face this problem to a large extent. It reveals that education helps the women entrepreneurs in selling the product in the market in an effective manner. The value of chi-square is statistically significant at 1 per cent level of significance. Age-wise information further shows that 39 per cent women entrepreneurs in the age group of above 40 feel that product sold by them fetches low price. On the other hand, 48 per cent women entrepreneurs in the lower age groups face this problem to some extent. It may be due to more knowledge and skill possessed by women entrepreneurs in lower age groups to sell their product. The value of chi-square is statistically significant at 1 per cent level of significance. 46 per cent women entrepreneurs hailing from urban areas have been encountering this problem to some extent. On the other hand, 31 per cent women entrepreneurs coming from rural

TABLE 6.2

Extent of Problem of Low Price of Product Faced by Women Entrepreneurs

Group	To great extent	To large extent	To some extent	To little extent	Not at all
1	2	3	4	5	6
All Data	31 (6.89)	81 (18.00)	197 (43.78)	108 (24.00)	33 (7.33)
Education					
Primary	3 (12.50)	5 (20.83)	8 (33.33)	7 (29.17)	1 (4.17)
Matric	13 (16.25)	24 (30.00)	24 (30.00)	16 (20.00)	3 (3.75)
Graduate	10 (5.32)	29 (15.43)	92 (49.47)	44 (23.40)	12 (6.38)
Post Graduate	5 (3.16)	23 (14.56)	72 (45.57)	41 (25.95)	17 (10.76)
Chi-square = 34.508; df = 12; Significant at 1 per cent level					
Age (years)					
Below 30	4 (2.84)	16 (11.35)	68 (48.23)	33 (23.40)	20 (14.18)
30-40	7 (4.58)	24 (15.69)	76 (49.67)	38 (24.84)	8 (5.23)
Above 40	20 (12.82)	41 (26.28)	53 (33.97)	37 (23.72)	5 (3.21)
Chi-square = 41.305; df = 8; Significant at 1 per cent level					
Place of Origin					
Rural	3 (3.45)	24 (27.59)	28 (32.18)	24 (27.59)	8 (9.20)
Urban	28 (7.71)	57 (15.70)	169 (46.56)	84 (23.14)	25 (6.89)
Chi-square = 11.759; df = 4; Significant at 1 per cent level					
Type of Family					
Joint	11 (5.26)	38 (18.18)	92 (44.02)	52 (24.88)	16 (7.66)
Nuclear	20 (8.30)	43 (17.84)	105 (43.57)	56 (23.24)	17 (7.05)
Chi-square = 1.691; df = 4; Insignificant					
Form of Business Organization					
Sole	15 (4.85)	54 (17.48)	141 (45.63)	78 (25.24)	21 (6.80)
Others	16 (11.35)	27 (19.15)	56 (39.72)	30 (21.28)	12 (8.51)
Chi-square = 7.873; df = 4; Insignificant					
Investment (Lacs)					
<1	5 (4.07)	16 (13.01)	54 (43.90)	40 (32.52)	8 (6.50)
1-2	12 (8.33)	32 (22.22)	58 (40.28)	32 (22.22)	10 (6.94)
2-3	7 (9.09)	10 (12.99)	32 (41.56)	21 (27.27)	7 (9.09)
3-5	5 (7.81)	11 (17.19)	33 (51.56)	8 (12.50)	7 (10.94)

(Contd.)

1	2	3	4	5	6
5-10	2 (6.45)	8 (25.81)	13 (41.94)	7 (22.58)	1 (3.23)
Above 10	—	4 (36.36)	7 (63.64)	—	—

Chi-square = 26.546; df = 20; Insignificant

Income (Rs.)

<7500	4 (7.41)	10 (18.52)	21 (38.89)	16 (29.63)	3 (5.56)
7500-10000	10 (6.62)	30 (19.87)	62 (41.06)	37 (24.50)	12 (7.95)
10000-15000	10 (10.31)	21 (21.65)	41 (42.27)	24 (24.74)	1 (1.03)
15000-20000	6 (6.00)	10 (10.00)	46 (46.00)	21 (21.00)	17 (17.00)
20000+	1 (2.08)	10 (20.83)	27 (56.25)	10 (20.83)	—

Chi-square = 33.768; df = 16; Significant at 1 per cent level

Training

Got Training	9 (3.83)	44 (18.72)	100 (42.55)	62 (26.38)	20 (8.51)
No Training	22 (10.23)	37 (17.21)	97 (45.∴_)	46 (21.40)	13 (6.05)

Chi-square = 9.087; df = 4; Insignificant

Sources of Finance

Formal	6 (5.00)	28 (23.33)	51 (42.50)	25 (20.83)	10 (8.33)
Informal	25 (7.58)	53 (16.06)	146 (44.24)	83 (25.15)	23 (6.97)

Chi-square = 4.401; df = 4; Insignificant

Age of Enterprise

Below 10 years	15 (5.02)	46 (15.38)	126 (42.14)	86 (28.76)	26 (8.70)
Above 10 years	16 (10.60)	35 (23.18)	71 (47.02)	22 (14.57)	7 (4.64)

Chi-square = 19.142; df = 4; Significant at 1 per cent level

areas face this problem to a large extent. The value of chi-square is statistically significant at 1 per cent level of significance. Almost same proportion of women entrepreneurs coming from joint and nuclear families face this problem to some extent. The value of chi-square is statistically insignificant. Women entrepreneurs managing business under other than individual forms of business organizations (30 per cent) face this problem on higher side than other women entrepreneurs (22 per cent). The value of chi-square is statistically insignificant. Level of investment made by women entrepreneurs further highlights that one-third women entrepreneurs investing more than Rs. 10 lacs in business face this problem to a large extent and 63 per cent face this problem to some extent. On the other hand, 40 per cent to 52 per cent women entrepreneurs investing different levels of money in business face this problem to some extent. The value of chi-square is statistically insignificant. It shows that these two variables are independent. One-fourth women entrepreneurs earning income upto Rs. 10,000 per month face this problem to a large extent. 42 per cent to 56 per cent of women entrepreneurs earning more than Rs. 10,000 per month face this problem to some extent. It depicts that availability of money helps women entrepreneurs in hiring services of experts to sort out this problem. The value of chi-square is statistically significant at 1 per cent level of significance. Almost same proportion of women entrepreneurs irrespective of their level of training faces this problem to some extent. 27 per cent of untrained women entrepreneurs face this problem to a great extent. The value of chi-square is statistically insignificant. Almost same proportion of women entrepreneurs (42 per cent) faces this problem to some extent irrespective of sources of finance taken by them. The value of chi-square is statistically insignificant. Women entrepreneurs having younger enterprises have been able to manage this problem in an effective manner than other women entrepreneurs. It reveals that women entrepreneurs having younger enterprises command more knowledge and skills to solve this problem. The value of chi-square is statistically significant at 1 per cent level of significance.

Table 6.3 shows that 49 per cent of women entrepreneurs face the problem of availability of spurious products to a large extent and other 28 per cent to some extent. Only 8 per cent of women entrepreneurs do not face this problem. Education-wise information further projects that women entrepreneurs (54 per cent to 62 per cent) possessing low level of education face this problem relatively more than educated women entrepreneurs (44 per cent to 46 per cent). The reason being, educated women entrepreneurs might be able to provide better quality products to customers. The value of chi-square is statistically significant at 5 per cent level of significance. Women entrepreneurs (61 per cent) in higher age group face this problem relatively more than women entrepreneurs in lower age groups (28 per cent). 13 per cent of women entrepreneurs in the age group of less than 30 years do not face this problem. It seems that younger women entrepreneurs might be more quality conscious and do not bother about availability of spurious products. The value of chi-square is

TABLE 6.3

Extent of Problem of Availability of Spurious Products Faced by Women Entrepreneurs

Group	To great extent	To large extent	To some extent	To little extent	Not at all
1	2	3	4	5	6
All Data	28 (6.22)	192 (42.67)	126 (28.00)	65 (14.44)	39 (8.67)
Education					
Primary	1 (4.17)	12 (50.00)	4 (16.67)	6 (25.00)	1 (4.17)
Matric	7 (8.75)	43 (53.75)	18 (22.50)	8 (10.00)	4 (5.00)
Graduate	12 (6.38)	74 (39.36)	65 (34.57)	18 (9.57)	19 (10.11)
Post Graduate	8 (5.06)	63 (39.87)	39 (24.68)	33 (20.89)	15 (9.49)
Chi-square = 23.144; df = 12; Significant at 5 per cent level					
Age (years)					
Below 30	3 (2.13)	36 (25.53)	49 (34.75)	34 (24.11)	19 (13.48)
30-40	12 (7.84)	74 (48.37)	39 (25.49)	21 (13.73)	7 (4.58)
Above 40	13 (8.33)	82 (52.56)	38 (24.36)	10 (6.41)	13 (8.33)
Chi-square = 46.279; df = 8; Significant at 1 per cent level					
Place of Origin					
Rural	5 (5.75)	39 (44.83)	22 (25.29)	15 (17.24)	6 (6.90)
Urban	23 (6.34)	153 (42.15)	104 (28.65)	50 (13.77)	33 (9.09)
Chi-square = 1.415; df = 4; Insignificant					
Type of Family					
Joint	8 (3.83)	93 (44.50)	55 (26.32)	30 (14.35)	23 (11.00)
Nuclear	20 (8.30)	99 (41.08)	71 (29.46)	35 (14.52)	16 (6.64)
Chi-square = 6.762; df = 4; Insignificant					
Form of Business Organization					
Sole	23 (7.44)	117 (37.86)	99 (32.04)	45 (14.56)	25 (8.09)
Others	5 (3.55)	75 (53.19)	27 (19.15)	20 (14.18)	14 (9.93)
Chi-square = 13.827; df = 4; Significant at 1 per cent level					
Investment (Lacs)					
<1	5 (4.07)	39 (31.71)	42 (34.15)	25 (20.33)	12 (9.76)
1-2	10 (6.94)	64 (44.44)	45 (31.25)	20 (13.89)	5 (3.47)
2-3	4 (5.19)	39 (50.65)	15 (19.48)	9 (11.69)	10 (12.99)
3-5	9 (14.06)	29 (45.31)	10 (15.62)	5 (7.81)	11 (17.19)

1	2	3	4	5	6
5-10	—	15 (48.39)	11 (35.48)	4 (12.90)	1 (3.23)
Above 10	—	6 (54.55)	3 (27.27)	2 (18.18)	—

Chi-square = 43.025; df = 20; Significant at 1 per cent level

Income (Rs.)					
<7500	4 (7.41)	20 (37.04)	18 (33.33)	9 (16.67)	3 (5.56)
7500-10000	9 (5.96)	53 (35.10)	50 (33.11)	21 (13.91)	18 (11.92)
10000-15000	4 (4.12)	54 (55.67)	18 (18.56)	17 (17.53)	4 (4.12)
15000-20000	6 (6.00)	41 (41.00)	30 (30.00)	11 (11.00)	12 (12.00)
20000+	5 (10.42)	24 (50.00)	10 (20.83)	7 (14.58)	2 (4.17)

Chi-square = 24.039; df = 16; Insignificant

Training					
Got Training	9 (3.83)	99 (42.13)	62 (26.38)	46 (19.57)	19 (8.09)
No Training	19 (8.84)	93 (43.26)	64 (29.77)	19 (8.84)	20 (9.30)

Chi-square = 14.171; df = 4; Significant at 1 per cent level

Sources of Finance					
Formal	7 (5.83)	55 (45.83)	35 (29.17)	13 (10.83)	10 (8.33)
Informal	21 (6.36)	137 (41.52)	91 (27.58)	52 (15.76)	29 (8.79)

Chi-square = 2.002; df = 4; Insignificant

Age of Enterprise					
Below 10 years	12 (4.01)	121 (40.47)	83 (27.76)	52 (17.39)	31 (10.37)
Above 10 years	16 (10.60)	71 (47.02)	43 (28.48)	13 (8.61)	8 (5.30)

Chi-square = 16.347; df = 4; Significant at 1 per cent level

statistically significant at 1 per cent level of significance. Almost same proportion of women entrepreneurs irrespective of place of origin (49 per cent each) face this problem. It shows that this problem is faced by all type of women entrepreneurs. The value of chi-square is statistically insignificant. Women entrepreneurs hailing from nuclear families face this problem slightly on higher side than women entrepreneurs coming from joint families. The value of chi-square is statistically insignificant. Women entrepreneurs managing business under other than individual forms of business organizations face this problem relatively more than women entrepreneurs managing business on individual basis. The value of chi-square is statistically significant at 1 per cent level of significance. More than 50 per cent of women entrepreneurs investing more than Rs. 1 lacs in business face this problem. It reveals that post reform period has observed availability of large number of close substitutes in the market and in this process small enterprises face this problem. The value of chi-square is statistically significant at 1 per cent level of significance. As high as 50 per cent of women entrepreneurs earning more than Rs. 10,000-15,000 and more than Rs. 20,000 per month face this problem to a large extent and more than 40 per cent of women entrepreneurs earning less than Rs. 10,000 per month face this problem. Effort should be made to develop the better quality products so that spurious products vanish from the market. The value of chi-square is statistically insignificant. Untrained women entrepreneurs (52 per cent) face this problem relatively more than trained women entrepreneurs (46 per cent). It shows that training helps the women entrepreneurs to provide better quality products to customers. The value of chi-square is statistically significant at 1 per cent level of significance. Women entrepreneurs (51 per cent) who have used formal sources of finance face this problem relatively more than women entrepreneurs (48 per cent) using informal sources of finance. Institutes providing finance to entrepreneurs should take into consideration quality aspects so that problem of spurious products should not act as hurdle in business. The value of chi-square is statistically insignificant. The women entrepreneurs having enterprises more than 10 years old face this problem relatively more as compared to women entrepreneurs possessing enterprises less than 10 years old. Information reveals that older enterprises flourished under controlled regime are now finding difficulty in selling product under new economic regime. The value of chi-square is statistically significant at 1 per cent level of significance. It shows that these two variables vary significantly.

Table 6.4 shows that 35 per cent of women entrepreneurs agree that there is decline in profit margin to a large extent, another 35 per cent feel that profit margin has declined to some extent. On the other hand, 16 per cent of women entrepreneurs observe that profit margin has not declined at all. Education-wise information further highlights that 52 per cent to 45 per cent of women entrepreneurs having low level of education feel that profit margin has declined in business. It may be due to increase in competition, availability of substitutes and use of modern

TABLE 6.4

Extent of Problem of Decline in Profit Margin Faced by Women Entrepreneurs

Group	To great extent	To large extent	To some extent	To little extent	Not at all
1	2	3	4	5	6
All Data	21 (4.67)	138 (30.67)	156 (34.67)	63 (14.00)	72 (16.00)
Education					
Primary	1 (4.17)	10 (41.67)	6 (25.00)	3 (12.50)	4 (16.67)
Matric	13 (16.25)	29 (36.25)	23 (28.75)	9 (11.25)	6 (7.50)
Graduate	5 (2.66)	64 (34.04)	62 (32.98)	29 (15.43)	28 (14.89)
Post Graduate	2 (1.27)	35 (22.15)	65 (41.14)	22 (13.92)	34 (21.52)
Chi-square = 45.781; df = 12; Significant at 1 per cent level					
Age (years)					
Below 30	3 (2.13)	31 (21.99)	50 (35.46)	25 (17.73)	32 (22.70)
30-40	—	39 (25.49)	66 (43.14)	16 (10.46)	32 (20.92)
Above 40	18 (11.54)	68 (43.59)	40 (25.64)	22 (14.10)	8 (5.13)
Chi-square = 65.587; df = 8; Significant at 1 per cent level					
Place of Origin					
Rural	5 (5.75)	34 (39.08)	21 (24.14)	11 (12.64)	16 (18.39)
Urban	16 (4.41)	104 (28.65)	135 (37.19)	52 (14.53)	56 (15.43)
Chi-square = 6.735; df = 4; Insignificant					
Type of Family					
Joint	12 (5.74)	60 (28.71)	81 (38.76)	29 (13.88)	27 (12.92)
Nuclear	9 (3.73)	78 (32.37)	75 (31.12)	34 (14.11)	45 (18.67)
Chi-square = 5.657; df = 4; Insignificant					
Form of Business Organization					
Sole	18 (5.83)	85 (27.51)	110 (35.60)	46 (14.89)	
Others	3 (2.13)	53 (37.59)	46 (32.62)	17 (12.06)	50 (16.18)
22 (15.60)					
Chi-square = 6.866; df = 4; Insignificant					
Investment (Lacs)					
<1	3 (2.44)	20 (16.26)	49 (39.84)	22 (17.89)	29 (23.58)
1-2	11 (7.64)	43 (29.86)	44 (30.56)	32 (22.22)	14 (9.72)
2-3	1 (1.30)	30 (38.96)	26 (33.77)	4 (5.19)	16 (20.78)

(Contd.)

1	2	3	4	5	6
3-5	6 (9.38)	27 (42.19)	18 (28.12)	1 (1.56)	12 (18.75)
5-10	—	15 (48.39)	11 (35.48)	4 (12.90)	1 (3.23)
Above 10	—	3 (27.27)	8 (72.73)	—	—

Chi-square = 69.502; df = 20; Significant at 1 per cent level

Income (Rs.)

<7500	—	14 (25.93)	26 (48.15)	10 (18.52)	4 (7.41)
7500-10000	11 (7.28)	40 (26.49)	49 (32.45)	26 (17.22)	25 (16.56)
10000-15000	6 (6.19)	36 (37.11)	34 (35.05)	11 (11.34)	10 (10.31)
15000-20000	4 (4.00)	34 (34.00)	26 (26.00)	12 (12.00)	24 (24.00)
20000+	—	14 (29.17)	21 (42.75)	4 (8.33)	9 (18.75)

Chi-square = 29.371; df = 16; Significant at 5 per cent level

Training

Got Training	4 (1.70)	57 (24.26)	83 (35.32)	33 (14.04)	58 (24.68)
No Training	17 (7.91)	81 (37.67)	73 (33.95)	30 (13.95)	14 (6.51)

Chi-square = 39.083; df = 4; Significant at 1 per cent level

Sources of Finance

Formal	—	50 (41.67)	36 (30.00)	14 (11.67)	20 (16.67)
Informal	21 (6.36)	88 (26.67)	120 (36.36)	49 (14.85)	52 (15.76)

Chi-square = 15.803; df = 4; Significant at 1 per cent level

Age of Enterprise

Below 10 years	6 (2.01)	75 (25.08)	105 (35.12)	52 (17.39)	61 (20.40)
Above 10 years	15 (9.93)	63 (41.72)	51 (33.77)	11 (7.28)	11 (7.28)

Chi-square = 40.728; df = 4; Significant at 1 per cent level

methods of marketing by entrepreneurs. On the other hand, 24 per cent of women entrepreneurs possessing post-graduate level of education observe that there is a decline in profit margin in the business. It seems that women entrepreneurs having higher level of education are handling business in an effective manner as compared to other women entrepreneurs. The value of chi-square is statistically significant at 1 per cent level of significance. 55 per cent women entrepreneurs in the age group of more than 40 feel that profit margin has declined in business to a large extent, whereas only one-fourth women entrepreneurs in lower age groups agree with this statement. The value of chi-square is statistically significant at 1 per cent level of significance. Women entrepreneurs (33 per cent) hailing from urban areas face this problem relatively less than women entrepreneurs (45 per cent) coming from rural areas. 37 per cent of women entrepreneurs hailing from urban areas have been able to reduce this problem to some extent. It may be due to better facilities available to women entrepreneurs coming from urban areas. The value of chi-square is statistically insignificant. Almost same proportion of women entrepreneurs coming from joint and nuclear families are facing this problem to a large extent. The value of chi-square is statistically insignificant. It reveals that these two variables are not associated with each other. Women entrepreneurs (39 per cent) managing business under other than individual forms of business organizations have been facing this problem more intensively than women entrepreneurs (33 per cent) managing business on individual basis. The reason being, joint business tries to incur expenditure on various heads and in era of intensive competition profit margin declines in this process. The value of chi-square is statistically insignificant. Almost same proportion of women entrepreneurs investing money in the range of Rs. 3-5 lacs and Rs. 5-10 lacs face this problem to a large extent. On the other hand, women entrepreneurs (72 per cent) spending more than Rs. 10 lacs in business have been facing this problem to some extent. It may be due to large scale production or rendering of better services that these enterprises are able to maintain profitability. The value of chi-square is statistically significant at 1 per cent level of significance. 43 per cent of women entrepreneurs earning income in the range of Rs. 10,000-15,000 per month and 38 per cent women entrepreneurs earning income Rs. 15,000-20,000 per month are facing this problem to large extent, whereas this ratio is 29 per cent in case of women entrepreneurs earning more than Rs. 20,000 per month. The value of chi-square is statistically significant at 5 per cent level of significance. Untrained women entrepreneurs (45 per cent) face this problem relatively more than trained women entrepreneurs (26 per cent). It may be due to better management practices used by trained women entrepreneurs and in this process they are able to reduce the cost of product. The value of chi-square is statistically significant at 1 per cent level of significance. 42 per cent of women entrepreneurs who have taken assistance from financial institutions face this problem relatively more than other women entrepreneurs (33 per cent). The value of chi-square is statistically significant at 1 per cent level of significance. Women entrepreneurs having enterprises less than 10 years old face this problem to less extent than other women entrepreneurs. It clearly depicts that younger generation of women entrepreneurs are having more knowledge and skill to observe the changing market conditions and are able to manage business in an efficient manner. There is a need to refresh the knowledge and skill of women entrepreneurs having enterprises more than 10 years old so that they may be able to utilize modern techniques of management. The value of chi-square is statistically significant at 1 per cent level of significance.

Table 6.5 shows that only small proportion of women entrepreneurs (20 per cent) face the problem of getting training in business to a large extent and 26 per cent women entrepreneurs face this problem to some extent. It reveals that post-reform period has observed the spread to large number of institutes providing training to new and existing women entrepreneurs. Information further shows that growth of entrepreneurship has opened the vast opportunities for educated skilled professionals. Education-wise information further shows that women entrepreneurs possessing higher level of education do not face this problem to a large extent than other women entrepreneurs. It may be due to lack of information related to availability of training institutes among less educated women entrepreneurs. There is a need to increase the level of awareness of various institutes imparting training for the growth of entrepreneurship. Public sector institutes should use modern communication media so that existing and potential women entrepreneurs can have training at low cost. The value of chi-square is statistically significant at 1 per cent level of significance. 24 per cent to 28 per cent women entrepreneurs in the age group of more than 30 face this problem to a large extent. It may be due to better education facilities available to women entrepreneurs in lower age groups and even less need felt by them. The value of chi-square is statistically significant at 1 per cent level of significance. Women entrepreneurs (26 per cent) hailing from rural area face this problem relatively more than women entrepreneurs (18 per cent) coming from urban areas. It may be due to location of training institutes in urban areas and lack of mobility among rural women entrepreneurs. Efforts should be made to open training institutes providing training

TABLE 6.5

Extent of Problem of Getting Training Faced by Women Entrepreneurs

Group	To great extent	To large extent	To some extent	To little extent	Not at all
1	2	3	4	5	6
All Data	42 (9.33)	47 (10.44)	119 (26.44)	135 (30.00)	107 (23.78)
Education					
Primary	10 (41.67)	1 (4.17)	6 (25.00)	2 (8.33)	5 (20.83)
Matric	18 (22.50)	15 (18.75)	17 (21.25)	22 (27.50)	8 (10.00)
Graduate	7 (3.72)	11 (5.85)	54 (28.72)	68 (36.17)	48 (25.53)
Post Graduate	7 (4.43)	20 (12.66)	42 (26.58)	43 (27.22)	46 (29.11)
Chi-square = 79.411; df = 12; Significant at 1 per cent level					
Age (years)					
Below 30	1 (0.71)	7 (4.96)	28 (19.86)	51 (36.17)	54 (38.33)
30-40	18 (11.76)	19 (12.42)	40 (26.14)	54 (32.29)	22 (14.38)
Above 40	23 (14.74)	21 (13.46)	51 (32.69)	30 (19.23)	31 (19.87)
Chi-square = 56.139; df = 8; Significant at 1 per cent level					
Place of Origin					
Rural	15 (17.24)	8 (9.20)	31 (35.63)	19 (21.84)	14 (16.09)
Urban	27 (7.44)	39 (10.74)	88 (24.24)	16 (31.96)	93 (25.62)
Chi-square = 15.904; df = 4; Significant at 1 per cent level					
Type of Family					
Joint	22 (10.53)	25 (11.96)	58 (27.75)	70 (33.49)	34 (16.27)
Nuclear	20 (8.30)	22 (9.13)	61 (25.31)	65 (26.97)	73 (30.29)
Chi-square = 12.550; df = 4; Significant at 1 per cent level					
Form of Business Organization					
Sole	27 (8.74)	30 (9.71)	68 (22.01)	100 (32.36)	84 (27.18)
Others	15 (10.64)	17 (12.06)	51 (36.17)	35 (24.82)	23 (16.31)
Chi-square = 14.879; df = 4; Significant at 1 per cent level					
Investment (Lacs)					
<1	7 (5.69)	6 (4.88)	26 (21.14)	58 (47.15)	26 (21.14)
1-2	17 (11.81)	27 (18.75)	36 (25.00)	41 (28.47)	23 (15.97)
2-3	9 (11.69)	10 (12.99)	28 (36.36)	16 (20.78)	14 (18.18)
3-5	5 (7.81)	2 (3.12)	15 (23.44)	12 (18.75)	30 (46.88)

(Contd.)

1	2	3	4	5	6
5-10	4 (12.90)	—	9 (29.03)	4 (12.90)	14 (45.16)
Above 10	—	2 (18.18)	5 (45.45)	4 (36.36)	—

Chi-square = 79.862; df = 20; Significant at 1 per cent level

Income (Rs.)

	2	3	4	5	6
<7500	—	6 (11.11)	11 (20.37)	28 (51.85)	9 (16.67)
7500-10000	10 (6.62)	17 (11.26)	41 (27.15)	40 (26.49)	43 (28.48)
10000-15000	23 (23.71)	8 (8.25)	17 (17.53)	31 (31.96)	18 (18.56)
15000-20000	—	13 (13.00)	30 (30.00)	26 (26.00)	31 (31.00)
20000+	9 (18.75)	3 (6.25)	20 (41.67)	10 (20.83)	6 (12.50)

Chi-square = 71.633; df = 16; Significant at 1 per cent level

Training

	2	3	4	5	6
Got Training	9 (3.83)	18 (7.66)	62 (26.38)	104 (44.26)	42 (17.87)
No Training	33 (15.35)	29 (13.49)	57 (26.51)	31 (14.42)	65 (30.23)

Chi-square = 60.147; df = 4; Significant at 1 per cent level

Sources of Finance

	2	3	4	5	6
Formal	—	9 (7.50)	29 (24.17)	30 (25.00)	52 (43.33)
Informal	42 (12.73)	38 (11.52)	90 (27.27)	105 (31.82)	55 (16.67)

Chi-square = 44.633; df = 4; Significant at 1 per cent level

Age of Enterprise

	2	3	4	5	6
Below 10 years	22 (7.36)	30 (10.23)	70 (23.41)	99 (33.11)	78 (26.09)
Above 10 years	20 (13.25)	17 (11.26)	49 (32.45)	36 (23.84)	29 (19.21)

Chi-square = 11.841 ; df = 4; Significant at 1 per cent level

in hi-tech and emerging areas in rural areas. The value of chi-square is statistically significant at 1 per cent level of significance. Women entrepreneurs (22 per cent) hailing from joint families face this problem relatively more than women entrepreneurs (17 per cent) coming from nuclear families. The value of chi-square is statistically significant at 1 per cent level of significance. Women entrepreneurs (22 per cent) managing business under other than individual forms of business organizations face this problem more than women entrepreneurs (17 per cent) doing business on individual basis. The reason being, large business needs training in wider areas than small business and in this process they face problem. The value of chi-square is statistically significant at 1 per cent level. 23 per cent to 29 per cent women entrepreneurs having made investment in the range of Rs. 1-2 lacs and Rs. 2-3 lacs in business face this problem to a large extent. It reveals that problem of getting training is felt more by small entrepreneurs and on the other hand, women entrepreneurs investing more money in business may be able to hire experts in different fields to manage business effectively. Small entrepreneurs have to perform all the management functions themselves. Suitable policies need to be formulated to fulfil the training requirements of micro and small enterprises. The value of chi-square is statistically significant at 1 per cent level of significance. 18 per cent to 32 per cent women entrepreneurs earning income in the range of Rs. 7,500-10,000 and Rs. 10,000-15,000 per month face this problem to a large extent. The value of chi-square is statistically significant at 1 per cent level of significance. Women entrepreneurs, who have not taken training before start of their business face this problem relatively more. Similarly, women entrepreneurs using informal sources of finance face this problem more than women entrepreneurs using formal sources of finance. The values of chi-square are statistically significant at 1 per cent level of significance in both cases. Women entrepreneurs possessing enterprises more than 10 years old face this problem relatively more than other women entrepreneurs. The reason to this may be attributed to difficulty in understanding the new concepts of business. The value of chi-square is statistically significant at 1 per cent level of significance.

Table 6.6 shows that slightly less than one-fourth women entrepreneurs face the problem of indifferent attitude of customers. Information shows that people do not make gender difference while buying commodities and most of time they are conscious of quality and better services. Education-wise information further shows that 25 per cent to 34 per cent women entrepreneurs possessing education upto matric level face this problem to a large extent. On the other hand, one-fifth women entrepreneurs possessing higher level of education also feel that customers show indifferent attitude. The value of chi-square is statistically significant at 1 per cent level of significance. Women entrepreneurs beyond age of 30 feel that customers show indifferent attitude. The value of chi-square is statistically significant at 5 per cent level of significance. Almost same proportion of women entrepreneurs coming from rural and urban

TABLE 6.6

Extent of Problem of Indifferent Attitude of Customers Faced by Women Entrepreneurs

Group	To great extent	To large extent	To some extent	To little extent	Not at all
1	2	3	4	5	6
All Data	21 (4.67)	86 (19.11)	106 (23.56)	141 (31.33)	96 (21.33)
Education					
Primary	—	6 (25.00)	5 (20.83)	8 (33.33)	5 (20.83)
Matric	6 (7.50)	21 (26.25)	28 (35.00)	19 (23.75)	6 (7.50)
Graduate	15 (7.98)	28 (14.89)	31 (16.49)	65 (34.57)	49 (26.06)
Post Graduate	—	31 (19.62)	42 (26.58)	49 (31.01)	36 (22.78)
Chi-square = 39.193; df = 12; Significant at 1 per cent level					
Age (years)					
Below 30	2 (1.42)	18 (12.77)	35 (24.82)	46 (32.62)	40 (28.37)
30-40	11 (7.19)	36 (23.53)	30 (19.61)	51 (33.33)	25 (16.34)
Above 40	8 (5.13)	32 (20.51)	41 (26.28)	44 (28.21)	31 (19.87)
Chi-square = 17.614; df = 8; Significant at 5 per cent level					
Place of Origin					
Rural	2 (2.30)	17 (19.54)	26 (29.89)	30 (34.48)	12 (13.79)
Urban	19 (5.23)	69 (19.01)	80 (22.04)	111 (30.58)	84 (23.14)
Chi-square = 6.356; df = 4; Insignificant					
Type of Family					
Joint	13 (6.22)	39 (18.66)	50 (23.92)	72 (34.45)	35 (16.75)
Nuclear	8 (3.32)	47 (19.50)	56 (23.24)	69 (28.63)	61 (25.31)
Chi-square = 7.140; df = 4; Insignificant					
Form of Business Organization					
Sole	19 (6.15)	59 (19.09)	62 (20.06)	100 (32.36)	69 (22.33)
Others	2 (1.42)	27 (19.15)	44 (31.21)	41 (29.08)	27 (19.15)
Chi-square = 10.537; df = 4; Significant at 5 per cent level					
Investment (Lacs)					
<1	10 (8.13)	26 (21.14)	25 (20.33)	43 (34.96)	19 (15.45)
1-2	6 (4.17)	42 (29.17)	39 (27.08)	39 (27.08)	18 (12.50)
2-3	2 (2.60)	13 (16.88)	17 (22.08)	33 (42.86)	12 (15.58)
3-5	2 (3.12)	5 (7.81)	10 (15.62)	15 (23.44)	32 (50.00)

1	2	3	4	5	6
5-10	1 (3.23)	—	10 (32.26)	6 (19.35)	14 (45.16)
Above 10	—	—	5 (45.45)	5 (45.45)	1 (9.09)

Chi-square = 81.766; df = 20; Significant at 1 per cent level

Income (Rs.)

<7500	10 (18.52)	16 (29.63)	12 (22.22)	11 (20.37)	5 (9.26)
7500-10000	6 (3.97)	33 (21.85)	27 (17.88)	41 (27.15)	44 (29.14)
10000-15000	2 (2.06)	27 (27.84)	21 (21.65)	30 (30.93)	17 (17.53)
15000-20000	2 (2.00)	5 (5.00)	25 (25.00)	44 (44.00)	24 (24.00)
20000+	1 (2.08)	5 (10.42)	21 (43.75)	15 (31.25)	6 (12.50)

Chi-square = 75.324; df = 16; Significant at 1 per cent level

Training

Got Training	10 (4.26)	38 (16.17)	70 (29.79)	76 (32.34)	41 (17.45)
No Training	11 (5.12)	48 (22.33)	36 (16.74)	65 (30.23)	55 (25.58)

Chi-square = 14.155; df = 4; Significant at 1 per cent level

Sources of Finance

Formal	2 (1.67)	11 (9.17)	27 (22.50)	34 (28.33)	46 (38.33)
Informal	19 (5.76)	75 (22.73)	79 (23.94)	107 (32.42)	50 (15.15)

Chi-square = 34.338; df = 4; Significant at 1 per cent level

Age of Enterprise

Below 10 years	13 (4.35)	56 (18.73)	67 (22.41)	98 (32.78)	65 (21.74)
Above 10 years	8 (5.30)	30 (19.87)	39 (25.83)	43 (28.48)	31 (20.53)

Chi-square = 1.421 ; df = 4; Insignificant

areas face this problem to a large extent. The value of chi-square is statistically insignificant. 23 per cent to 25 per cent women entrepreneurs hailing from nuclear and joint families face this problem. The value of chi-square is statistically insignificant. Women entrepreneurs (25 per cent) managing business on individual basis face this problem relatively more as compared to women entrepreneurs (21 per cent) managing business under other than individual forms of business organizations. The value of chi-square is statistically significant at 5 per cent level of significance. Women entrepreneurs investing less money in business face this problem relatively more as compared to other women entrepreneurs. It shows that people take into consideration various aspect of product. Women entrepreneurs earning lower level of income face this problem more than women entrepreneurs earning higher level of income. The values of chi-square are statistically significant at 1 per cent level of significance. Untrained women entrepreneurs (27 per cent) face this problem relatively more than trained women entrepreneurs (20 per cent). It may be due to lack of training that these entrepreneurs face this problem. The value of chi-square is statistically significant at 1 per cent level of significance. Women entrepreneurs (28 per cent) who have used informal sources of finance face this problem relatively more as compared to women entrepreneurs (11 per cent) using formal sources of finance. The value of chi-square is statistically significant at 1 per cent level of significance. Women entrepreneurs managing business for a longer period of time face this problem slightly more than other women entrepreneurs. The value of chi-square is statistically insignificant.

Table 6.7 shows that only 20 per cent of women entrepreneurs face the problem of estimation of demand for their product to a large extent, 36 per cent to some extent and 15 per cent do not face this problem. Education-wise information further shows that problem of estimation of demand for product is felt less intensively among educated women entrepreneurs than less educated women entrepreneurs. It shows that education helps in solving the problem of estimation of demand for product. Information further shows that educated women entrepreneurs might be managing business differently than less educated women entrepreneurs. The value of chi-square is statistically significant at 1 per cent level of significance. Only small proportion of women entrepreneurs (8 per cent) in the age group of less than 30 are facing this problem to a great extent, whereas this ratio is more than one-fourth among women entrepreneurs in the age group of more than 40. It shows that entrepreneurial skill is high among younger generation of women entrepreneurs. The value of chi-square is statistically significant at 1 per cent level of significance. It shows that these two variables differ significantly. Women entrepreneurs coming from rural areas (25 per cent) face this problem more intensively than women entrepreneurs coming from urban areas (18 per cent). The reason to this may be attributed to education difference and fast changing environment, which women entrepreneurs from rural areas find it difficult to forecast. The value of chi-square is statistically significant at 5 per

TABLE 6.7

Extent of Problem of Estimation of Demand for Product Faced by Women Entrepreneurs

Group	To great extent	To large extent	To some extent	To little extent	Not at all
1	2	3	4	5	6
All Data	23 (5.11)	67 (14.89)	164 (36.44)	128 (28.44)	68 (15.11)
Education					
Primary	2 (8.33)	4 (16.67)	8 (33.33)	7 (29.17)	3 (12.50)
Matric	5 (6.25)	28 (35.00)	26 (32.50)	15 (18.75)	6 (7.50)
Graduate	14 (7.45)	21 (11.17)	63 (33.51)	59 (31.38)	31 (16.49)
Post Graduate	2 (1.27)	14 (8.86)	67 (42.41)	47 (29.75)	28 (17.72)
Chi-square = 44.479; df = 12; Significant at 1 per cent level					
Age (years)					
Below 30	2 (1.42)	10 (7.09)	59 (41.84)	41 (29.08)	29 (20.57)
30-40	10 (6.54)	25 (16.34)	49 (32.03)	53 (34.64)	16 (10.46)
Above 40	11 (7.05)	32 (20.51)	56 (35.90)	34 (21.79)	23 (14.74)
Chi-square = 26.260; df = 8; Significant at 1 per cent level					
Place of Origin					
Rural	2 (2.30)	20 (22.99)	33 (37.93)	26 (29.89)	6 (6.90)
Urban	21 (5.79)	47 (12.95)	131 (36.09)	102 (28.10)	62 (17.08)
Chi-square = 11.381; df = 4; Significant at 5 per cent level					
Type of Family					
Joint	14 (6.70)	35 (16.75)	77 (36.84)	50 (23.92)	33 (15.79)
Nuclear	9 (3.73)	32 (13.28)	87 (36.10)	78 (32.37)	35 (14.52)
Chi-square = 5.768; df = 4; Insignificant					
Form of Business Organization					
Sole	21 (6.80)	45 (14.56)	108 (34.95)	88 (28.48)	47 (15.21)
Others	2 (1.42)	22 (15.60)	56 (39.72)	40 (28.37)	21 (14.89)
Chi-square = 6.159; df = 4; Insignificant					
Investment (Lacs)					
<1	14 (11.38)	10 (8.13)	48 (39.02)	39 (31.71)	12 (9.76)
1-2	6 (4.17)	24 (16.67)	58 (40.28)	41 (28.47)	15 (10.42)
2-3	2 (2.60)	18 (23.38)	24 (31.17)	21 (27.27)	12 (15.58)
3-5	—	11 (17.19)	21 (32.81)	14 (21.88)	18 (28.12)

(Contd.)

1	2	3	4	5	6
5-10	1 (3.23)	4 (12.90)	9 (29.03)	7 (22.58)	10 (32.26)
Above 10	—	—	4 (36.36)	6 (54.55)	1 (9.09)

Chi-square = 48.952; df = 20; Significant at 1 per cent level

Income (Rs.)

<7500	10 (18.52)	3 (5.56)	25 (46.30)	11 (20.37)	5 (9.26)
7500-10000	3 (1.99)	22 (14.57)	60 (39.74)	41 (27.15)	25 (16.56)
10000-15000	5 (5.15)	20 (20.62)	32 (32.99)	27 (27.84)	13 (13.40)
15000-20000	2 (2.00)	17 (17.00)	25 (25.00)	35 (35.00)	21 (21.00)
20000+	3 (6.25)	5 (10.42)	22 (45.83)	14 (29.17)	4 (8.33)

Chi-square = 45.336; df = 16; Significant at 1 per cent level

Training

Got Training	10 (4.26)	19 (8.09)	93 (39.57)	84 (35.74)	29 (12.34)
No Training	13 (6.05)	48 (22.33)	71 (33.02)	44 (20.47)	39 (18.14)

Chi-square = 29.034; df = 4; Significant at 1 per cent level

Sources of Finance

Formal	1 (0.83)	8 (6.67)	45 (37.50)	39 (32.50)	27 (22.50)
Informal	22 (6.67)	59 (17.88)	119 (36.06)	89 (26.97)	41 (12.42)

Chi-square = 20.197; df = 4; Significant at 1 per cent level

Age of Enterprise

Below 10 years	15 (5.02)	33 (11.04)	120 (40.13)	81 (27.09)	50 (16.72)
Above 10 years	8 (5.30)	34 (22.52)	44 (29.14)	47 (31.13)	18 (11.92)

Chi-square = 14.329; df = 4; Significant at 1 per cent level

cent level of significance. Only 23 per cent women entrepreneurs belonging to joint families and 17 per cent from nuclear families face this problem to a large extent. Almost same proportion of women entrepreneurs (36 per cent each) coming from joint and nuclear families have been able to reduce this problem to some extent. Almost same proportion of women entrepreneurs coming from nuclear and joint families do not face this problem. The value of chi-square is statistically insignificant. Only 21 per cent women entrepreneurs managing business under individual forms of business organizations face this problem to a large extent. The value of chi-square is statistically insignificant. Women entrepreneurs investing more than Rs. 5 lacs in business face this problem less intensively as compared to women entrepreneurs investing money upto Rs. 3 lacs. It shows that women entrepreneurs managing business on large scale may be able to hire the expert persons to estimate the demand for their product. The value of chi-square is statistically significant at 1 per cent level of significance. Women entrepreneurs earning more income face this problem less than women entrepreneurs earning lower level of income. 46 per cent of women entrepreneurs earning less than Rs. 7,500 per month are able to solve this problem to some extent. The value of chi-square is statistically significant at 1 per cent level of significance. It shows that these two variables vary significantly. Trained women entrepreneurs have been facing this problem less intensively than untrained women entrepreneurs. Information throws light on the fact that training helps in understanding basic concepts of business. Further, training also helps in understanding the changing market conditions. The value of chi-square is statistically significant at 1 per cent level of significance. Women entrepreneurs who have taken assistance from financial institutions face this problem less as compared to other women entrepreneurs. It shows that women entrepreneurs using formal sources of finance are using various methods to maintain the demand for their products so that they may be able to repay their loans easily. The value of chi-square is statistically significant at 1 per cent level of significance. Women entrepreneurs having enterprises less than 10 years old face this problem less than other women entrepreneurs. It shows that recent established business might have done better market survey. The value of chi-square is statistically significant at 1 per cent level of significance.

Table 6.8 shows that only small proportion of women entrepreneurs (18 per cent) face the problem of identification of customers and one-fourth face this problem to little extent. Information vividly highlights that women entrepreneurs are choosing only those business lines which have better scope in the market. It may also be due to spread of consultancy in the field of business. Education-wise information further reveals that almost same proportion of women entrepreneurs (29 per cent each) possessing primary and matric level of education face this problem to a large extent. It may be due to wrong choice of product. The value of chi-square is statistically significant at 1 per cent level of significance. One-fourth women entrepreneurs in higher age group face this problem to a large extent. The reason

TABLE 6.8

Extent of Problem of Identification of Customers Faced by Women Entrepreneurs

Group	To great extent	To large extent	To some extent	To little extent	Not at all
1	2	3	4	5	6
All Data	10 (2.22)	70 (15.56)	152 (33.78)	122 (27.11)	96 (21.33)
Education					
Primary	—	7 (29.17)	8 (33.33)	4 (16.67)	5 (20.83)
Matric	4 (5.00)	19 (23.75)	27 (33.75)	22 (27.50)	8 (10.00)
Graduate	5 (2.66)	23 (12.23)	55 (29.26)	63 (33.51)	42 (22.34)
Post Graduate	1 (0.63)	21 (13.29)	62 (39.24)	33 (20.89)	41 (25.95)
Chi-square = 28.526; df = 12; Significant at 1 per cent level					
Age (years)					
Below 30	1 (0.71)	10 (7.09)	40 (28.37)	52 (36.88)	38 (26.95)
30-40	5 (3.27)	24 (15.69)	61 (39.87)	37 (24.18)	26 (16.99)
Above 40	4 (2.56)	36 (23.08)	51 (32.69)	33 (21.15)	32 (20.51)
Chi-square = 28.385; df = 8; Significant at 1 per cent level					
Place of Origin					
Rural	—	18 (20.69)	30 (34.48)	30 (34.48)	9 (10.34)
Urban	10 (2.75)	52 (14.33)	122 (33.61)	92 (25.34)	87 (23.97)
Chi-square = 12.506; df = 4; Significant at 1 per cent level					
Type of Family					
Joint	5 (2.39)	42 (20.10)	70 (33.49)	59 (28.23)	33 (15.79)
Nuclear	5 (2.07)	28 (11.62)	82 (34.02)	63 (26.14)	63 (26.14)
Chi-square = 11.034; df = 4; Significant at 5 per cent level					
Form of Business Organization					
Sole	9 (2.91)	35 (11.33)	110 (35.60)	88 (28.48)	67 (21.68)
Others	1 (0.71)	35 (24.82)	42 (29.79)	34 (24.11)	29 (20.57)
Chi-square = 15.157; df = 4; Significant at 1 per cent level					
Investment (Lacs)					
<1	4 (3.25)	11 (8.94)	47 (38.21)	39 (31.71)	22 (17.89)
1-2	2 (1.39)	23 (15.97)	55 (38.19)	42 (29.17)	22 (15.28)
2-3	3 (3.90)	23 (29.87)	22 (28.57)	17 (22.08)	12 (15.58)
3-5	—	9 (14.06)	15 (23.44)	13 (20.31)	27 (42.19)

1	2	3	4	5	6
5-10	1 (3.23)	4 (12.90)	8 (25.81)	6 (19.35)	12 (38.71)
Above 10	—	—	5 (45.45)	5 (45.45)	1 (9.09)

Chi-square = 52.200; df = 20; Significant at 1 per cent level

Income (Rs.)

<7500	2 (3.70)	7 (12.96)	25 (46.30)	11 (20.37)	9 (16.67)
7500-10000	2 (1.32)	17 (11.26)	56 (37.09)	35 (23.18)	41 (27.15)
10000-15000	—	23 (23.71)	23 (23.71)	34 (35.05)	17 (17.53)
15000-20000	3 (3.00)	15 (15.00)	27 (27.00)	30 (30.00)	25 (25.00)
20000+	3 (6.25)	8 (16.67)	21 (43.75)	12 (25.00)	4 (8.330

Chi-square = 34.371; df = 16; Significant at 1 per cent level

Training

Got Training	4 (1.70)	33 (14.04)	89 (37.87)	66 (28.09)	43 (18.30)
No Training	6 (2.79)	37 (17.21)	63 (29.00)	56 (26.05)	53 (24.65)

Chi-square = 6.060; df = 4; Insignificant

Sources of Finance

Formal	1 (0.83)	7 (5.83)	26 (21.67)	38 (31.67)	48 (40.00)
Informal	9 (2.73)	63 (19.09)	126 (38.18)	84 (25.45)	48 (14.55)

Chi-square = 46.449; df = 4; Significant at 1 per cent level

Age of Enterprise

Below 10 years	6 (2.01)	40 (13.38)	98 (32.78)	87 (29.10)	68 (22.74)
Above 10 years	4 (2.65)	30 (19.87)	54 (35.76)	35 (23.18)	28 (18.54)

Chi-square = 5.293; df = 4; Insignificant

to this may be assigned to lack of proper market survey and poor identification of product. The value of chi-square is statistically significant at 1 per cent level of significance. Women entrepreneurs (21 per cent) hailing from rural areas face this problem relatively more than women entrepreneurs coming from urban areas (17 per cent). It may be due to difference in place of region and lack of opportunity to get proper information relating to product. The value of chi-square is statistically significant at 1 per cent level of significance. Women entrepreneurs (22 per cent) hailing from joint families face this problem relatively more as compared to their counterparts coming from nuclear families (14 per cent). The value of chi-square is statistically significant at 5 per cent level of significance. Women entrepreneurs (25 per cent) managing business under other than individual form of business organization face this problem relatively more than other women entrepreneurs (14 per cent). The value of chi-square is statistically insignificant. One-third women entrepreneurs investing money in the range of Rs. 2-3 lacs face this problem to a large extent. On the other hand, 45 per cent women entrepreneurs investing more than Rs. 10 lacs in business face this problem to some extent. It shows that these women entrepreneurs might have surveyed in the market effectively due to availability of resources. The value of chi-square is statistically significant at 1 per cent level of significance. 23 per cent women entrepreneurs earning income in the range of Rs. 10,000-15,000 per month face this problem to a large extent. It may be the urge of women entrepreneurs to increase revenue in their business. On the other hand, only small proportion of women entrepreneurs earning income in the other ranges face this problem. The value of chi-square is statistically significant at 1 per cent level of significance. Almost same proportion of trained and untrained women entrepreneurs face this problem to a little extent. The value of chi-square is statistically insignificant. Women entrepreneurs (22 per cent) those who have used informal sources of finance face this problem more than women entrepreneurs (6 per cent) using formal sources of finance. It may be due to better project formulation and proper survey of market in case of women entrepreneurs in latter case. The value of chi-square is statistically significant at 1 per cent level of significance. One-fifth women entrepreneurs having enterprises more than 10 years old face this problem to a large extent. It seems that products offered by them might be in the declining stage of their life cycle and failure to compete in the free market economies. The value of chi-square is statistically insignificant.

Table 6.9 shows that one-fifth women entrepreneurs face the problem of getting work regularly, 34 per cent to some extent and 27 per cent face this problem to little extent. Education-wise information further reveals that 25 per cent to 38 per cent women entrepreneurs possessing education upto matric level face this problem to a large extent. On the other hand, less than 20 per cent women entrepreneurs possessing higher level of education face this problem to a large extent. But almost same proportion of women entrepreneurs beyond matric level of education has been able to reduce this problem to some extent. It reveals that educated

TABLE 6.9

Extent of Problem of Getting Work Regularly Faced by Women Entrepreneurs

Group	To great extent	To large extent	To some extent	To little extent	Not at all
1	2	3	4	5	6
All Data	7 (1.56)	94 (20.89)	155 (34.44)	124 (27.56)	70 (15.56)
Education					
Primary	1 (4.17)	5 (20.83)	6 (25.00)	9 (37.50)	3 (12.50)
Matric	3 (3.75)	28 (35.00)	30 (37.50)	10 (12.50)	9 (11.25)
Graduate	3 (1.60)	30 (15.96)	65 (34.57)	55 (29.26)	35 (18.62)
Post Graduate	—	31 (19.62)	54 (34.18)	50 (31.65)	23 (14.56)
Chi-square = 27.697; df = 12; Significant at 1 per cent level					
Age (years)					
Below 30	—	12 (8.51)	48 (34.04)	51 (36.17)	30 (21.28)
30-40	4 (2.61)	32 (20.92)	54 (35.29)	44 (28.76)	19 (12.42)
Above 40	3 (1.92)	50 (32.05)	53 (33.97)	29 (18.59)	21 (13.46)
Chi-square = 35.331; df = 8; Significant at 1 per cent level					
Place of Origin					
Rural	1 (1.15)	21 (24.14)	30 (34.48)	19 (21.84)	16 (18.39)
Urban	6 (1.65)	73 (20.11)	125 (34.44)	105 (28.93)	54 (14.88)
Chi-square = 2.496; df = 4; Insignificant					
Type of Family					
Joint	7 (3.35)	51 (24.40)	61 (29.19)	61 (21.84)	29 (13.88)
Nuclear	—	43 (17.84)	94 (39.00)	63 (26.14)	41 (17.01)
Chi-square = 14.594; df = 4; Significant at 1 per cent level					
Form of Business Organization					
Sole	6 (1.94)	63 (20.39)	102 (33.01)	91 (29.45)	47 (15.21)
Others	1 (0.71)	31 (21.99)	53 (37.59)	33 (23.40)	23 (16.31)
Chi-square = 3.013; df = 4; Insignificant					
Investment (Lacs)					
<1	7 (5.69)	20 (16.26)	41 (33.33)	35 (28.46)	20 (16.26)
1-2	—	38 (26.39)	42 (29.17)	44 (30.56)	20 (13.89)
2-3	—	19 (24.68)	30 (38.96)	21 (27.27)	7 (9.09)
3-5	—	11 (17.19)	26 (40.62)	9 (14.06)	18 (28.12)

(Contd.)

1	2	3	4	5	6
5-10	—	5 (16.3)	12 (38.71)	9 (29.03)	5 (16.13)
Above 10	—	1 (9.09)	4 (36.36)	6 (54.55)	—

Chi-square = 44.777; df = 20; Significant at 1 per cent level

Income (Rs.)

<7500	5 (9.26)	10 (18.52)	17 (31.48)	13 (24.07)	9 (16.67)
7500-10000	1 (0.66)	41 (27.15)	38 (25.17)	40 (26.49)	31 (30.53)
10000-15000	1 (1.03)	15 (15.46)	40 (41.24)	32 (32.99)	9 (9.28)
15000-20000	—	19 (19.00)	37 (37.00)	25 (25.00)	19 (19.00)
20000+	—	9 (18.75)	23 (47.92)	14 (29.17)	2 (4.17)

Chi-square = 47.693; df = 16; Significant at 1 per cent level

Training

Got Training	4 (1.70)	37 (15.74)	91 (38.72)	68 (28.94)	35 (14.89)
No Training	3 (1.40)	57 (26.51)	64 (29.77)	56 (26.05)	35 (16.28)

Chi-square = 9.392; df = 4; Insignificant

Sources of Finance

Formal	—	12 (10.00)	52 (43.33)	33 (27.50)	23 (19.17)
Informal	7 (2.12)	82 (24.85)	103 (31.21)	91 (27.58)	47 (14.24)

Chi-square = 16.959; df = 4; Significant at 1 per cent level

Age of Enterprise

Below 10 years	2 (0.67)	53 (17.73)	114 (38.13)	85 (28.43)	45 (15.05)
Above 10 years	5 (3.31)	41 (27.15)	41 (27.15)	39 (25.83)	25 (16.56)

Chi-square = 12.672; df = 4; Significant at 1 per cent level

women entrepreneurs have been able to explore market in a much better manner than other women entrepreneurs. Analysis further shows that education helps in understanding the consumer behaviour and frequent change in market conditions. The value of chi-square is statistically significant at 1 per cent level of significance. Only small proportion of women entrepreneurs less than 30 years face this problem to a large extent as compared to women entrepreneurs having more than 30 years age. The value of chi-square is statistically significant at 1 per cent level of significance. Almost same proportion of women entrepreneurs hailing from urban and rural areas face this problem to some extent. The value of chi-square is statistically insignificant. 18 per cent women entrepreneurs hailing from nuclear families face this problem to a large extent, whereas this ratio is 28 per cent in case of other women entrepreneurs. It may be due to more exposure and better understanding of working of market among urban women entrepreneurs. The value of chi-square further shows that these two variables vary significantly. Almost same proportion of women entrepreneurs managing business under different forms of business organization face this problem to a large extent. The value of chi-square is statistically insignificant. Women entrepreneurs investing more than Rs. 10 lacs in business are facing this problem to a little extent. On the other hand, women entrepreneurs investing less money in business face this problem to a large extent. The value of chi-square is statistically significant at 1 per cent level of significance. It shows that level of investment and problem of getting work irregularly are positively associated. Slightly, more than 16 per cent women entrepreneurs earning income beyond Rs. 10,000 per month face this problem to large extent. It may be due to desire to have more work, these women entrepreneurs might have expressed this problem. The value of chi-square is statistically significant at 1 per cent level of significance. 28 per cent untrained women entrepreneurs are facing this problem to a large extent, whereas this ratio is 17 per cent in case of trained women entrepreneurs. The value of chi-square is statistically insignificant. 27 per cent women entrepreneurs using informal sources of finance face this problem to a large extent, whereas this proportion is just 10 per cent in case of women entrepreneurs using formal sources of finance. The value of chi-square is statistically significant at 1 per cent level of significance. Women entrepreneurs having enterprises more than 10 years old face this problem relatively more as compared to other women entrepreneurs. It shows that women entrepreneurs established enterprises recently are managing their business more successfully. The value of chi-square is statistically significant at 1 per cent level of significance.

Table 6.10 shows that 45 per cent of women entrepreneurs face the problem of competition from big producers to a large extent. Education-wise information further shows that more than 43 per cent women entrepreneurs possessing education beyond matric level face this problem to a large extent and 66 per cent women entrepreneurs having primary level of education also face this problem. Information lucidly reveals that competition from

TABLE 6.10

Extent of Problem of Competition from Big Producers Faced by Women Entrepreneurs

Group	To great extent	To large extent	To some extent	To little extent	Not at all
1	2	3	4	5	6
All Data	39 (8.67)	166 (36.89)	172 (38.22)	56 (12.44)	17 (3.78)
Education					
Primary	5 (20.83)	11 (45.83)	7 (29.17)	—	1 (4.17)
Matric	7 (8.75)	30 (37.50)	34 (42.50)	5 (6.25)	4 (5.00)
Graduate	13 (6.91)	71 (37.77)	68 (36.17)	27 (14.36)	9 (4.79)
Post Graduate	14 (8.86)	54 (34.18)	63 (39.87)	24 (15.19)	3 (1.90)
Chi-square = 16.148; df = 12; Insignificant					
Age (years)					
Below 30	7 (4.96)	47 (33.33)	51 (36.17)	30 (21.28)	6 (4.26)
30-40	14 (9.15)	57 (37.25)	54 (35.29)	20 (13.07)	8 (5.23)
Above 40	18 (11.54)	62 (39.74)	67 (42.95)	6 (3.85)	3 (1.92)
Chi-square = 26.512; df = 8; Significant at 1 per cent level					
Place of Origin					
Rural	2 (2.30)	29 (33.33)	38 (43.68)	14 (16.09)	4 (4.60)
Urban	37 (10.19)	137 (37.74)	134 (36.91)	42 (11.57)	13 (3.58)
Chi-square = 7.601; df = 4; Insignificant					
Type of Family					
Joint	19 (9.09)	79 (37.80)	78 (37.32)	27 (12.92)	6 (2.87)
Nuclear	20 (8.30)	87 (36.10)	94 (39.00)	29 (12.03)	11 (4.56)
Chi-square = 1.172; df = 4; Insignificant					
Form of Business Organization					
Sole	25 (8.09)	119 (38.51)	116 (37.54)	43 (13.92)	6 (1.94)
Others	14 (9.93)	47 (33.33)	56 (39.72)	13 (9.22)	11 (7.80)
Chi-square = 11.717; df = 4; Significant at 1 per cent level					
Investment (Lacs)					
<1	14 (11.38)	53 (43.09)	29 (23.58)	23 (18.70)	4 (3.25)
1-2	9 (6.25)	46 (31.94)	65 (45.14)	23 (15.97)	1 (0.69)
2-3	14 (18.18)	15 (19.48)	40 (51.95)	4 (5.19)	4 (5.19)
3-5	2 (3.12)	25 (39.06)	29 (45.31)	1 (1.56)	7 (10.94)

1	2	3	4	5	6
5-10	—	22 (70.97)	3 (9.68)	5 (16.13)	1 (3.23)
Above 10	—	5 (45.45)	6 (54.55)	—	—

Chi-square = 84.912; df = 20; Significant at 1 per cent level

Income (Rs.)

<7500	13 (24.07)	23 (42.59)	7 (12.96)	8 (14.81)	3 (5.56)
7500-10000	9 (5.96)	59 (39.07)	48 (31.79)	28 (18.54)	7 (4.64)
10000-15000	13 (13.40)	27 (27.84)	52 (53.61)	4 (4.12)	1 (1.03)
15000-20000	4 (4.00)	30 (30.00)	48 (48.00)	12 (12.00)	6 (6.00)
20000+	—	27 (56.25)	17 (35.42)	4 (8.33)	—

Chi-square = 70.123; df = 16; Significant at 1 per cent level

Training

Got Training	20 (8.51)	91 (38.72)	77 (32.77)	37 (15.74)	10 (4.26)
No Training	19 (8.84)	75 (34.88)	95 (44.19)	19 (8.84)	7 (3.26)

Chi-square = 8.895; df = 4; Insignificant

Sources of Finance

Formal	3 (2.50)	57 (47.50)	43 (35.83)	9 (7.50)	8 (6.67)
Informal	36 (10.91)	109 (33.03)	129 (39.09)	47 (14.24)	9 (2.73)

Chi-square = 19.249; df = 4; Significant at 1 per cent level

Age of Enterprise

Below 10 years	25 (8.36)	107 (35.79)	106 (35.45)	47 (15.72)	14 (4.68)
Above 10 years	14 (9.27)	59 (39.07)	66 (43.71)	9 (5.96)	3 (1.99)

Chi-square = 11.787; df = 4; Significant at 1 per cent level

big producers is a problem, which can be tackled by improving the quality of product and making provisions for better technology to small enterprises. Priority should be given by the various institutions to purchase the products produced by women entrepreneurs. The value of chi-square is statistically insignificant. Age-wise information further shows that problem of competition from big producers are faced relatively more by women entrepreneurs in higher age groups. The reason to this may be attributed to failure of women entrepreneurs to compete the products produced by big producers and lack of proper management techniques adopted by these women entrepreneurs. The value of chi-square is statistically significant at 1 per cent level of significance. Competition from big producers is faced relatively more by women entrepreneurs (48 per cent) from urban areas than women entrepreneurs (36 per cent) from urban areas. The reason to this may be assigned to more competition with small enterprises. The value of chi-square is statistically insignificant. Almost same proportion of women entrepreneurs belonging to joint and nuclear families face this problem. The value of chi-square is statistically insignificant. Women entrepreneurs managing business on individual basis face this problem relatively more as compared to other women entrepreneurs. It reveals that small enterprises need more facilities to improve their business process. The value of chi-square is statistically significant at 1 per cent level of significance. Women entrepreneurs investing more money in business also face this problem. It may be due to technological superiority, economies of scale and brand image of the product manufactured by big producers. The value of chi-square is statistically significant at 1 per cent level of significance. 66 per cent women entrepreneurs earning less than Rs. 7,500 per month and 56 per cent women entrepreneurs earning more than Rs. 20,000 per month also face this problem. The value of chi-square is statistically significant at 1 per cent level of significance. Trained women entrepreneurs also face this problem on slightly higher side than other trained women entrepreneurs. The value of chi-square is statistically insignificant. It shows that these two variables are independent. Women entrepreneurs using formal sources of finance also face this problem relatively more than women entrepreneurs using informal sources of finance. It seems that women entrepreneurs having taken assistance from formal sources of finance are more alert to return their money to these institutions. The value of chi-square is statistically insignificant. Women entrepreneurs (48 per cent) possessing enterprises more than 10 years old face this problem relatively more than other women entrepreneurs. It may be due to failure of these entrepreneurs to bring change in products and services rendered by them and use of traditional methods of management practices in their organizations. The value of chi-square is statistically significant at 1 per cent level of significance.

Table 6.11 shows that 40 per cent of women entrepreneurs face the problem of publicity of product to a large extent and another 38 per cent face this problem to some extent. It reveals that women entrepreneurs face problem of publicity of product.

TABLE 6.11

Extent of Problem of Publicity of Product Faced by Women Entrepreneurs

Group	To great extent	To large extent	To some extent	To little extent	Not at all
1	2	3	4	5	6
All Data	16 (3.56)	165 (36.67)	169 (37.56)	69 (15.33)	31 (6.89)
Education					
Primary	1 (4.17)	9 (37.50)	10 (41.67)	3 (12.50)	1 (4.17)
Matric	7 (8.75)	35 (43.75)	25 (31.25)	9 (11.25)	4 (5.00)
Graduate	3 (1.60)	69 (36.70)	79 (42.02)	23 (12.23)	14 (7.45)
Post Graduate	5 (3.16)	52 (32.91)	55 (34.81)	34 (21.52)	12 (7.59)
Chi-square = 19.160; df = 12; Insignificant					
Age (years)					
Below 30	4 (2.84)	38 (26.95)	59 (41.84)	25 (17.73)	15 (10.64)
30-40	7 (4.58)	59 (38.56)	60 (39.22)	19 (12.42)	8 (5.23)
Above 40	5 (3.21)	68 (43.59)	50 (32.05)	25 (16.03)	8 (5.13)
Chi-square = 14.203; df = 8; Insignificant					
Place of Origin					
Rural	2 (2.30)	37 (42.53)	28 (32.18)	16 (18.39)	4 (4.60)
Urban	14 (3.86)	128 (35.26)	141 (38.84)	5 (14.60)	27 (7.44)
Chi-square = 3.798; df = 4; Insignificant					
Type of Family					
Joint	9 (4.31)	77 (36.84)	74 (35.41)	36 (17.22)	13 (6.22)
Nuclear	7 (2.90)	88 (36.51)	95 (39.42)	33 (13.69)	18 (7.47)
Chi-square = 2.266; df = 4; Insignificant					
Form of Business Organization					
Sole	12 (3.88)	113 (36.57)	116 (37.54)	49 (15.86)	19 (6.15)
Others	4 (2.84)	52 (36.88)	53 (37.59)	20 (14.18)	12 (8.51)
Chi-square = 1.262; df = 4; Insignificant					
Investment (Lacs)					
<1	11 (8.94)	45 (36.59)	47 (38.21)	9 (7.32)	11 (8.94)
1-2	5 (3.47)	51 (35.42)	47 (32.64)	35 (24.31)	6 (4.17)
2-3	—	31 (40.26)	30 (38.96)	10 (12.99)	6 (7.79)
3-5	—	24 (37.50)	26 (40.62)	7 (10.94)	7 (10.94)

(Contd.)

1	2	3	4	5	6
5-10	—	14 (45.16)	12 (38.71)	4 (12.90)	1 (3.23)
Above 10	—	—	7 (63.64)ʹ	4 (36.36)	—

Chi-square = 47.052; df = 20; Significant at 1 per cent level

Income (Rs.)

<7500	2 (3.70)	29 (53.70)	16 (29.63)	4 (7.41)	3 (5.56)
7500-10000	7 (4.64)	45 (29.80)	57 (37.75)	27 (17.88)	15 (9.93)
10000-15000	7(7.22)	35 (36.08)	39 (40.21)	13 (13.40)	3 (3.09)
15000-20000	—	39 (39.00)	34 (34.00)	17 (17.00)	10 (10.00)
20000+	—	17 (35.42)	23 (47.92)	8 (16.67)	—

Chi-square = 30.843; df = 16; Significant at 1 per cent level

Training

Got Training	11 (4.68)	91 (38.72)	85 (36.17)	28 (11.91)	20 (8.51)
No Training	5 (2.33)	74 (34.42)	84 (39.07)	41 (19.07)	11 (5.12)

Chi-square = 8.197; df = 4; Insignificant

Sources of Finance

Formal	2 (1.67)	40 (33.33)	57 (47.50)	9 (7.50)	12 (10.00)
Informal	14 (4.24)	125 (37.88)	112 (33.94)	60 (18.18)	19 (5.76)

Chi-square = 15.294; df = 4; Significant at 1 per cent level

Age of Enterprise

Below 10 years	7 (2.34)	111 (37.12)	116 (38.80)	43 (14.38)	22 (7.36)
Above 10 years	9 (5.96)	54 (35.76)	53 (35.10)	26 (17.22)	9 (5.96)

Chi-square = 4.923; df = 4; Insignificant

It may be due to lack of availability of finance, awareness and increase in expenditure on publicity. More than 50 per cent women entrepreneurs having matric level of education face this problem and on the other hand, less than 40 per cent of women entrepreneurs possessing other levels of education face this problem to a large extent. 29 per cent women entrepreneurs possessing post-graduate level of education have completely overcome this problem. It may be due to lack of awareness among women entrepreneurs to use various means to advertise their products having low level of education. The value of chi-square is statistically insignificant. Women entrepreneurs in higher age groups face this problem relatively more as compared to women entrepreneurs in lower age groups. It may be due to different management practices used by these women entrepreneurs. The value of chi-square is statistically significant at 1 per cent level of significance. 45 per cent women entrepreneurs hailing from rural areas and 39 per cent from urban areas face this problem to a large extent. The reason to this may be assigned to lack of exposure among women entrepreneurs from the rural areas to use various means of advertisement. Almost same proportion of women entrepreneurs hailing from joint and nuclear families face this problem to a large extent. The values of chi-square are statistically insignificant. It shows that type of family and problem of publicity of product are not associated with each other. Almost same proportion of women entrepreneurs managing business under different forms of business organizations face this problem. It reveals that women entrepreneurs irrespective of different forms of business organizations face this problem. The value of chi-square is statistically insignificant. Major proportion of women entrepreneurs (63 per cent) investing more than Rs. 10 lacs in business face this problem to a small extent, whereas 35 per cent to 45 per cent women entrepreneurs investing upto Rs. 10 lacs in business face this problem to a large extent. It shows that women entrepreneurs investing more money in business are able to use various forms of advertisements to give publicity to their product. The value of chi-square is statistically significant at 1 per cent level of significance. Women entrepreneurs earning low level of income face this problem more intensively than women entrepreneurs earning higher level of income. It may be due to paucity of funds among women entrepreneurs earning lower level of income. The value of chi-square is statistically significant at 1 per cent level of significance. Trained women entrepreneurs (43 per cent) face this problem more intensively than untrained women entrepreneurs (36 per cent). It may be due to lack of information available to them. The value of chi-square is statistically insignificant. Women entrepreneurs who have not taken financial assistance from formal sources face this problem relatively more than other women entrepreneurs. It shows that women entrepreneurs might be facing this problem due to increase in cost of finance. The value of chi-square is statistically significant at 1 per cent level of significance. It shows that these two variables vary significantly. Almost same proportion of women entrepreneurs irrespective of their life of enterprise face this problem. It may also be due to increase in cost of publication and competition in the market. The value of chi-square is statistically insignificant.

Table 6.12 shows that only one-fourth women entrepreneurs face the problem of frequently changing market conditions, 39 per cent to some extent and another 28 per cent to little extent. Education-wise information further reveals that more than 41 per cent women entrepreneurs possessing lower level of education face this problem. On the other hand, educated women entrepreneurs are facing this problem to some extent. It shows that educated women entrepreneurs are able to understand the frequent changes in market conditions and use of modern techniques of management to solve this problem. The value of chi-square is statistically significant at 1 per cent level of significance. Only 17 per cent of women entrepreneurs in the age group of less than 30 face this problem to a large extent, whereas this ratio is 35 per cent among women entrepreneurs in higher age group. It shows that women entrepreneurs in higher age group face this problem more intensively. It may be due to lack of proper knowledge of change in market conditions. The value of chi-square is statistically significant at 1 per cent level of significance. 36 per cent of women entrepreneurs coming from rural areas face this problem to a large extent, whereas it is 22 per cent in case of women entrepreneurs hailing from urban areas. It may be due to lack of awareness of market conditions and difficulties in selling their products due to availability of large number of substitutes. The value of chi-square is statistically significant at 5 per cent level of significance. Women entrepreneurs coming from joint families face this problem slightly on higher side than women entrepreneurs coming from nuclear families. The value of chi-square is statistically insignificant. Women entrepreneurs managing the business under other than individual forms of business organizations face this problem more intensively than women entrepreneurs managing business under individual forms of business organizations. It shows that competition is more intense in case of other forms of business organizations. The value of chi-square is statistically insignificant. 63 per cent women entrepreneurs investing more than Rs. 10 lacs in business are facing this problem to a little extent, whereas 44 per cent women entrepreneurs investing money in the range of Rs. 2-3 lacs face this problem to a little extent. The value of chi-square is

TABLE 6.12

**Extent of Problem of Frequently Changing Market Condition
Faced by Women Entrepreneurs**

Group	To large extent	To some extent	To little extent	Not at all
1	2	3	4	5
All Data	113 (25.11)	177 (39.33)	126 (28.00)	34 (7.56)
Education				
Primary	11 (45.83)	5 (20.83)	7 (29.17)	1 (4.17)
Matric	33 (41.25)	26 (32.50)	13 (16.25)	8 (10.00)
Graduate	42 (22.34)	85 (45.21)	49 (26.06)	12 (6.38)
Post Graduate	27 (17.09)	61 (38.61)	57 (36.08)	13 (8.23)
Chi-square = 31.060; df = 9; Significant at 1 per cent level				
Age (years)				
Below 30	24 (17.02)	61 (43.26)	43 (30.50)	13 (9.22)
30-40	34 (22.22)	49 (32.03)	58 (37.91)	12 (7.84)
Above 40	55 (35.26)	67 (42.95)	25 (16.03)	9 (5.77)
Chi-square = 28.586; df = 6; Significant at 1 per cent level				
Place of Origin				
Rural	32 (36.78)	28 (32.18)	24 (27.59)	3 (3.45)
Urban	81 (22.31)	149 (41.05)	102 (28.10)	31 (8.54)
Chi-square = 9.666; df = 3; Significant at 5 per cent level				
Type of Family				
Joint	57 (27.27)	80 (38.28)	58 (27.75)	14 (6.70)
Nuclear	56 (23.24)	97 (40.25)	68 (28.22)	20 (8.30)
Chi-square = 1.225; df = 3; Insignificant				
Form of Business Organization				
Sole	69 (22.33)	121 (39.16)	95 (30.74)	24 (7.77)
Others	44 (31.21)	56 (39.72)	31 (21.99)	10 (7.09)
Chi-square = 5.756; df = 3; Insignificant				
Investment (Lacs)				
'<1	32 (26.02)	44 (35.77)	37 (30.08)	10 (8.13)
1-2	45 (31.25)	65 (45.14)	26 (18.06)	8 (5.56)
2-3	21 (27.27)	18 (23.38)	34 (44.16)	4 (5.19)
3-5	8 (12.50)	31 (48.44)	16 (25.00)	9 (14.06)

(Contd.)

1	2	3	4	5
5-10	7 (22.58)	15 (48.39)	6 (19.35)	3 (9.68)
Above 10	—	4 (36.36)	7 (63.64)	—

Chi-square = 42.336; df = 15; Significant at 1 per cent level

Income (Rs.)

<7500	16 (29.63)	24 (44.44)	11 (20.37)	3 (5.56)
7500-10000	42 (27.81)	61 (40.40)	36 (23.84)	12 (7.95)
10000-15000	37 (38.14)	37 (38.14)	17 (17.53)	6 (6.19)
15000-20000	13 (13.00)	41 (41.00)	37 (37.00)	9 (9.00)
20000+	5 (10.42)	14 (29.17)	25 (52.08)	4 (8.33)

Chi-square = 38.742; df = 12; Significant at 1 per cent level

Training

Got Training	43 (18.33)	93 (39.57)	75 (31.91)	24 (10.21)
No Training	70 (32.56)	84 (39.07)	51 (23.72)	10 (4.65)

Chi-square = 16.389; df = 3; Significant at 1 per cent level

Sources of Finance

Formal	22 (18.33)	57 (47.50)	28 (23.33)	13 (10.83)
Informal	91 (27.58)	120 (36.36)	98 (29.70)	21 (6.36)

Chi-square = 9.368; df = 3; Significant at 5 per cent level

Age of Enterprise

Below 10 years	69 (23.08)	111 (37.12)	96 (32.11)	23 (7.69)
Above 10 years	44 (29.14)	66 (43.71)	30 (19.87)	11 (7.28)

Chi-square = 7.964; df = 3; Significant at 5 per cent level

statistically significant at 1 per cent level of significance. Women entrepreneurs earning lower level of income face this problem more than women entrepreneurs earning higher level of income. It shows that availability of finance helps the women entrepreneurs in seeking the assistance of outside experts to solve the problem of change in market conditions. Easy availability of literature on market conditions can be helpful to women entrepreneurs in this direction. The value of chi-square is statistically significant at 1 per cent level of significance. Untrained women entrepreneurs (32 per cent) face this problem relatively more as compared to trained women entrepreneurs (18 per cent). It shows that training might have helped them in overcoming this problem. The value of chi-square is statistically significant at 1 per cent level of significance. Women entrepreneurs using informal sources of finance are facing this problem relatively more than other women entrepreneurs. It may be due to paucity of resources available to them. The value of chi-square is statistically significant at 5 per cent level of significance. Women entrepreneurs who have been in business even for a longer period of time face this problem more than other women entrepreneurs. The value of chi-square is statistically significant at 5 per cent level of significance.

Table 6.13 shows that only one-fourth women entrepreneurs face the problem of fixed capital in business upto a large extent, 22 per cent face this problem to some extent and more than 50 per cent women entrepreneurs have been able to solve this problem. It shows that entrepreneurs have chosen fixed locations,

TABLE 6.13

Extent of Problem of Fixed Capital Faced by Women Entrepreneurs

Group	To great extent	To large extent	To some extent	To little extent	Not at all
1	2	3	4	5	6
All Data	18 (4.00)	90 (20.00)	100 (22.22)	118 (26.22)	124 (27.56)
Education					
Primary	1 (4.17)	6 (25.00)	2 (8.33)	6 (25.00)	9 (37.50)
Matric	6 (7.50)	13 (16.25)	23 (28.75)	19 (23.75)	19 (23.75)
Graduate	10 (5.32)	38 (20.21)	36 (19.15)	52 (27.66)	52 (27.66)
Post Graduate	1 (0.63)	33 (20.89)	39 (24.68)	41 (25.95)	44 (27.85)
Chi-square = 15.164; df = 12; Insignificant					
Age (years)					
Below 30	1 (0.71)	18 (12.77)	35 (24.82)	49 (34.75)	38 (26.95)
30-40	10 (6.54)	37 (24.18)	23 (15.03)	31 (20.26)	52 (33.99)
Above 40	7 (4.49)	35 (22.44)	42 (26.92)	38 (24.36)	34 (21.79)
Chi-square = 27.785; df = 8; Significant at 1 per cent level					
Place of Origin					
Rural	5 (5.75)	14 (16.09)	23 (26.44)	25 (28.74)	20 (22.99)
Urban	13 (3.58)	76 (20.94)	77 (21.21)	93 (25.62)	104 (28.65)
Chi-square = 3.585; df = 4; Insignificant					

(Contd.)

1	2	3	4	5	6
Type of Family					
Joint	10 (4.78)	45 (21.53)	50 (23.92)	56 (26.79)	48 (22.97)
Nuclear	8 (3.32)	45 (18.67)	50 (20.75)	62 (25.73)	76 (31.54)
Chi-square = 4.598; df = 4; Insignificant					
Form of Business Organization					
Sole	14 (4.53)	64 (20.71)	63 (20.39)	86 (27.83)	82 (26.54)
Others	4 (2.84)	26 (18.44)	37 (26.24)	32 (22.70)	42 (29.79)
Chi-square = 3.782; df = 4; Insignificant					
Investment (Lacs)					
<1	8 (6.50)	31 (25.20)	39 (31.71)	24 (19.51)	21 (17.07)
1-2	8 (5.56)	34 (23.61)	34 (23.61)	47 (32.64)	21 (14.58)
2-3	2 (2.60)	19 (24.68)	10 (12.99)	21 (27.27)	25 (32.47)
3-5	—	4 (6.25)	11 (17.19)	12 (18.75)	37 (57.81)
5-10	—	2 (6.45)	6 (19.35)	5 (16.13)	18 (58.06)
Above 10	—	—	—	9 (81.82)	2 (18.18)
Chi-square = 99.704; df = 20; Significant at 1 per cent level					
Income (Rs.)					
<7500	3 (5.56)	13 (24.07)	15 (27.78)	17 (31.48)	6 (11.11)
7500-10000	3 (1.99)	40 (26.49)	33 (21.85)	48 (31.79)	27 (17.88)
10000-15000	8 (8.25)	22 (22.68)	25 (25.77)	19 (19.59)	23 (23.71)
15000-20000	2 (2.00)	13 (13.00)	19 (19.00)	22 (22.00)	44 (44.00)
20000+	2 (4.17)	2 (4.17)	8 (16.67)	12 (25.00)	24 (50.00)
Chi-square = 56.348; df = 16; Significant at 1 per cent level					
Training					
Got Training	7 (2.98)	50 (21.28)	54 (22.98)	66 (28.09)	58 (24.68)
No Training	11 (5.12)	40 (18.60)	46 (21.40)	52 (24.19)	66 (30.70)
Chi-square = 3.936; df = 4; Insignificant					
Sources of Finance					
Formal	—	16 (13.33)	28 (23.33)	31 (25.83)	45 (37.50)
Informal	18 (5.45)	74 (22.42)	72 (21.82)	87 (26.36)	79 (23.94)
Chi-square = 16.155; df = 4; Significant at 1 per cent level					
Age of Enterprise					
Below 10 years	12 (4.01)	57 (19.06)	65 (21.74)	79 (26.42)	86 (28.76)
Above 10 years	6 (3.97)	33 (21.85)	35 (23.18)	39 (25.83)	38 (25.17)
Chi-square = 0.969; df = 4; Insignificant					

before start of business. Education-wise information further shows that almost same proportion of women entrepreneurs possessing different levels of education face this problem to a little extent. Only one-fourth women entrepreneurs having education upto graduation level face this problem to a large extent. The value of chi-square is statistically insignificant. Only small proportion of women entrepreneurs (13 per cent) in lower age group face the problem of fixed capital to a large extent. It shows that women entrepreneurs in lower age group are giving top priority to fixed capital in business. The value of chi-square is statistically significant at 1 per cent level of significance. Almost same proportion of women entrepreneurs hailing from rural and urban areas face this problem to a large extent. It shows that women entrepreneurs lay more emphasis to have fixed location of business. The value of chi-square is statistically insignificant. Only one-fourth and one-fifth women entrepreneurs coming from joint and nuclear families face this problem to a large extent. The value of chi-square is statistically insignificant. Forms of business organizations further reveal that one-fifth and one-fourth women entrepreneurs managing business under individual and other forms of business organizations face this problem to a large extent. But 27 per cent women entrepreneurs managing business on individual basis face this problem to a little extent. The value of chi-square is statistically insignificant. 81 per cent women entrepreneurs investing more than Rs. 10 lacs in business face this problem to a little extent. It shows that these women entrepreneurs on account of availability of finance do not face this problem. On the other hand, women entrepreneurs investing less money in business face this problem more intensively. It may be due to high risk involved in small business and women entrepreneurs do not want to spend more money on fixed capital and they prefer to start their business on rented buildings. The value of chi-square is statistically significant at 1 per cent level of significance. More than 44 per cent women entrepreneurs earning more than Rs. 15,000 per month in business not at all face this problem. On the other hand, slightly more than one-fourth women entrepreneurs earning income upto Rs. 15,000 per month face this problem to a large extent. The value of chi-square is statistically significant at 1 per cent level of significance. Almost same proportion of women entrepreneurs irrespective of their level of training face this problem to a large extent. It shows that women entrepreneurs prefer to go for fixed location first. The value of chi-square is statistically insignificant. Women entrepreneurs who have taken assistance from financial institutions face this problem relatively less than other women entrepreneurs. It shows that financial institutions help women entrepreneurs in solving the problem of fixed capital. The value of chi-square is statistically significant at 1 per cent level of significance. Almost same proportion of women entrepreneurs (24 per cent) irrespective of age of their enterprises face this problem to a large extent. It reveals that women entrepreneurs want to have fixed location of business to avoid the cost of shifting business from one place to other. The value of chi-square is statistically insignificant.

Table 6.14 shows that only one-fifth women entrepreneurs are facing the problem of working capital in business and another slightly more than one-fourth women entrepreneurs face this problem to some extent. 22 per cent of women entrepreneurs do not face this problem. It shows that free market economies help women entrepreneurs in earning sufficient income to solve the problem of working capital. Education-wise information further shows that 28 per cent women entrepreneurs possessing higher level of education face this problem to some extent. 20 per cent to 33 per cent women entrepreneurs having studied upto primary and matric level of education face this problem to a large extent. The value of chi-square is statistically significant at 1 per cent level of significance. 20 per cent of women entrepreneurs in the age group of 30-40 face this problem to a large extent as compared to 32 per cent of women entrepreneurs belonging to higher age groups. It may be due to decline in demand for their product and difficulty faced by them to manage business under new markets. The value of chi-square is statistically significant at 1 per cent level of significance. Only 20 per cent women entrepreneurs coming from urban areas and 25 per cent from rural areas face this problem upto a large extent. Almost same proportion of women entrepreneurs irrespective of place of region face this problem to some extent. The value of chi-square is statistically insignificant. Almost same proportion of women entrepreneurs hailing from joint and nuclear families face this problem upto large and some extent respectively. The value of chi-square is statistically insignificant. It shows that these two variables are not associated

TABLE 6.14

**Extent of Problem of Working Capital Faced by Women
Entrepreneurs**

Group	To great extent	To large extent	To some extent	To little extent	Not at all
1	2	3	4	5	6
All Data	12 (2.67)	85 (18.89)	127 (28.22)	124 (27.56)	102 (22.67)
Education					
Primary	—	5 (20.83)	6 (25.00)	6 (25.00)	7 (29.17)
Matric	2 (2.50)	24 (30.00)	24 (30.00)	14 (17.50)	16 (20.00)
Graduate	10 (5.32)	36 (19.15)	54 (28.72)	52 (27.66)	36 (19.15)
Post Graduate	—	20 (12.66)	43 (27.22)	52 (32.91)	43 (27.22)
Chi-square = 26.409; df = 12; Significant at 1 per cent level					
Age (years)					
Below 30	2 (1.42)	14 (9.93)	46 (32.62)	45 (31.91)	34 (24.11)
30-40	10 (6.54)	21 (13.73)	33 (21.57)	48 (31.37)	41 (26.80)
Above 40	—	50 (32.05)	48 (30.77)	31 (19.87)	27 (17.31)
Chi-square = 48.123; df = 8; Significant at 1 per cent level					
Place of Origin					
Rural	2 (2.30)	20 (22.99)	22 (25.29)	26 (29.89)	17 (19.54)
Urban	10 (2.75)	65 (17.91)	105 (28.93)	98 (27.00)	85 (23.42)
Chi-square = 2.021; df = 4; Insignificant					
Type of Family					
Joint	6 (2.87)	42 (20.10)	59 (28.23)	61 (29.19)	41 (19.62)
Nuclear	6 (2.49)	43 (17.84)	68 (28.22)	63 (26.14)	61 (25.31)
Chi-square = 2.340; df = 4; Insignificant					
Form of Business Organization					
Sole	12 (3.30)	58 (18.77)	86 (27.83)	83 (26.86)	70 (22.65)
Others	—	27 (19.15)	41 (29.08)	41 (29.08)	32 (22.70)
Chi-square = 5.709; df = 4; Insignificant					
Investment (Lacs)					
<1	10 (8.13)	21 (17.07)	27 (21.95)	46 (37.40)	19 (15.45)
1-2	2 (1.39)	40 (27.78)	57 (39.58)	25 (17.36)	20 (13.89)
2-3	—	13 (16.88)	20 (25.97)	22 (28.57)	22 (28.57)
3-5	—	6 (9.38)	10 (15.62)	19 (29.69)	29 (45.31)

(Contd.)

1	2	3	4	5	6
5-10	—	5 (16.13)	11 (35.48)	5 (16.13)	10 (32.26)
Above 10	—	—	2 (18.18)	7 (63.64)	2 (18.18)

Chi-square = 85.509; df = 20; Significant at 1 per cent level

Income (Rs.)

<7500	4 (7.41)	11 (20.37)	16 (29.63)	17 (31.48)	6 (11.11)
7500-10000	6 (3.97)	32 (21.19)	50 (33.11)	36 (23.84)	27 (17.88)
10000-15000	2 (2.06)	25 (25.77)	24 (24.74)	25 (25.77)	21 (21.65)
15000-20000	—	14 (14.00)	26 (26.00)	26 (26.00)	34 (34.00)
20000+	—	3 (6.25)	11 (22.92)	20 (41.67)	14 (29.17)

Chi-square = 36.270; df = 16; Significant at 1 per cent level

Training

Got Training	12 (5.11)	37 (15.74)	65 (27.66)	70 (29.79)	51 (21.70)
No Training	—	48 (22.33)	62 (28.84)	54 (25.12)	51 (23.72)

Chi-square = 14.699; df = 4; Significant at 1 per cent level

Sources of Finance

Formal	2 (1.67)	13 (10.83)	38 (31.67)	29 (24.17)	38 (31.67)
Informal	10 (3.03)	72 (21.82)	89 (26.97)	95 (28.79)	64 (19.39)

Chi-square = 13.453; df = 4; Significant at 1 per cent level

Age of Enterprise

Below 10 years	6 (2.01)	52 (17.39)	75 (25.08)	90 (30.10)	76 (25.42)
Above 10 years	6 (3.97)	33 (21.85)	52 (34.44)	34 (22.52)	26 (17.22)

Chi-square = 10.694; df = 4; Significant at 1 per cent level

with each other. Almost same proportion of women entrepreneurs irrespective of forms of business organizations face this problem to a large extent. The value of chi-square is statistically insignificant. Only small proportion of women entrepreneurs investing more than Rs. 10 lacs in business face this problem to some extent. It reveals that women entrepreneurs managing business on large scale are utilizing the services of experts to minimize the problem of working capital. On the other hand, one-fourth of women entrepreneurs investing upto Rs. 2 lacs in business face this problem to a large extent. The value of chi-square is statistically significant at 1 per cent level of significance. 42 per cent women entrepreneurs earning more than Rs. 20,000 per month face this problem to a little extent. It shows that higher level of income solves the problem of working capital in business. On the other hand, slightly more than one-fourth women entrepreneurs earning lower level of income face this problem to a large extent. It highlights that level of earnings affect the availability of working capital in business. The value of chi-square is statistically significant at 1 per cent level of significance. Almost same proportion of women entrepreneurs irrespective of their level of training face this problem to a large extent. The value of chi-square is statistically significant at 1 per cent level of significance. Women entrepreneurs who have been able to avail financial assistance from financial institutions face this problem relatively less as compared to other women entrepreneurs. It shows that availability of finance helps in solving the problem of working capital. The value of chi-square is statistically significant at 1 per cent level of significance. 30 per cent of women entrepreneurs having enterprises less than 10 years old face this problem to a little extent and another 25 per cent not at all face this problem. It shows that women entrepreneurs having younger enterprises are managing business in a much effective manner. The value of chi-square is statistically significant at 5 per cent level of significance.

Table 6.15 shows that only 16 per cent women entrepreneurs face the problem of collateral security to a large extent and one-third to some extent. It reveals that collateral security is no longer a problem for women entrepreneurs. Education-wise information further shows that women entrepreneurs having lower level of education face this problem relatively more than women entrepreneurs having higher level of education. The reason to this may be assigned to change in policy of financial institutions to provide more liberal loans to educated women entrepreneurs. The value of chi-square is statistically significant at 1 per cent level of significance. It shows that these two variables are closely associated with each other. Only one-fourth women entrepreneurs in the age group of more than 40 face the problem of collateral security, whereas it is 15 per cent in case of other women entrepreneurs. It reveals that women entrepreneurs in younger age group might be getting co-operation from their family members in giving security to various institutions. The value of chi-square is statistically significant at 1 per cent level of significance. It shows that these two variables are positively associated.

TABLE 6.15

Extent of Problem of Collateral Security Faced by Women Entrepreneurs

Group	To great extent	To large extent	To some extent	To little extent	Not at all
1	2	3	4	5	6
All Data	10 (2.22)	61 (13.56)	142 (31.56)	119 (26.44)	118 (26.22)
Education					
Primary	—	6 (25.00)	3 (12.50)	8 (33.33)	7 (29.17)
Matric	2 (2.50)	24 (30.00)	24 (30.00)	14 (17.50)	16 (20.00)
Graduate	6 (3.19)	22 (11.70)	57 (30.32)	44 (23.40)	59 (31.38)
Post Graduate	2 (1.27)	9 (5.70)	58 (36.71)	53 (33.54)	36 (22.78)

Chi-square = 42.606; df = 12; Significant at 1 per cent level

Age (years)					
Below 30	2 (1.42)	5 (3.55)	35 (24.82)	53 (37.59)	46 (32.62)
30-40	6 (3.92)	16 (10.46)	59 (38.56)	33 (21.57)	39 (25.49)
Above 40	2 (1.28)	40 (25.64)	48 (30.77)	33 (21.15)	33 (21.15)

Chi-square = 49.180; df = 8; Significant at 1 per cent level

Place of Origin					
Rural	2 (2.30)	14 (16.09)	29 (33.33)	27 (31.03)	15 (17.24)
Urban	8 (2.20)	47 (12.95)	113 (31.33)	92 (25.34)	103 (28.37)

Chi-square = 4.799; df = 4; Insignificant

Type of Family					
Joint	6 (2.87)	33 (15.79)	71 (33.97)	52 (24.88)	47 (22.49)
Nuclear	4 (1.66)	28 (11.62)	71 (29.46)	67 (27.80)	71 (29.46)

Chi-square = 5.333; df = 4; Insignificant

Form of Business Organization					
Sole	6 (1.94)	36 (11.65)	95 (30.74)	86 (27.83)	86 (27.83)
Others	4 (2.84)	25 (17.73)	47 (33.33)	33 (23.40)	32 (22.70)

Chi-square = 4.887; df = 4; Insignificant

Investment (Lacs)					
<1	6 (4.88)	14 (11.38)	43 (34.96)	33 (26.83)	27 (21.95)
1-2	2 (1.39)	25 (17.36)	58 (40.28)	36 (25.00)	23 (15.97)
2-3	2 (2.60)	14 (18.18)	17 (22.08)	21 (27.27)	23 (29.87)
3-5	—	3 (4.69)	13 (20.31)	18 (28.12)	30 (46.88)

1	2	3	4	5	6
5-10	—	5 (16.13)	6 (19.35)	7 (22.58)	13 (41.94)
Above 10	—	—	5 (45.45)	4 (36.36)	2 (18.18)

Chi-square = 47.521; df = 20; Significant at 1 per cent level

Income (Rs.)

1	2	3	4	5	6
<7500	4 (7.41)	8 (14.81)	19 (35.19)	7 (12.96)	16 (29.63)
7500-10000	—	20 (13.25)	54 (35.76)	44 (29.14)	33 (21.85)
10000-15000	4 (4.12)	20 (20.62)	30 (30.93)	22 (22.68)	21 (21.65)
15000-20000	2 (2.00)	12 (12.00)	18 (18.00)	30 (30.00)	38 (38.00)
20000+	—	1 (2.08)	21 (43.75)	16 (33.33)	10 (20.83)

Chi-square = 44.126; df = 16; Significant àt 1 per cent level

Training

1	2	3	4	5	6
Got Training	6 (2.55)	28 (11.91)	71 (30.21)	74 (31.49)	56 (23.83)
No Training	4 (1.86)	33 (15.35)	71 (33.02)	45 (20.93)	62 (28.84)

Chi-square = 7.308; df = 4; Insignificant

Sources of Finance

1	2	3	4	5	6
Formal	—	16 (13.33)	32 (26.67)	28 (23.33)	44 (36.67)
Informal	10 (3.03)	45 (13.64)	110 (33.33)	91 (27.58)	74 (22.42)

Chi-square = 12.288; df = 4; Significant at 1 per cent level

Age of Enterprise

1	2	3	4	5	6
Below 10 years	6 (2.01)	25 (8.36)	98 (32.78)	86 (28.76)	84 (28.09)
Above 10 years	4 (2.65)	36 (23.84)	44 (29.14)	33 (21.85)	34 (22.52)

Chi-square = 21.343; df = 4; Significant at 1 per cent level

Almost same proportion of women entrepreneurs irrespective of place of origin face this problem to some extent. The value of chi-square is statistically insignificant. Women entrepreneurs hailing from joint families face this problem slightly on higher side than women entrepreneurs coming from nuclear families. It may.be due to property jointly held by more than one family member and women entrepreneurs might face problem to provide collateral security in this process. The value of chi-square is statistically insignificant. Women entrepreneurs managing business under other forms of business organizations face this problem relatively more than women entrepreneurs managing business on individual basis. It shows that joint business needs more security than small businesses and in this process this type of businesses faces problem. The value of chi-square is statistically insignificant. 45 per cent of women entrepreneurs investing more than Rs. .10 lacs in business face this problem to some extent, whereas this ratio is one-fourth among women entrepreneurs investing money in the range of Rs. 2-10 lacs in business. The value of chi-square is statistically significant at 1 per cent level of significance. It shows that these two variables vary significantly. 43 per cent women entrepreneurs earning more than Rs. 20,000 per month in business face this problem to some extent. On the other hand, one-third women entrepreneurs earning income upto Rs. 15,000 per month face this problem to some extent. It shows that high income helps in solving the problem of collateral security among women entrepreneurs. The value of chi-square is statistically significant at 1 per cent level of significance. Untrained women entrepreneurs face this problem to a large and some extent more than trained women entrepreneurs. The value of chi-square is statistically insignificant. Women entrepreneurs who have taken financial assistance from financial institutions face this problem relatively less than other women entrepreneurs. The value of chi-square is statistically significant at 1 per cent level of significance. Women entrepreneurs having enterprises more than 10 years old face this problem relatively more than women entrepreneurs having enterprises less 10 years old. It shows that the post-reform period has observed liberal attitude of financial institutions towards growth of women entrepreneurship. The value of chi-square is statistically significant at 1 per cent level of significance.

Table 6.16 highlights that only 18 per cent women entrepreneurs face the problem of too much paper formalities by financial institutions and another 23 per cent face this problem to some extent. 38 per cent women entrepreneurs do not face this problem at all. It reveals that financial institutions have been reducing paper formality work under new-economic regime. Education-wise information further shows that more than one-third women entrepreneurs are not at all facing this problem. It reveals that reduction in paper formalities have been felt by women entrepreneurs irrespective of their level of education. The value of chi-square is statistically significant at 1 per cent level of significance. Less than one-fourth women entrepreneurs in different age groups face this problem to a large extent and more than one-third women entrepreneurs not at all face this problem.

TABLE 6.16

Extent of Problem Relating to too much Paper Work Faced by Women Entrepreneurs

Group	To great extent	To large extent	To some extent	To little extent	Not at all
1	2	3	4	5	6
All Data	14 (3.11)	67 (14.89)	105 (23.33)	89 (19.78)	175 (38.89)
Education					
Primary	—	7 (29.17)	3 (12.50)	4 (16.67)	10 (41.67)
Matric	—	19 (23.75)	20 (25.00)	10 (12.50)	31 (38.75)
Graduate	6 (3.19)	18 (9.57)	51 (27.13)	34 (18.09)	79 (42.02)
Post Graduate	8 (5.06)	23 (14.56)	31 (19.62)	41 (25.95)	55 (34.81)
Chi-square = 26.427; df = 12; Significant at 1 per cent level					
Age (years)					
Below 30	5 (3.55)	16 (11.35)	30 (21.28)	22 (15.60)	68 (48.23)
30-40	4 (2.61)	24 (15.69)	36 (23.53)	35 (22.88)	54 (35.29)
Above 40	5 (3.21)	27 (17.31)	39 (25.00)	32 (20.51)	53 (33.97)
Chi-square = 9.188; df = 8; Insignificant					
Place of Origin					
Rural	3 (3.45)	18 (20.69)	24 (27.59)	14 (16.09)	28 (32.18)
Urban	11 (3.03)	49 (13.50)	81 (22.31)	75 (20.66)	147 (40.50)'
Chi-square = 5.300 ; df = 4; Insignificant					
Type of Family					
Joint	4 (1.91)	31 (14.83)	53 (25.36)	55 (26.32)	66 (31.58)
Nuclear	10 (4.15)	36 (14.94)	52 (21.58)	34 (14.11)	109 (45.23)
Chi-square = 16.282; df = 4; Significant at 1 per cent level					
Form of Business Organization					
Sole	12 (3.88)	30 (9.71)	66 (21.36)	63 (20.39)	138 (44.66)
Others	2 (1.42)	37 (26.24)	39 (27.66)	26 (18.44)	37 (26.24)
Chi-square = 29.944; df = 4; Significant at 1 per cent level					
Investment (Lacs)					
<1	6 (4.88)	27 (21.95)	24 (19.51)	13 (10.57)	53 (43.09)
1-2	4 (2.78)	15 (10.42)	44 (30.56)	31 (21.53)	50 (34.72)
2-3	3 (3.90)	14 (18.18)	18 (23.38)	26 (33.77)	16 (20.78)
3-5	—	7 (10.94)	8 (12.50)	9 (14.06)	40 (62.50)

(Contd.)

1	2	3	4	5	6
5-10	1 (3.23)	4 (12.90)	6 (19.35)	6 (19.35)	14 (45.16)
Above 10	—	—	5 (45.45)	4 (36.36)	2 (18.18)

Chi-square = 56.605; df = 20; Significant at 1 per cent level

Income (Rs.)

<7500	3 (5.56)	8 (14.81)	8 (14.81)	5 (9.26)	30 (55.56)
7500-10000	4 (2.65)	15 (9.93)	41 (27.15)	36 (23.84)	55 (36.42)
10000-15000	5 (5.15)	20 (20.62)	17 (17.53)	14 (14.43)	41 (42.27)
15000-20000	1 (1.00)	15 (15.00)	25 (25.00)	25 (25.00)	34 (34.00)
20000+	1 (2.08)	9 (18.75)	14 (29.17)	9 (18.75)	15 (31.25)

Chi-square = 26.793; df = 16; Significant at 5 per cent level

Training

Got Training	9 (3.83)	37 (15.74)	58 (24.68)	53 (22.55)	78 (33.19)
No Training	5 (2.33)	30 (13.95)	47 (21.86)	36 (16.74)	97 (45.12)

Chi-square = 7.462; df = 4; Insignificant

Sources of Finance

Formal	9 (7.50)	10 (8.33)	25 (20.83)	23 (19.17)	53 (44.17)
Informal	5 (1.52)	57 (17.27)	80 (24.24)	66 (20.00)	122 (36.97)

Chi-square = 16.496; df = 4; Significant at 1 per cent level

Age of Enterprise

Below 10 years	13 (4.35)	50 (16.72)	61 (20.40)	54 (18.06)	121 (40.47)
Above 10 years	1 (0.66)	17 (11.26)	44 (29.14)	35 (23.18)	54 (35.76)

Chi-square = 11.576; df = 4; Significant at 5 per cent level

The value of chi-square is statistically insignificant. Women entrepreneurs (24 per cent) coming from rural areas face this problem to a large extent more than women entrepreneurs (17 per cent) hailing from urban areas. It may also be due to lack of awareness and low level of availing financial facilities from financial institutions. The value of chi-square is statistically insignificant. 45 per cent women entrepreneurs hailing from nuclear families not at all face this problem, whereas this ratio is 32 per cent in case of women entrepreneurs coming from joint families. It may be due to more knowledge and less dependency as compared to women entrepreneurs coming from joint families. The value of chi-square is statistically significant at 1 per cent level of significance. Women entrepreneurs managing business under joint ventures (28 per cent) face this problem relatively more than women entrepreneurs managing business on individual basis (13 per cent). It may be due to large requirements of big business. The value of chi-square is statistically significant at 1 per cent level of significance. It shows that these two variables vary significantly. 26 per cent women entrepreneurs investing less than Rs. 1 lac face this problem to a large extent. It shows that financial institutions may be reluctant to provide financial assistance to small enterprises due to more risk involved or small enterprises face this problem due to lack of resources to fulfil various conditions. There is a need to formulate policies for small and micro enterprises relating to problem of collateral security keeping in view tendency of people to start business on small scale at initial phases. The value of chi-square is statistically significant at 1 per cent level of significance. Level of income earned by women entrepreneurs further show that almost same proportion of women entrepreneurs earning less than Rs. 7,500 per month and more than Rs. 20,000 per month face this problem to a large extent. On the other hand, more than one-third women entrepreneurs earning different levels of income not at all face this problem. It shows that problem of provision of too much paper formalities vary among different levels of income earned by women entrepreneurs. The value of chi-square is statistically significant at 5 per cent level of significance. Trained women entrepreneurs face this problem to a large extent slightly on higher side than other women entrepreneurs. It shows that training is not found to be beneficial in case of security against loan is concerned. The value of chi-square is statistically insignificant. 44 per cent women entrepreneurs who have availed financial assistance from financial institutions do not face this problem, whereas it is 37 per cent in case of other women entrepreneurs. The value of chi-square is statistically significant at 1 per cent level of significance. Women entrepreneurs having enterprises less than 10 years old face this problem relatively more than other women entrepreneurs. The value of chi-square is statistically significant at 1 per cent level of significance.

Table 6.17 shows that slightly more than one-fourth women entrepreneurs face the problem of delay in release of payments upto a large extent and one-third to some extent. It shows that financial institutions are releasing the payments as early as

TABLE 6.17

Extent of Problem of Delay in Release of Payments Faced by Women Entrepreneurs

Group	To great extent	To large extent	To some extent	To little extent	Not at all
1	2	3	4	5	6
All Data	20 (4.44)	110 (24.44)	135 (30.00)	78 (17.33)	107 (23.78)
Education					
Primary	4 (16.67)	7 (29.17)	5 (20.83)	3 (12.50)	5 (20.83)
Matric	3 (3.75)	25 (31.25)	31 (38.75)	9 (11.25)	12 (15.00)
Graduate	4 (2.13)	39 (20.74)	54 (28.72)	35 (18.62)	56 (29.79)
Post Graduate	9 (5.70)	39 (24.68)	45 (28.48)	31 (19.62)	34 (21.52)
Chi-square = 25.271; df = 12; Significant at 1 per ...nt level					
Age (years)					
Below 30	7 (4.96)	35 (24.82)	35 (24.82)	21 (14.89)	43 (30.50)
30-40	5 (3.27)	38 (24.84)	55 (35.95)	26 (16.99)	29 (18.95)
Above 40	8 (5.13)	37 (23.72)	45 (28.45)	31 (19.87)	35 (22.44)
Chi-square = 9.277; df = 8; Insignificant					
Place of Origin					
Rural	7 (8.05)	26 (29.89)	35 (40.23)	14 (16.09)	5 (5.75)
Urban	13 (3.58)	84 (23.14)	100 (27.55)	64 (17.63)	102 (28.10)
Chi-square = 23.058; df = 4; Significant at 1 per cent level					
Type of Family					
Joint	10 (4.78)	54 (25.84)	72 (34.45)	35 (16.75)	38 (18.18)
Nuclear	10 (4.15)	56 (23.24)	63 (26.14)	43 (17.84)	69 (28.63)
Chi-square = 8.204 ; df = 4; Insignificant					
Form of Business Organization					
Sole	16 (5.18)	73 (23.62)	86 (27.83)	53 (17.15)	81 (26.21)
Others	4 (2.84)	37 (26.24)	49 (34.75)	25 (17.73)	26 (18.44)
Chi-square = 4.887; df = 4; Insignificant					
Investment (Lacs)					
<1	5 (4.07)	38 (30.89)	36 (29.27)	18 (14.63)	26 (21.14)
1-2	11 (7.64)	42 (29.17)	43 (29.86)	22 (15.28)	26 (18.06)
2-3	4 (5.19)	21 (27.27)	23 (29.87)	19 (24.68)	10 (12.99)
3-5	—	5 (7.81)	17 (26.56)	11 (17.19)	31 (48.94)

1	2	3	4	5	6
5-10	—	4 (12.90)	11 (35.48)	4 (12.90)	12 (38.71)
Above 10	—	—	5 (45.45)	4 (36.36)	2 (18.18)

Chi-square = 56.342; df = 20; Significant at 1 per cent level

Income (Rs.)

1	2	3	4	5	6
<7500	2 (3.70)	12 (22.22)	14 (25.93)	10 (18.52)	16 (29.63)
7500-10000	5 (3.31)	52 (34.44)	37 (24.50)	22 (14.57)	35 (23.18)
10000-15000	7 (7.22)	20 (20.62)	29 (29.90)	19 (19.59)	22 (22.68)
15000-20000	6 (6.00)	18 (18.00)	26 (26.00)	22 (22.00)	28 (28.00)
20000+	—	8 (16.67)	29 (60.42)	5 (10.42)	6 (12.50)

Chi-square = 39.500; df = 16; Significant at 1 per cent level

Training

1	2	3	4	5	6
Got Training	6 (2.55)	63 (26.81)	67 (28.51)	54 (22.98)	45 (19.15)
No Training	14 (6.51)	47 (21.86)	68 (31.63)	24 (11.16)	62 (28.84)

Chi-square = 18.923; df = 4; Significant at 1 per cent level

Sources of Finance

1	2	3	4	5	6
Formal	2 (1.67)	24 (20.00)	28 (23.33)	18 (15.00)	48 (40.00)
Informal	18 (5.45)	86 (26.06)	107 (32.42)	60 (18.18)	59 (17.88)

Chi-square = 25.212; df = 4; Significant at 1 per cent level

Age of Enterprise

1	2	3	4	5	6
Below 10 years	12 (4.01)	73 (24.41)	88 (29.43)	53 (17.73)	73 (24.41)
Above 10 years	8 (5.30)	37 (24.50)	47 (31.13)	25 (16.56)	34 (22.52)

Chi-square = 0.700; df = 4; Insignificant

possible after completion of all the formalities. It also highlights that there has been a remarkable shift in the policies of financial institutions during post-reform period. Education-wise information further shows that 46 per cent women entrepreneurs possessing primary and one-third matric and post-graduate level of education face this problem to a large extent. The value of chi-square is statistically significant at 1 per cent level of significance. It shows that these two variables vary significantly. Almost same proportion of women entrepreneurs irrespective of their age groups face this problem to a large extent. 30 per cent women entrepreneurs in the age group of less than 30 years not at all face this problem, whereas it is slightly more than one-fifth among other women entrepreneurs. It shows that women entrepreneurs in higher age groups are facing problem of delay in release of payments. The value of chi-square is statistically insignificant. Proportion of women entrepreneurs (38 per cent) hailing from rural areas faces this problem relatively more than their urban counterparts (27 per cent). There is a need to liberalize the policies for women entrepreneurs coming from rural areas. 28 per cent women entrepreneurs hailing from urban areas not at all face this problem. The value of chi-square is statistically significant at 1 per cent level of significance. Almost same proportion of women entrepreneurs hailing from joint and nuclear families face this problem upto a large extent. 28 per cent women entrepreneurs coming from nuclear families do not face this problem, whereas this ratio is 18 per cent in case of other women entrepreneurs. It shows that women entrepreneurs hailing from nuclear families are more enlightened than other women entrepreneurs. The value of chi-square is statistically insignificant. Almost same proportion of women entrepreneurs managing business under different forms of business organization face this problem to a large extent. The value of chi-square is statistically insignificant. Women entrepreneurs investing more money in business do not face much problem related to delay in payments. It may be due to more capacity of large business to manage things inspite of delay in payments. On the other hand, slightly more than one-third women entrepreneurs investing money upto Rs. 3 lacs in business face this problem to a large extent. It shows that small business cannot withstand in case of delay in payments. It may also be due to lack of financial resources to manage of business for a longer period of time. Similarly, almost same proportion of women entrepreneurs investing upto Rs. 5 lacs in business also face this problem to some extent. The value of chi-square is statistically significant at 1 per cent level of significance. 60 per cent women entrepreneurs earning higher level of income face this problem of some extent. One-fourth women entrepreneurs earning income in the range of Rs. 7,500 and 15,000-20,000 per month face this problem to a large extent. It seems that women entrepreneurs earning low level of income have less capacity to continue in business due to delay in payments. The value of chi-square is statistically significant at 1 per cent level of significance. It shows that these variables vary significantly. Almost same proportion of women entrepreneurs (28 per cent) irrespective of level of training face this problem to a large extent. It shows that financial payments need more skill than managing other things. One-fifth women entrepreneurs who have taken assistance from financial institutions face this problem to a large extent. The value of chi-square is statistically significant at 1 per cent level of significance. Almost same proportion of women entrepreneurs irrespective of their age of enterprise face this problem to a large extent. The analysis reveals that financial institutions should monitor disbursement of money well in time to women entrepreneurs. The value of chi-square is statistically insignificant.

Table 6.18 shows that only one-third women entrepreneurs feel that there is a lack of coordination among financial institutions. It shows that under new economic regime financial institutions are trying to provide all services through single window. Education-wise information further shows that women entrepreneurs possessing low level of education face this problem to a large extent. It seems that less educated women entrepreneurs face this problem due to lack of awareness and difficulty in approaching these institutions. The value of chi-square vary significantly. Only one-fourth women entrepreneurs in higher age group face this problem to a large extent whereas, this ratio is 42 per cent in case of women entrepreneurs in the age group of 30-40. The value of chi-square is statistically significant at 1 per cent level of significance. Women entrepreneurs hailing from rural areas face this problem more than women entrepreneurs coming from urban areas. It may also be due to difference in place of origin and less exposure to business procedure. 31 per cent of women entrepreneurs coming from urban areas not at all face this problem. The value of chi-square is statistically significant at 1 per cent level of significance. It shows that these two variables are independent. Women entrepreneurs coming from joint families face this problem more than other women entrepreneurs. The value of chi-square is statistically insignificant. Women entrepreneurs managing business on individual basis face this problem slightly on higher side as compared to other women entrepreneurs. It shows that large business faces less problems. It may be due to ability to take the services of experts and more contacts. The value of chi-square is statistically significant at 5 per cent level of significance. Women entrepreneurs investing less money in business face this problem more than other women

TABLE 6.18

Extent of Problem of Coordination among Financial Institutions Faced by Women Entrepreneurs

Group	To great extent	To large extent	To some extent	To little extent	Not at all
1	2	3	4	5	6
All Data	24 (5.33)	128 (28.44)	76 (16.89)	96 (21.33)	126 (28.00)
Education					
Primary	—	13 (57.17)	—	4 (16.67)	7 (29.17)
Matric	12 (15.00)	12 (15.00)	19 (23.75)	17 (21.25)	20 (25.00)
Graduate	5 (2.66)	56 (29.79)	28 (14.89)	33 (17.55)	66 (35.11)
Post Graduate	7 (4.43)	47 (29.75)	29 (18.35)	42 (26.58)	33 (20.89)
Chi-square = 45.925; df = 12; Significant at 1 per cent level					
Age (years)					
Below 30	2 (1.42)	44 (31.21)	11 (7.80)	41 (29.08)	43 (30.50)
30-40	14 (9.15)	50 (32.68)	27 (17.65)	27 (17.65)	35 (22.88)
Above 40	8 (5.13)	34 (21.79)	38 (24.36)	28 (17.95)	48 (30.77)
Chi-square = 32.065; df = 8; Significant at 1 per cent level					
Place of Origin					
Rural	5 (5.75)	31 (35.63)	10 (11.49)	28 (32.18)	13 (14.94)
Urban	19 (5.23)	97 (26.72)	66 (18.18)	68 (18.73)	113 (31.13)
Chi-square = 16.371; df = 4; Significant at 1 per cent level					
Type of Family					
Joint	15 (7.18)	63 (30.14)	37 (17.70)	43 (20.57)	51 (24.40)
Nuclear	9 (3.73)	65 (26.97)	39 (16.18)	53 (21.99)	75 (31.12)
Chi-square = 4.946; df = 4; Insignificant					
Form of Business Organization					
Sole	16 (5.18)	91 (29.45)	40 (12.94)	69 (22.33)	93 (30.10)
Others	8 (5.67)	37 (26.24)	36 (25.53)	27 (19.15)	33 (23.40)
Chi-square = 11.486; df = 4; Significant at 5 per cent level					
Investment (Lacs)					
<1	5 (4.07)	47 (38.21)	11 (8.94)	31 (25.20)	29 (23.58)
1-2	12 (8.33)	40 (27.78)	29 (20.14)	35 (24.31)	28 (19.44)
2-3	3 (3.90)	29 (37.66)	17 (22.08)	14 (18.18)	14 (18.18)
3-5	—	12 (18.75)	9 (14.06)	5 (7.81)	38 (59.38)

1	2	3	4	5	6
5-10	4 (12.90)	—	6 (19.35)	5 (16.13)	16 (51.61)
Above 10	—	—	4 (36.36)	6 (54.55)	1 (9.09)

Chi-square = 91.286; df = 20; Significant at 1 per cent level

Income (Rs.)

<7500	—	13 (24.07)	7 (12.96)	17 (31.48)	17 (31.48)
7500-10000	7 (4.64)	46 (30.46)	16 (10.60)	32 (21.19)	50 (30.11)
10000-15000	8 (8.25)	30 (30.93)	27 (27.84)	12 (12.37)	20 (20.62)
15000-20000	3 (3.00)	25 (25.00)	17 (17.00)	23 (23.00)	32 (32.00)
20000+	6 (12.50)	14 (29.17)	9 (18.75)	12 (25.00)	7 (14.58)

Chi-square = 36.316; df = 16; Significant at 1 per cent level

Training

Got Training	14 (5.96)	68 (28.94)	39 (16.60)	63 (26.81)	51 (21.70)
No Training	10 (4.65)	60 (27.91)	37 (17.21)	33 (15.35)	75 (34.88)

Chi-square = 14.305; df = 4; Significant at 1 per cent level

Sources of Finance

Formal	3 (2.50)	9 (7.50)	24 (20.00)	34 (28.33)	50 (41.67)
Informal	21 (6.36)	119 (36.06)	52 (15.76)	62 (18.79)	76 (23.03)

Chi-square = 43.311; df = 4; Significant at 1 per cent level

Age of Enterprise

Below 10 years	20 (6.69)	94 (31.44)	43 (14.38)	62 (20.74)	80 (26.76)
Above 10 years	4 (2.65)	34 (22.52)	33 (21.85)	34 (22.52)	46 (30.46)

Chi-square = 9.837; df = 4; Significant at 5 per cent level

entrepreneurs. The value of chi-square is statistically significant at 1 per cent level of significance. It shows that these two variables vary significantly. Women entrepreneurs earning even higher level of income feel that there is lack of coordination among various financial institutions. It may be due to more urgent requirement of finance to fulfil various requirements. The value of chi-square is statistically significant at 1 per cent level of significance. Almost same proportion of trained and untrained women entrepreneurs face this problem to a large extent. It shows that training sometime doesn't prove to be beneficial in case of coordination with financial institutions. The value of chi-square is statistically significant at 1 per cent level of significance. 42 per cent women entrepreneurs who have not availed financial assistance from financial institutions face this problem. The value of chi-square is statistically significant at 1 per cent level of significance. Women entrepreneurs who have established their business recently feel that there is a lack of coordination among financial institutions. The value of chi-square is statistically significant at 5 per cent level of significance.

Table 6.19 shows that 26 per cent women entrepreneurs face the problem of high rate of interest to a large extent and another 23 per cent to some extent. It shows that problem of high rate of interest is prevalent among small and micro-level enterprises. The reason to this may be assigned to more dependence on informal sources of finance in business. Education-wise information further projects that women entrepreneurs possessing lower level of education face the problem of high rate of interest. On the other hand, women entrepreneurs having higher level of education do

TABLE 6.19
Extent of Problem of High Rate of Interest Faced by Women Entrepreneurs

Group	To great extent	To large extent	To some extent	To little extent	Not at all
1	2	3	4	5	6
All Data	5 (1.11)	114 (25.33)	102 (22.67)	136 (30.22)	93 (20.67)
Education					
Primary	—	7 (29.17)	7 (29.17)	7 (29.17)	3 (12.50)
Matric	—	30 (37.50)	22 (27.50)	16 (20.00)	12 (15.00)
Graduate	5 (2.66)	47 (25.00)	34 (18.09)	58 (30.85)	44 (23.40)
Post Graduate	—	30 (18.99)	39 (24.68)	55 (38.81)	34 (21.52)
Chi-square = 24.253; df = 12; Significant at 1 per cent level					
Age (years)					
Below 30	1 (0.71)	22 (15.60)	22 (15.60)	59 (41.84)	37 (26.24)
30-40	2 (1.31)	40 (26.14)	41 (26.80)	45 (29.41)	25 (16.34)
Above 40	2 (1.28)	52 (33.33)	39 (25.00)	32 (20.51)	31 (19.87)
Chi-square = 28.934; df = 8; Significant at 1 per cent level					
Place of Origin					
Rural	—	23 (26.44)	31 (35.63)	19 (21.84)	14 (16.09)
Urban	5 (1.38)	91 (25.07)	71 (19.56)	117 (32.23)	79 (21.76)
Chi-square = 12.849; df = 4; Significant at 1 per cent level					

1	2	3	4	5	6
Type of Family					
Joint	1 (0.48)	56 (26.79)	60 (28.71)	64 (30.62)	28 (13.40)
Nuclear	4 (1.66)	58 (24.07)	42 (17.43)	72 (29.88)	65 (26.97)
Chi-square = 18.018; df = 4; Significant at 1 per cent level					
Form of Business Organization					
Sole	4 (1.29)	71 (22.98)	69 (22.33)	96 (31.07)	69 (22.33)
Others	1 (0.71)	43 (30.50)	33 (23.40)	40 (28.37)	24 (17.02)
Chi-square = 4.062; df = 4; Insignificant					
Investment.(Lacs)					
<1	3 (2.44)	33 (26.83)	20 (16.26)	41 (33.33)	26 (21.14)
1-2	—	51 (35.42)	42 (29.17)	32 (22.22)	19 (13.19)
2-3	1 (1.30)	15 (19.48)	26 (33.77)	22 (28.57)	13 (16.88)
3-5	1 (1.56)	8 (12.50)	5 (7.81)	25 (39.06)	25 (39.06)
5-10	—	7 (22.58)	4 (12.90)	12 (38.71)	8 (25.81)
Above 10	—	—	5 (45.45)	4 (36.36)	2 (18.18)
Chi-square = 58.670; df = 20; Significant at 1 per cent level					
Income (Rs.)					
<7500	1 (1.85)	17 (31.48)	6 (11.11)	14 (25.93)	16 (29.63)
7500-10000	2 (1.32)	42 (27.81)	42 (27.81)	38 (25.17)	27 (17.88)
10000-15000	1 (1.03)	31 (31.96)	22 (22.68)	20 (20.62)	23 (23.71)
15000-20000	1 (1.00)	19 (19.00)	18 (18.00)	40 (40.00)	22 (22.00)
20000+	—	5 (10.42)	14 (29.17)	24 (50.00)	5 (10.42)
Chi-square = 35.904; df = 16; Significant at 1 per cent level					
Training					
Got Training	3 (1.28)	46 (19.57)	53 (22.55)	92 (39.15)	41 (17.45)
No Training	2 (0.93)	68 (31.63)	49 (22.79)	44 (20.47)	52 (24.19)
Chi-square = 21.999; df = 4; Significant at 1 per cent level					
Sources of Finance					
Formal	2 (1.67)	21 (17.50)	22 (18.33)	38 (31.67)	37 (30.83)
Informal	3 (0.91)	93 (28.18)	80 (24.24)	98 (29.70)	56 (16.97)
Chi-square = 14.071; df = 4; Significant at 1 per cent level					
Age of Enterprise					
Below 10 years	3 (1.00)	70 (23.41)	60 (20.07)	101 (33.78)	65 (21.74)
Above 10 years	2 (1.32)	44 (29.14)	42 (29.14)	35 (23.18)	28 (18.54)
Chi-square = 8.276; df = 4; Insignificant					

not face this problem. It seems that women entrepreneurs possessing higher level of education might be using their financial resources more judiciously. The value of chi-square is statistically significant at 1 per cent level of significance. Women entrepreneurs in lower age group face this problem less than women entrepreneurs in middle and higher age group. It seems that women entrepreneurs in lower age groups might be using their own resources or taking assistance from their parents and institutional sources. The value of chi-square is statistically significant at 1 per cent level of significance. Almost same proportion of women entrepreneurs (26 per cent) hailing from rural and urban areas face the problem of higher rate of interest to a large extent. The value of chi-square is statistically significant at 1 per cent level of significance. Similarly, almost same proportion of women entrepreneurs coming from joint and nuclear families also face this problem to a large extent. The value of chi-square is statistically significant at 1 per cent level of significance. Women entrepreneurs managing business under other than individual forms of business organizations face this problem relatively more as compared to their counterparts managing business on individual basis. The value of chi-square is statistically significant at 1 per cent level of significance. Women entrepreneurs investing less money in business face this problem relatively more as compared to women entrepreneurs investing more money in business. It reveals that the problem of high rate of interest is no longer faced by women entrepreneurs investing more money in business. Suitable policies need to be formulated to cater to the needs of small and micro-level enterprises. The value of chi-square is statistically significant at 1 per cent level of significance. Women entrepreneurs earning moderate and lower level of income face the problem of high rate of interest. The value of chi-square is statistically significant at 1 per cent level of significance. Untrained women entrepreneurs (32 per cent) face the problem of high rate of interest more than trained women entrepreneurs (21 per cent). It seems that training enhances the knowledge of availability of various sources of finance and women entrepreneurs might be able to get assistance from formal sources of finance. The value of chi-square is statistically significant at 1 per cent level of significance. It seems logical that women entrepreneurs using informal sources of finance face the problem of high rate of interest. The value of chi-square is statistically significant at 1 per cent level of significance. Similarly, women entrepreneurs having older enterprises face the problem of high rate of interest. It seems that younger generation of women entrepreneurs are more alert, knowledgeable and informative and utilizing this information in their business to overcome the problem of high rate of interest. The value of chi-square is statistically insignificant. Analysis vividly reveals that women entrepreneurs in micro and small enterprises face the problem of high rate of interest. There is a need to provide more credit facilities on low rate of interest to this sector. This sector has more potential to generate gainful employment opportunities along with large number of other benefits.

Table 6.20 highlights that only one-fourth women entrepreneurs face the problem of labour absenteeism to a large extent and 39 per cent to some extent. It reveals that problem of labour absenteeism is prevalent in micro and small enterprises. It may be due to increase in availability of alternative job opportunities for labour in the market. Education-wise information further shows that one-third women entrepreneurs having education upto matric level face this problem to a large extent than other women entrepreneurs. Analysis shows that problem of labour absenteeism has been found to be decline with increase in education level. It reveals that education enhances the skill among women entrepreneurs to manage labour effectively. The value of chi-square is statistically significant at 1 per cent level of significance. Age-wise information further reveals that problem of labour absenteeism is found to be more among women entrepreneurs in higher age groups. It may be due to difference in leadership style among women entrepreneurs of different age groups. The value of chi-square is statistically significant at 1 per cent level of significance. Almost same proportion of women entrepreneurs (35 per cent) hailing from rural and urban areas not at all face this problem. On the other hand, women entrepreneurs coming from urban areas face this problem slightly on higher side than women entrepreneurs coming from rural areas. According to some women entrepreneurs labour seems to become more mobile and leave job whenever they find some better alternatives. The value of chi-square is statistically insignificant. 25 per cent women entrepreneurs coming from joint and nuclear families face

TABLE 6.20

Extent of Problem of Labour Absenteeism Faced by Women Entrepreneurs

Group	To great extent	To large extent	To some extent	To little extent	Not at all
1	2	3	4	5	6
All Data	20 (4.44)	94 (20.89)	176 (39.11)	136 (30.22)	24 (5.33)
Education					
Primary	—	7 (29.17)	7 (29.17)	7 (29.17)	3 (12.50)
Matric	2 (2.50)	25 (31.25)	31 (38.75)	16 (20.00)	6 (7.50)
Graduate	14 (7.45)	26 (13.83)	86 (45.74)	51 (27.13)	11 (5.85)
Post Graduate	4 (2.53)	36 (22.78)	52 (32.91)	62 (39.24)	4 (2.53)
Chi-square = 33.851; df = 12; Significant at 1 per cent level					
Age (years)					
Below 30	—	15 (10.64)	50 (35.46)	71 (50.35)	5 (3.55)
30-40	12 (7.84)	27 (17.65)	56 (36.60)	49 (32.03)	9 (5.88)
Above 40	8 (5.13)	52 (33.33)	70 (44.87)	16 (10.26)	10 (6.41)
Chi-square = 72.806; df = 8; Significant at 1 per cent level					
Place of Origin					
Rural	—	19 (21.84)	37 (42.53)	26 (29.89)	5 (5.75)
Urban	20 (5.51)	75 (20.66)	139 (38.29)	110 (30.30)	19 (5.23)
Chi-square = 5.201; df = 4; Insignificant					
Type of Family					
Joint	10 (4.78)	47 (22.49)	83 (39.71)	61 (29.19)	8 (3.83)
Nuclear	10 (4.15)	47 (19.50)	93 (38.59)	75 (31.12)	16 (6.64)
Chi-square = 2.413; df = 4; Insignificant					
Form of Business Organization					
Sole	16 (5.18)	56 (18.12)	124 (40.13)	98 (31.72)	15 (4.85)
Others	4 (2.84)	38 (26.95)	52 (36.88)	38 (26.95)	9 (6.38)
Chi-square = 6.219; df = 4; Insignificant					
Investment (Lacs)					
<1	10 (8.13)	21 (17.07)	32 (26.02)	54 (43.90)	6 (4.88)
1-2	6 (4.17)	32 (22.22)	68 (47.22)	34 (23.61)	4 (2.78)
2-3	4 (5.19)	22 (28.57)	25 (32.47)	24 (31.17)	2 (2.60)
3-5	—	11 (17.19)	32 (50.00)	13 (20.31)	8 (12.50)

1	2	3	4	5	6
5-10	—	8 (25.81)	8 (25.81)	11 (35.48)	4 (12.90)
Above 10	—	—	11 (100.0)	—	—

Chi-square = 65.662; df = 20; Significant at 1 per cent level

Income (Rs.)

<7500	8 (14.81)	12 (22.22)	20 (37.04)	10 (18.52)	4 (7.41)
7500-10000	4 (2.65)	27 (17.88)	77 (50.99)	35 (23.18)	8 (5.30)
10000-15000	2 (2.06)	32 (32.99)	26 (26.80)	32 (32.99)	5 (5.15)
15000-20000	4 (4.00)	18 (18.00)	30 (30.00)	43 (43.00)	5 (5.00)
20000+	2 (4.17)	5 (10.42)	23 (47.92)	16 (33.33)	2 (4.17)

Chi-square = 49.527; df = 16; Significant at 1 per cent level

Training

Got Training	14 (5.96)	40 (17.02)	74 (31.49)	100 (42.55)	7 (2.98)
No Training	6 (2.79)	54 (25.12)	102 (47.44)	36 (16.74)	17 (7.91)

Chi-square = 43.220; df = 4; Significant at 1 per cent level

Sources of Finance

Formal	2 (1.67)	23 (19.17)	53 (44.17)	29 (24.17)	13 (10.83)
Informal	18 (5.45)	71 (21.52)	123 (37.27)	107 (32.42)	11 (3.33)

Chi-square = 15.409; df = 4; Significant at 1 per cent level

Age of Enterprise

Below 10 years	12 (4.01)	57 (19.06)	99 (33.11)	116 (38.80)	15 (5.02)
Above 10 years	8 (5.30)	37 (24.50)	77 (50.99)	20 (13.25)	9 (5.96)

Chi-square = 31.838; df = 4; Significant at 1 per cent level

this problem to a large extent. The value of chi-square is statistically insignificant. Women entrepreneurs managing business under other than individual forms of business organizations face this problem slightly on higher side than other women entrepreneurs. It shows that problem of labour absenteeism is more among small enterprises. It may be due to lack of coordination and incentives required to maintain labour under free market economies. The value of chi-square is statistically insignificant. One-fourth women entrepreneurs investing upto Rs. 3 lacs in business face this problem to a large extent. It may be due to less incentives provided to them. On the other hand, all women entrepreneurs investing more than Rs. 10 lacs in business face this problem to some extent. It shows that big enterprises may be able to provide better incentives to labour. The value of chi-square is statistically significant at 1 per cent level of significance. Women entrepreneurs earning higher level of income do not face this problem to a large extent than other women entrepreneurs. It may be due to more paying capacity among women entrepreneurs earning higher level of income. The value of chi-square is statistically significant at 1 per cent level of significance. Almost same proportion of trained and untrained women entrepreneurs face this problem to a large extent. 47 per cent women entrepreneurs who have taken training before start of business face this problem to some extent. It shows that training improves the skill to manage labour in a proper manner. The value of chi-square is statistically significant at 1 per cent level of significance. One-fourth women entrepreneurs who have taken assistance from informal sources face this problem to a large extent. On the other hand, women entrepreneurs having taken assistance from financial institutions face this problem of some extent. It shows that availability of money at low cost improves the financial conditions and women entrepreneurs have been able to solve the problem of labour absenteeism. The value of chi-square is statistically insignificant. One-third women entrepreneurs having enterprises more than 10 years old face this problem more than their counterparts having enterprises less than 10 years old. The reason to this may be assigned to professional management practices adopted by women entrepreneurs in former case. The value of chi-square is statistically significant at 1 per cent level of significance.

Table 6.21 shows that 38 per cent women entrepreneurs face the problem of non-availability of skilled labour to a large extent and another 36 per cent to some extent. It shows that skilled labour is still in short supply in new economic regime and there is a need to formulate policies to improve human capital base of labour. Women entrepreneurs possessing low level of education face this problem relatively more than other women entrepreneurs. The reason to this may be assigned to lack of incentives provided to skilled labour, less future scope of labour in these enterprises and in this process they face this problem. The value of chi-square is statistically significant at 1 per cent level of significance. Women entrepreneurs in higher age group face this problem relatively more than women entrepreneurs in lower age groups. It may be

TABLE 6.21

**Extent of Problem of Non-availability of Skilled Labour Faced by
Women Entrepreneurs**

Group	To great extent	To large extent	To some extent	To little extent	Not at all
1	2	3	4	5	6
All Data	42 (9.33)	127 (28.22)	165 (36.67)	76 (16.89)	40 (8.89)
Education					
Primary	1 (4.17)	12 (50.00)	8 (33.33)	—	3 (12.50)
Matric	13 (16.25)	22 (27.50)	29 (36.25)	13 (16.25)	3 (3.75)
Graduate	20 (10.64)	51 (27.13)	60 (31.91)	32 (17.02)	25 (13.30)
Post Graduate	8 (5.06)	42 (26.58)	68 (43.04)	31 (19.62)	9 (5.70)
Chi-square = 28.903; df = 12; Significant at 1 per cent level					
Age (years)					
Below 30	1 (0.71)	41 (29.08)	53 (37.59)	35 (24.82)	11 (7.80)
30-40	16 (10.46)	39 (25.49)	66 (43.14)	10 (6.54)	22 (14.38)
Above 40	25 (16.03)	47 (30.13)	46 (29.49)	31 (19.87)	7 (4.49)
Chi-square = 48.107; df = 8; Significant at 1 per cent level					
Place of Origin					
Rural	3 (3.45)	33 (37.93)	31 (35.63)	13 (14.94)	7 (8.05)
Urban	39 (10.74)	94 (25.90)	134 (36.91)	63 (17.36)	33 (9.09)
Chi-square = 7.964; df = 4; Insignificant					
Type of Family					
Joint	24 (11.48)	51 (24.40)	75 (35.89)	42 (20.10)	17 (8.13)
Nuclear	18 (7.47)	76 (31.54)	90 (37.34)	34 (14.11)	23 (9.54)
Chi-square = 6.642; df = 4; Insignificant					
Form of Business Organization					
Sole	28 (9.06)	78 (25.24)	123 (39.81)	55 (17.80)	25 (8.09)
Others	14 (9.93)	49 (34.75)	42 (29.79)	21 (14.89)	15 (10.64)
Chi-square = 7.022; df = 4; Insignificant					
Investment (Lacs)					
<1	13 (10.57)	43 (34.96)	30 (24.39)	24 (19.51)	13 (10.57)
1-2	17 (11.81)	32 (22.22)	72 (50.00)	19 (13.19)	4 (2.78)
2-3	6 (7.79)	24 (31.17)	19 (24.68)	19 (24.68)	9 (11.69)
3-5	4 (6.25)	17 (26.56)	25 (39.06)	10 (15.62)	8 (12.50)

(Contd.)

1	2	3	4	5	6
5-10	2 (6.45)	9 (29.03)	10 (32.26)	4 (12.90)	6 (19.35)
Above 10	—	2 (18.18)	9 (81.82)	—	—
Chi-square = 48.742; df = 20; Significant at 1 per cent level					

Income (Rs.)

<7500	14 (25.93)	20 (37.04)	10 (18.52)	8 (14.81)	2 (3.70)
7500-10000	9 (5.96)	43 (28.48)	55 (36.42)	30 (19.87)	14 (9.27)
10000-15000	7 (7.22)	28 (28.87)	39 (40.21)	18 (18.56)	5 (5.15)
15000-20000	8 (8.00)	22 (22.00)	38 (38.00)	15 (15.00)	17 (17.00)
20000+	4 (8.33)	14 (29.17)	23 (47.92)	5 (10.42)	2 (4.17)
Chi-square = 42.536; df = 16; Significant at 1 per cent level					

Training

Got Training	22 (9.36)	67 (28.51)	76 (32.34)	41 (17.45)	29 (12.34)
No Training	20 (9.30)	60 (27.91)	89 (41.40)	35 (16.28)	11 (5.12)
Chi-square = 9.208; df = 4; Insignificant					

Sources of Finance

Formal	7 (5.83)	40 (33.33)	41 (34.17)	13 (10.83)	19 (15.83)
Informal	35 (10.61)	87 (26.36)	124 (37.58)	63 (19.09)	21 (6.36)
Chi-square = 16.372; df = 4; Significant at 1 per cent level					

Age of Enterprise

Below 10 years	20 (6.69)	82 (27.42)	104 (34.78)	60 (20.07)	33 (11.04)
Above 10 years	22 (14.57)	45 (29.80)	61 (40.40)	16 (10.60)	7 (4.64)
Chi-square = 17.693; df = 4; Significant at 1 per cent level					

due to traditional style of management of enterprise and failure to motivate workers. The value of chi-square is statistically significant at 1 per cent level of significance. Women entrepreneurs hailing from rural areas face this problem slightly on higher side than women entrepreneurs coming from urban areas. It may be due to difference in education and difference in attitude to manage skilled labour in business. The value of chi-square is statistically insignificant. Almost same proportion of women entrepreneurs hailing from joint and nuclear families face this problem to a large and some extent. It shows that emerging markets provide intense competition for women entrepreneurs to retain skilled labour. The value of chi-square is statistically insignificant. Women entrepreneurs managing business on large scale face this problem more intensively as compared to other women entrepreneurs. The reason to this may be assigned to more demand for skilled labour in big businesses. The value of chi-square is statistically insignificant. Women entrepreneurs investing more money in business face this problem relatively less than other women entrepreneurs. It shows that women entrepreneurs investing less money face this problem due to lack of capacity to pay higher wages to skilled labour. The value of chi-square is statistically significant at 1 per cent level of significance. Women entrepreneurs earning higher level of income face this problem less intensively as compared to other women entrepreneurs. In case of middle level of income, proportion is almost same. The value of chi-square is statistically significant at 1 per cent level of significance. Almost same proportion of women entrepreneurs irrespective of level of training face this problem to a large extent. The value of chi-square is statistically insignificant. Almost same proportion of women entrepreneurs using various sources of finance face this problem to a large extent. Women entrepreneurs having enterprises more than 10 years old face this problem more intensively as compared to women entrepreneurs having enterprises 10 years old. The values of chi-square vary statistically significantly.

Table 6.22 reveals that 21 per cent of women entrepreneurs face the problem of labour turnover to a large extent and another 45 per cent to some extent. It reveals that in competitive markets cost as well as demand for labour has increased. Education-wise information further depicts that one-fourth women entrepreneurs having primary level of education face this problem to a large extent and 21 per cent of women entrepreneurs possessing graduate level of education also face this problem. The value of chi-square is statistically insignificant. 48 per cent of women entrepreneurs in age group of less than 30 and 30-40 face this problem to some extent. 35 per cent women entrepreneurs in the age group of more than 40 also face this problem to a large extent. The reason being, women entrepreneurs in higher age group might be using traditional methods to manage their enterprise and labour force. The value of chi-square is statistically significant at 1 per cent level of significance. 14 per cent and 22 per cent women entrepreneurs hailing from rural and urban areas face this problem to a large extent. Only small proportion of women entrepreneurs not at all face this problem. The value of chi-square is statistically insignificant. Women entrepreneurs hailing from joint families (24 per cent) face this problem to a great extent relatively more than their counterparts coming from nuclear families (18 per cent). It shows that labour is becoming more mobile and aware of increase in their demand over a period of time. The value of chi-square is statistically insignificant. Women entrepreneurs managing business under other than individual form of business organizations face this problem relatively more. It may be due to joint forms of business organizations and more requirement of skilled labour to maintain quality of product. The value of chi-square is statistically insignificant. 21 per cent to 25 per cent of women entrepreneurs investing money upto Rs. 3 lacs in

TABLE 6.22

Extent of Problem of Labour Turnove. Faced by Women Entrepreneurs

Group	To great extent	To large extent	To some extent	To little extent	Not at all
1	2	3	4	5	6
All Data	32 (7.11)	63 (14.00)	204 (45.33)	97 (21.56)	54 (12.00)
Education					
Primary	1 (4.17)	5 (20.83)	9 (37.50)	6 (25.00)	3 (12.50)
Matric	7 (8.75)	12 (15.00)	27 (33.75)	27 (33.75)	7 (8.75)
Graduate	17 (9.04)	23 (12.23)	93 (49.47)	30 (15.96)	25 (13.30)
Post Graduate	7 (4.43)	23 (14.56)	75 (47.47)	34 (21.52)	19 (12.03)
Chi-square = 17.407; df = 12; Insignificant					
Age (years)					
Below 30	—	12 (8.51)	68 (48.23)	37 (26.24)	24 (17.02)
30-40	17 (11.11)	12 (7.84)	75 (49.02)	32 (20.92)	17 (11.11)
Above 40	15 (9.62)	39 (25.00)	61 (39.10)	28 (17.95)	13 (8.33)
Chi-square = 44.778; df = 8; Significant at 1 per cent level					
Place of Origin					
Rural	—	13 (14.94)	40 (45.98)	20 (22.99)	14 (16.09)
Urban	32 (8.82)	50 (13.77)	164 (45.18)	77 (21.21)	40 (11.02)
Chi-square = 9.355; df = 4; Insignificant					

1	2	3	4	5	6
Type of Family					
Joint	16 (7.66)	36 (17.22)	75 (35.89)	63 (30.14)	19 (9.09)
Nuclear	16 (6.64)	27 (11.20)	129 (53.53)	34 (14.11)	35 (14.52)
Chi-square = 26.851 ; df = 4; Insignificant					
Form of Business Organization					
Sole	21 (6.80)	35 (11.33)	146 (47.25)	69 (22.33)	38 (12.30)
Others	11 (7.80)	28 (19.86)	58 (41.13)	28 (19.86)	16 (11.35)
Chi-square = 6.317; df = 4; Significant at 1 per cent level					
Investment (Lacs)					
<1	15 (12.20)	11 (8.94)	42 (34.15)	32 (26.02)	23 (18.70)
1-2	10 (6.94)	19 (13.19)	71 (49.31)	34 (23.61)	10 (6.94)
2-3	4 (5.19)	15 (19.48)	35 (45.45)	16 (20.78)	7 (9.09)
3-5	3 (4.69)	8 (12.50)	36 (56.25)	7 (10.94)	10 (15.62)
5-10	—	8 (25.81)	11 (35.48)	8 (25.81)	4 (12.90)
Above 10	—	2 (18.18)	9 (81.82)	—	—
Chi-square = 42.824; df = 20; Significant at 1 per cent level					
Income (Rs.)					
<7500	12 (22.22)	9 (16.67)	22 (40.74)	7 (12.96)	4 (7.41)
7500-10000	8 (5.30)	15 (9.93)	73 (48.34)	35 (23.18)	20 (13.25)
10000-15000	5 (5.15)	20 (20.62)	38 (39.18)	20 (20.62)	14 (14.43)
15000-20000	5 (5.00)	12 (12.00)	44 (44.00)	27 (27.00)	12 (12.00)
20000+	2 (4.17)	7 (14.58)	27 (56.25)	8 (16.67)	4 (8.33)
Chi-square = 33.969; df = 16; Significant at 1 per cent level					
Training					
Got Training	19 (8.09)	34 (14.47)	108 (45.96)	41 (17.45)	33 (14.04)
No Training	13 (6.05)	29 (13.49)	94 (44.65)	56 (26.05)	21 (9.77)
Chi-square = 6.338; df = 4; Insignificant					
Sources of Finance					
Formal	4 (3.33)	19 (15.83)	51 (42.50)	27 (22.50)	19 (15.83)
Informal	28 (8.48)	44 (13.33)	153 (46.36)	70 (21.21)	35 (10.61)
Chi-square = 6.038; df = 4; Insignificant					
Age of Enterprise					
Below 10 years	16 (5.35)	35 (11.71)	131 (43.81)	77 (25.75)	40 (13.38)
Above 10 years	16 (10.60)	28 (18.54)	73 (48.34)	20 (13.25)	14 (9.27)
Chi-square = 16.377; df = 4; Significant at 1 per cent level					

business face this problem. It may be due to lack of paying capacity. 81 per cent of women entrepreneurs investing more than Rs. 10 lacs in business face this problem to some extent. Analysis lucidly reveals that this problem seems to be on decline with increase in level of investment. The value of chi-square is statistically significant at 1 per cent level of significance. Women entrepreneurs earning lower level of income face this problem relatively more than other women entrepreneurs. It seems that availability of money helps in solving the problem of labour turnover. The value of chi-square is statistically significant at 1 per cent level of significance. Almost same proportion of trained and untrained women entrepreneurs face this problem to large and some extent. The value of chi-square is statistically insignificant. 46 per cent women entrepreneurs who have not availed financial assistance from formal sources of finance face this problem to a some extent, whereas this proportion is 42 in case of other women entrepreneurs. The value of chi-square is statistically insignificant. It shows that these variables are independent. 29 per cent women entrepreneurs who have been in business for more than 10 years face this problem to a large extent, whereas this ratio is 17 per cent in case of other women entrepreneurs. It shows that labour turnover has increased among older enterprises. The value of chi-square is statistically insignificant.

Table 6.23 shows that 23 per cent women entrepreneurs face the problem of negative attitude of labour to a large extent and 26 per cent to some extent. It shows that negative attitude of labour is a problem for women entrepreneurs. It may also be due to gender difference. Education-wise information further shows that women entrepreneurs possessing lower level of education face this problem more than women entrepreneurs possessing higher level of education. The reason to this may be assigned to difference in level of education and difficulty in management of labour. The value of chi-square is statistically insignificant. Women entrepreneurs in higher age group face this problem more than women entrepreneurs in lower age group. The value of chi-square is statistically significant at 1 per cent level of significance. Women entrepreneurs hailing from urban areas face this problem relatively more as compared to their counterparts coming from rural areas. The value of chi-square is statistically insignificant. Women entrepreneurs coming from nuclear families face this

TABLE 6.23

Extent of Problem of Negative Attitude of Labour Faced by Women Entrepreneurs

Group	To great extent	To large extent	To some extent	To little extent	Not at all
1	2	3	4	5	6
All Data	22 (4.89)	85 (18.89)	120 (26.67)	113 (25.11)	110 (24.44)
Education					
Primary	1 (4.17)	9 (37.50)	2 (8.33)	5 (20.83)	7 (29.17)
Matric	7 (8.75)	12 (15.00)	27 (33.75)	20 (25.00)	14 (17.50)
Graduate	10 (5.32)	31 (16.49)	53 (28.19)	51 (27.13)	43 (22.87)
Post Graduate	4 (2.53)	33 (20.89)	38 (24.05)	37 (23.42)	46 (29.11)
Chi-square = 19.437; df = 12; Insignificant					
Age (years)					
Below 30	2 (1.42)	24 (17.02)	20 (14.18)	47 (33.33)	48 (34.04)
30-40	9 (5.88)	23 (15.03)	40 (26.14)	34 (22.22)	47 (30.72)
Above 40	11 (7.05)	38 (24.36)	60 (38.46)	32 (20.51)	15 (9.62)
Chi-square = 53.033; df = 8; Significant at 1 per cent level					
Place of Origin					
Rural	—	14 (16.09)	25 (28.74)	21 (24.14)	27 (31.03)
Urban	22 (6.06)	71 (19.56)	95 (26.17)	92 (25.34)	83 (22.87)
Chi-square = 7.849; df = 4; Insignificant					
Type of Family					
Joint	12 (5.74)	28 (13.40)	70 (33.49)	47 (22.49)	52 (24.88)
Nuclear	10 (4.15)	57 (23.65)	50 (20.75)	66 (27.39)	58 (24.07)
Chi-square = 14.730; df = 4; Significant at 1 per cent level					
Form of Business Organization					
Sole	15 (4.85)	46 (14.89)	87 (28.16)	86 (27.83)	75 (24.27)
Others	7 (4.96)	39 (27.66)	33 (23.40)	27 (19.15)	35 (24.82)
Chi-square = 12.103; df = 4; Significant at 1 per cent level					
Investment (Lacs)					
<1	10 (8.13)	20 (16.26)	31 (25.20)	22 (17.89)	40 (32.52)
1-2	8 (5.56)	21 (14.58)	47 (32.64)	46 (31.94)	22 (15.28)
2-3	2 (2.60)	19 (24.68)	16 (20.78)	20 (25.97)	20 (25.97)
3-5	—	12 (18.75)	21 (32.81)	13 (20.31)	18 (28.12)

(Contd.)

1	2	3	4	5	6
5-10	2 (6.45)	6 (19.35)	4 (12.90)	9 (29.03)	10 (32.26)
Above 10	—	7 (63.64)	1 (9.09)	3 (27.27)	—
Chi-square = 47.902; df = 20; Significant at 1 per cent level					

Income (Rs.)

<7500	8 (14.81)	8 (14.81)	23 (42.59)	7 (12.96)	8 (14.81)
7500-10000	3 (1.99)	21 (13.91)	51 (33.77)	46 (30.46)	30 (19.87)
10000-15000	9 (9.28)	24 (24.74)	20 (20.62)	23 (23.71)	21 (21.65)
15000-20000	—	19 (19.00)	22 (22.00)	30 (30.00)	29 (29.00)
20000+	2 (4.17)	13 (27.08)	4 (8.33)	7 (14.58)	22 (45.83)
Chi-square = 65.893; df = 16; Significant at 1 per cent level					

Training

Got Training	11 (4.68)	39 (16.60)	60 (25.53)	57 (24.26)	68 (28.94)
No Training	11 (5.12)	46 (21.40)	60 (27.91)	56 (26.05)	42 (19.53)
Chi-square = 5.853; df = 4; Insignificant					

Sources of Finance

Formal	3 (2.50)	29 (24.17)	31 (25.83)	29 (24.17)	28 (23.33)
Informal	19 (5.76)	56 (16.97)	89 (26.97)	84 (25.45)	82 (24.85)
Chi-square = 4.507; df = 4; Insignificant					

Age of Enterprise

Below 10 years	10 (3.34)	53 (17.73)	63 (21.07)	82 (27.42)	91 (30.43)
Above 10 years	12 (7.95)	32 (21.19)	57 (37.75)	31 (20.53)	19 (12.58)
Chi-square = 30.431; df = 4; Significant at 1 per cent level					

problem more than women entrepreneurs coming from joint families. It may be due to availability of more persons in joint families that these women entrepreneurs area able to manage this problem. The value of chi-square is statistically significant at 1 per cent level of significance. Women entrepreneurs managing business even under other forms of business organizations face this problem relatively more than their counterparts managing business on individual basis. The value of chi-square is statistically significant at 1 per cent level of significance. Similarly, women entrepreneurs investing even more money in business face this problem more than women entrepreneurs investing less money in business. It may be due to less need felt by women entrepreneurs in latter case. On the other hand, women entrepreneurs in large business may face problem to manage labour more effectively. The value of chi-square is statistically significant at 1 per cent level of significance. Women entrepreneurs earning moderate and higher level of income face this problem more than women entrepreneurs earning lower level of income. The value of chi-square is statistically significant at 1 per cent level of significance. Untrained women entrepreneurs face this problem to a large extent more than trained women entrepreneurs. It may be due to better training taken by women entrepreneurs. But almost same proportion of women entrepreneurs face this problem to some extent. The value of chi-square is statistically insignificant. Women entrepreneurs who have availed financial assistance from formal sources face this problem slightly on higher side than women entrepreneurs using informal sources of finance. But almost same proportion of women entrepreneurs face this problem to some extent. The value of chi-square is statistically insignificant. Women entrepreneurs having enterprises more than 10 years old face this problem relatively more as compared to their counterparts having enterprises less than 10 years old. It may be due to difference in management practices used by women entrepreneurs. The value of chi-square is statistically significant at 1 per cent level of significance.

Table 6.24 shows that only 10 per cent women entrepreneurs face the problem of record keeping to a large extent and another 20 per cent to some extent. It reveals that due to spread of education, persons in the field of commerce background are easily available. Only small proportion of women entrepreneurs irrespective of their level of education face this problem to a large extent. The value of chi-square is statistically significant at 1 per cent level of significance. Women entrepreneurs in higher age groups face this problem on slightly higher side than other women entrepreneurs. It may be due to lack of awareness of maintenance of accounts in a standardized form. The value of chi-square is statistically significant at 1 per cent level of significance. Less than 11 per cent women entrepreneurs coming from rural and urban areas face this problem to a large extent. The value of chi-square is statistically insignificant. Similar types of conclusions have been observed in case of women entrepreneurs coming from different type of families. The value of chi-square is statistically insignificant. Slightly less than one-third women entrepreneurs

TABLE 6.24

Extent of Problem of Record Keeping Faced by Women Entrepreneurs

Group	To great extent	To large extent	To some extent	To little extent	Not at all
1	2	3	4	5	6
All Data	5 (1.11)	41 (9.11)	91 (20.22)	161 (35.78)	152 (33.78)
Education					
Primary	—	2 (8.33)	12 (50.00)	1 (4.17)	9 (37.50)
Matric	2 (2.50)	5 (6.25)	19 (23.75)	28 (35.00)	26 (32.50)
Graduate	3 (1.60)	13 (6.91)	30 (15.96)	78 (41.49)	64 (34.04)
Post Graduate	—	21 (13.29)	30 (18.99)	54 (34.18)	53 (33.54)
Chi-square = 30.082; df = 12; Significant at 1 per cent level					
Age (years)					
Below 30	—	9 (6.38)	23 (16.31)	57 (40.43)	52 (36.88)
30-40	4 (2.61)	12 (7.84)	21 (13.73)	56 (36.60)	60 (39.22)
Above 40	1 (0.64)	20 (12.82)	47 (30.13)	48 (30.77)	40 (25.64)
Chi-square = 27.369; df = 8; Significant at 1 per cent level					
Place of Origin					
Rural	—	5 (5.75)	20 (22.99)	38 (43.68)	24 (27.59)
Urban	5 (1.38)	36 (9.92)	71 (19.56)	123 (33.88)	128 (35.26)
Chi-square = 6.052; df = 4; Insignificant					
Type of Family					
Joint	3 (1.44)	20 (9.57)	45 (21.53)	73 (34.93)	68 (32.54)
Nuclear	2 (0.83)	21 (8.71)	46 (19.09)	88 (36.51)	84 (34.85)
Chi-square = 1.047; df = 4; Insignificant					
Form of Business Organization					
Sole	5 (1.62)	33 (10.68)	49 (15.86)	106 (34.30)	116 (37.54)
Others	—	8 (5.67)	42 (29.79)	55 (39.01)	36 (25.53)
Chi-square = 18.966; df = 4; Significant at 1 per cent level					
Investment (Lacs)					
<1	5 (4.07)	14 (11.38)	26 (21.14)	33 (26.83)	45 (36.59)
1-2	—	15 (10.42)	27 (18.75)	73 (50.69)	29 (20.14)
2-3	—	9 (11.69)	20 (25.97)	17 (22.08)	31 (40.26)
3-5	—	3 (4.69)	8 (12.50)	25 (39.06)	28 (43.75)

1	2	3	4	5	6
5-10	—	—	7 (22.58)	6 (19.35)	18 (58.06)
Above 10	—	—	3 (27.27)	7 (63.64)	1 (9.09)
Chi-square = 62.850; df = 20; Significant at 1 per cent level					
Income (Rs.)					
<7500	3 (5.56)	12 (22.22)	6 (11.11)	9 (16.67)	24 (44.44)
7500-10000	2 (1.32)	10 (6.62)	25 (16.56)	74 (49.01)	40 (26.49)
10000-15000	—	15 (15.46)	28 (28.87)	36 (37.11)	18 (8.56)
15000-20000	—	4 (4.00)	21 (21.00)	28 (28.00)	47 (47.00)
20000+	—	—	11 (22.92)	14 (29.17)	23 (47.92)
Chi-square = 76.229; df = 16; Significant at 1 per cent level					
Training					
Got Training	4 (1.70)	25 (10.64)	38 (16.17)	85 (36.17)	83 (35.32)
No Training	1 (0.47)	16 (7.44)	53 (24.65)	76 (35.35)	69 (32.09)
Chi-square = 7.166; df = 4; Insignificant					
Sources of Finance					
Formal	—	4 (3.33)	26 (21.67)	48 (40.00)	42 (35.00)
Informal	5 (1.52)	37 (11.21)	65 (19.70)	113 (34.24)	110 (33.33)
Chi-square = 8.870; df = 4; Insignificant					
Age of Enterprise					
Below 10 years	—	26 (8.70)	52 (17.39)	109 (36.45)	112 (37.46)
Above 10 years	5 (3.31)	15 (9.93)	39 (25.83)	52 (34.44)	40 (26.49)
Chi-square = 17.288; df = 4; Significant at 1 per cent level					

managing business on joint basis face this problem to some extent. Only 15 per cent of women entrepreneurs managing business on individual basis face this problem to some extent. It may be due to small scale nature of business. The value of chi-square is statistically significant at 1 per cent level of significance. Only small proportion of women entrepreneurs investing money upto Rs. 3 lacs in business face this problem to a large extent. 63 per cent women entrepreneurs investing more than Rs. 10 lacs in business face this problem to little extent. The value of chi-square is statistically significant at 1 per cent level of significance. Women entrepreneurs earning lower level of income face jobs problem more than women entrepreneurs earning higher level of income. It shows that availability of finance helps women entrepreneurs in taking the services of experts. The value of chi-square is statistically significant at 1 per cent level of significance. Less than 12 per cent women entrepreneurs irrespective of their level of training face this problem to a large extent. 24 per cent untrained women entrepreneurs face this problem to some extent. It may be due to lack of knowledge to maintain records. The value of chi-square is statistically insignificant. Women entrepreneurs who are dependent on informal sources of finance face this problem relatively more as compared to other women entrepreneurs. The value of chi-square is statistically insignificant. Women entrepreneurs having enterprises more than 10 years old face this problem more than women entrepreneurs possessing enterprises less than 10 years old. The value of chi-square is statistically significant at 1 per cent level of significance. It reveals that age of enterprises affects the cost of maintenance of records of business.

Table 6.25 shows that only one-fifth women entrepreneurs are facing the problem of inventory management to a large extent and another one-third to some extent. Information vividly reveals that inventory management is no longer a problem for women entrepreneurs. It may be due to easy availability of inputs and other related services. Women entrepreneurs possessing lower level of education face this problem more than women entrepreneurs having higher level of education. It may be due to lack of expertise in inventory management or paucity of resources to keep advance inventory for business. The value of chi-square is statistically insignificant. Women entrepreneurs belonging to lower age group face this problem relatively less than other women entrepreneurs. It may be due to better management practices adopted by younger generation of women entrepreneurs. The value of chi-square is statistically significant at 1 per cent level of significance. Less than 20 per cent women entrepreneurs hailing from joint and nuclear families and also from rural and urban areas face this problem to a large extent. The value of chi-square is statistically insignificant. Almost same proportion of women entrepreneurs doing business under individual and other forms of business organizations face this problem to a large extent but this problem to some extent has been faced relatively more by women entrepreneurs managing business on large scale. The value of chi-square is statistically significant at 1 per cent level of significance. It shows that these two variables are positively

TABLE 6.25

Extent of Problem of Inventory Management Faced by Women Entrepreneurs

Group	To great extent	To large extent	To some extent	To little extent	Not at all
1	2	3	4	5	6
All Data	15 (3.33)	74 (16.44)	138 (30.67)	163 (36.22)	60 (13.33)
Education					
Primary	—	8 (33.33)	9 (37.50)	4 (16.67)	3 (12.50)
Matric	2 (2.50)	17 (21.25)	29 (36.25)	20 (25.00)	12 (15.00)
Graduate	9 (4.79)	25 (13.30)	53 (28.19)	71 (37.77)	30 (15.96)
Post Graduate	4 (2.53)	24 (15.19)	47 (29.75)	68 (43.04)	15 (9.49)
Chi-square = 20.993; df = 12; Insignificant					
Age (years)					
Below 30	1 (0.71)	10 (7.09)	39 (27.66)	61 (43.26)	30 (21.28)
30-40	5 (3.27)	27 (17.65)	53 (34.64)	54 (35.29)	14 (9.15)
Above 40	9 (5.77)	37 (23.72)	46 (29.49)	48 (30.77)	16 (10.26)
Chi-square = 32.653; df = 8; Significant at 1 per cent level					
Place of Origin					
Rural	2 (2.30)	13 (14.94)	25 (28.74)	29 (33.33)	18 (20.69)
Urban	13 (3.58)	61 (16.80)	113 (31.13)	134 (36.91)	42 (11.57)
Chi-square = 5.251; df = 4; Insignificant					
Type of Family					
Joint	9 (4.31)	37 (17.70)	58 (27.75)	74 (35.41)	31 (14.83)
Nuclear	6 (2.49)	37 (15.35)	80 (33.20)	89 (36.93)	29 (12.03)
Chi-square = 3.295; df = 4; Insignificant					
Form of Business Organization					
Sole	13 (4.21)	50 (16.18)	81 (26.21)	124 (40.13)	41 (13.27)
Others	2 (1.42)	24 (17.02)	57 (40.43)	39 (27.66)	19 (13.48)
Chi-square = 12.837; df = 4; Significant at 1 per cent level					
Investment (Lacs)					
<1	6 (4.88)	29 (23.58)	27 (21.95)	49 (39.84)	12 (9.76)
1-2	7 (4.86)	25 (17.36)	51 (35.42)	47 (32.64)	14 (9.72)
2-3	—	13 (16.88)	30 (38.96)	24 (31.17)	10 (12.99)
3-5	2 (3.12)	5 (7.81)	16 (25.00)	25 (39.06)	16 (25.00)

(Contd.)

1	2	3	4	5	6
5-10	—	2 (6.45)	10 (32.26)	11 (35.48)	8 (25.81)
Above 10	—	—	4 (36.36)	7 (63.64)	—

Chi-square = 41.128; df = 20; Significant at 1 per cent level

Income (Rs.)

<7500	10 (18.52)	14 (25.93)	13 (24.07)	9 (16.67)	8 (14.81)
7500-10000	3 (1.99)	24 (15.89)	42 (27.81)	60 (39.74)	22 (14.57)
10000-15000	2 (2.06)	23 (23.71)	25 (25.77)	40 (41.24)	7 (7.22)
15000-20000	—	13 (13.00)	37 (37.00)	29 (29.00)	21 (21.00)
20000+	—	—	21 (43.75)	25 (52.08)	2 (4.17)

Chi-square = 86.281; df = 16; Significant at 1 per cent level

Training

Got Training	7 (2.98)	25 (10.64)	74 (31.49)	96 (40.85)	33 (14.04)
No Training	8 (3.72)	49 (22.79)	64 (29.77)	67 (31.16)	27 (12.56)

Chi-square = 13.472; df = 4; Significant at 1 per cent level

Sources of Finance

Formal	2 (1.67)	7 (5.83)	41 (34.17)	48 (40.00)	22 (18.33)
Informal	13 (3.94)	67 (20.30)	97 (29.39)	115 (34.85)	38 (11.52)

Chi-square = 16.934; df = 4; Significant at 1 per cent level

Age of Enterprise

Below 10 years	10 (3.34)	40 (13.38)	97 (32.44)	111 (37.12)	41 (13.71)
Above 10 years	5 (3.31)	34 (22.52)	41 (27.15)	52 (34.44)	19 (12.58)

Chi-square = 6.307; df = 4; Insignificant

associated. Women entrepreneurs investing money upto Rs. 2 lacs in business face this problem relatively more than women entrepreneurs investing more than Rs. 2 lacs in business. It may be due to financial constraints to maintain adequate inventory. The value of chi-square is statistically significant at 1 per cent level of significance. Women entrepreneurs earning lower and moderate level of income face this problem more than women entrepreneurs earning higher level of income. It shows that more income helps in reducing the problem of inventory management to a large extent. The value of chi-square further corroborates our findings. Untrained women entrepreneurs (26 per cent) face this problem relatively more as compared to trained women entrepreneurs (13 per cent). It projects that training helps in reducing the problem of inventory management in business. The value of chi-square is statistically significant at 1 per cent level of significance. Women entrepreneurs using other than formal sources of finance face this problem more intensively. It reveals that availability of finance helps in reducing the problem to a large extent. The value of chi-square is statistically significant at 1 per cent level of significance. It shows that these two variables vary significantly. Women entrepreneurs having enterprises more than 10 years old face this problem more than women entrepreneurs possessing enterprises less than 10 years old. It shows that these women entrepreneurs might be managing their enterprises on traditional lines and consequently face the problem of inventory management.

Table 6.26 shows that 28 per cent women entrepreneurs face the problem of infrastructure to a large extent and 42 per cent to some extent. Information highlights that infrastructure bottlenecks affect the business operations. One-third women entrepreneurs possessing matric and graduate level of education face the infrastructure problem to a great extent than other women entrepreneurs. But almost same proportion of women entrepreneurs possessing different levels of education face this problem to some extent. The value of chi-square is statistically insignificant. Around one-third women entrepreneurs in the age group of more than 30 face this problem to a large extent. It shows that women entrepreneurs in lower age group might be having resources to overcome these constraints. The value of chi-square is statistically insignificant. Women entrepreneurs hailing from urban areas face this problem relatively more than women entrepreneurs coming from rural areas. It shows that women entrepreneurs from urban areas may need more infrastructural facilities due to different management practices used by them. The value of chi-square is statistically insignificant. One-third women entrepreneurs coming from joint families face this problem to a large extent than women entrepreneurs coming from nuclear families. On the other hand, 37 per cent of women entrepreneurs coming from nuclear families face this problem to some extent. The value of chi-square is statistically insignificant. Women entrepreneurs managing business under other than individual forms of business organization face this problem more than their counterparts managing business on individual basis. The value

TABLE 6.26

Extent of Problem of Infrastructural Constrains Faced by Women Entrepreneurs

Group	To great extent	To large extent	To some extent	To little extent	Not at all
1	2	3	4	5	6
All Data	17 (3.78)	111 (24.67)	190 (42.22)	109 (24.22)	23 (5.11)
Education					
Primary	—	6 (25.00)	10 (41.67)	7 (29.17)	1 (4.17)
Matric	2 (2.50)	26 (32.50)	34 (42.50)	14 (17.50)	4 (5.00)
Graduate	11 (5.85)	48 (25.53)	75 (39.89)	44 (23.40)	10 (5.32)
Post Graduate	4 (2.53)	31 (19.62)	71 (44.94)	44 (27.85)	8 (5.06)
Chi-square = 10.945; df = 12; Insignificant					
Age (years)					
Below 30	4 (2.84)	26 (18.44)	60 (42.55)	41 (29,08)	10 (7.09)
30-40	8 (5.23)	39 (25.49)	66 (43.14)	30 (19.61)	10 (6.54)
Above 40	5 (3.21)	46 (29.49)	64 (41.03)	38 (24.36)	3 (1.92)
Chi-square = 12.645; df = 8; Insignificant					
Place of Origin					
Rural	2 (2.30)	19 (21.84)	35 (40.23)	30 (34.48)	1 (1.15)
Urban	15 (4.13)	92 (25.34)	155 (42.70)	79 (21.76)	22 (6.06)
Chi-square = 9.075; df = 4; Insignificant					
Type of Family					
Joint	10 (4.78)	58 (27.75)	79 (37.80)	55 (26.32)	7 (3.35)
Nuclear	7 (2.90)	53 (21.99)	111 (46.06)	54 (22.41)	16 (6.64)
Chi-square = 7.437; df = 4; Insignificant					
Form of Business Organization					
Sole	13 (4.21)	66 (21.36)	133 (43.04)	82 (26.54)	15 (4.85)
Others	4 (2.84)	45 (31.91)	57 (40.43)	27 (19.15)	8 (5.67)
Chi-square = 7.321; df = 4; Insignificant					
Investment (Lacs)					
<1	11 (8.94)	24 (19.51)	48 (39.02)	38 (30.89)	2 (1.63)
1-2	4 (2.78)	29 (20.14)	71 (49.31)	36 (25.00)	4 (2.78)
2-3	—	18 (23.38)	34 (44.16)	22 (28.57)	3 (3.90)
3-5	2 (3.12)	23 (35.94)	22 (34.38)	6 (9.38)	11 (17.19)

1	2	3	4	5	6
5-10	—	13 (41.94)	10 (32.26)	5 (16.13)	3 (9.68)
Above 10	—	4 (36.36)	5 (45.45)	2 (18.18)	—
Chi-square = 62.124; df = 20; Significant at 1 per cent level					

Income (Rs.)					
<7500	10 (18.52)	15 (27.78)	17 (31.48)	8 (14.81)	4 (7.41)
7500-10000	5 (3.31)	28 (18.54)	75 (49.67)	37 (24.50)	6 (3.97)
10000-15000	2 (2.06)	19 (19.59)	48 (49.48)	26 (26.80)	2 (2.06)
15000-20000	—	28 (28.00)	33 (33.00)	30 (30.00)	9 (9.00)
20000+	—	21 (43.75)	17 (35.42)	8 (16.67)	2 (4.17)
Chi-square = 66.265; df = 16; Significant at 1 per cent level					

Training					
Got Training	10 (4.26)	54 (22.98)	85 (36.17)	70 (29.79)	16 (6.81)
No Training	7 (3.26)	57 (26.51)	105 (48.84)	39 (18.14)	7 (3.26)
Chi-square = 14.193; df = 4; Significant at 1 per cent level					

Sources of Finance					
Formal	—	36 (30.00)	54 (45.00)	14 (11.67)	16 (13.33)
Informal	17 (5.15)	75 (22.73)	136 (41.21)	95 (28.79)	7 (2.12)
Chi-square = 40.662; df = 4; Significant at 1 per cent level					

Age of Enterprise					
Below 10 years	9 (3.01)	62 (20.74)	128 (42.81)	80 (26.76)	20 (6.69)
Above 10 years	8 (5.30)	49 (32.45)	62 (41.06)	29 (19.21)	3 (1.99)
Chi-square = 13.747; df = 4; Significant at 1 per cent level					

of chi-square is statistically insignificant. Women entrepreneurs investing even more money in business face this problem. It shows that large business needs more infrastructural facilities. The value of chi-square is statistically significant at 1 per cent level of significance. It reveals that these two variables vary significantly. Similarly, women entrepreneurs earning higher level of income also face this problem. It shows that women entrepreneurs earning higher level of income needs better facilities to face the intensive competition in the free markets. The value of chi-square is statistically significant at 1 per cent level of significance. Untrained women entrepreneurs face this problem slightly on higher side than trained women entrepreneurs. It reveals that trained women entrepreneurs try to find alternatives to infrastructure facilities.

The value of chi-square is statistically significant at 1 per cent level of significance. Almost same proportion of women entrepreneurs using formal and informal sources of finance face this problem to a large extent. The value of chi-square is statistically significant at 1 per cent level of significance. 38 per cent of women entrepreneurs having enterprises more than 10 years old face this problem to a large extent, whereas this proportion is 23 per cent in case of women entrepreneurs having enterprises less than 10 years old. It seems that women entrepreneurs in former case might be using traditional methods of management and in this process, they face this problem. The value of chi-square is statistically significant at 1 per cent level of significance.

Table 6.27 shows that 40 per cent of women entrepreneurs face the problem of high cost of land and 37 per cent to some extent. Education wise information further shows that women entrepreneurs having different levels of education face the problem of high cost of land. It seems that educated women entrepreneurs prefer to locate their business at better place and in this process they face this problem. The value of chi-square is statistically insignificant. 35 per cent to 42 per cent of women entrepreneurs in all age groups face the problem of high cost of land. The value of chi-square is statistically significant at 1 per cent level of significance. Women entrepreneurs hailing from urban areas face this problem relatively more than women entrepreneurs hailing from rural areas. The reason being, women entrepreneurs in rural areas might be having easy availability of land. The value of chi-square is statistically insignificant. Women entrepreneurs hailing from joint families (45 per cent) face this problem relatively more than women entrepreneurs coming from nuclear families (35 per cent). The reason to this may be assigned to the use of joint resources. The value of chi-square is statistically significant at 5 per cent level of significance. It shows that these two variables are positively associated. Almost same proportion of women entrepreneurs managing business under different forms of business organizations face this problem to a large extent. The value of chi-square is statistically significant at 1 per cent level of significance. It shows that these two variables vary significantly. Women entrepreneurs investing more money in business do not face this problem more intensively. It shows that availability of money helps in solving the problem of land. The value of chi-

TABLE 6.27

Extent of Problem of High Cost of Land Faced by Women Entrepreneurs

Group	To great extent	To large extent	To some extent	To little extent	Not at all
1	2	3	4	5	6
All Data	42 (9.33)	137 (30.44)	169 (37.56)	73 (16.22)	29 (6.44)
Education					
Primary	1 (4.17)	10 (41.67)	5 (20.83)	7 (29.17)	1 (4.17)
Matric	6 (7.50)	31 (38.75)	33 (41.25)	8 (10.00)	2 (2.50)
Graduate	18 (9.57)	50 (26.60)	74 (39.36)	27 (14.36)	19 (10.11)
Post Graduate	17 (10.76)	46 (29.11)	57 (36.08)	31 (19.62)	7 (4.43)
Chi-square = 20.421; df = 12; Insignificant					
Age (years)					
Below 30	10 (7.09)	40 (28.37)	63 (44.68)	14 (9.93)	14 (9.93)
30-40	21 (13.73)	42 (27.45)	48 (31.37)	32 (20.92)	10 (6.54)
Above 40	11 (7.05)	55 (35.26)	58 (37.18)	27 (17.31)	5 (3.21)
Chi-square = 20.929; df = 8; Significant at 1 per cent level					
Place of Origin					
Rural	8 (9.20)	20 (22.99)	33 (37.93)	22 (25.29)	4 (4.60)
Urban	34 (9.37)	117 (32.23)	136 (37.47)	51 (14.05)	25 (6.89)
Chi-square = 8.010; df = 4; Insignificant					
Type of Family					
Joint	16 (7.66)	78 (37.32)	67 (32.06)	36 (17.22)	12 (5.74)
Nuclear	26 (10.79)	59 (24.48)	102 (42.32)	37 (15.35)	17 (7.05)
Chi-square = 10.920; df = 4; Significant at 5 per cent level					
Form of Business Organization					
Sole	39 (12.62)	81 (26.21)	116 (37.54)	53 (17.15)	20 (6.47)
Others	3 (2.13)	56 (39.72)	53 (37.59)	20 (14.18)	9 (6.38)
Chi-square = 17.748; df = 4; Significant at 1 per cent level					
Investment (Lacs)					
<1	21 (17.07)	44 (35.77)	35 (28.46)	13 (10.57)	10 (8.13)
1-2	12 (8.33)	30 (20.83)	61 (42.36)	39 (27.08)	2 (1.39)
2-3	3 (3.90)	34 (44.16)	26 (33.77)	11 (14.29)	3 (3.90)
3-5	5 (7.81)	21 (32.81)	22 (34.38)	5 (7.81)	11 (17.19)

(Contd.)

1	2	3	4	5	6
5-10	1 (3.23)	8 (25.81)	16 (51.61)	3 (9.68)	3 (9.68)
Above 10	—	—	9 (81.82)	2 (18.18)	—

Chi-square = 74.713; df = 20; Significant at 1 per cent level

Income (Rs.)

<7500	13 (24.07)	22 (40.74)	13 (24.07)	1 (1.85)	5 (9.26)
7500-10000	12 (7.95)	36 (23.84)	67 (44.37)	24 (15.89)	12 (7.95)
10000-15000	7 (7.22)	30 (30.93)	33 (34.02)	25 (25.77)	2 (2.06)
15000-20000	4 (4.00)	33 (33.00)	36 (36.00)	19 (19.00)	8 (8.00)
20000+	6 (12.50)	16 (33.33)	20 (41.67)	4 (8.33)	2 (4.17)

Chi-square = 45.894; df = 16; Significant at 1 per cent level

Training

Got Training	26 (11.06)	84 (35.74)	80 (34.04)	29 (12.34)	16 (6.81)
No Training	16 (7.44)	53 (24.65)	8(,41.40)	44 (20.47)	13 (6.05)

Chi-square = 12.403; df = 4; Significant at 1 per cent level

Sources of Finance

Formal ·	14 (11.67)	24 (20.00)	56 (46.67)	11 (9.17)	15 (12.50)
Informal	28 (8.48)	113 (34.24)	113 (34.24)	62 (18.79)	14 (4.24)

Chi-square = 24.767; df = 4; Significant at 1 per cent level

Age of Enterprise

Below 10 years	27 (9.03)	91 (30.43)	111 (37.12)	45 (15.05)	25 (8.36)
Above 10 years	15 (9.93)	46 (30.46)	58 (38.41)	28 (18.54)	4 (2.65)

Chi-square = 5.967; df = 4; Insignificant

square is statistically significant at 1 per cent level of significance. 64 per cent women entrepreneurs earning less than Rs. 7500 per month face the problem of high cost of land and 45 per cent women entrepreneurs earning more than Rs. 20,000 per month also face this problem. The value of chi-square is statistically significant at 1 per cent level of significance. Trained women entrepreneurs (47 per cent) face this problem more than their untrained counterparts (32 per cent). It seems that trained women entrepreneurs want better location of enterprise. The value of chi-square is statistically significant at 1 per cent level of significance. Women entrepreneurs using informal sources of finance agree with this statement more than other women entrepreneurs. The value of chi-square is statistically significant at 1 per cent level of significance. Almost same proportion of women entrepreneurs irrespective of life of their enterprises agree with this statement. The value of chi-square is statistically insignificant. Table 6.28 shows that 42 per cent women entrepreneurs face the problem of better technology to a great extent and another 36 per cent to some extent. It shows that availability of better technology is a problem for small and micro-level enterprises. Women entrepreneurs possessing low level of education face this problem more than women entrepreneurs possessing higher level of education. The reason to this may be attributed to lack of awareness or financial constrains among women entrepreneurs in former case. Efforts should be made to make available better technology to these enterprises by various agencies. The value of chi-square is statistically significant at 1 per cent level of significance. Women entrepreneurs in higher age group face this problem more than other women entrepreneurs. The value of chi-square is statistically significant at 1 per cent level of significance. Women entrepreneurs (46 per cent) hailing from rural areas face this problem slightly on higher side than other women entrepreneurs (41 per cent). It seems that problem of availability of technology is a problem for women entrepreneurs irrespective of place of their origin. The value of chi-square is statistically insignificant. Women entrepreneurs (50 per cent) coming from joint families face this problem relatively more as compared to women entrepreneurs (36 per cent) coming from nuclear families. The value of chi-square is statistically significant at 1 per cent level of significance. 48 per cent women entrepreneurs managing business under other than individual forms of business organizations face this problem to a large extent, whereas this ratio is 39 per cent in case of women entrepreneurs managing business on individual basis. The value of chi-square is statistically significant at 1 per cent level of significance. 50 per cent to 45 per cent women entrepreneurs investing money in the range of Rs. 3-5 lacs, 5-10 lacs and less than 1 lac face the problem of availability of better technology to a large extent. It seems that problem of availability of better technology is not only confined to women entrepreneurs investing less money in business. The value of chi-square is statistically significant at 1 per cent level of significance. More than 50 per cent women entrepreneurs earning lower and higher level of income face this problem more than other women entrepreneurs.

TABLE 6.28

Upto what Extent Women Entrepreneurs Face the Problem of Better Technology

Group	To great extent	To large extent	To some extent	To little extent	Not at all
1	2	3	4	5	6
All Data	18 (4.00)	173 (38.44)	163 (36.22)	51 (11.33)	45 (10.00)
Education					
Primary	2 (8.33)	13 (54.17)	8 (33.33)	—	1 (4.17)
Matric	3 (3.75)	46 (57.50)	23 (28.75)	6 (7.50)	2 (2.50)
Graduate	10 (5.32)	59 (31.38)	74 (39.36)	19 (10.11)	26 (13.83)
Post Graduate	3 (1.90)	55 (34.81)	58 (36.71)	26 (16.46)	16 (10.13)

Chi-square = 33.334; df = 12; Significant at 1 per cent level

Age (years)					
Below 30	4 (2.84)	36 (25.53)	62 (43.97)	17 (12.06)	22 (15.60)
30-40	9 (5.88)	65 (42.48)	48 (31.37)	12 (7.84)	19 (12.42)
Above 40	5 (3.21)	72 (46.15)	53 (33.97)	22 (14.10)	4 (2.56)

Chi-square = 31.515; df = 8; Significant at 1 per cent level

Place of Origin					
Rural	2 (2.30)	38 (43.68)	25 (28.74)	14 (16.09)	8 (9.20)
Urban	16 (4.41)	135 (37.19)	138 (38.02)	37 (10.19)	37 (10.19)

Chi-square = 5.442; df = 4; Insignificant

Type of Family					
Joint	12 (5.74)	93 (44.50)	66 (31.58)	26 (12.44)	12 (5.74)
Nuclear	6 (2.49)	80 (33.20)	97 (40.25)	25 (10.37)	33 (13.69)

Chi-square = 16.500; df = 4; Significant at 1 per cent level

Form of Business Organization					
Sole	18 (5.83)	105 (33.98)	120 (38.83)	33 (10.68)	33 (10.68)
Others	—	68 (48.23)	43 (30.50)	18 (12.77)	12 (8.51)

Chi-square = 16.011; df = 4; Significant at 1 per cent level

Investment (Lacs)					
<1	7 (5.69)	50 (40.65)	41 (33.33)	9 (7.32)	16 (13.01)
1-2	8 (5.56)	53 (36.81)	58 (40.28)	18 (12.50)	7 (4.86)
2-3	2 (2.60)	25 (32.47)	30 (38.96)	14 (18.18)	6 (7.79)
3-5	—	32 (50.00)	16 (25.00)	5 (7.81)	11 (17.19)

1	2	3	4	5	6
5-10	1 (3.23)	13 (41.94)	9 (29.03)	3 (9.68)	5 (16.13)
Above 10	—	—	9 (81.82)	2 (18.18)	—

Chi-square = 39.978; df = 20; Significant at 1 per cent level

Income (Rs.)

<7500	7 (12.96)	25 (46.30)	12 (22.22)	4 (7.41)	6 (11.11)
7500-10000	3 (1.99)	61 (40.40)	57 (37.75)	14 (9.27)	16 (10.60)
10000-15000	5 (5.15)	32 (32.99)	41 (42.27)	13 (13.40)	6 (6.19)
15000-20000	2 (2.00)	31 (31.00)	34 (34.00)	18 (18.00)	15 (15.00)
20000+	1 (2.08)	24 (50.00)	19 (39.58)	2 (4.17)	2 (4.17)

Chi-square = 36.727; df = 16; Significant at 1 per cent level

Training

Got Training	10 (4.26)	91 (38.72)	90 (38.30)	15 (6.38)	29 (12.34)
No Training	8 (3.72)	82 (38.14)	73 (33.95)	36 (16.74)	16 (7.44)

Chi-square = 14.005; df = 4; Significant at 1 per cent level

Sources of Finance

Formal	—	46 (38.33)	48 (40.00)	5 (4.17)	21 (17.50)
Informal	18 (5.45)	127 (38.48)	115 (34.85)	46 (13.94)	24 (7.27)

Chi-square = 23.811; df = 4; Significant at 1 per cent level

Age of Enterprise

Below 10 years	9 (3.01)	104 (34.78)	111 (37.12)	39 (13.04)	36 (12.04)
Above 10 years	9 (5.96)	69 (45.70)	52 (34.44)	12 (7.95)	9 (5.96)

Chi-square = 11.499; df = 4; Significant at 5 per cent level

The value of chi-square is statistically significant at 1 per cent level of significance. Almost same proportion of trained and untrained women entrepreneurs face this problem to a large extent. The value of chi-square is statistically significant at 1 per cent level of significance. Women entrepreneurs (44 per cent) using informal sources of finance face this problem more than other women entrepreneurs (38 per cent). It shows that availability of finance at low cost might be preventing women entrepreneurs in former case to adopt better technology. The value of chi-square is statistically significant at 1 per cent level of significance. Women entrepreneurs (51 per cent) who have been in business for a longer period of time face this problem relatively more than other women entrepreneurs (38 per cent). It seems that availability of better technology is out of reach of women entrepreneurs in former case. The value of chi-square is statistically significant at 5 per cent level of significance.

Table 6.29 shows that one-fourth women entrepreneurs face the problem of time management in business. It may be due to dual role performed by them and lack of guidance related to time management techniques to be used in business. 42 per cent women entrepreneurs face this problem to some extent. Information clearly shows that time management is a problem for women entrepreneurs. Education-wise information further highlights that less educated women entrepreneurs face this problem more than other women entrepreneurs. It may be due to lack of training in the area of time management. In the era of intensive competition women entrepreneurs have to spend more time in business. On the other hand, educated women entrepreneurs face this problem less intensively due to better time management practices used by them. The value of chi-square is statistically significant at 1 per cent level of significance. It shows that these two variables vary significantly. Women entrepreneurs in lower age group face this problem less than women entrepreneurs in middle and higher age groups. It may be due to less responsibilities and more exposure of knowledge. The value of chi-square is statistically significant at 1 per cent level of significance. Women entrepreneurs coming from rural areas face this problem slightly on higher side as compared to their urban counterparts. It shows that problem of time management is felt more by women entrepreneurs in the former case. It may be due to lack of knowledge of various techniques of management. The value of chi-square is statistically insignificant. Women entrepreneurs coming from joint families face this problem more intensively as compared to women entrepreneurs belonging to nuclear families. It may be due to less responsibilities among women entrepreneurs in the latter case. The value of chi-square is statistically significant at 1 per cent level of significance. Women entrepreneurs managing business under other than individual forms of business organizations face this problem more than women entrepreneurs managing business on individual basis. The value of chi-square is statistically significant at 1 per cent level of significance. Women entrepreneurs investing more money in business face this problem less as compared to women

TABLE 6.29

Extent of Problem of Time Management Faced by Women Entrepreneurs

Group	To great extent	To large extent	To some extent	To little extent	Not at all
1	2	3	4	5	6
All Data	22 (4.89)	87 (19.33)	188 (41.78)	108 (24.00)	45 (10.00)
Education					
Primary	2 (8.33)	6 (25.00)	11 (45.83)	4 (16.67)	1 (4.17)
Matric	5 (6.25)	26 (32.50)	34 (42.50)	10 (12.50)	5 (6.25)
Graduate	13 (6.91)	33 (17.55)	74 (39.36)	50 (26.60)	18 (9.57)
Post Graduate	2 (1.27)	22 (13.92)	69 (43.67)	44 (27.85)	21 (13.29)
Chi-square = 27.616; df = 12; Significant at 1 per cent level					
Age (years)					
Below 30	4 (2.84)	9 (6.38)	59 (41.84)	44 (31.21)	25 (17.73)
30-40	10 (6.54)	37 (24.18)	60 (39.22)	33 (21.57)	13 (8.50)
Above 40	8 (5.13)	41 (26.28)	69 (44.23)	31 (19.87)	7 (4.49)
Chi-square = 38.584; df = 8; Significant at 1 per cent level					
Place of Origin					
Rural	5 (5.75)	18 (20.69)	37 (42.53)	19 (21.84)	8 (9.20)
Urban	17 (4.68)	69 (19.01)	151 (41.60)	89 (24.52)	37 (10.19)
Chi-square = 0.559; df = 4; Insignificant					
Type of Family					
Joint	14 (6.70)	57 (27.27)	78 (37.32)	43 (20.57)	17 (8.13)
Nuclear	8 (3.32)	30 (12.45)	110 (45.64)	65 (26.97)	28 (11.62)
Chi-square = 20.461; df = 4; Significant at 1 per cent level					
Form of Business Organization					
Sole	20 (6.47)	44 (14.24)	129 (41.75)	83 (26.86)	33 (10.68)
Others	2 (1.42)	43 (30.50)	59 (41.84)	25 (17.73)	12 (8.51)
Chi-square = 22.113; df = 4; Significant at 1 per cent level					
Investment (Lacs)					
<1	10 (8.13)	30 (24.39)	34 (27.64)	38 (30.89)	11 (8.94)
1-2	11 (7.64)	24 (16.67)	71 (49.31)	29 (20.14)	9 (6.25)
2-3	—	13 (16.88)	39 (50.65)	22 (28.57)	3 (3.90)
3-5	—	11 (17.19)	27 (42.19)	7 (10.94)	19 (29.69)

(Contd.)

1	2	3	4	5	6
5-10	1 (3.23)	7 (22.58)	9 (29.03)	11 (35.48)	3 (9.68)
Above 10	—	2 (18.18)	8 (72.73)	1 (9.09)	—

Chi-square = 70.432; df = 20; Significant at 1 per cent level

Income (Rs.)

<7500	6 (11.11)	12 (22.22)	21 (38.89)	9 (16.67)	6 (11.11)
7500-10000	5 (3.31)	28 (18.54)	56 (37.09)	44 (29.14)	18 (11.92)
10000-15000	11 (11.34)	22 (22.68)	42 (43.30)	20 (20.62)	2 (2.06)
15000-20000	—	13 (13.00)	43 (43.00)	27 (27.00)	17 (17.00)
20000+	—	12 (25.00)	26 (54.17)	8 (16.67)	2 (4.17)

Chi-square = 45.064; df = 16; Significant at 1 per cent level

Training

Got Training	8 (3.40)	39 (16.60)	100 (42.55)	63 (26.81)	25 (10.64)
No Training	14 (6.51)	48 (22.33)	88 (40.93)	45 (20.93)	20 (9.30)

Chi-square = 6.012; df = 4; Insignificant

Sources of Finance

Formal	1 (0.83)	16 (13.33)	62 (51.67)	21 (17.50)	20 (16.67)
Informal	21 (6.36)	71 (21.52)	126 (38.18)	87 (26.36)	25 (7.58)

Chi-square = 22.536; df = 4; Significant at 1 per cent level

Age of Enterprise

Below 10 years	13 (4.35)	49 (16.39)	118 (39.46)	84 (28.09)	35 (11.71)
Above 10 years	9 (5.96)	38 (25.17)	70 (46.36)	24 (15.89)	10 (6.62)

Chi-square = 14.487; df = 4; Significant at 1 per cent level

entrepreneurs investing less money in business. It may be due to hiring of services of various experts, women entrepreneurs may be able to manage their time effectively. The value of chi-square is statistically significant at 1 per cent level of significance. Women entrepreneurs earning lower and moderate level of income face this problem relatively more than women entrepreneurs earning higher level of income. It seems that availability of money enable the women entrepreneurs to shift various responsibilities to hired persons. The value of chi-square is statistically significant at 1 per cent level of significance. Untrained women entrepreneurs (29 per cent) face the problem of time management more than trained women entrepreneurs (20 per cent). The reason to this may be attributed to learning of various techniques of time management by trained women entrepreneurs during training period. The value of chi-square is statistically insignificant. Women entrepreneurs using informal sources of finance face this problem relatively more as compared to women entrepreneurs using formal sources of finance. It seems that availability of finance at low cost helps the women entrepreneurs in overcoming the problem of time management. The value of chi-square is statistically significant at 1 per cent level of significance. 31 per cent women entrepreneurs having enterprises more than 10 years old face this problem to a large extent, whereas this ratio is 21 per cent in case of women entrepreneurs having enterprises less than 10 years old. It may be due to difference in various techniques of management used by women entrepreneurs in the latter case. The value of chi-square is statistically significant at 1 per cent level of significance.

Table 6.30 shows that 26 per cent women entrepreneurs face the problem of fulfilment of legal formalities in business and another one-third face this problem to some extent. It shows that women entrepreneurs in small and micro enterprises still face the problem of legal formalities in business. It may be due to lack of awareness and difficulty in understanding various legal processes. Education-wise information further shows that women entrepreneurs possessing lower level of education face this problem more than women entrepreneurs possessing higher level of education. It shows that education helps in solving various problems faced by women entrepreneurs in the latter case. The value of chi-square is statistically insignificant. Women entrepreneurs in lower age groups face this problem less as compared to women entrepreneurs in other age groups. It shows that women entrepreneurs in the former case may possess better knowledge of business laws. The value of chi-square is statistically significant at 1 per cent level of significance. It shows that these two variables vary significantly. Women entrepreneurs hailing from rural areas face this problems more than their counterparts coming from urban areas. It may be due to easy availability of various sources to complete legal formalities among women entrepreneurs in latter case. The value of chi-square is statistically significant at 1 per cent level of significance. 29 per cent women entrepreneurs hailing from joint families and 25 per cent from nuclear families face this problem to a large extent.

TABLE 6.30

Extent of Problem of Legal Formalities Faced by Women Entrepreneurs

Group	To great extent	To large extent	To some extent	To little extent	Not at all
1	2	3	4	5	6
All Data	31 (6.89)	89 (19.78)	147 (32.67)	107 (23.78)	76 (16.89)
Education					
Primary	2 (8.33)	9 (37.50)	8 (33.33)	2 (8.33)	3 (12.50)
Matric	7 (8.75)	23 (28.75)	21 (26.25)	18 (22.50)	11 (13.75)
Graduate	11 (5.85)	26 (13.83)	67 (35.64)	44 (23.40)	40 (21.28)
Post Graduate	11 (6.96)	31 (19.62)	51 (32.28)	43 (27.22)	22 (13.92)
Chi-square = 19.694; df = 12; Insignificant					
Age (years)					
Below 30	9 (6.38)	19 (13.48)	55 (39.01)	38 (25.95)	20 (14.18)
30-40	19 (12.42)	29 (18.95)	37 (24.18)	38 (24.84)	30 (19.61)
Above 40	3 (1.92)	41 (26.28)	55 (35.26)	31 (19.87)	26 (16.67)
Chi-square = 27.030; df = 8; Significant and 1 per cent level					
Place of Origin					
Rural	4 (4.60)	22 (25.29)	41 (47.13)	13 (14.94)	7 (8.05)
Urban	27 (7.44)	67 (18.46)	106 (29.30)	94 (25.90)	69 (19.01)
Chi-square = 17.915; df = 4; Significant and 1 per cent level					
Type of Family					
Joint	16 (7.66)	44 (21.05)	74 (35.41)	46 (22.01)	29 (13.88)
Nuclear	15 (6.22)	45 (18.67)	73 (30.29)	61 (25.31)	47 (19.50)
Chi-square = 4.162; df = 4; Insignificant					
Form of Business Organization					
Sole	22 (7.12)	56 (18.12)	99 (32.04)	81 (26.21)	51 (16.50)
Others	9 (6.38)	33 (23.40)	48 (34.04)	26 (18.44)	25 (17.73)
Chi-square = 4.108; df = 4; Insignificant					
Investment (Lacs)					
<1	19 (15.45)	18 (14.63)	33 (26.83)	29 (23.58)	24 (19.51)
1-2	2 (1.39)	43 (29.86)	52 (36.11)	38 (26.39)	9 (6.25)
2-3	6 (7.79)	14 (18.18)	31 (40.26)	15 (19.48)	11 (14.29)
3-5	3 (4.69)	6 (9.38)	17 (26.56)	15 (23.44)	23 (35.94)

1	2	3	4	5	6
5-10	1 (3.23)	8 (25.81)	7 (22.58)	7 (22.58)	8 (25.81)
Above 10	—	—	7 (63.64)	3 (27.27)	1 (9.09)

Chi-square = 71.946; df = 20; Significant and 1 per cent level

Income (Rs.)

<7500	3 (5.56)	4 (7.41)	12 (22.22)	16 (29.63)	19 (35.19)
7500-10000	14 (9.27)	33 (21.85)	50 (33.11)	35 (23.18)	19 (12.58)
10000-15000	5 (5.15)	28 (28.87)	20 (20.62)	32 (32.99)	12 (12.37)
15000-20000	2 (2.00)	9 (9.00)	53 (53.00)	18 (18.00)	18 (18.00)
20000+	7 (14.58)	15 (31.25)	12 (25.00)	6 (12.50)	8 (16.67)

Chi-square = 68.512; df = 16; Significant and 1 per cent level

Training

Got Training	24 (10.21)	33 (14.04)	76 (32.34)	66 (28.09)	36 (15.32)
No Training	7 (3.26)	56 (26.05)	71 (33.02)	41 (19.07)	40 (18.60)

Chi-square = 20.640; df = 4; Significant and 1 per cent level

Sources of Finance

Formal	6 (5.00)	12 (10.00)	38 (31.67)	34 (28.33)	30 (25.00)
Informal	25 (7.58)	77 (23.33)	109 (33.03)	73 (22.12)	46 (13.94)

Chi-square = 16.610; df = 4; Significant and 1 per cent level

Age of Enterprise

Below 10 years	21 (7.02)	58 (19.40)	91 (30.43)	81 (27.09)	48 (16.05)
Above 10 years	10 (6.62)	31 (20.53)	56 (37.09)	26 (17.22)	28 (18.54)

Chi-square = 5.927; df = 4; Insignificant

But proportion of women entrepreneurs facing this problem to little extent is found to be less in case of joint families. The value of chi-square is statistically insignificant. Women entrepreneurs managing business under other than individual forms of business organizations face this problem slightly on higher side. The value of chi-square is statistically insignificant. Level of investment made by women entrepreneurs further show that women entrepreneurs investing less money in business face this problem more than other women entrepreneurs. It shows that availability of finance helps women entrepreneurs in availing services of experts to complete the legal formalities in business. The value of chi-square is statistically significant at 1 per cent level of significance. Level of income earned by women entrepreneurs further show that women entrepreneurs earning higher level of income face this problem more than women entrepreneurs earning other levels of income. It may be due to more requirements to be fulfiled in case of women entrepreneurs earning higher level of income. The value of chi-square is statistically significant at 1 per cent level of significance. Untrained women entrepreneurs (29 per cent) face this problem more than trained women entrepreneurs (24 per cent). It reveals that training increases the knowledge of various aspects of business. Efforts should be made to increase the level of awareness of legal formalities through short-term specialized courses to existing and potential women entrepreneurs. Book-lets containing various legal aspects written in common language should be given to existing and potential women entrepreneurs at minimum prices. The value of chi-square is statistically significant at 1 per cent level of significance. It seems logical that due to the problem of various legal formalities, overwhelming proportion of women entrepreneurs depend on informal sources of finance to run their enterprises. In this table slightly less than one-third women entrepreneurs using informal sources of finance face this problem to large extent. The value of chi-square is statistically significant at 1 per cent level of significance. Almost same proportion of women entrepreneurs having enterprises more than and less than 10 years old face this problem to a large extent. But this problem to little extent and beyond is faced by women entrepreneurs who have been in business for less than 10 years. Information vividly shows that problem of legal formalities is less felt by younger generation of women entrepreneurs. It may also be due to more exposure of knowledge among younger generation of women entrepreneurs. The value of chi-square is statistically insignificant. To overcome the problem of legal formalities, various business laws should be translated in common language which are easily understood by people and these small booklets should be made available to women entrepreneurs. Availability of various business laws in common language will be helpful to women entrepreneurs in overcoming the various problems faced by them relating to business laws and cost of hiring experts will also be reduced.

Table 6.31 shows that 27 per cent women entrepreneurs feel that lack of higher education act as an obstacle in business. 29 per cent women entrepreneurs face this problem to some extent.

TABLE 6.31

Upto what Extent Women Entrepreneurs Face the Problem of Higher Education

Group	To great extent	To large extent	To some extent	To little extent	Not at all
1	2	3	4	5	6
All Data	15 (3.33)	109 (24.22)	134 (29.78)	103 (22.89)	89 (19.78)
Education					
Primary	2 (8.33)	7 (29.17)	5 (20.83)	7 (29.17)	3 (12.50)
Matric	3 (3.75)	25 (31.25)	19 (23.75)	21 (26.25)	12 (15.00)
Graduate	7 (3.72)	30 (15.96)	62 (32.98)	42 (22.34)	47 (25.00)
Post Graduate	3 (1.90)	47 (29.75)	48 (30.38)	33 (20.89)	27 (17.09)
Chi-square = 20.202; df = 12; Insignificant					
Age (years)					
Below 30	3 (2.13)	45 (31.91)	30 (21.28)	36 (25.33)	27 (19.15)
30-40	7 (4.58)	28 (18.30)	49 (32.03)	35 (22.88)	34 (22.22)
Above 40	5 (3.21)	36 (23.08)	55 (35.26)	32 (20.51)	28 (17.95)
Chi-square = 13.898; df = 8; Insignificant					
Place of Origin					
Rural	5 (5.75)	26 (29.89)	36 (41.38)	9 (10.34)	11 (12.64)
Urban	10 (2.75)	83 (23.87)	98 (27.00)	94 (25.90)	78 (21.49)
Chi-square = 18.378; df = 4; Significant at 1 per cent level					
Type of Family					
Joint	8 (3.83)	44 (21.05)	78 (37.32)	44 (21.05)	35 (16.75)
Nuclear	7 (2.90)	65 (26.97)	56 (23.24)	59 (24.48)	54 (22.41)
Chi-square = 11.749; df = 4; Significant at 1 per cent level					
Form of Business Organization					
Sole	15 (4.85)	74 (23.95)	83 (26.86)	74 (23.95)	63 (20.39)
Others	—	35 (24.82)	51 (36.17)	29 (20.57)	26 (18.44)
Chi-square = 10.362; df = 4; Significant at 5 per cent level					
Investment (Lacs)					
<1	5 (4.07)	35 (28.46)	19 (15.45)	30 (24.9)	34 (27.64)
1-2	8 (5.56)	43 (29.86)	55 (38.19)	25 (17.36)	13 (9.03)
2-3	2 (2.60)	19 (24.68)	26 (33.77)	22 (28.57)	8 (10.39)
3-5	—	8 (12.50)	17 (26.56)	16 (25.00)	23 (35.94)

(Contd.)

1	2	3	4	5	6
5-10	—	4 (12.90)	10 (32.26)	7 (22.58)	10 (32.26)
Above 10	—	—	7 (63.64)	3 (27.27)	1 (9.09)

Chi-square = 64.139; df = 20; Significant at 1 per cent level

Income (Rs.)

<7500	—	5 (9.26)	9 (16.67)	17 (31.48)	23 (42.59)
7500-10000	10 (6.62)	44 (29.14)	42 (27.81)	27 (17.88)	28 (18.54)
10000-15000	3 (3.09)	21 (21.65)	38 (39.18)	24 (24.74)	11 (11.34)
15000-20000	2 (2.00)	29 (29.00)	31 (31.00)	18 (18.00)	20 (20.00)
20000+	—	10 (20.83)	14 (29.17)	17 (35.42)	7 (14.58)

Chi-square = 49.385; df = 16; Significant at 1 per cent level

Training

Got Training	10 (4.6)	45 (19.15)	67 (28.51)	63 (26.81)	50 (21.28)
No Training	5 (2.33)	64 (29.77)	67 (31.16)	40 (18.60)	39 (18.14)

Chi-square = 10.606; df = 4; Significant at 5 per cent level

Sources of Finance

Formal	3 (2.50)	21 (17.50)	30 (25.00)	28 (23.33)	38 (31.67)
Informal	12 (3.64)	88 (26.67)	104 (31.52)	75 (22.73)	51 (15.45)

Chi-square = 16.357; df = 4; Significant at 1 per cent level

Age of Enterprise

Below 10 years	4 (1.34)	75 (25.08)	85 (28.43)	76 (25.42)	59 (19.73)
Above 10 years	11 (7.28)	34 (22.52)	49 (32.45)	27 (17.88)	30 (19.87)

Chi-square = 13.954; df = 4; Significant at 1 per cent level

Women entrepreneurs possessing lower level of education face this problem relatively more as compared to women entrepreneurs. It shows that education helps in overcoming various obstacles in business. It becomes easy for an educated women to take the reference of various business-related sources by themselves. The value of chi-square is statistically insignificant. Women entrepreneurs in lower age group face this problem more than women entrepreneurs in middle and higher age group. The value of chi-square is statistically insignificant. 35 per cent women entrepreneurs hailing from rural areas face this problem to a large extent, whereas this ratio is 25 per cent in case of women entrepreneurs coming from urban areas. The reason to this may be attributed to lack of education and opportunity to get information in case of women entrepreneurs in former case. The value of chi-square is statistically significant at 1 per cent level of significance. It shows that these two variables vary significantly. Women entrepreneurs (29 per cent) coming from nuclear families face this problem more than women entrepreneurs (25 per cent) coming from joint families. It may be due to availability of more persons in joint families. The value of chi-square is statistically significant at 1 per cent level of significance. Women entrepreneurs managing business on individual basis face this problem to a large extent. The value of chi-square is statistically significant at 5 per cent level of significance. Women entrepreneurs investing less money in business face this problem more intensively than women entrepreneurs having made more investment in business. It seems that less educated women entrepreneurs are more involved in micro and small enterprises. The value of chi-square is statistically significant at 1 per cent level of significance. Women entrepreneurs earning moderate level of income face this problem more intensively than women entrepreneurs earning lower and higher level of income. It shows that due to availability of more money women entrepreneurs in higher income groups might be able to get higher services of various experts. The value of chi-square is statistically significant at 1 per cent level of significance. Trained women entrepreneurs face this problem less intensively than untrained women entrepreneurs. It seems that training fulfils the various requirements of women in business. The value of chi-square is statistically significant at 5 per cent level of significance. Women entrepreneurs (30 per cent) using informal sources of finance face this problem relatively more as compared to women entrepreneurs (20 per cent) using formal sources of finance. The value of chi-square is statistically significant at 1 per cent level of significance. Women entrepreneurs having enterprises more than 10 years old face this problem more than other women entrepreneurs. It shows that women entrepreneurs in former case understand the value of higher education The value of chi-square is statistically significant at 1 per cent level of significance.

Table 6.32 shows that 38 per cent women entrepreneurs face the problem of gender discrimination while doing business. More than 35 per cent women entrepreneurs irrespective of their level of education agree with this statement. The value of chi-square is

TABLE 6.32

Extent of Problem of Gender Bias Faced by Women Entrepreneurs

Group	To great extent	To large extent	To some extent	To little extent	Not at all
1	2	3	4	5	6
All Data	63 (14.00)	110 (24.44)	134 (29.78)	81 (18.00)	62 (13.78)
Education					
Primary	4 (16.67)	7 (29.17)	6 (25.00)	4 (16.67)	3 (12.50)
Matric	10 (12.50)	22 (27.50)	20 (25.00)	19 (23.75)	9 (11.25)
Graduate	24 (12.77)	42 (22.34)	58 (30.85)	31 (16.49)	33 (17.55)
Post Graduate	25 (15.82)	39 (24.68)	50 (31.65)	27 (17.09)	17 (10.76)
Chi-square = 7.947; df = 12; Insignificant					
Age (years)					
Below 30	14 (9.93)	21 (14.89)	59 (41.84)	25 (17.73)	22 (15.60)
30-40	35 (22.88)	52 (33.99)	24 (15.69)	26 (16.99)	16 (10.46)
Above 40	14 (8.97)	37 (23.72)	51 (32.69)	30 (19.23)	24 (15.38)
Chi-square = 43.710; df = 8; Significant at 1 per cent level					
Place of Origin					
Rural	9 (10.34)	20 (22.99)	33 (37.93)	14 (16.09)	11 (12.64)
Urban	54 (14.88)	90 (24.79)	101 (27.82)	67 (18.46)	51 (14.05)
Chi-square = 3.849; df = 4; Insignificant					
Type of Family					
Joint	31 (14.83)	53 (25.36)	66 (31.58)	33 (15.79)	2o (12.44)
Nuclear	32 (13.28)	57 (23.65)	68 (28.22)	48 (19.92)	36 (14.94)
Chi-square = 2.318; df = 4; Insignificant					
Form of Business Organization					
Sole	45 (14.56)	80 (25.89)	92 (29.77)	53 (17.15)	39 (12.62)
Others	18 (12.77)	30 (21.28)	42 (29.79)	28 (19.86)	23 (16.31)
Chi-square = 2.417; df = 4; Insignificant					
Investment (Lacs)					
<1	23 (18.70)	39 (31.71)	31 (25.20)	15 (12.20)	15 (12.20)
1-2	16 (11.11)	41 (28.47)	57 (39.58)	24 (16.67)	6 (4.17)
2-3	17 (22.08)	19 (24.68)	19 (24.68)	16 (20.78)	6 (7.79)
3-5	3 (4.69)	6 (9.38)	15 (23.44)	15 (23.44)	25 (39.06)

1	2	3	4	5	6
5-10	4 (12.90)	5 (16.13)	3 (9.68)	10 (32.26)	9 (29.03)
Above 10	—	—	9 (81.82)	1 (9.09)	1 (9.09)
Chi-square = 101.104; df = 20; Significant at 1 per cent level					

Income (Rs.)

<7500	10 (18.52)	14 (25.93)	12 (22.22)	9 (16.67)	9 (16.67)
7500-10000	10 (6.62)	39 (25.83)	51 (33.77)	26 (17.22)	25 (16.56)
10000-15000	14 (14.43)	33 (34.02)	26 (26.80)	20 (20.62)	4 (4.12)
15000-20000	18 (18.00)	13 (13.00)	30 (30.00)	21 (21.00)	18 (18.00)
20000+	11 (22.92)	11 (22.92)	15 (31.25)	5 (10.42)	6 (12.50)
Chi-square = 33.512; df = 16; Significant at 1 per cent level					

Training

Got Training	55 (23.40)	48 (20.43)	71 (30.21)	34 (14.47)	27 (11.49)
No Training	8 (3.72)	62 (28.84)	63 (29.30)	47 (21.86)	35 (16.28)
Chi-square = 39.631; df = 4; Significant at 1 per cent level					

Sources of Finance

Formal	9 (7.50)	10 (8.33)	43 (35.83)	27 (22.50)	31 (25.83)
Informal	54 (16.36)	100 (30.30)	91 (27.58)	54 (16.36)	31 (9.39)
Chi-square = 43.432; df = 4; Significant at 1 per cent level					

Age of Enterprise

Below 10 years	47 (15.72)	75 (25.08)	86 (28.76)	54 (18.06)	37 (12.37)
Above 10 years	16 (10.60)	35 (23.18)	48 (31.79)	27 (17.88)	25 (16.56)
Chi-square = 3.613; df = 4; Significant at 1 per cent level					

statistically insignificant. Age-wise information further reveals that this problem is faced more by women entrepreneurs in middle and higher age groups. Analysis reveals that women entrepreneurs may face this problem due to difference in perceptions. The value of chi-square is statistically significant at 1 per cent level of significance. Women entrepreneurs hailing from urban areas face this problem more than their counterparts coming from rural areas. The value of chi-square is statistically insignificant. Almost same proportion of women entrepreneurs coming from joint and nuclear families face this problem to a large extent. But this problem to some extent has been faced by women entrepreneurs hailing from joint families. It may be due to lack of exposure. The value of chi-square is statistically insignificant. Women entrepreneurs managing business on individual basis face this problem more than women entrepreneurs managing business under other forms of business organizations. The value of chi-square is statistically insignificant. Women entrepreneurs having made less investment in business face this problem more intensively than women entrepreneurs investing more money in business. The value of chi-square is statistically significant at 1 per cent level of significance. Almost same proportion of women entrepreneurs earning lower and higher level of income face this problem more than other women entrepreneurs. The value of chi-square is statistically significant at 1 per cent level of significance. Trained women entrepreneurs face this problem more than their untrained counterparts. It seems that trained women entrepreneurs due to more knowledge understand the working of various officials. The value of chi-square is statistically significant at 1 per cent level of significance. Women entrepreneurs using informal sources of finance face this problem more than other women entrepreneurs. The value of chi-square is statistically significant at 1 per cent level of significance. Women entrepreneurs having enterprises more than 10 years old face this problem less than women entrepreneurs having enterprises less than 10 years old. It seems that women entrepreneurs managing business under new economic regime might be facing more problems due to more knowledge and skill *vis-a-vis* officials of government departments. The value of chi-square is statistically significant at 1 per cent level of significance.

SUGGESTIONS AND POLICY IMPLICATIONS

Women entrepreneurs face one of the biggest problem in the field of marketing of their products. Problems relating to marketing of the product can be solved by formulating various strategies for micro and small enterprises. Problem relating to various marketing related aspects can be solved by organizing various conferences for existing women entrepreneurs. Various NGOs and women organizations should conduct seminar periodically at different cities. Industrial organizations should conduct various market related surveys on the future demand on the product of these enterprises and information should be provided to existing SMEs. Short-term courses relating to marketing of the product should be organized for existing women entrepreneurs. It will help them in understanding the trends and challenges faced by their enterprises. Institutes of higher learning should also provide help to SMEs. Workshops and seminars should be conducted at college levels. Training in general and specific areas should be made compulsory for women entrepreneurs who want to avail loans from financial institutions. It will also reduce the problem of industrial sickness which seems to be more in case of small and micro-level enterprises. With the spread of technical and professional education in Northern India, course curriculum should be made more business/self-employment oriented so that students after completing higher education can go for business ventures without much problems. Women entrepreneurs face the problem of fixed capital in business. Suitable policies need to be follow to allot plots/sheds for women entrepreneurs. It becomes more important due to sky rocketing prices of land. It becomes very difficult for the entrepreneurs to purchase plot/building to start their business and consequently have to take high rent. Due to dual role performed by women existing rules and regulation regarding the operation of business at home or near home. It will help them to perform dual functions effectively. The problem relating to working capital can be solved by providing loans against different assets. The problem relating to high rate of interest can be solved by following liberal policies by financial institutions. Micro and small enterprises should be given top priority while advancing loans. Financial institutions should not insist more on collateral securities while advancing loans. It will be useful to SMEs to sort out the various problems of finance. Small proportion of women entrepreneurs also faces problem of lack of coordination and problem relating to various other formalities. Financial institutions should increase the awareness of their schemes among small and micro level enterprises. Increase in awareness of these schemes can be more useful to these enterprises to avail various benefits. Schemes of various financial institutions should be published in local newspapers. Women entrepreneurs face the problem of labour absenteeism and labour turnover. Women entrepreneurs should manage their enterprises in a scientific manner. Worker should be trained as per requirements of business. Progressive wage structure and better leadership styles can act as an effective tool to sort out these problems. These techniques will also solve the problem of negative attitude of the labour. Large business associations should also provide training to the existing and potential women entrepreneurs so that they may be able to utilize modern human resource management practices in an efficient manner. Women entrepreneurs also face the problem of lack of availability of skilled labour. Government should lay more emphasis on vocational education to improve the skill and human capital base of the population. It will help in increasing supply of better quality of labour in the market, which is need of the free market economies. Women entrepreneurs are facing the large number of production-related problems. These problems can be solved by following liberal policies for SMEs. Infrastructure constraints are being faced by SMEs sector more intensively. Various infrastructural facilities should be provided to SMEs sector on liberal terms and conditions. Government should lay more emphasize for the development of infrastructure for SMEs sector. Availability of infrastructure will reduced the cost of product of SMEs. Latest technology should be made available to SMEs at low price. Availability of technology will improve competitiveness of SMEs. Productivity improvement through technological development will solve large number of problems faced by women entrepreneurs. Problem of time management can be solved by providing training in this field. Human capital base of female should be improved. Quality education should be provided at school level.

Perception of Women Towards Various Entrepreneurship Related Issues

Human resources are considered to be one of the main assets of the country. The economic development of the country chiefly relies on the development of human resources. The economic development of advanced countries of the world to a large extent has been attributed to growth of entrepreneurship in small and medium enterprises. Keeping the experience of western economies the government of India followed the policy for development of entrepreneurship among human resources of the country in general and women in particular during post-liberalisation regime. Government has set up large number of institutions to provide financial and other supportive measures for the growth of entrepreneurship among women. Post-reform period has seen the increase in participation of even NGOs for the growth of entrepreneurship among human resources of the country. Rate of participation is found to be low when compared with advanced countries of the world. The reason to low participation has been assigned to dual role performed by women and socio-cultural environment prevailing in our society. Keeping in view this fact in mind an attempt is being made to analyse the perception of women towards various entrepreneurship related issues.

The chapter analysis the perception of women entrepreneurs towards various entrepreneurship related issues. 26 statements are administered to women entrepreneurs of our sample. Likert five degree scale is used for the analysis purpose. Following are statements:

1. Product produced by women entrepreneurs should be given due publicity.
2. Women officials should deal with women.
3. There should be separate support agencies for women entrepreneurs.
4. Emerging areas have more scope than traditional ones.
5. Business incubators should be set-up.
6. Marketing of the product is a problem for women entrepreneurs.
7. Availing financial assistance from support system is a problem.
8. Ignorance of law is an obstacle.
9. Acquiring technical know how is a problem.
10. Management training is must for women.
11. Management should be a compulsory subject at graduate level.
12. With reduction of public sector self-employment is the only way.
13. Present policy provisions are sufficient for growth of women entrepreneurship.
14. EDPs can act as stimulator.
15. Women become entrepreneur out of compulsion.
16. Job is better than entrepreneurship.
17. Business family can act as motivator.
18. Social and cultural barriers act as hindrance in the growth of business.
19. Being a women is boon for becoming entrepreneur.
20. Women can compete with men.
21. Success results in neglect of children, family and home.
22. It is difficult to survive without help of husband.
23. Success stories of women entrepreneurs can act as motivator.

24. Home is the right place for women.
25. Women inspectors should deal with women.
26. Ideal stage to be an entrepreneur is before marriage.

Table 7.1 shows that 88 per cent women entrepreneurs fully agree with the statement that products produced by women entrepreneurs should be given due publicity. It may be due to various problems encountered by women entrepreneurs in selling their products. Education-wise information further reveals that women entrepreneurs possessing lower level of education agree with this statement relatively more than other women entrepreneurs. It seems that women entrepreneurs having lower level of education might be facing problem of marketing of their products. Almost same proportion of women entrepreneurs irrespective of their age group agree with this statement. Women entrepreneurs hailing from rural areas agree slightly on the higher side of this issue than women entrepreneurs coming from urban areas. It shows that the problem of publicity of product is felt more by women entrepreneurs coming from rural areas. The values of chi-square are statistically insignificant in all these cases. More than 80 per cent women entrepreneurs coming from joint and nuclear families agree with this statement. The value of chi-square is statistically significant at 1 per cent level of significance. Women entrepreneurs managing business on individual basis agree with this statement relatively more than women entrepreneurs managing business under other than individual forms of business organizations. It may be due to involvement of more persons in case of latter category of business organizations. The value of chi-square is statistically insignificant. Level of investment made by women entrepreneurs also highlights that women entrepreneurs investing different levels of money agree with this statement. It may be due to increase in competition, requirement of more information and guidance. The value of chi-square is statistically significant at 1 per cent level of significance. Women entrepreneurs earning lower level of income agree more with this statement than women entrepreneurs earning higher level of income. It may be due to availability of finance among women entrepreneurs in latter case. The value of chi-square is statistically significant at 1 per cent level of significance. It shows that these two variables vary significantly. Almost same proportion of women

TABLE 7.1

Products Produced by Women Entrepreneurs should be given Due Publicity

Group	Strongly agree	Agree	Indifferent	Disagree	Strongly disagree
1	2	3	4	5	6
All Data	118 (26.22)	281 (62.44)	16 (3.56)	32 (7.11)	3 (0.67)
Education					
Primary	7 (29.17)	16 (66.67)	—	1 (4.17)	—
Matric	21 (26.25)	51 (63.75)	5 (6.25)	3 (3.75)	—
Graduate	47 (25.00)	118 (62.77)	6 (3.19)	15 (7.98)	2 (1.06)
Post Graduate	43 (27.22)	96 (60.76)	5 (3.16)	13 (8.23)	1 (0.63)
Chi-square = 6.217; df = 12; Insignificant					
Age (years)					
Below 30	24 (17.02)	101 (71.63)	4 (2.84)	11 (7.80)	1 (0.71)
30-40	52 (33.99)	82 (53.59)	7 (4.58)	10 (6.54)	2 (1.31)
Above 40	42 (26.92)	98 (62.82)	5 (3.21)	11 (7.05)	—
Chi-square = 14.785; df = 8; Insignificant					
Place of Origin					
Rural	19 (21.84)	61 (70.11)	4 (4.60)	3 (3.45)	—
Urban	99 (27.27)	220 (60.61)	12 (3.31)	29 (7.99)	3 (0.83)
Chi-square = 4.890; df = 4; Insignificant					
Type of Family					
Joint	57 (27.27)	116 (55.50)	15 (7.18)	21 (10.05)	—
Nuclear	61 (25.31)	165 (68.46)	1 (0.41)	11 (4.56)	3 (1.24)
Chi-square = 24.905; df = 4; Significant at 1 per cent level					
Form of Business Organization					
Sole	79 (25.57)	200 (64.72)	12 (3.88)	17 (5.50)	1 (0.32)
Others	39 (27.66)	81 (57.45)	4 (2.84)	15 (10.64)	2 (1.42)
Chi-square = 6.615; df = 4; Insignificant					
Investment (Lacs)					
<1	33 (26.83)	84 (68.29)	2 (1.63)	2 (1.63)	2 (1.63)
1-2	48 (33.33)	86 (59.72)	3 (2.08)	7 (4.86)	—
2-3	19 (24.68)	44 (57.14)	4 (5.19)	10 (12.99)	—
3-5	15 (23.44)	41 (64.06)	1 (1.56)	7 (10.94)	—

1	2	3	4	5	6
5-10	3 (9.68)	17 (54.84)	6 (19.35)	4 (12.90)	1 (3.23)
Above 10	—	9 (81.82)	—	2 (18.18)	—
Chi-square = 58.318; df = 20; Significant at 1 per cent level					

Income (Rs.)					
<7500	7 (12.96)	41 (75.93)	1 (1.85)	3 (5.56)	2 (3.70)
7500-10000	37 (24.50)	97 (64.24)	5 (3.31)	12 (7.95)	—
10000-15000	42 (43.30)	53 (54.64)	—	2 (2.06)	—
15000-20000	23 (23.00)	60 (60.00)	4 (4.00)	12 (12.00)	1 (1.00)
20000+	9 (18.75)	30 (62.50)	6 (12.50)	3 (6.25)	—
Chi-square = 50.291; df = 16; Significant at 1 per cent level					

Training					
Got Training	56 (23.83)	155 (65.96)	11 (4.68)	13 (5.53)	—
No Training	62 (28.84)	126 (58.60)	5 (2.33)	19 (8.84)	3 (1.40)
Chi-square = 8.801; df = 4; Insignificant					

Sources of Finance					
Formal	28 (23.33)	76 (63.33)	5 (4.17)	8 (6.67)	3 (2.50)
Informal	90 (27.27)	205 (62.12)	11 (3.33)	24 (7.27)	—
Chi-square = 9.009; df = 4; Insignificant					

Age of Enterprise					
Below 10 years	84 (28.09)	181 (60.54)	11 (3.68)	20 (6.69)	3 (1.00)
Above 10 years	34 (22.52)	100 (66.23)	5 (3.31)	12 (7.95)	—
Chi-square = 3.487; df = 4; Insignificant					

entrepreneurs irrespective of their level of training agree with this statement. It shows that marketing of the product has become cumbersome over the period of time and women entrepreneurs want some agencies which can provide help to them in this field. The value of chi-square is statistically insignificant. Similar type of response has been obtained in case of women entrepreneurs using various sources of finance. The value of chi-square is statistically insignificant. Almost same proportion of women entrepreneurs who have been in business for more than and less than 10 years want the wider publicity of their product. The value of chi-square is statistically insignificant. Efforts are being made to give exposure to the products manufactured by women entrepreneurs in various national and international trade fairs, but interaction with women entrepreneurs reveal that still more needs to be done in this direction.

Table 7.2 shows that 65 per cent women entrepreneurs agree with this statement that women officials should deal with cases of women entrepreneurs. It may be due to gender bias and difficulty in dealing with male members in the offices. Women entrepreneurs possessing low level of education agree with this statement relatively more than women entrepreneurs having higher level of education. It may be due to difference in level of education that these women entrepreneurs face the problem. The value of chi-square is statistically insignificant. It shows that these two variables are independent. Women entrepreneurs in lower age group agree with this statement relatively less as compared to women entrepreneurs in higher age groups. It seems that women entrepreneurs in higher age groups prefer women officials to deal with their cases. The value of chi-square is statistically significant at 5 per cent level of significance. Women entrepreneurs hailing from rural areas agree with this statement slightly on higher side than women entrepreneurs coming from urban areas. It may be due to less exposure faced by women entrepreneurs coming from rural areas. The value of chi-square is statistically insignificant. Almost same proportion of women entrepreneurs coming from joint and nuclear families agree with this statement. The value of chi-square is statistically significant at 5 per cent level of significance. It shows that these two variables are positively associated. 62 per cent women entrepreneurs managing business on individual basis and 69 per cent under other than individual forms of business organizations agree with this statement. The value of chi-square is statistically insignificant. As high as, 54 per cent women entrepreneurs having made investment more than Rs. 10 lacs in business agree with this view. On the other hand, more than 55 per cent women entrepreneurs investing other levels of money agree with this statement. The value of chi-square is statistically significant at 1 per cent level of significance. Women entrepreneurs earning higher level of income agree with this statement relatively more than women entrepreneurs earning lower level of income. It may be due to large operations of business and more frequent contact with various government departments. The value of chi-square is statistically significant at 5 per cent level of significance. Untrained women entrepreneurs

(68 per cent) agree with this statement more than trained women entrepreneurs (60 per cent). It shows that training enhances skill to deal with people. The value of chi-square is statistically significant at 1 per cent level of significance. Women entrepreneurs using informal sources of finance face this problem relatively more as compared to other women entrepreneurs. The value of chi-square is statistically significant at 1 per cent level of significance. Women entrepreneurs who have been in business for more than 10 years also agree with this statement. The value of chi-square is statistically insignificant.

TABLE 7.2

Women Officials should Deal with Women

Group	Strongly agree	Agree	Indifferent	Disagree	Strongly disagree
1	2	3	4	5	6
All Data	93 (20.67)	201 (44.67)	30 (6.67)	123 (27.33)	3 (0.67)
Education					
Primary	4 (16.67)	13 (54.17)	3 (12.50)	4 (16.67)	—
Matric	18 (22.50)	40 (50.00)	3 (3.75)	18 (22.50)	1 (1.25)
Graduate	43 (22.87)	78 (41.49)	11 (5.85)	55 (29.26)	1 (0.53)
Post Graduate	28 (17.72)	70 (44.30)	13 (8.23)	46 (29.11)	1 (0.63)
Chi-square = 8.599; df = 12; Insignificant					
Age (years)					
Below 30	27 (19.15)	50 (35.46)	11 (7.80)	51 (36.17)	2 (1.42)
30-40	36 (23.53)	74 (48.37)	5 (3.27)	38 (24.84)	—
Above 40	30 (19.23)	77 (49.36)	14 (8.97)	34 (21.79)	1 (0.64)
Chi-square = 17.347; df = 8; Significant at 5 per cent level					
Place of Origin					
Rural	18 (20.69)	41 (47.13)	8 (9.20)	18 (20.69)	2 (2.30)
Urban	75 (20.66)	160 (44.08)	22 (6.06)	105 (28.93)	1 (0.28)
Chi-square = 7.232; df = 4; Insignificant					
Type of Family					
Joint	34 (16.27)	102 (48.80)	20 (9.57)	52 (24.88)	1 (0.48)
Nuclear	59 (24.48)	99 (41.08)	10 (4.15)	71 (29.46)	2 (0.83)
Chi-square = 11.148 ; df = 4; Significant at 5 per cent level					

(Contd.)

1	2	3	4	5	6
Form of Business Organization					
Sole	63 (20.39)	132 (42.72)	27 (8.74)	85 (27.51)	2 (0.65)
Others	30 (21.28)	69 (48.94)	3 (2.13)	38 (26.95)	1 (0.71)
Chi-square = 7.237; df = 4; Insignificant					
Investment (Lacs)					
<1	25 (20.33)	61 (49.59)	10 (8.13)	27 (21.95)	—
1-2	31 (21.53)	50 (34.72)	7 (4.86)	55 (38.19)	1 (0.69)
2-3	15 (19.48)	46 (59.74)	2 (2.60)	13 (16.88)	1 (1.30)
3-5	15 (23.44)	21 (32.81)	9 (14.06)	19 (29.69)	—
5-10	7 (22.58)	17 (54.84)	2 (6.45)	4 (12.90)	1 (3.23)
Above 10	—	6 (54.55)	—	5 (45.45)	—
Chi-square = 41.657; df = 20; Significant at 1 per cent level					
Income (Rs.)					
<7500	3 (5.56)	24 (44.44)	7 (12.96)	20 (37.04)	—
7500-10000	37 (24.50)	53 (35.10)	12 (7.95)	48 (31.79)	1 (0.66)
10000-15000	20 (20.62)	49 (50.52)	4 (4.12)	23 (23.71)	1 (1.03)
15000-20000	26 (26.00)	48 (48.00)	5 (5.00)	20 (20.00)	1 (1.00)
20000+	7 (14.58)	27 (56.25)	2 (4.17)	12 (25.00)	—
Chi-square = 26.721; df = 16; Significant at 5 per cent level					
Training					
Got Training	35 (14.89)	109 (46.38)	14 (5.96)	75 (31.91)	2 (0.85)
No Training	58 (26.98)	92 (42.79)	16 (7.44)	48 (22.33)	1 (0.47)
Chi-square = 12.656; df = 4; Significant at 1 per cent level					
Sources of Finance					
Formal	31 (25.83)	37 (30.83)	7 (5.83)	43 (35.83)	2 (1.67)
Informal	62 (18.79)	164 (49.70)	23 (6.97)	80 (24.24)	1 (0.30)
Chi-square = 16.075; df = 4; Significant at 1 per cent level					
Age of Enterprise					
Below 10 years	66 (22.07)	124 (41.47)	18 (6.02)	89 (29.77)	2 (0.67)
Above 10 years	27 (17.88)	77 (50.99)	12 (7.95)	34 (22.52)	1 (0.66)
Chi-square = 5.378; df = 4; Insignificant					

Table 7.3 shows that 70 per cent agree with this statement there should be separate support agencies for women entrepreneurs and only 15 per cent women entrepreneurs disagree with this statement. Women entrepreneurs possessing lower level

TABLE 7.3

There should be Separate Support Agencies for Women Entrepreneurs

Group	Strongly agree	Agree	Indifferent	Disagree	Strongly disagree
1	2	3	4	5	6
All Data	130 (28.89)	185 (41.11)	66 (14.67)	60 (13.33)	9 (2.00)
Education					
Primary	5 (20.83)	10 (41.67)	6 (25.00)	3 (12.50)	—
Matric	26 (32.50)	42 (52.50)	2 (2.50)	7 (8.75)	3 (3.75)
Graduate	55 (29.26)	75 (39.89)	32 (17.02)	23 (12.23)	4 (2.13)
Post Graduate	44 (27.85)	58 (36.71)	26 (16.46)	27 (17.09)	2 (1.27)
Chi-square = 20.165; df = 12; Insignificant					
Age (years)					
Below 30	35 (24.82)	52 (36.88)	22 (15.60)	27 (19.15)	5 (3.55)
30-40	53 (34.64)	63 (41.18)	22 (14.38)	13 (8.50)	2 (1.31)
Above 40	42 (26.92)	70 (44.87)	22 (14.10)	20 (12.82)	2 (1.28)
Chi-square = 12.792; df = 8; Insignificant					
Place of Origin					
Rural	18 (20.69)	50 (57.47)	9 (10.34)	7 (8.05)	3 (3.45)
Urban	112 (30.85)	135 (37.19)	57 (15.70)	53 (14.60)	6 (1.65)
Chi-square = 14.297; df = 4; Significant at 1 per cent level					
Type of Family					
Joint	55 (26.32)	95 (45.45)	27 (12.92)	27 (12.92)	5 (2.39)
Nuclear	75 (31.12)	90 (37.34)	39 (16.18)	33 (13.69)	4 (1.66)
Chi-square = 3.849; df = 4; Significant at 1 per cent level					
Form of Business Organization					
Sole	81 (26.21)	120 (38.83)	55 (17.80)	48 (15.53)	5 (1.62)
Others	49 (34.75)	65 (46.10)	11 (7.80)	12 (8.51)	4 (2.84)
Chi-square = 14.586; df = 4; Significant at 1 per cent level					
Investment (Lacs)					
<1	28 (22.76)	56 (45.53)	18 (14.63)	19 (15.45)	2 (1.63)
1-2	42 (29.17)	56 (38.89)	26 (18.06)	19 (13.19)	1 (0.69)
2-3	19 (24.68)	39 (50.65)	6 (7.79)	10 (12.99)	3 (3.90)
3-5	26 (40.62)	17 (26.56)	13 (20.31)	8 (12.50)	—

(Contd.)

1	2	3	4	5	6
5-10	13 (41.94)	13 (41.94)	3 (9.68)	1 (3.23)	1 (3.23)
Above 10	2 (18.18)	4 (36.36)	—	3 (27.27)	2 (18.18)

Chi-square = 43.394; df = 20; Significant at 1 per cent level

Income (Rs.)

<7500	7 (12.96)	23 (42.59)	9 (16.67)	13 (24.07)	2 (3.70)
7500-10000	44 (29.14)	64 (42.38)	32 (21.19)	10 (6.62)	1 (0.66)
10000-15000	30 (30.93)	36 (37.11)	15 (15.46)	15 (15.46)	1 (1.03)
15000-20000	34 (34.00)	38 (38.00)	9 (9.00)	16 (16.00)	3 (3.00)
20000+	15 (31.25)	24 (50.00)	1 (2.08)	6 (12.50)	2 (4.17)

Chi-square = 34.327; df = 16; Significant at 1 per cent level

Training

Got Training	64 (27.33)	108 (45.96)	25 (10.64)	30 (12.77)	8 (3.40)
No Training	66 (30.70)	77 (35.81)	41 (19.07)	30 (13.95)	1 (0.47)

Chi-square = 13.687; df = 4; Significant at 1 per cent level

Sources of Finance

Formal	43 (35.83)	31 (25.83)	14 (11.67)	28 (23.33)	4 (3.33)
Informal	87 (26.36)	154 (46.67)	52 (15.76)	32 (9.70)	5 (1.52)

Chi-square = 26.754; df = 4; Significant at 1 per cent level

Age of Enterprise

Below 10 years	92 (30.77)	121 (40.47)	40 (13.38)	41 (13.71)	5 (1.67)
Above 10 years	38 (25.17)	64 (42.38)	26 (17.22)	19 (12.58)	4 (2.65)

Chi-square = 2.764; df = 4; Insignificant

of education agree more with this statement than other women entrepreneurs. It may be due to difference in level of education. The value of chi-square is statistically insignificant. Women entrepreneurs in higher age group agree with this statement relatively more as compared to women entrepreneurs in lower age groups. It seems that women entrepreneurs in higher age group have old mindset towards government agencies. The value of chi-square is statistically insignificant. Women entrepreneurs (78 per cent) hailing from rural area agree with this statement more than women entrepreneurs (68 per cent) coming from urban areas. It may be due to less exposure, lack of education and stringent socio cultural environment prevailing in rural areas. The value of chi-square is statistically significant at 1 per cent level of significance.

Women entrepreneurs (72 per cent) hailing from joint families agree more with this statement than women entrepreneurs (68 per cent) hailing from nuclear families. The value of chi-square is statistically insignificant. Women entrepreneurs managing business under other than individual forms of business organizations agree with this statement more than women entrepreneurs managing business on individual basis. The reason being, less necessity felt by women entrepreneurs managing business on individual basis. The value of chi-square is statistically significant at 1 per cent level of significance. Women entrepreneurs investing money in the range of Rs. 5-10 lacs agree with this statement relatively more than women entrepreneurs investing other levels of money in business. The value of chi-square is statistically significant at 1 per cent level of significance. Similarly, women entrepreneurs earning higher level of income agree with this statement more than women entrepreneurs earning lower level of income. It may be due to more problems faced by women entrepreneurs in former case and in this process they feel that there should be separate support agencies. The value of chi-square is statistically significant at 1 per cent level of significance. Trained women entrepreneurs agree with this statement more than untrained women entrepreneurs. It seems that trained women entrepreneurs even having more knowledge face problems while dealing with officials in government departments. The value of chi-square is statistically significant at 1 per cent level of significance. Women entrepreneurs using informal sources of finance agree with this statement more than women entrepreneurs using formal sources of finance. It may be due to gender-based problems encountered by women entrepreneurs in the former case. The value of chi-square is statistically significant at 1 per cent level of significance. Women entrepreneurs who have enterprises less than 10 years old face this problem slightly on higher side than their counterparts having enterprises more than 10 years old. It shows that women entrepreneurs who have established enterprises recently, might be confronting with these problems. This problem can be solved by creating separate cells headed by women officers to deal with cases related to women entrepreneurs. The value of chi-square is statistically insignificant.

Table 7.4 shows that 92 per cent women entrepreneurs agree with this statement that emerging areas have more scope than traditional ones. It shows that there has been shift in pattern of use of goods and services used by consumers under new economic regime. People are demanding different types of goods and services. Women entrepreneurs irrespective of their level of education agree with this statement. Information vividly shows that women entrepreneurs even having lower level of education feel that people are demanding new styles of goods and services. The value of chi-square is statistically insignificant. Similar type of conclusion has been observed in case of women entrepreneurs in different age groups. The value of chi-square is statistically significant at 5 per cent level of significance. Women entrepreneurs hailing from urban and rural areas agree with this statement. It shows that women entrepreneurs irrespective of their place of

TABLE 7.4

Emerging Areas have more Scope than Traditional Ones

Group	Strongly agree	Agree	Indifferent	Disagree	Strongly disagree
1	2	3	4	5	6
All Data	78 (17.33)	341 (75.78)	18 (4.00)	10 (2.22)	3 (0.67)
Education					
Primary	6 (25.00)	15 (62.50)	1 (4.17)	2 (8.33)	—
Matric	11 (13.75)	65 (81.25)	2 (2.50)	2 (2.50)	—
Graduate	31 (16.49)	143 (76.06)	8 (4.26)	3 (1.60)	3 (1.60)
Post Graduate	30 (18.99)	118 (74.68)	7 (4.43)	3 (1.90)	—
Chi-square = 11.838; df = 12; Insignificant					
Age (years)					
Below 30	25 (17.73)	105 (74.47)	10 (7.09)	—	1 (0.71)
30-40	24 (15.69)	115 (75.16)	4 (2.61)	8 (5.23)	2 (1.31)
Above 40	29 (18.59)	121 (77.56)	4 (2.56)	2 (1.28)	—
Chi-square = 17.371; df = 8; Significant at 5 per cent level					
Place of Origin					
Rural	20 (20.99)	62 (71.26)	5 (5.75)	—	—
Urban	58 (15.98)	279 (76.86)	13 (3.58)	10 (2.75)	3 (0.83)
Chi-square = 6.219; df = 4; Insignificant					

1	2	3	4	5	6
Type of Family					
Joint	42 (20.10)	153 (73.21)	13 (6.22)	1 (0.48)	—
Nuclear	36 (14.94)	188 (78.01)	5 (2.07)	9 (3.73)	3 (1.24)
Chi-square = 14.809; df = 4; Significant at 1 per cent level					
Form of Business Organization					
Sole	49 (15.86)	246 (79.61)	11 (3.56)	2 (0.65)	1 (0.32)
Others	29 (20.57)	95 (67.38)	7 (4.96)	8 (5.67)	2 (1.42)
Chi-square = 16.378; df = 4; Significant at 1 per cent level					
Investment (Lacs)					
<1	29 (23.58)	85 (69.11)	4 (3.25)	3 (2.44)	2 (1.63)
1-2	29 (20.14)	110 (76.39)	4 (2.78)	1 (0.69)	—
2-3	18 (23.38)	52 (67.53)	5 (6.49)	2 (2.60)	—
3-5	2 (3.12)	57 (89.06)	1 (1.56)	4 (6.25)	—
5-10	—	26 (83.87)	4 (12.90)	—	1 (3.23)
Above 10	—	11 (100.0)	—	—	—
Chi-square = 47.158; df = 20; Significant at 1 per cent level					
Income (Rs.)					
<7500	8 (14.81)	41 (75.93)	2 (3.70)	1 (1.85)	2 (3.70)
7500-10000	26 (17.22)	121 (80.13)	3 (1.99)	1 (0.66)	—
10000-15000	26 (26.80)	64 (65.98)	6 (6.19)	—	1 (1.03)
15000-20000	16 (16.00)	74 (74.00)	7 (7.00)	3 (3.00)	—
20000+	2 (4.17)	41 (85.42)	—	5 (10.42)·	—
Chi-square = 47.505; df = 16; Significant at 1 per cent level					
Training					
Got Training	41 (17.45)	179 (76.17)	7 (2.98)	7 (2.98)	1 (0.43)
No Training	37 (17.21)	162 (75.35)	11 (5.12)	3 (1.40)	2 (0.93)
Chi-square = 2.992; df = 4; Insignificant					
Sources of Finance					
Formal	10 (8.33)	103 (85.83)	4 (3.33)	—	3 (2.50)
Informal	68 (20.61)	238 (72.12)	14 (4.24)	10 (3.03)	—
Chi-square = 21.899; df = 4; Significant at 1 per cent level					
Age of Enterprise					
Below 10 years	55 (18.39)	221 (73.91)	13 (4.35)	7 (2.34)	3 (1.00)
Above 10 years	23 (15.23)	120 (79.47)	5 (3.31)	3 (1.99)	—
Chi-square = 2.829; df = 4; Insignificant					

origin agree with this statement. The value of chi-square is statistically insignificant. Almost same proportion of women entrepreneurs hailing from joint and nuclear families agree with this statement. The value of chi-square is statistically significant at 1 per cent level of significance. Women entrepreneurs managing business under individual forms of business organizations agree with this statement more than their counterparts managing business under other than individual forms of business organizations. It reveals that micro and small enterprises might be facing the problem of decline in the demand for their products. The value of chi-square is statistically significant at 1 per cent level of significance. It shows that these two variables vary significantly. All women entrepreneurs investing more than Rs. 10 lacs in business agree with this statement and more than 80 per cent women entrepreneurs investing other range of income also agree with this statement. The value of chi-square is statistically significant at 1 per cent level of significance. It shows that requirements of people are changing vary fast and women entrepreneurs in business feel that new areas offer more scope in the market. Overwhelming proportion of women entrepreneurs earning different levels of income agree with this statement. It shows that new areas have more potential and demand. It also reveals the fast changing taste and preferences of people. The value of chi-square is statistically significant at 1 per cent level of significance. It shows that these two variables are positively associated. Almost same proportion of women entrepreneurs irrespective of their level of training agree with this statement. It throws light on the fact that even untrained women entrepreneurs have started understanding the change in market conditions. The value of chi-square is statistically insignificant. Similarly, women entrepreneurs using formal and informal sources of finance agree with this statement. The value of chi-square is statistically significant at 1 per cent level of significance. Women entrepreneurs possessing enterprises less than 10 years old agree slightly on higher side with the statement than their counterparts having enterprises more than 10 years old. It seems that entrepreneurs who have established business recently understand the change in trends of market. The value of chi-square is statistically insignificant.

Table 7.5 shows that 93 per cent women entrepreneurs agree with this statement that business incubators should be established so that women entrepreneurs may not face problems right from planning to final operation of the enterprises. More than 90 per cent women entrepreneurs possessing matric to post-graduate level of education agree with this statement and all the women entrepreneurs possessing primary level of education fully agree with this statement. It shows that women entrepreneurs possessing lower level of education face more problem right from establishment to final operation of enterprises. They need a system which can look after their enterprises from the initial phases to final establishment. The value of chi-square is statistically significant at 1 per cent level of significance. More than 84 per cent of women entrepreneurs in different age groups strongly agree with this statement. The value of chi-square is statistically insignificant. Women entrepreneurs hailing from urban areas agree relatively more with this statement than women

TABLE 7.5
Business Incubators should be Set-up

Group	Strongly agree	Agree	Indifferent	Disagree
1	2	3	4	5
All Data	130 (28.89)	288 (64.00)	17 (3.78)	15 (3.33)
Education				
Primary	11 (45.83)	13 (54.17)	—	—
Matric	16 (20.00)	56 (70.00)	8 (10.00)	—
Graduate	51 (27.13)	124 (65.96)	8 (4.26)	5 (2.66)
Post Graduate	52 (32.91)	95 (60.13)	1 (0.63)	10 (6.33)
Chi-square = 28.288; df = 9; Significant at 1 per cent level				
Age (years)				
Below 30	39 (27.66)	89 (63.12)	6 (4.26)	7 (4.96)
30-40	53 (34.64)	95 (62.09)	3 (1.96)	2 (1.31)
Above 40	38 (24.36)	104 (60.13)	8 (5.13)	6 (3.85)
Chi-square = 8.520; df = 6; Insignificant				
Place of Origin				
Rural	29 (33.33)	49 (56.32)	7 (8.05)	2 (2.30)
Urban	101 (27.82)	239 (65.84)	10 (2.75)	13 (3.58)
Chi-square = 7.278; df = 3; Insignificant				

(Contd.)

1	2	3	4	5
Type of Family				
Joint	47 (22.49)	141 (67.46)	14 (6.70)	7 (3.35)
Nuclear	83 (34.44)	147 (61.00)	3 (1.24)	8 (3.32)
Chi-square = 15.079; df = 3; Significant at 1 per cent level				
Form of Business Organization				
Sole	93 (30.10)	192 (62.14)	12 (3.88)	12 (3.88)
Others	37 (26.24)	96 (68.09)	5 (3.55)	3 (2.13)
Chi-square = 1.958; df = 3; Insignificant				
Investment (Lacs)				
<1	34 (27.64)	82 (66.67)	2 (1.63)	5 (4.07)
1-2	35 (24.21)	97 (67.36)	6 (4.17)	6 (4.17)
2-3	26 (33.77)	47 (61.04)	3 (3.90)	1 (1.30)
3-5	27 (42.19)	31 (48.44)	3 (4.69)	3 (4.69)
5-10	8 (25.81)	20 (64.52)	3 (9.68)	—
Above 10	—	11 (100.0)	—	—
Chi-square = 22.278; df = 15; Insignificant				
Income (Rs.)				
<7500	5 (9.26)	41 (75.93)	—	8 (14.81)
7500-10000	42 (27.81)	96 (63.58)	9 (5.96)	4 (2.65)
10000-15000	29 (29.90)	66 (68.04)	2 (2.06)	—
15000-20000	34 (34.00)	59 (59.00)	4 (4.00)	3 (3.00)
20000+	20 (41.67)	26 (54.17)	2 (4.17)	—
Chi-square = 44.648; df = 12; Significant at 1 per cent level				
Training				
Got Training	69 (29.36)	157 (66.81)	5 (2.13)	4 (1.70)
No Training	61 (28.37)	131 (60.93)	12 (5.58)	11 (5.12)
Chi-square = 8.116; df = 3; Significant at 5 per cent level				
Sources of Finance				
Formal	35 (29.17)	77 (64.17)	4 (3.33)	4 (3.33)
Informal	95 (28.79)	211 (63.94)	13 (3.94)	11 (3.33)
Chi-square = 0.091; df = 3; Insignificant				
Age of Enterprise				
Below 10 years	92 (30.77)	187 (62.54)	9 (3.01)	11 (3.68)
Above 10 years	38 (25.17)	101 (66.89)	8 (5.30)	4 (2.65)
Chi-square = 3.096; df = 3; Insignificant				

entrepreneurs coming from urban areas. It may be due to more competition prevailing in urban areas. The value of chi-square is statistically insignificant. Women entrepreneurs coming from joint families agree less with this statement than women entrepreneurs hailing from nuclear families. It may be due to less exposure in the business process. The value of chi-square is statistically insignificant. Women entrepreneurs managing business on individual basis agree slightly less with this statement. The value of chi-square is statistically insignificant. Majority of women entrepreneurs investing various levels of money agree with this statement and all the women entrepreneurs investing more than Rs. 10 lacs in business need such type of assistance at initial stages of business. The value of chi-square is statistically insignificant. More than 96 per cent women entrepreneurs earning income in the range of Rs. 10,000-15,000 per month and more than Rs. 20,000 per month agree more with this statement, whereas this ratio is more than 85 per cent in other cases. The value of chi-square is statistically significant at 1 per cent level of significance. Trained women entrepreneurs agree relatively more with this statement as compared to untrained women entrepreneurs. It shows that trained women entrepreneurs still need expertise in the field of management at initial stages. The value of chi-square is statistically significant at 5 per cent level of significance. Almost same proportion of women entrepreneurs using formal and informal sources of finance fully agree with this statement. The value of chi-square is statistically insignificant. Similar type of observations have been observed in case of women entrepreneurs possessing enterprises with different age groups. The value of chi-square is statistically insignificant.

Table 7.6 shows that 63 per cent of women entrepreneurs agree with the statement that marketing of the product is a problem. It may be due to increase in competition or increase in cost of advertisement of their product. Education-wise information further shows that women entrepreneurs having low level of education face this problem relatively more than other women entrepreneurs. It may be due to lack of awareness of accessibility to various means of advertisement. The value of chi-square is statistically significant at 1 per cent level of significance. Women entrepreneurs in the age group of more than 40 face this problem more than women entrepreneurs in other age groups. It seems that

TABLE 7.6

Marketing of the Product is a Problem for Women Entrepreneurs

Group	Strongly agree	Agree	Indifferent	Disagree	Strongly disagree
1	2	3	4	5	6
All Data	44 (9.78)	241 (53.56)	52 (11.56)	104 (23.11)	9 (2.00)
Education					
Primary	4 (16.67)	15 (62.50)	—	3 (12.50)	2 (8.33)
Matric	8 (10.00)	43 (53.75)	7 (8.75)	22 (27.50)	—
Graduate	13 (6.91)	101 (53.72)	34 (18.09)	33 (17.55)	7 (3.72)
Post Graduate	19 (12.03)	82 (51.90)	11 (6.96)	46 (29.11)	—
Chi-square = 36.319; df = 12; Significant at 1 per cent level					
Age (years)					
Below 30	5 (3.55)	73 (51.77)	17 (12.06)	42 (29.79)	4 (2.84)
30-40	25 (16.34)	64 (41.83)	18 (11.76)	44 (28.76)	2 (1.31)
Above 40	14 (8.97)	104 (66.67)	17 (10.90)	18 (11.54)	3 (1.92)
Chi-square = 36.291; df = 8; Significant at 1 per cent level					
Place of Origin					
Rural	12 (13.79)	42 (48.28)	3 (3.45)	27 (31.03)	3 (3.45)
Urban	32 (8.82)	199 (54.82)	49 (13.50)	77 (21.21)	6 (1.65)
Chi-square = 12.535; df = 4; Significant at 1 per cent level					
Type of Family					
Joint	28 (13.40)	105 (50.24)	23 (11.00)	46 (22.01)	7 (3.35)
Nuclear	16 (6.54)	136 (56.43)	29 (12.03)	58 (24.07)	2 (0.83)
Chi-square = 9.898 ; df = 4; Significant at 5 per cent level					
Form of Business Organization					
Sole	28 (9.06)	162 (52.43)	40 (12.94)	75 (24.27)	4 (1.29)
Others	16 (11.35)	79 (56.03)	12 (8.51)	29 (20.57)	5 (3.55)
Chi-square = 5.429; df = 4; Insignificant					
Investment (Lacs)					
<1	7 (5.69)	63 (51.22)	22 (17.89)	29 (23.58)	2 (1.63)
1-2	29 (20.14)	69 (47.92)	12 (8.33)	31 (21.53)	3 (2.08)
2-3	5 (6.49)	45 (58.44)	6 (7.79)	21 (27.27)	—
3-5	2 (3.12)	42 (65.62)	6 (9.38)	12 (18.75)	2 (3.12)

1	2	3	4	5	6
5-10	1 (3.23)	14 (45.16)	6 (19.35)	8 (25.81)	2 (6.45)
Above 10	—	8 (72.73)	—	3 (27.27)	—

Chi-square = 44.770; df = 20; Significant at 1 per cent level

Income (Rs.)					
<7500	1 (1.85)	36 (66.67)	8 (14.81)	9 (16.67)	—
7500-10000	20 (13.25)	79 (52.32)	15 (9.93)	35 (23.18)	2 (1.32)
10000-15000	15 (15.46)	58 (59.79)	6 (6.19)	15 (15.46)	3 (3.09)
15000-20000	7 (7.00)	43 (43.00)	15 (15.00)	32 (32.00)	3 (3.00)
20000+	1 (2.08)	25 (52.0)	8 (16.67)	13 (27.08)	1 (2.08).

Chi-square = 31.860; df = 16; Significant at 1 per cent level

Training					
Got Training	14 (5.96)	112 (47.66)	34 (14.47)	71 (30.21)	4 (1.70)
No Training	30 (13.95)	129 (60.00)	18 (8.37)	33 (15.35)	5 (2.33)

Chi-square = 25.097; df = 4; Significant at 1 per cent level

Sources of Finance					
Formal	9 (7.50)	65 (54.17)	16 (13.33)	27 (22.50)	3 (2.50)
Informal	35 (10.61)	176 (53.33)	36 (10.91)	77 (23.33)	6 (1.82)

Chi-square = 1.558; df = 4; Insignificant

Age of Enterprise					
Below 10 years	28 (9.36)	147 (49.16)	36 (12.04)	82 (27.42)	6 (2.01)
Above 10 years	16 (10.60)	94 (62.25)	16 (10.60)	22 (14.57)	3 (1.99)

Chi-square = 10.720; df = 4; Significant at 5 per cent level

due to increase in competition and change in expectations of the people, these women entrepreneurs face the problem in advertisement of their product. The value of chi-square is statistically significant at 1 per cent level of significance. Almost same proportion of women entrepreneurs hailing from rural and urban areas face this problem. It shows that advertisement of the product is almost difficult for women entrepreneurs irrespective of their place of origin. The value of chi-square is statistically significant at 1 per cent level of significance. Similarly, women entrepreneurs coming from joint and nuclear families also agree with this statement. The value of chi-square is statistically significant at 5 per cent level of significance. Women entrepreneurs managing business under other than of business organizations face this problem relatively more as compared to women entrepreneurs managing business on individual basis. It may be due to less need felt by women entrepreneurs managing business on individual basis. Information clearly shows that marketing of the product is even more difficult for women entrepreneurs doing business under other than individual forms of business organizations. The value of chi-square is statistically insignificant. Women entrepreneurs investing more than Rs. 10 lacs in business face this problem relatively more than women entrepreneurs investing other ranges of money. It may be due to availability of large number of substitutes and large-scale opening up of same enterprises. The value of chi-square is statistically significant at 1 per cent level of significance. Women entrepreneurs earning lower level of income face this problem relatively more than other women entrepreneurs. It shows that due to higher level of income, women entrepreneurs may have more capacity to spend money on advertisements. The value of chi-square is statistically significant at 1 per cent level of significance. Untrained women entrepreneurs (74 per cent) face this problem relatively more as compared to trained women entrepreneurs (53 per cent). It shows that training helps in overcoming the problem of advertisement. There is a need to formulate the policies which should increase the training facilities for women entrepreneurs. Almost same proportion of women entrepreneurs who have used formal and informal sources of finance to run their enterprises face the problem of marketing of their product. The value of chi-square is statistically insignificant. Women entrepreneurs having enterprises more than 10 years old face this problem more intensively than women entrepreneurs having enterprises less than 10 years old. It may be due to traditional methods of marketing used by women entrepreneurs or inability to cope with intensive competition. The value of chi-square is statistically significant at 5 per cent level of significance.

Table 7.7 shows that slightly less than one-third women entrepreneurs agree with the statement that availing financial assistance from support system is a problem and 47 per cent of women entrepreneurs disagree with this statement. Information clearly reveals that their has been shift in attitude of financial institutions to provide finance to small enterprises during post-reform period. Financial institutions are adopting liberal policies while giving loans to small enterprises. Education-wise information further shows that women entrepreneurs having low level of education agree more with this statement more than women entrepreneurs possessing higher level of education. It may be due to difference in attitude of women entrepreneurs having different level of education. The value of chi-square is statistically significant at 5 per cent level of significance. It shows that these two variables vary significantly. Women entrepreneurs in lower age groups face this problem relatively less as compared to women entrepreneurs in higher age groups. It may be due to

TABLE 7.7

Availing Financial Assistance from Support System is a Problem

Group	Strongly agree	Agree	Indifferent	Disagree	Strongly disagree
1	2	3	4	5	6
All Data	37 (8.22)	96 (21.33)	105 (23.33)	146 (32.44)	66 (14.67)
Education					
Primary	2 (8.33)	6 (25.00)	9 (37.50)	5 (20.83)	2 (8.33)
Matric	11 (13.75)	16 (20.00)	18 (22.50)	23 (28.75)	12 (15.00)
Graduate	13 (6.91)	43 (22.87)	49 (26.06)	48 (25.53)	35 (18.62)
Post Graduate	11 (6.96)	31 (19.62)	29 (18.35)	70 (44.30)	17 (10.76)
Chi-square = 23.940; df = 12; Significant at 5 per cent level					
Age (years)					
Below 30	4 (2.84)	28 (19.86)	38 (26.95)	45 (31.91)	26 (18.44)
30-40	21 (13.73)	24 (15.69)	31 (20.26)	52 (33.99)	25 (16.34)
Above 40	12 (7.69)	44 (28.21)	36 (23.08)	49 (31.41)	15 (9.62)
Chi-square = 22.510; df = 8; Significant at 1 per cent level					
Place of Origin					
Rural	9 (10.34)	21 (24.14)	16 (18.39)	36 (41.38)	5 (5.75)
Urban	28 (7.71)	75 (20.66)	89 (24.52)	110 (30.30)	61 (16.00)
Chi-square = 10.622; df = 4; Significant at 5 per cent level					
Type of Family					
Joint	23 (11.00)	45 (21.53)	46 (22.01)	65 (31.10)	30 (14.35)
Nuclear	14 (5.81)	51 (21.16)	59 (24.48)	81 (33.61)	36 (14.94)
Chi-square = 4.218; df = 4; Insignificant					

(Contd.)

1	2	3	4	5	6
Form of Business Organization					
Sole	24 (7.77)	56 (18.12)	80 (25.89)	110 (35.60)	39 (12.62)
Others	13 (9.22)	40 (28.37)	25 (17.73)	36 (25.53)	54 (14.84)
Chi-square = 11.372; df = 4; Significant at 1 per cent level					
Investment (Lacs)					
<1	6 (4.88)	27 (21.95)	38 (30.89)	45 (36.59)	7 (5.69)
1-2	21 (14.58)	36 (25.00)	30 (20.83)	40 (27.78)	17 (11.81)
2-3	5 (6.49)	23 (29.87)	12 (15.58)	22 (28.57)	15 (19.49)
3-5	5 (7.81)	4 (6.25)	18 (28.12)	21 (32.81)	16 (25.00)
5-10	—	4 (12.90)	7 (22.58)	9 (29.03)	11 (35.48)
Above 10	—	2 (18.18)	—	9 (81.82)	—
Chi-square = 67.120; df = 20; Significant at 1 per cent level					
Income (Rs.)					
<7500	3 (5.56)	7 (12.96)	19 (35.19)	22 (40.74)	3 (5.56)
7500-10000	17 (11.26)	29 (19.21)	44 (29.14)	47 (31.13)	14 (9.27)
10000-15000	11 (11.34)	31 (31.96)	18 (18.56)	31 (31.96)	6 (6.19)
15000-20000	1 (1.00)	23 (23.00)	17 (17.00)	23 (23.00)	36 (36.00)
20000+	5 (10.42)	6 (12.50)	7 (14.58)	23 (47.92)	7 (14.58)
Chi-square = 78.085; df = 16; Significant at 1 per cent level					
Training					
Got Training	15 (6.38)	46 (19.57)	54 (22.98)	79 (33.62)	41 (17.45)
No Training	22 (10.23)	50 (23.26)	51 (23.72)	67 (31.16)	25 (11.63)
Chi-square = 5.564; df = 4; Insignificant					
Sources of Finance					
Formal	5 (4.17)	17 (14.17)	14 (11.67)	60 (50.00)	24 (20.00)
Informal	32 (9.70)	79 (23.94)	91 (27.58)	86 (26.06)	42 (12.73)
Chi-square = 35.476; df = 4; Significant at 1 per cent level					
Age of Enterprise					
Below 10 years	26 (8.70)	63 (21.07)	61 (20.40)	99 (33.11)	50 (16.72)
Above 10 years	11 (7.28)	33 (21.85)	44 (29.14)	47 (31.13)	16 (10.60)
Chi-square = 6.244; df = 4; Insignificant					

stereotype attitude of women entrepreneurs in higher age groups towards financial institutes. The value of chi-square is statistically significant at 1 per cent level of significance. Women entrepreneurs hailing from rural areas agree relatively more with this statement than women entrepreneurs coming from urban areas. It may be due to lack of awareness and difficulty in approaching financial institutions to avail assistance. The value of chi-square is statistically significant at 5 per cent level of significance. It shows that these two variables vary significantly. One-third women entrepreneurs hailing from joint families agree with this statement, whereas this ratio is 27 per cent in case of women entrepreneurs coming from nuclear families. It may be due to lack of mobility among women entrepreneurs in former case. The value of chi-square is statistically insignificant. 38 per cent women entrepreneurs managing business under other than individual forms of business organization agree with this statement more than women entrepreneurs managing business on individual basis (26 per cent). It may be due to less necessity felt by women entrepreneurs managing business on individual basis. The value of chi-square is statistically significant at 1 per cent level of significance. Only small proportion of women entrepreneurs investing money beyond Rs. 3 lacs agree with this statement, whereas 26 per cent to 40 per cent women entrepreneurs investing upto Rs. 3 lacs agree with this statement. It reveals that financial institutes still hesitate to provide loans to small and micro-level enterprises. It may be due to poor paying capacity and inability of small enterprises to fulfil various requirements of financial institutes. The value of chi-square is statistically significant at 1 per cent level of significance. Women entrepreneurs earning moderate level of income face this problem relatively more than women entrepreneurs earning higher level of income. It shows that the problem of financial assistance is felt more by small enterprises. The value of chi-square is statistically significant at 1 per cent level of significance. It reveals that these two variables are associated with each other. Women entrepreneurs who have undergone training before the start of their business face this problem relatively less than untrained women entrepreneurs. It reveals that training helps in solving financial problems faced by women entrepreneurs. Moreover, training also increases the awareness of various sources of finance available to small enterprises and procedure of getting loans from these institutions. The value of chi-square is statistically insignificant. Women entrepreneurs who are dependent on informal sources of finance feel that availing financial assistance from formal sources is a problem. The value of chi-square is statistically significant at 1 per cent level of significance. Almost same proportion of women entrepreneurs irrespective of age of their enterprises fully agree with this statement. The value of chi-square is statistically insignificant. It shows that these two variables are independent.

Table 7.8 shows that 72 per cent women entrepreneurs feel that ignorance of law is a problem and only 17 per cent women entrepreneurs disagree with this statement. It shows that women entrepreneurs still face the problem of ignorance of law inspite of relaxation in rules and regulations. It may also be due to lack of opportunities to get adequate information relating to business laws. Education-wise information further shows that more than 65 per cent women entrepreneurs irrespective of their level of education agree with this statement. But this problem is faced relatively more by less educated women entrepreneurs. The value of chi-square is statistically significant at 1 per cent level of significance. Women entrepreneurs in higher age groups face the problem of ignorance of law relatively more than women entrepreneurs in lower age groups. It may be due to difference in age and difficulty in understanding various business laws. The value of chi-square is statistically insignificant. Women entrepreneurs coming from rural areas face this problem relatively more than their urban counterparts. It may be due to difference in education and less exposure to business world. The value of chi-square is statistically significant at 1 per cent level of significance. Women entrepreneurs coming from nuclear families face this problem relatively more as compared to women entrepreneurs hailing from joint families. It may be due to availability of more persons and links of joint families. The value of chi-square is statistically insignificant. Almost same proportion of women entrepreneurs managing business under different forms of business organizations face this problem. It shows that understanding of law is cumbersome and complicated even for women entrepreneurs managing business on joint basis. It may also be due to increase in cost of hiring of legal experts in business. The value of chi-square is statistically significant at 1 per cent level of significance. Women entrepreneurs investing less money in business face this problem relatively more than other women entrepreneurs. It may be due to lack of finances and lack of knowledge of business law among entrepreneurs of small

TABLE 7.8

Ignorance of Law is an Obstacle

Group	Strongly agree	Agree	Indifferent	Disagree	Strongly disagree
1	2	3	4	5	6
All Data	43 (9.56)	283 (62.89)	46 (10.22)	69 (15.33)	9 (2.00)
Education					
Primary	2 (8.33)	15 (62.50)	4 (16.67)	3 (12.50)	—
Matric	3 (3.75)	69 (86.25)	—	8 (10.00)	—
Graduate	20 (10.64)	102 (54.26)	29 (15.43)	30 (15.96)	7 (3.72)
Post Graduate	18 (11.39)	97 (61.39)	13 (8.23)	28 (17.72)	2 (1.27)
Chi-square = 35.165; df = 12; Significant at 1 per cent level					
Age (years)					
Below 30	18 (12.77)	83 (58.87)	12 (8.51)	24 (17.02)	4 (2.84)
30-40	10 (6.54)	92 (60.13)	21 (13.73)	25 (16.34)	5 (3.27)
Above 40	15 (9.62)	108 (69.23)	13 (8.33)	20 (12.82)	—
Chi-square = 13.162; df = 8; Insignificant					
Place of Origin					
Rural	17 (19.54)	50 (57.47)	6 (6.90)	14 (16.09)	—
Urban	26 (7.16)	233 (64.19)	40 (11.02)	55 (15.15)	9 (2.48)
Chi-square = 15.120; df = 4; Significant at 1 per cent level					
Type of Family					
Joint	21 (10.05)	126 (60.29)	24 (11.48)	36 (17.22)	2 (0.96)
Nuclear	22 (9.13)	157 (65.15)	22 (9.13)	33 (3.69)	7 (2.90)
Chi-square = 4.160; df = 4; Insignificant					
Form of Business Organization					
Sole	31 (10.03)	192 (62.14)	40 (12.94)	39 (12.62)	7 (2.27)
Others	12 (8.51)	91 (64.54)	6 (4.26)	30 (21.28)	2 (1.42)
Chi-square = 12.553; df = 4; Significant at 1 per cent level					
Investment (Lacs)					
<1	18 (14.63)	73 (59.35)	16 (13.01)	13 (10.57)	3 (2.44)
1-2	12 (8.33)	107 (74.31)	7 (4.86)	18 (12.50)	—
2-3	11 (14.29)	39 (50.65)	11 (14.29)	13 (16.88)	3 (3.90)
3-5	1 (1.56)	47 (73.44)	3 (4.69)	13 (20.31)	—

(Contd.)

1	2	3	4	5	6
5-10	1 (3.23)	14 (45.16)	7 (22.58)	6 (19.35)	3 (9.68)
Above 10	—	3 (27.27)	2 (18.18)	6 (54.55)	—

Chi-square = 65.506; df = 20; Significant at 1 per cent level

Income (Rs.)

<7500	4 (7.41)	34 (62.96)	10 (18.52)	4 (7.41)	2 (3.70)
7500-10000	15 (9.93)	108 (71.52)	5 (3.31)	23 (15.23)	—
10000-15000	15 (15.46)	65 (67.01)	5 (5.15)	11 (11.34)	1 (1.03)
15000-20000	7 (7.00)	48 (48.00)	19 (19.00)	22 (22.00)	4 (4.00)
20000+	2 (4.17)	28 (58.33)	7 (14.58)	9 (18.75)	2 (4.17)

Chi-square = 47.135; df = 16; Significant at 1 per cent level

Training

Got Training	34 (14.47)	131 (55.74)	28 (11.91)	40 (17.02)	2 (0.85)
No Training	9 (4.19)	152 (70.70)	18 (8.37)	29 (13.49)	7 (3.26)

Chi-square = 21.953; df = 4; Significant at 1 per cent level

Sources of Finance

Formal	7 (5.83)	71 (59.17)	8 (6.67)	29 (24.17)	5 (4.17)
Informal	36 (10.91)	212 (64.24)	38 (11.52)	40 (12.12)	4 (1.21)

Chi-square = 16.925; df = 4; Significant at 1 per cent level

Age of Enterprise

Below 10 years	32 (10.70)	185 (61.87)	25 (8.36)	48 (16.05)	9 (3.01)
Above 10 years	11 (7.28)	98 (64.90)	21 (13.91)	21 (13.91)	—

Chi-square = 9.238; df = 4; Insignificant

enterprises. The value of chi-square is statistically significant at 1 per cent level of significance. More than 62 per cent women entrepreneurs earning different levels of income except in the range of Rs. 15,000-20,000 per month face this problem. The value of chi-square is statistically significant at 1 per cent level of significance. More than 70 per cent trained and untrained women entrepreneurs face the problem of ignorance of law. It shows that even after getting training related to business, women entrepreneurs still face the problem of ignorance of law. Efforts should be made to put more emphasis on knowledge of law by various training institutes. Various business laws written in common language should be made available to women entrepreneurs so that they may also be able to understand these complicated laws. It will be helpful to them to reduce the cost of hiring the experts in this field. It will help the women entrepreneurs in dealing with various departments of the government. Women entrepreneurs who have availed assistance from financial institutions face this problem relatively less as compared to women entrepreneurs who are dependent on informal sources of finance. It reveals that due to lack of knowledge of various laws these women entrepreneurs are dependent on informal sources of finance. The value of chi-square is statistically significant at 1 per cent level of significance. Almost same proportion of women entrepreneurs irrespective of their life of enterprises face this problem. It shows that even under new economic policies, understanding of business law is still a problem for women entrepreneurs. There is a need to make business laws easier so that even less educated women entrepreneurs may be able to understand the working of these laws.

Table 7.9 shows that 72 per cent women entrepreneurs agree with the statement that acquiring technology is a problem for women entrepreneurs. Information reveals that in the era of globalization, liberalization and privatization, technology is still out of reach of small and micro-level enterprises. Education-wise information further depicts that more than 69 per cent women entrepreneurs irrespective of their level of education face the problem of acquiring latest technology. It shows that technology is not easily available to even highly educated women entrepreneurs. It may be due to increase in cost and rapid change in technology over the period of time. Efforts should be made to develop technology exclusively for small and micro-level enterprises. It will help this sector to improve its productivity by adopting the better technology, which is needed under new economic scenario. Moreover, improvement in productivity will make this sector more viable and competitive. The value of chi-square is statistically insignificant. 81 per cent women entrepreneurs in higher age group face the problem of acquiring latest technology. The reason to this may be assigned to lack of acquiring knowledge and use of technology. The value of chi-square is statistically significant at 1 per cent level of significance. Almost same proportion of women entrepreneurs hailing from urban and rural areas face the problem of acquiring technology. It shows that the problem of having latest know-how is faced by

TABLE 7.9

Acquiring Technical Know-how is a Problem

Group	Strongly agree	Agree	Indifferent		Disagree
1	2	3	4	5	6
All Data	90 (20.00)	236 (52.44)	64 (14.22)		60 (13.33)
Education					
Primary	4 (16.67)	13 (54.17)	6 (25.00)		1 (4.17)
Matric	17 (21.25)	50 (62.50)	6 (7.50)		7 (8.75)
Graduate	37 (19.68)	96 (51.06)	28 (14.89)		27 (14.36)
Post Graduate	32 (20.25)	77 (48.73)	24 (15.19)		25 (15.82)
Chi-square = 10.572; df = 9; Insignificant					
Age (years)					
Below 30	18 (12.77)	69 (48.94)	26 (18.44)		28 (19.86)
30-40	40 (26.14)	72 (47.06)	18 (11.76)		23 (15.03)
Above 40	32 (20.51)	95 (60.90)	20 (12.82)		9 (5.77)
Chi-square = 24.056; df = 6; Significant at 1 per cent level					
Place of Origin					
Rural	11 (12.64)	50 (57.47)	8 (9.20)		18 (20.69)
Urban	79 (21.76)	186 (51.24)	56 (15.43)		42 (11.57)
Chi-square = 9.731; df = 3; Significant at 5 per cent level					
Type of Family					
Joint	40 (19.14)	110 (52.63)	25 (11.96)		34 (16.27)
Nuclear	50 (20.75)	126 (52.28)	39 (16.18)		26 (10.79)
Chi-square = 4.070; df = 3; Insignificant					
Form of Business Organization					
Sole	63 (20.39)	158 (51.13)	45 (14.56)		43 (13.92)
Others	27 (19.15)	78 (55.32)	19 (13.48)		17 (12.06)
Chi-square = 0.729; df = 3; Insignificant					
Investment (Lacs)					
<1	26 (21.14)	48 (39.02)	25 (20.33)		24 (19.51)
1-2	34 (23.61)	76 (52.78)	18 (12.50)		16 (11.11)
2-3	13 (16.88)	51 (66.23)	2 (2.60)		11 (14.29)
3-5	10 (15.62)	39 (60.94)	10 (15.62)		5 (7.81)
5-10	5 (16.13)	14 (45.16)	9 (29.03)		3 (9.68)
Above 10	2 (18.13)	8 (72.73)	—		1 (9.09)
Chi-square = 34.663; df = 15; Significant at 1 per cent level					

1	2	3	4	5	6
Income (Rs.)					
<7500	11 (20.37)	25 (46.30)	10 (18.52)		8 (14.81)
7500-10000	33 (21.85)	84 (55.63)	12 (7.95)		22 (14.57)
10000-15000	22 (22.68)	54 (55.67)	12 (12.37)		9 (9.28)
15000-20000	18 (18.00)	51 (51.00)	19 (19.00)		12 (12.00)
20000+	6 (12.50)	22 (45.83)	11 (22.92)		9 (18.75)
Chi-square = 15.395; df = 12; Insignificant					
Training					
Got Training	41 (17.45)	115 (48.94)	33 (14.04)		46 (19.57)
No Training	49 (22.79)	121 (56.28)	31 (14.42)		14 (6.51)
Chi-square = 17.138; df = 3; Significant at 1 per cent level					
Sources of Finance					
Formal	24 (20.00)	63 (52.50)	19 (15.83)		14 (11.67)
Informal	66 (20.00)	173 (52.42)	45 (13.64)		46 (13.94)
Chi-square = 0.640; df = 3; Insignificant					
Age of Enterprise					
Below 10 years	58 (19.40)	151 (50.50)	44 (14.72)		46 (15.38)
Above 10 years	32 (21.19)	85 (56.29)	20 (13.25)		14 (9.27)
Chi-square = 3.767; df = 3; Insignificant					

women entrepreneurs irrespective of their place of origin. The value of chi-square is statistically significant at 5 per cent level of significance. Almost same proportion of women entrepreneurs coming from nuclear and joint families face the problem of acquiring technology. The value of chi-square is statistically insignificant. 74 per cent women entrepreneurs managing business under other than individual forms of business organizations face this problem, whereas this ratio is 71 per cent in case of women entrepreneurs managing business on individual basis. It shows that acquisition of technology is difficult for women entrepreneurs managing business under different forms of business organizations. The value of chi-square is statistically insignificant. Women entrepreneurs investing even more money are facing the problem of acquiring technology. It may be due to increase in cost and technology is fast becoming obsolete, as revealed by women entrepreneurs. The value of chi-square is statistically significant at 1 per cent level of significance. Almost same proportion of women entrepreneurs earning income in the range of Rs. 7,500-15,000 per month face this problem. 66 per cent women entrepreneurs earning income less than Rs. 7500 per month also face this problem. 58 per cent women entrepreneurs earning more than Rs. 20,000 per month in business face this problem. There is a need to formulate policies for technological development by various organizations and efforts should be made to provide this technology to small and micro-level enterprises. The value of chi-square is statistically insignificant. Untrained women entrepreneurs (79 per cent) face this problem more than trained women entrepreneurs (66 per cent). The value of chi-square is statistically significant at 1 per cent level of significance. Almost same proportion of women entrepreneurs using formal and informal sources of finance face this problem. In 'ormation depicts that technology is still out of reach to small enterprises. Financial institutions should ensure the availability of technology to small enterprises managed by women entrepreneurs while sanctioning loans. Women entrepreneurs (77 per cent) having enterprises more than 10 years old face this problem relatively more as compared to women entrepreneurs having enterprises less than 10 years old (69 per cent). It may be due to difficulty in using technology among entrepreneurs in older enterprises. The value of chi-square is statistically insignificant. Efforts should be made to increase the knowledge of using latest technical know-how through various seminars and workshops to these already established enterprises by women entrepreneurs.

Table 7.10 shows that 79 per cent women entrepreneurs agree with the statement that management training is must. It shows that women entrepreneurs want to minimize the risk, involved in business. Overwhelming proportion of women entrepreneurs irrespective of their level of education agree with this statement. It shows that women entrepreneurs even possessing higher level of education want to learn basics of business. The value of chi-square is statistically insignificant. Women entrepreneurs in higher age group agree with this statement slightly on higher side than women entrepreneurs in lower age group. It reveals that women entrepreneurs in higher age group want to brush their knowledge and want to increase confidence in business. The value of chi-square is statistically significant at 1 per cent level of significance.

It shows that these two variables vary significantly. Women entrepreneurs hailing from rural areas agree relatively more with this statement than their counterparts coming from urban areas. It may be due to less exposure in business. The value of chi-square is statistically insignificant. Women entrepreneurs hailing from nuclear families agree with this statement more than women entrepreneurs coming from joint families. It may be due to availability of more persons in joint families for guidance. The value of chi-square is statistically significant at 1 per cent level of

TABLE 7.10

Management Training is must for Women Entrepreneurs

Group	Strongly agree	Agree	Indifferent	Disagree	Strongly disagree
1	2	3	4	5	6
All Data	127 (28.22)	229 (50.89)	44 (9.78)	41 (9.11)	9 (2.00)
Education					
Primary	6 (25.00)	13 (54.17)	4 (16.67)	1 (4.17)	—
Matric	22 (27.50)	41 (51.25)	6 (7.50)	8 (10.00)	3 (3.75)
Graduate	52 (27.66)	97 (51.60)	21 (11.17)	14 (7.45)	4 (2.13)
Post Graduate	47 (29.75)	78 (49.37)	13 (8.23)	18 (11.39)	2 (1.27)
Chi-square = 7.081; df = 12; Insignificant					
Age (years)					
Below 30	24 (17.02)	86 (60.99)	14 (9.93)	10 (7.09)	7 (4.96)
30-40	60 (39.22)	58 (37.91)	15 (9.80)	18 (11.76)	2 (1.31)
Above 40	43 (27.56)	85 (54.49)	15 (9.62)	13 (8.33)	—
Chi-square = 32.743; df = 8; Significant at 1 per cent level					
Place of Origin					
Rural	23 (26.44)	50 (57.47)	3 (3.45)	8 (9.20)	3 (3.45)
Urban	104 (28.65)	179 (49.31)	41 (11.29)	33 (9.09)	6 (1.65)
Chi-square = 6.591; df = 4; Insignificant					
Type of Family					
Joint	53 (25.36)	101 (48.33)	19 (9.09)	33 (15.79)	3 (1.44)
Nuclear	74 (30.71)	128 (53.11)	25 (10.37)	8 (3.32)	6 (2.49)
Chi-square = 21.551; df = 4; Significant at 1 per cent level					

(Contd.)

1	2	3	4	5	6
Form of Business Organization					
Sole	83 (26.86)	156 (50.49)	32 (10.36)	33 (10.68)	5 (1.62)
Others	44 (31.21)	73 (51.77)	12 (8.51)	8 (5.67)	4 (2.84)
Chi-square = 4.398; df = 4; Insignificant					
Investment (Lacs)					
<1	34 (27.64)	55 (44.72)	14 (11.38)	20 (16.26)	—
1-2	40 (27.78)	75 (52.08)	14 (9.72)	10 (6.94)	5 (3.47)
2-3	21 (27.27)	47 (61.04)	4 (5.19)	2 (2.60)	3 (3.90)
3-5	16 (25.00)	34 (53.12)	9 (14.06)	5 (7.81)	—
5-10	12 (38.71)	11 (35.48)	3 (9.68)	4 (12.90)	1 (3.23)
Above 10	4 (36.36)	7 (63.64)	—	—	—
Chi-square = 30.362; df = 20; Insignificant					
Income (Rs.)					
<7500	13 (24.07)	30 (55.56)	6 (11.11)	5 (9.26)	—
7500-10000	40 (26.49)	79 (52.32)	19 (12.58)	11 (7.28)	2 (1.32)
10000-15000	32 (32.99)	45 (46.39)	7 (7.22)	10 (10.31)	3 (3.09)
15000-20000	24 (24.00)	53 (53.00)	9 (9.00)	11 (11.00)	3 (3.00)
20000+	18 (37.50)	22 (45.83)	3 (6.25)	4 (8.33)	1 (2.08)
Chi-square = 10.645; df = 16; Insignificant					
Training					
Got Training	66 (28.09)	128 (54.47)	18 (7.66)	14 (5.96)	9 (3.83)
No Training	61 (28.37)	101 (46.98)	26 (12.09)	27 (12.56)	—
Chi-square = 17.102; df = 4; Significant at 1 per cent level					
Sources of Finance					
Formal	38 (31.67)	62 (51.67)	12 (10.00)	6 (5.00)	2 (1.67)
Informal	89 (26.97)	167 (50.61)	32 (9.70)	35 (10.61)	7 (2.12)
Chi-square = 3.842; df = 4; Insignificant					
Age of Enterprise					
Below 10 years	89 (29.77)	143 (47.83)	25 (8.36)	33 (11.04)	9 (3.01)
Above 10 years	38 (25.17)	86 (56.95)	19 (12.58)	8 (5.30)	—
Chi-square = 12.395; df = 4; Significant at 1 per cent level					

significance. It shows that these two variables are positively associated. Women entrepreneurs managing business under other than individual forms of business organizations agree with this statement relatively more as compared to women entrepreneurs managing business under individual forms of business organizations. The value of chi-square is statistically insignificant. All the women entrepreneurs investing more than Rs. 10 lacs in business agree with this statement. It seems that women entrepreneurs investing more money want to avoid business risk completely. The value of chi-square is statistically insignificant. More than 70 per cent women entrepreneurs earning different levels of income agree with this statement. It shows that women entrepreneurs want to earn more income by learning various techniques of business. The value of chi-square is statistically insignificant. Trained women entrepreneurs (82 per cent) agree relatively more with this statement than untrained women entrepreneurs (75 per cent). It shows the importance of training expressed by women entrepreneurs. The value of chi-square is statistically significant at 1 per cent level of significance. It shows that these two variables are positively associated. Women entrepreneurs using formal sources of finance agree relatively more with this statement than their counterparts using informal sources of finance. The reason being, women entrepreneurs using formal sources of finance feel it necessary to manage resources effectively. The value of chi-square is statistically insignificant. Women entrepreneurs who have been in business for more than 10 years agree with this statement more than women entrepreneurs who have been in business for less than 10 years. It seems that women entrepreneurs who have been in business line for more than 10 years might be facing the problem of management of small enterprises. The value of chi-square is statistically significant at 1 per cent level of significance. It shows that these two variables vary significantly.

Table 7.11 shows that overwhelming proportion of women entrepreneurs agree with this statement that management should be compulsory subject at graduate level. It shows that women entrepreneurs understand the significance of this area in the business. Education-wise information further shows that more than 75 per cent women entrepreneurs irrespective of their level of education agree with this statement. It shows that even highly educated women entrepreneurs might be facing problem in the management of small enterprises. The value of chi-square is statistically significant at 5 per cent level of significance. It shows that these two variables vary positively. Almost same proportion

TABLE 7.11

Management should be a Compulsory Subject at Graduate Level

Group	Strongly agree	Agree	Indifferent	Disagree	Strongly disagree
1	2	3	4	5	6
All Data	89 (19.78)	257 (57.11)	30 (6.67)	65 (14.44)	9 (2.00)
Education					
Primary	2 (8.33)	17 (70.83)	2 (8.33)	3 (12.50)	—
Matric	8 (10.00)	55 (68.75)	4 (5.00)	13 (16.25)	—
Graduate	38 (20.21)	105 (55.85)	18 (9.57)	23 (12.23)	4 (2.13)
Post Graduate	41 (25.95)	80 (50.63)	6 (3.80)	26 (16.46)	5 (3.16)
Chi-square = 21.677; df = 12; Significant at 5 per cent level					
Age (years)					
Below 30	41 (29.08)	67 (47.52)	12 (8.51)	16 (11.35)	5 (3.55)
30-40	33 (21.57)	85 (55.56)	8 (5.23)	25 (16.34)	2 (1.31)
Above 40	15 (9.62)	105 (67.31)	10 (6.41)	24 (15.38)	2 (1.28)
Chi-square = 24.813; df = 8; Significant at 1 per cent level					
Place of Origin					
Rural	26 (29.89)	47 (54.02)	3 (3.45)	11 (12.64)	—
Urban	63 (17.36)	210 (57.85)	27 (7.44)	54 (14.88)	9 (2.48)
Chi-square = 9.826; df = 4; Significant at 5 per cent level					
Type of Family					
Joint	49 (23.44)	106 (50.72)	17 (8.13)	35 (16.75)	2 (0.96)
Nuclear	40 (16.60)	151 (62.66)	13 (5.39)	30 (12.45)	7 (2.90)
Chi-square = 9.826; df = 4; Significant at 5 per cent level					
Form of Business Organization					
Sole	62 (20.06)	172 (55.66)	25 (8.09)	43 (13.92)	7 (2.27)
Others	27 (19.15)	85 (60.28)	5 (3.55)	22 (15.60)	2 (1.42)
Chi-square = 3.940; df = 4; Insignificant					
Investment (Lacs)					
<1	36 (29.27)	63 (51.22)	10 (8.13)	8 (6.50)	6 (4.88)
1-2	32 (22.22)	92 (63.89)	5 (3.47)	15 (10.42)	—
2-3	14 (18.18)	44 (57.14)	7 (9.09)	12 (15.58)	—
3-5	6 (9.38)	33 (51.56)	3 (4.69)	22 (34.38)	—

1	2	3	4	5	6
5-10	1 (3.23)	17 (54.84)	5 (16.13)	5 (16.13)	3 (9.68)
Above 10	—	8 (72.73)	—	3 (27.27)	—
Chi-square = 73.527; df = 20; Significant at 1 per cent level					
Income (Rs.)					
<7500	10 (18.52)	29 (53.70)	4 (7.41)	5 (9.26)	6 (11.11)
7500-10000	41 (27.15)	71 (47.02)	8 (5.30)	31 (20.53)	—
10000-15000	9 (19.59)	67 (69.07)	2 (2.06)	9 (9.28)	—
15000-20000	1 (13.22)	56 (56.00)	15 (15.00)	15 (15.00)	1 (1.00)
20000+	6 (12.50)	34 (70.83)	1 (2.08)	5 (10.42)	2 (4.17)
Chi-square = 66.354; df = 16; Significant at 1 per cent level					
Training					
Got Training	61 (25.96)	117 (49.79)	16 (6.81)	39 (16.60)	2 (0.85)
No Training	28 (13.04)	140 (65.12)	14 (6.51)	26 (12.09)	7 (3.26)
Chi-square = 18.954; df = 4; Significant at 1 per cent level					
Sources of Finance					
Formal	11 (9.17)	74 (61.67)	6 (5.00)	24 (20.00)	5 (4.17)
Informal	78 (23.64)	183 (55.45)	24 (7.27)	41 (12.42)	4 (1.21)
Chi-square = 17.930; df = 4; Significant at 1 per cent level					
Age of Enterprise					
Below 10 years	72 (24.08)	157 (52.51)	21 (7.02)	41 (13.71)	8 (2.68)
Above 10 years	17 (11.26)	100 (66.23)	9 (5.96)	24 (15.89)	1 (0.66)
Chi-square = 14.180; df = 4; Significant at 1 per cent level					

of women entrepreneurs in different age groups agree with this statement. The value of chi-square is statistically significant at 1 per cent level of significance. Women entrepreneurs hailing from rural area agree more with this statement than their counterparts coming from urban areas. It seems that women entrepreneurs coming from rural areas might be facing more problems. The value of chi-square is statistically significant at 5 per cent level of significance. Women entrepreneurs (79 per cent) coming from nuclear families agree more with this statement than women entrepreneurs (74 per cent) hailing from joint families. It seems that women entrepreneurs in former case want to understand various concepts of business. The value of chi-square is statistically significant at 5 per cent level of significance. Women entrepreneurs even managing business under other than individual forms of business organization agree more than their counterparts managing business on individual basis. It reveals that women entrepreneurs managing business under different forms of business organizations also want to understand various concepts of business to reduce the cost of hiring of services of experts in the former case. The value of chi-square is statistically insignificant. Women entrepreneurs having made low and higher level of investment agree relatively more with this statement as compared to women entrepreneurs investing moderate level of money. The value of chi-square is statistically significant at 1 per cent level of significance. It shows that these two variables vary significantly. 82 per cent to 88 per cent women entrepreneurs earning income in the range of Rs. 20,000 per month and Rs. 10,000-15,000 per month agree with this statement. It shows that women entrepreneurs want to further increase their level of income. The value of chi-square is statistically significant at 1 per cent level of significance. Untrained women entrepreneurs agree with this statement slightly on higher side than their counterparts, who have undergone training before the start of their business. The reason being women entrepreneurs in former case, might be facing problems in business. The value of chi-square is statistically significant at 1 per cent level of significance. It shows that these two variables are positively associated. Women entrepreneurs using informal sources of finance agree with this statement more than women entrepreneurs using formal sources of finance. The reason being, women entrepreneurs want to increase their knowledge about various agencies available to them so that cost of loans may be reduced. The value of chi-square is statistically significant at 1 per cent level of significance. Almost same proportion of women entrepreneurs irrespective of their life of enterprises agree with this statement. It shows that business related information is required by all the women entrepreneurs. The value of chi-square is statistically significant at 1 per cent level of significance. It shows that these two variables are positively associated.

Table 7.12 shows that 72 per cent of women entrepreneurs agree with this statement that with the reduction in size of public sector self-employment is the only way. Education-wise information clearly shows that there has been shift in attitude of

TABLE 7.12

With Reduction of Public Sector, Self-employment is the only Way

Group	Strongly agree	Agree	Indifferent	Disagree	Strongly disagree
1	2	3	4	5	6
All Data	34 (7.56)	289 (64.22)	17 (3.78)	99 (22.00)	11 (2.44)
Education					
Primary	4 (16.67)	13 (54.17)	—	7 (29.17)	—
Matric	6 (7.50)	59 (73.75)	—	15 (18.75)	—
Graduate	16 (8.51)	118 (62.77)	9 (4.79)	35 (18.62)	10 (5.32)
Post Graduate	8 (5.06)	99 (62.66)	8 (5.06)	42 (26.58)	1 (0.630
Chi-square = 25.371; df = 12; Significant at 1 per cent level					
Age (years)					
Below 30	12 (8.51)	88 (62.41)	10 (7.09)	28 (19.86)	3 (2.13)
30-40	12 (7.84)	87 (56.86)	2 (1.31)	48 (31.37)	4 (2.61)
Above 40	10 (6.41)	114 (73.08)	5 (3.21)	23 (14.74)	4 (2.56)
Chi-square = 20.654; df = 8; Significant at 1 per cent level					
Place of Origin					
Rural	8 (9.20)	53 (60.92)	5 (5.75)	21 (24.14)	—
Urban	26 (7.16)	236 (65.01)	12 (3.31)	78 (21.49)	11 (3.03)
Chi-square = 4.535; df = 4; Insignificant					
Type of Family					
Joint	15 (7.18)	129 (61.72)	9 (4.31)	53 (25.36)	3 (1.44)
Nuclear	19 (7.88)	160 (66.39)	8 (3.32)	46 (19.09)	8 (3.32)
Chi-square = 4.3698 ; df = 4; Insignificant					
Form of Business Organization					
Sole	26 (8.41)	192 (62.14)	9 (2.91)	74 (23.95)	8 (2.59)
Others	8 (5.67)	97 (68.79)	8 (5.67)	25 (17.73)	3 (2.13)
Chi-square = 5.370; df = 4; Insignificant					
Investment (Lacs)					
<1	20 (16.26)	68 (55.28)	5 (4.07)	26 (21.14)	4 (3.25)
1-2	10 (6.94)	107 (74.31)	5 (3.47)	22 (15.28)	—
2-3	2 (2.60)	44 (57.14)	—	30 (38.96)	1 (1.30)
3-5	—	45 (70.31)	2 (3.12)	14 (21.88)	3 (4.69)

(Contd.)

1	2	3	4	5	6
5-10	2 (6.45)	18 (58.06)	2 (6.45)	6 (19.35)	3 (9.68)
Above 10	—	7 (63.64)	3 (27.27)	1 (9.09)	—

Chi-square = 71.778; df = 20; Significant at 1 per cent level

Income (Rs.)

<7500	2 (3.70)	34 (62.96)	4 (7.41)	12 (22.22)	2 (3.70)
7500-10000	18 (11.92)	102 (67.55)	1 (0.66)	26 (17.22)	4 (2.65)
10000-15000	9 (9.28)	74 (76.29)	—	12 (12.37)	2 (2.06)
15000-20000	2 (2.00)	55 (55.00)	7 (7.00)	35 (35.00)	1 (1.00)
20000+	3 (6.25)	24 (50.00)	5 (10.42)	14 (29.17)	2 (4.17)

Chi-square = 48.858; df = 16; Significant at 1 per cent level

Training

Got Training	26 (11.06)	144 (61.28)	10 (4.26)	51 (21.70)	4 (1.70)
No Training	8 (3.72)	145 (67.44)	7 (3.26)	48 (22.33)	7 (3.26)

Chi-square = 10.102; df = 4; Significant at 5 per cent level

Sources of Finance

Formal	14 (11.67)	73 (60.83)	10 (8.33)	17 (14.17)	6 (5.00)
Informal	20 (6.06)	216 (65.45)	7 (2.12)	82 (24.85)	5 (1.52)

Chi-square = 21.878; df = 4; Significant at 1 per cent level

Age of Enterprise

Below 10 years	23 (7.69)	184 (61.54)	12 (4.01)	72 (24.08)	8 (2.68)
Above 10 years	11 (7.28)	105 (69.54)	5 (3.31)	27 (17.88)	3 (1.99)

Chi-square = 3.100; df = 4; Insignificant

women entrepreneurs towards public sector irrespective of their level of education. It is an indication of positive development. The value of chi-square is statistically significant at 1 per cent level of significance. It shows that these two variables vary significantly. Women entrepreneurs (more than 70 per cent) in the age-group of below 30 and above 40 agree with this statement than women entrepreneurs in the age group of 30-40 (63 per cent). It reveals that women entrepreneurs in middle age group still have expectations from public sector in case of employment generation. The value of chi-square is statistically significant at 1 per cent level of significance. More than 70 per cent of women entrepreneurs hailing from urban and rural areas fully agree with this statement. It shows that women entrepreneurs irrespective of place of origin have changed their attitude towards public sector. The value of chi-square is statistically insignificant. 69 per cent to 74 per cent women entrepreneurs coming from joint and nuclear families agree with this statement. The value of chi-square is statistically insignificant. Similar type of conclusions have been observed in case of women entrepreneurs managing business under various forms of business organizations. The value of chi-square is statistically insignificant. Women entrepreneurs investing less money in business agree with this statement relatively more than women entrepreneurs investing moderate and higher level of money in business. It shows that women entrepreneurs investing less money understand the decline employment opportunities in the formal sector. The value of chi-square is statistically significant at 1 per cent level of significance. It shows that these two variables vary significantly. Women entrepreneurs earning lower level of income agree relatively more with this statement than women entrepreneurs earning higher level of income. It shows that women entrepreneurs might be comparing their opportunity cost with job or with other occupations. The value of chi-square is statistically significant at 1 per cent level of significance. Information further shows that trained women entrepreneurs (72 per cent) agree with this statement slightly less than untrained women entrepreneurs (70 per cent). The value of chi-square is statistically significant at 5 per cent level of significance. Similarly, women entrepreneurs using various sources of finance also fully agree with this statement. The value of chi-square is statistically significant at 1 per cent level of significance. Women entrepreneurs doing business for a longer period of time fully agree with this statement than women entrepreneurs who have started business recently. It may be due to stagnation in business or difficulty in management of business during post-reform period. The value of chi-square is statistically insignificant.

Table 7.13 shows that slightly less than one-third women entrepreneurs fully agree with this statement that present policy provisions are sufficient for the growth of entrepreneurship among women and another slightly more than one-third women entrepreneurs are indifferent. Education-wise information further shows that proportion of women entrepreneurs having low level of education agree with this statement more than women entrepreneurs having higher level of education. It may be due to more expectations of more educated women entrepreneurs towards government policies and procedures. The value of chi-square is statistically significant at 1 per cent level of significance. Women entrepreneurs in lower age group agree relatively less with this statement than women entrepreneurs in higher age groups. It may be due to increase in awareness of various policies of government by this section of women entrepreneurs. The value of chi-square is statistically significant at 1 per cent level of significance. It reveals that these two variables affect each other significantly. 42 per cent women entrepreneurs hailing from rural areas agree with this statement, whereas only 27 per cent women entrepreneurs coming from urban areas agree with this statement.

TABLE 7.13

Present Policy Provisions are Sufficient

Group	Strongly agree	Agree	Indifferent	Disagree	Strongly disagree
1	2	3	4	5	6
All Data	18 (4.00)	119 (26.44)	167 (37.11)	108 (24.00)	38 (8.44)
Education					
Primary	4 (16.67)	6 (25.00)	9 (37.50)	5 (20.83)	—
Matric	4 (5.00)	22 (27.50)	28 (35.00)	18 (22.50)	8 (10.00)
Graduate	7 (3.72)	44 (23.40)	85 (45.21)	33 (17.55)	19 (10.11)
Post Graduate	3 (1.90)	47 (29.75)	45 (28.48)	52 (32.91)	11 (6.96)
Chi-square = 31.502; df = 12; Significant at 1 per cent level					
Age (years)					
Below 30	10 (7.09)	30 (21.28)	58 (41.13)	33 (23.40)	10 (7.09)
30-40	3 (1.96)	31 (20.26)	53 (34.64)	53 (34.64)	13 (8.50)
Above 40	5 (3.21)	58 (37.18)	56 (35.90)	22 (14.10)	15 (9.62)
Chi-square = 30.735; df = 8; Significant at 1 per cent level					
Place of Origin					
Rural	4 (4.60)	33 (37.93)	18 (20.69)	25 (28.74)	7 (8.05)
Urban	14 (3.86)	86 (23.69)	149 (41.05)	83 (22.87)	31 (8.54)
Chi-square = 14.342; df = 4; Significant at 1 per cent level					

1	2	3	4	5	6
Type of Family					
Joint	9 (4.31)	50 (23.92)	84 (40.19)	45 (21.53)	7 (8.05)
Nuclear	9 (3.73)	69 (28.63)	83 (34.44)	63 (26.14)	31 (8.54)
Chi-square = 4.206; df = 4; Insignificant					
Form of Business Organization					
Sole	14 (4.53)	75 (24.27)	118 (38.19)	73 (23.62)	29 (9.39)
Others	4 (2.84)	44 (31.21)	49 (34.75)	35 (24.82)	9 (6.38)
Chi-square = 3.854; df = 4; Insignificant					
Investment (Lacs)					
<1	6 (4.88)	30 (24.39)	51 (41.46)	32 (26.02)	4 (3.25)
1-2	8 (6.56)	42 (29.17)	58 (40.28)	29 (20.14)	7 (4.86)
2-3	1 (1.30)	17 (22.08)	28 (36.36)	21 (27.27)	10 (12.99)
3-5	3 (4.69)	19 (29.69)	18 (28.12)	13 (20.31)	11 (17.19)
5-10	—	8 (25.81)	10 (32.26)	7 (22.58)	6 (19.35)
Above 10	—	3 (27.27)	2 (18.18)	6 (54.55)	—
Chi-square = 34.568; df = 20; Significant at 5 per cent level					
Income (Rs.)					
<7500	2 (3.70)	14 (25.93)	28 (51.85)	7 (12.96)	3 (5.56)
7500-10000	6 (3.97)	37 (24.50)	67 (44.37)	27 (17.88)	14 (9.27)
10000-15000	2 (2.06)	41 (42.27)	29 (29.90)	21 (21.65)	4 (4.12)
15000-20000	6 (6.00)	17(17.00)	31 (31.00)	31 (31.00)	15 (15.00)
20000+	2 (4.17)	10 (20.83)	12 (25.00)	22 (45.83)	2 (4.17)
Chi-square = 50.671; df = 16; Significant at 1 per cent level					
Training					
Got Training	4 (1.70)	60 (25.53)	87 (37.02)	58 (24.68)	26 (11.06)
No Training	14 (6.51)	59 (27.44)	80 (37.21)	50 (23.26)	12 (5.58)
Chi-square = 10.740; df = 4; Significant at 5 per cent level					
Sources of Finance					
Formal	5 (4.17)	43 (35.83)	35 (29.17)	25 (20.83)	12 (10.00)
Informal	13 (3.94)	76 (23.03)	132 (40.00)	83 (25.15)	26 (7.88)
Chi-square = 9.402; df = 4; Insignificant					
Age of Enterprise					
Below 10 years	14 (4.68)	66 (22.07)	113 (37.79)	83 (27.76)	23 (7.69)
Above 10 years	4 (2.65)	33 (35.10)	54 (35.76)	25 (16.56)	15 (9.93)
Chi-square = 13.429; df = 4; Significant at 1 per cent level					

The value of chi-square is statistically significant at 1 per cent level of significance. Women entrepreneurs hailing from nuclear families agree with this statement slightly more than women entrepreneurs coming from joint families. The value of chi-square is statistically insignificant. Women entrepreneurs managing business under other than individual forms of business organizations agree more with this statement than women entrepreneurs managing business on individual basis. It shows that women entrepreneurs doing business on joint basis need more help than other women entrepreneurs and in this process they are more aware of policies of government. The value of chi-square is statistically insignificant. Women entrepreneurs investing less money in business more agree relatively more with this statement than women entrepreneurs investing more money in business. It clearly shows that women entrepreneurs investing more money in business have to consult various policies of government more rigorously than other women entrepreneurs. The value of chi-square is statistically significant at 5 per cent level of significance. Women entrepreneurs earning moderate level of income agree relatively more with this statement than women entrepreneurs earning lower and higher level of income. It shows that women entrepreneurs earning lower level of income want to increase their level of income and in this process they need more help from government. Similarly, women entrepreneurs earning higher level of income want to increase their income further. The value of chi-square vary significantly. One-third women entrepreneurs who have not undertaken training before start of their business agree with this statement more than trained women entrepreneurs. The value of chi-square is statistically significant at 5 per cent level of significance. Women entrepreneurs (41 per cent) who have taken assistance from financial institutions agree with this statement relatively more than other women entrepreneurs. The reason being, women entrepreneurs depending on informal sources of finance face more problem in managing business due to high cost of finance. The value of chi-square is statistically insignificant. 38 per cent of women entrepreneurs possessing older enterprises agree relatively more with statement as compared to women entrepreneurs possessing younger enterprises. It may be due to more expectations of younger generation of women entrepreneurs from government agencies.

The value of chi-square is statistically significant at 1 per cent level of significance.

Table 7.14 shows that 90 per cent of women entrepreneurs fully agree with this statement that EDP programmes can act as stimulator. It shows the significance expressed by women entrepreneurs towards these programmes. It may be due to exposure received by women entrepreneurs during these programmes. Women entrepreneurs possessing higher level of education agree with this statement relatively more than other women entrepreneurs. It seems that educated women entrepreneurs have evinced keen interest in this programmes. Analysis show that organizations responsible for conducting EDP programmes should be strengthened further. The value of chi-square is statistically insignificant. Women entrepreneurs in different age groups fully agree with this statement. It shows that women in different age groups desire to understand various business concepts before entering in business field. The value of chi-square is statistically insignificant. Almost same proportion of women entrepreneurs hailing from rural and urban areas agree with statement. Similar type of conclusions have been observed in case of women entrepreneurs coming from joint and 'nuclear families respectively. Women entrepreneurs managing business under different forms of business organizations agree with this statement. The values of chi-square are statistically insignificant in these cases. Women entrepreneurs investing more money in business agree relatively more with this statement. It shows that women entrepreneurs want to minimize risk in business by having more understanding of business process. The value of chi-square further justifies this argument. All the women entrepreneurs earning more than Rs. 20,000 per month in business agree with this statement and in other cases more than 81 per cent of women entrepreneurs fully agree with this statement. It seems that women entrepreneurs are in the constant search of sources which can provide information relating to business to them. The value of chi-square is statistically significant at 1 per cent level of significance. More than 80 per cent trained and untrained women entrepreneurs agree with this statement. The reason to this may be attributed to the desire of women entrepreneurs to get information relating to business, so that difficulties in

TABLE 7.14

EDPs can act as Stimulators

Group	Strongly agree	Agree	Indifferent	Disagree	Strongly disagree
1	2	3	4	5	6
All Data	80 (17.78)	329 (73.11)	28 (6.22)	10 (2.22)	3 (0.67)
Education					
Primary	3 (12.50)	16 (66.67)	4 (16.67)	1 (4.17)	—
Matric	13 (16.25)	58 (72.50)	8 (10.00)	1 (1.25)	—
Graduate	30 (15.96)	145 (77.13)	8 (4.26)	2 (1.06)	3 (1.60)
Post Graduate	34 (21.52)	110 (69.62)	8 (5.06)	6 (3.80)	—
Chi-square = 18.276; df = 12; Insignificant					
Age (years)					
Below 30	26 (18.44)	101 (71.63)	8 (5.67)	5 (3.55)	1 (0.71)
30-40	27 (17.65)	110 (71.90)	10 (6.54)	4 (2.61)	2 (1.31)
Above 40	27 (17.31)	118 (75.64)	10 (6.41)	1 (0.64)	—
Chi-square = 5.325; df = 8; Insignificant					
Place of Origin					
Rural	15 (17.24)	64 (73.56)	8 (9.20)	—	—
Urban	65 (17.91)	265 (73.00)	20 (5.51)	10 (2.75)	3 (0.83)
Chi-square = 4.668; df = 4; Insignificant					
Type of Family					
Joint	35 (16.75)	157 (75.12)	12 (5.74)	5 (2.39)	—
Nuclear	45 (18.67)	172 (71.37)	16 (6.64)	5 (2.07)	3 (1.24)
Chi-square = 3.246; df = 4; Insignificant					
Form of Business Organization					
Sole	53 (17.15)	228 (73.79)	23 (7.44)	4 (1.29)	1 (0.32)
Others	27 (19.15)	101 (71.63)	5 (3.55)	6 (4.26)	2 (1.42)
Chi-square = 8.202; df = 4; Insignificant					
Investment (Lacs)					
<1	24 (19.51)	83 (67.48)	14 (11.38)	—	2 (1.63)
1-2	25 (17.36)	106 (73.61)	10 (6.94)	3 (2.08)	—
2-3	21 (27.27)	49 (63.64)	1 (1.30)	6 (7.79)	—
3-5	8 (12.50)	54 (84.38)	1 (1.56)	1 (1.56)	—

1	2	3	4	5	6
5-10	1 (3.23)	27 (87.10)	2 (6.45)	—	1 (3.23)
Above 10	1 (9.09)	10 (90.91)	—	—	—
Chi-square = 45.765; df = 20; Significant at 1 per cent level					

Income (Rs.)

<7500	6 (11.11)	39 (72.22)	7 (12.96)	—	2 (3.70)
7500-10000	22 (14.57)	123 (81.46)	4 (2.65)	2 (1.32)	—
10000-15000	31 (31.96)	50 (51.55)	12 (12.37)	3 (3.09)	1 (1.03)
15000-20000	16 (16.00)	74 (74.00)	5 (5.00)	5 (5.00)	—
20000+	5 (10.42)	43 (89.58)	—	—	—
Chi-square = 56.682; df = 16; Significant at 1 per cent level					

Training

Got Training	45 (19.15)	181 (77.02)	6 (2.55)	2 (0.85)	1 (0.43)
No Training	35 (16.28)	148 (68.84)	22 (10.23)	8 (3.72)	2 (0.93)
Chi-square = 16.780; df = 4; Significant at 1 per cent level					

Sources of Finance

Formal	17 (14.17)	95 (79.17)	5 (4.17)	—	3 (2.50)
Informal	63 (19.09)	234 (70.91)	23 (6.97)	10 (3.03)	—
Chi-square = 15.019; df = 4; Significant at 1 per cent level					

Age of Enterprise

Below 10 years	58 (19.40)	209 (69.90)	20 (6.69)	9 (3.01)	3 (1.00)
Above 10 years	22 (14.57)	120 (79.47)	8 (5.30)	1 (0.66)	—
Chi-square = 6.888; df = 4; Insignificant					

management of business can be minimized. The value of chi-square is statistically significant at 1 per cent level of significance. It reveals that these two variables are positively associated. More than 90 per cent of women entrepreneurs using formal and informal sources of finance fully agree with this statement. The value of chi-square is statistically significant at 1 per cent level of significance. More than 90 per cent women entrepreneurs irrespective of life of their enterprises fully agree with this statement. It shows that all women entrepreneurs in business also want to brush their knowledge by attending various EDP programmes in order to survive in the market.

Table 7.15 shows that 22 per cent of women entrepreneurs agree with the statement that women become entrepreneurs out

TABLE 7.15

Women become Entrepreneurs out of Compulsion

Group	Strongly agree	Agree	Indifferent	Disagree	Strongly disagree
1	2	3	4	5	6
All Data	12 (2.67)	88 (19.56)	68 (15.11)	191 (42.44)	91 (20.22)
Education					
Primary	—	10 (41.67)	3 (12.50)	10 (41.67)	1 (4.17)
Matric	3 (3.75)	27 (33.75)	8 (10.00)	24 (30.00)	18 (22.50)
Graduate	7 (3.72)	27 (14.36)	36 (19.15)	85 (45.21)	33 (17.50)
Post Graduate	2 (1.27)	24 (15.19)	21 (13.29)	72 (45.57)	39 (24.68)

Chi-square = 34.291; df = 12; Significant at 1 per cent level

Age (years)					
Below 30	4 (2.84)	13 (9.22)	26 (18.44)	67 (47.52)	31 (21.99)
30-40	3 (1.96)	37 (24.18)	18 (11.76)	55 (35.95)	40 (26.14)
Above 40	5 (3.21)	38 (24.36)	24 (15.38)	69 (44.23)	20 (12.82)

Chi-square = 23.454; df = 8; Significant at 1 per cent level

Place of Origin					
Rural	—	22 (25.29)	7 (8.05)	34 (39.08)	24 (27.59)
Urban	12 (3.31)	66 (18.18)	61 (16.80)	157 (43.25)	67 (18.46)

Chi-square = 11.430; df = 4; Significant at 5 per cent level

Type of Family					
Joint	5 (2.39)	47 (22.49)	34 (16.27)	77 (36.84)	46 (22.01)
Nuclear	7 (2.90)	41 (17.01)	34 (14.11)	114 (47.30)	45 (18.67)

Chi-square = 5.674; df = 4; Insignificant

Form of Business Organization					
Sole	7 (2.27)	64 (20.71)	52 (16.83)	120 (38.63)	66 (21.36)
Others	5 (3.55)	24 (17.02)	16 (11.35)	71 (50.35)	25 (17.73)

Chi-square = 6.852; df = 4; Insignificant

Investment (Lacs)					
<1	—	20 (16.26)	22 (17.89)	49 (39.84)	32 (26.02)
1-2	2 (1.39)	25 (17.36)	19 (13.19)	63 (43.75)	35 (24.31)
2-3	4 (5.19)	28 (36.36)	6 (7.79)	28 (36.36)	11 (14.29)
3-5	4 (6.25)	9 (14.06)	11 (17.19)	31 (48.44)	9 (14.06)

1	2	3	4	5	6
5-10	2 (6.45)	6 (19.35)	8 (25.81)	14 (45.16)	1 (3.23)
Above 10	—	—	2 (18.18)	6 (54.55)	3 (27.27)

Chi-square = 45.024; df = 20; Significant at 1 per cent level

Income (Rs.)					
<7500	—	15 (27.78)	14 (25.93)	23 (42.59)	2 (3.70)
7500-10000	3 (1.99)	29 (19.21)	17 (11.26)	59 (39.07)	43 (28.48)
10000-15000	1 (1.03)	20 (20.62)	14 (14.43)	38 (39.18)	24 (24.74)
15000-20000	6 (6.00)	21 (21.00)	13 (13.00)	49 (49.00)	11 (11.00)
20000+	2 (4.17)	3 (6.25)	10 (20.83)	22 (45.83)	11 (22.92)

Chi-square = 40.182; df = 16; Significant at 1 per cent level

Training					
Got Training	4 (1.70)	45 (19.15)	36 (15.32)	96 (40.85)	54 (22.98)
No Training	8 (3.72)	43 (20.00)	32 (14.88)	95 (44.19)	37 (17.21)

Chi-square = 3.914; df = 4; Insignificant

Sources of Finance					
Formal	4 (3.33)	9 (7.50)	19 (15.83)	67 (55.83)	21 (17.50)
Informal	8 (2.42)	79 (23.94)	49 (14.85)	124 (37.58)	70 (21.21)

Chi-square = 20.001; df = 4; Significant at 1 per cent level

Age of Enterprise					
Below 10 years	10 (3.34)	50 (16.72)	45 (15.05)	125 (41.81)	69 (23.08)
Above 10 years	2 (1.32)	38 (25.17)	23 (15.23)	66 (43.71)	22 (14.57)

Chi-square = 8.871; df = 4; Insignificant

of compulsion and 63 per cent of women entrepreneurs disagree with this statement. It shows that women are entering in business line to achieve something. It may be due to change in perceptions of women entrepreneurs towards business. It may also be due to decline in employment opportunities in formal sector of economy. Education-wise information further shows that women entrepreneurs possessing lower level of education agree with this statement relatively more than other women entrepreneurs. It may be due to lack of alternative employment opportunities available to women entrepreneurs having low level of education. The value of chi-square is statistically significant at 1 per cent level of significance. It shows that these two variables are positively associated. Women entrepreneurs in higher age group agreed relatively more with this statement than women entrepreneurs in lower age group. It may be due to difference in age of women entrepreneurs and women entrepreneurs in higher age group might be facing difficulties in management of business under changing economic scenario. The value of chi-square is statistically significant at 1 per cent level of significance. Women entrepreneurs (25 per cent) hailing from rural area agree relatively more with this statement than other women entrepreneurs (21 per cent). It may be due to stagnation of employment opportunities in rural areas, low wages in agriculture sector and lack of industrial and commercial activities. The value of chi-square is statistically significant at 5 per cent level of significance. Women entrepreneurs (25 per cent) coming from joint families agree with this statement more than other women entrepreneurs (20 per cent). It may be due to more restrictions and elders in family tak' major decisions. The value of chi-square is statistically insignificant. Women entrepreneurs managing business under other than individual forms of business organizations disagree more with this statement as compared to women entrepreneurs managing business on individual basis. It may be due to involvement of more than one per cent in joint business. The value of chi-square is statistically insignificant. Women entrepreneurs investing money in the range of Rs. 2-3 lacs agree more with this statement than women entrepreneurs investing money upto Rs. 2 lacs in business. On the other hand, women entrepreneurs investing more than Rs. 10 lacs in business fully disagree with this statement. It shows that women entrepreneurs investing more money in business are more serious and take things not under compulsions. The value of chi-square is statistically significant at 1 per cent level of significance. The women entrepreneurs earning lower level of income agree with this statement relatively more than women entrepreneurs earning higher level of income. The reason to this may be attributed to lower level of income and difficulties in fulfilment of various business obligations. The value of chi-square is statistically significant at 1 per cent level of significance. Untrained women entrepreneurs agree with this statement slightly more than trained women entrepreneurs. The value of chi-square is statistically insignificant. Women entrepreneurs (26 per cent) who have been using informal sources of finance agree with this statement more than women entrepreneurs (11 per cent) using formal sources of finance. It may be due to lack of availability of finance at low interest. The value of chi-square is statistically significant at 1 per cent level of significance. Women entrepreneurs who have enterprises more than 10 years old agree with this statement more than other women entrepreneurs. The reason to this may be assigned to decline in profit of older enterprises. The value of chi-square is statistically insignificant.

Table 7.16 shows that 47 per cent women entrepreneurs agree with this statement that job is better than business. It may be due to more complexities involved in business and a lot of time is required to perform business effectively. Education-wise information further shows that women entrepreneurs possessing education upto graduate level agree with this statement more than women entrepreneurs possessing post-graduate level of

TABLE 7.16

Job is Better than Entrepreneurship

Group	Strongly agree	Agree	Indifferent	Disagree	Strongly disagree
1	2	3	4	5	6
All Data	50 (11.11)	162 (36.00)	55 (12.22)	153 (34.00)	30 (6.67)
Education					
Primary	2 (8.33)	14 (58.33)	1 (4.17)	6 (25.00)	1 (4.17)
Matric	9 (11.25)	37 (46.25)	6 (7.50)	28 (35.00)	—
Graduate	29 (15.43)	63 (33.51)	25 (13.30)	56 (29.79)	15 (7.98)
Post Graduate	10 (6.33)	48 (30.38)	23 (14.56)	63 (39.87)	14 (8.86)
Chi-square = 27.920; df = 12; Significant at 1 per cent level					
Age (years)					
Below 30	13 (9.22)	52 (36.88)	17 (12.06)	45 (31.91)	14 (9.93)
30-40	15 (9.80)	63 (41.18)	19 (12.42)	44 (28.76)	12 (7.84)
Above 40	22 (14.10)	47 (30.13)	19 (12.18)	64 (41.03)	4 (2.56)
Chi-square = 14.806; df = 8; Insignificant					
Place of Origin					
Rural	7 (8.05)	31 (35.63)	8 (9.20)	39 (44.83)	2 (2.30)
Urban	43 (11.85)	131 (36.09)	47 (12.95)	114 (31.40)	28 (7.71)
Chi-square = 8.530; df = 4; Insignificant					

(Contd.)

1	2	3	4	5	6
Type of Family					
Joint	20 (9.57)	81 (38.76)	31 (14.83)	71 (33.97)	6 (2.87)
Nuclear	30 (12.45)	81 (33.61)	24 (9.96)	82 (34.02)	24 (9.96)
Chi-square = 12.268; df = 4; Significant at 1 per cent level					
Form of Business Organization					
Sole	41 (13.27)	105 (33.98)	42 (13.59)	99 (32.04)	22 (7.12)
Others	9 (6.38)	57 (40.43)	13 (9.22)	54 (38.00)	8 (5.67)
Chi-square = 8.182; df = 4; Insignificant					
Investment (Lacs)					
<1	8 (6.50)	48 (39.02)	20 (16.26)	37 (30.08)	10 (8.13)
1-2	10 (6.94)	63 (43.75)	17 (11.81)	52 (36.11)	2 (1.39)
2-3	9 (11.69)	35 (45.45)	2 (2.60)	25 (32.47)	6 (7.79)
3-5	16 (25.00)	11 (17.19)	8 (12.50)	20 (31.25)	9 (14.06)
5-10	5 (16.13)	2 (6.45)	5 (16.13)	16 (51.61)	3 (9.68)
Above 10	2 (18.18)	3 (27.27)	3 (27.27)	3 (27.27)	—
Chi-square = 62.407; df = 20; Significant at 1 per cent level					
Income (Rs.)					
<7500	5 (9.26)	22 (40.74)	8 (14.81)	15 (27.78)	4 (7.41)
7500-10000	18 (11.92)	63 (41.72)	16 (10.60)	47 (31.13)	7 (4.64)
10000-15000	10 (10.31)	37 (38.14)	7 (7.22)	35 (36.08)	8 (8.25)
15000-20000	15 (15.00)	24 (24.00)	17 (17.00)	34 (34.00)	10 (10.00)
20000+	2 (4.17)	16 (33.33)	7 (14.58)	22 (45.83)	1 (2.08)
Chi-square = 21.988; df = 16; Insignificant					
Training					
Got Training	21 (8.94)	92 (39.15)	28 (11.91)	77 (32.77)	17 (7.23)
No Training	29 (13.49)	70 (32.56)	27 (12.56)	76 (35.35)	13 (6.05)
Chi-square = 3.945; df = 4; Insignificant					
Sources of Finance					
Formal	11 (9.17)	36 (30.00)	13 (10.83)	42 (35.00)	18 (15.00)
Informal	39 (11.82)	126 (38.18)	42 (12.73)	111 (33.64)	12 (3.64)
Chi-square = 19.545; df = 4; Significant at 1 per cent level					
Age of Enterprise					
Below 10 years	32 (10.70)	108 (36.12)	33 (11.04)	100 (33.44)	26 (8.70)
Above 10 years	18 (11.92)	54 (35.76)	22 (14.57)	53 (35.10)	4 (2.65)
Chi-square = 6.745; df = 4; Insignificant					

education. It may be due to fixed income and various facilities available in job and on the other hand, income in business is highly fluctuating. The value of chi-square is statistically significant at 1 per cent level of significance. Women entrepreneurs in the middle age group agree with this statement more than women entrepreneurs in lower and higher age groups. It may be due to difference in attitude of women. The value of chi-square is statistically insignificant. 44 per cent women entrepreneurs hailing from rural areas and 48 per cent from urban areas agree with the statement. It may be due to availability of better facilities in job. The value of chi-square is statistically insignificant. Almost same proportion of women entrepreneurs hailing from joint and nuclear families fully agree with this statement. It seems that job is still a preference for women entrepreneurs. The value of chi-square is statistically significant at 1 per cent level of significance. Similar type of conclusions have been observed in case of women entrepreneurs managing business under various forms of business organizations. The value of chi-square is statistically insignificant. Women entrepreneurs investing lower level of money agree more with statement. It may be due to increase in competition and failure to fulfil various assignments. The value of chi-square is statistically significant at 1 per cent level of significance. More than 48 per cent of women entrepreneurs earning income upto Rs. 15,000 per month in business fully agree with this statement. On the other hand, women entrepreneurs earning higher level of income do not give more weightage to this factor. The reason being, these women entrepreneurs are earning better income and enjoying better status. The value of chi-square is statistically insignificant. Almost same proportion of women entrepreneurs irrespective of their level of training fully agree with this statement. It seems that craze of job is still in the minds of people. The value of chi-square is statistically insignificant. Women entrepreneurs who have used informal sources of finance agree with this statement relatively more as compared to women entrepreneurs who have used formal sources of finance. The reason to this may be assigned to the lack of availability of financial facilities, increase in cost of credit and poor return on investment. The value of chi-square is statistically significant at 1 per cent level of significance. Almost same proportion of women entrepreneurs irrespective of life of their enterprises agree with this statement. It may be due to intensive competition and increase in dual responsibilities. The value of chi-square is statistically insignificant. It shows that these two variables are independent.

Table 7.17 shows that 82 per cent of women entrepreneurs agree with this statement that business family can be a motivating factor and only small proportion of women entrepreneurs disagree with this statement. It may be due to availability of business knowledge at home. Education-wise information reveals that women entrepreneurs possessing higher level of education agree with this statement relatively more than other women entrepreneurs. It may be due to more necessity felt by highly educated women entrepreneurs. On the other hand, women entrepreneurs having low level of education may not think it necessary. The value of chi-square is statistically significant at

TABLE 7.17

Business Family can Act as Motivator

Group	Strongly agree	Agree	Indifferent	Disagree	Strongly disagree
1	2	3	4	5	6
All Data	103 (22.89)	269 (59.78)	21 (4.67)	51 (11.33)	6 (1.33)
Education					
Primary	5 (20.83)	10 (41.67)	6 (25.00)	3 (12.50)	—
Matric	17 (21.25)	54 (67.50)	1 (1.25)	8 (10.00)	—
Graduate	33 (17.55)	111 (59.04)	12 (6.38)	26 (13.83)	6 (3.19)
Post Graduate	48 (30.83)	94 (59.49)	2 (1.27)	14 (8.86)	—
Chi-square = 47.253; df = 12; Significant at 1 per cent level					
Age (years)					
Below 30	32 (22.70)	87 (61.70)	6 (4.26)	14 (9.93)	2 (1.42)
30-40	36 (23.53)	91 (59.48)	8 (5.23)	14 (9.15)	4 (2.61)
Above 40	35 (22.44)	91 (58.33)	7 (4.49)	23 (14.74)	—
Chi-square = 6.814; df = 8; Insignificant					
Place of Origin					
Rural	19 (21.84)	50 (57.47)	8 (9.20)	10 (11.49)	—
Urban	84 (23.14)	219 (60.33)	13 (3.58)	41 (11.29)	6 (1.65)
Chi-square = 6.328; df = 4; Insignificant					

1	2	3	4	5	6
Type of Family					
Joint	50 (23.92)	123 (58.85)	7 (3.35)	28 (13.40)	1 (0.48)
Nuclear	53 (21.99)	146 (60.58)	14 (5.81)	23 (9.54)	5 (2.07)
Chi-square = 6.328; df = 4; Insignificant					
Form of Business Organization					
Sole	65 (21.04)	188 (60.84)	18 (5.83)	35 (11.33)	3 (0.97)
Others	38 (26.95)	81 (57.45)	3 (2.13)	16 (11.35)	3 (2.13)
Chi-square = 5.475; df = 4; Insignificant					
Investment (Lacs)					
<1	35 (28.46)	75 (60.98)	5 (4.07)	4 (3.25)	4 (3.25)
1-2	26 (18.06)	103 (71.53)	5 (3.47)	10 (6.94)	—
2-3	20 (25.97)	39 (50.65)	7 (9.09)	10 (12.99)	1 (1.30)
3-5	13 (20.31)	31 (48.44)	1 (1.56)	19 (29.69)	—
5-10	6 (19.35)	13 (41.94)	3 (9.68)	8 (25.81)	1 (3.23)
Above 10	3 (27.27)	4 (72.73)	—	—	—
Chi-square = 61.805; df = 20; Significant at 1 per cent level					
Income (Rs.)					
<7500	14 (25.93)	30 (55.56)	3 (5.56)	3 (5.56)	4 (7.41)
7500-10000	34 (22.52)	93 (61.59)	2 (1.32)	22 (14.57)	—
10000-15000	29 (29.90)	54 (55.67)	8 (8.25)	4 (4.12)	2 (2.06)
15000-20000	10 (10.00)	63 (63.00)	8 (8.00)	19 (19.00)	—
20000+	16 (33.33)	29 (60.42)	—	3 (6.25)	—
Chi-square = 56.570; df = 16; Significant at 1 per cent level					
Training					
Got Training	68 (28.94)	132 (56.17)	10 (4.26)	24 (10.21)	1 (0.43)
No Training	35 (16.28)	137 (63.72)	11 (5.12)	27 (12.56)	5 (2.33)
Chi-square = 12.693; df = 4; Significant at 1 per cent level					
Sources of Finance					
Formal	19 (15.83)	74 (61.67)	6 (5.00)	18 (15.00)	3 (2.50)
Informal	84 (25.45)	195 (59.09)	15 (4.55)	33 (10.00)	3 (0.91)
Chi-square = 7.307; df = 4; Insignificant					
Age of Enterprise					
Below 10 years	77 (25.75)	176 (58.86)	14 (4.68)	28 (9.36)	4 (1.34)
Above 10 years	26 (17.22)	93 (61.59)	7 (4.64)	23 (15.23)	2 (1.32)
Chi-square = 6.365; df = 4; Insignificant					

1 per cent level of significance. Almost same proportion of women entrepreneurs in different age groups fully agree with this statement. The value of chi-square is statistically insignificant. Women entrepreneurs hailing from urban areas agree relatively more with this statement than women entrepreneurs belonging to rural areas. It may be due to more competition and difficulties in understanding business processes. Almost same proportion of women entrepreneurs hailing from joint and nuclear families agree with this statement. Almost same proportion of women entrepreneurs managing business under various forms of business organizations agree with this statement. The values of chi-square are statistically insignificant. All the women entrepreneurs investing more than Rs. 10 lacs in business fully agree with this statement than women entrepreneurs investing other slabs of investment. It may be due to more necessity felt by women entrepreneurs investing more money in business. On the other hand, women entrepreneurs investing less money in business may not feel it necessity. The value of chi-square is statistically significant at 1 per cent level of significance. Women entrepreneurs earning higher level of income agree with this statement more than women entrepreneurs earning lower level of income. The reason being, women entrepreneurs earning low level of income might be having various sources to fill the gap of business background families. The value of chi-square is statistically significant at 1 per cent level of significance. Trained women entrepreneurs agree relatively more with this statement as compared to their untrained counterparts. It shows that trained women entrepreneurs have more desire to learn basics of business. The value of chi-square is statistically significant at 1 per cent level of significance. Women entrepreneurs, who have used formal sources of finance agree with this statement less than women entrepreneurs using informal sources of finance. It may be due to less need felt by women entrepreneurs in former case. The value of chi-square is statistically insignificant. Women entrepreneurs having enterprises more than 10 years old agree relatively more with this statement than other women entrepreneurs. It seems that the women entrepreneurs who have been associated with business for a longer period of time need more assistance under new economic regime.

Table 7.18 shows that 54 per cent women entrepreneurs agree

with the statement that social and cultural barriers come in the way while doing business and slightly more than one-third women entrepreneurs disagree with this statement. Only small proportion of women entrepreneurs feel indifferent on this issue. Information reveals that mindset of people has not changed over the period of time. Women entrepreneurs possessing low level of education face this problem relatively more than other women entrepreneurs. It may be due to difference in level of education. The value of chi-square is statistically insignificant. It shows that these two variables are independent. Women entrepreneurs in middle age-group face this problem relatively more as compared to women entrepreneurs in lower and higher age groups. The value of chi-square is statistically significant at 1 per cent level of

TABLE 7.18

Social and Cultural Barriers Act as Hindrance in Business

Group	Strongly agree	Agree	Indifferent	Disagree	Strongly disagree
1	2	3	4	5	6
All Data	78 (17.33)	166 (36.89)	44 (9.78)	148 (32.89)	14 (3.11)
Education					
Primary	2 (8.33)	13 (54.17)	2 (8.33)	7 (29.17)	—
Matric	14 (17.50)	26 (32.50)	2 (2.50)	36 (45.00)	2 (5.67)
Graduate	29 (15.43)	69 (36.70)	22 (11.70)	58 (30.85)	10 (5.32)
Post Graduate	33 (20.89)	58 (36.71)	18 (11.39)	47 (29.75)	2 (1.27)
Chi-square = 20.448; df = 12; Insignificant					
Age (years)					
Below 30	17 (12.06)	49 (34.75)	21 (14.89)	46 (32.62)	8 (5.67)
30-40	47 (30.72)	59 (38.56)	9 (5.88)	34 (22.22)	4 (2.61)
Above 40	14 (8.97)	58 (37.18)	14 (8.97)	68 (43.59)	2 (1.28)
Chi-square = 46.417; df = 8; Significant at 1 per cent level					
Place of Origin					
Rural	21 (24.14)	27 (31.03)	5 (5.75)	32 (36.78)	2 (2.30)
Urban	57 (15.70)	139 (38.29)	39 (10.74)	116 (31.96)	12 (3.31)
Chi-square = 6.401; df = 4; Insignificant					

(Contd.)

1	2	3	4	5	6
Type of Family					
Joint	33 (15.79)	76 (36.36)	28 (13.40)	65 (31.10)	7 (3.35)
Nuclear	45 (18.67)	90 (37.34)	16 (6.64)	83 (34.44)	7 (2.90)
Chi-square = 6.245; df = 4; Insignificant					
Form of Business Organization					
Sole	59 (19.09)	106 (34.30)	34 (11.00)	100 (32.36)	10 (3.24)
Others	19 (13.48)	60 (42.55)	10 (7.09)	48 (34.04)	4 (2.84)
Chi-square = 5.197; df = 4; Insignificant					
Investment (Lacs)					
<1	21 (17.07)	55 (44.72)	18 (14.63)	22 (17.89)	7 (5.69)
1-2	29 (20.14)	65 (45.14)	4 (2.78)	45 (31.25)	1 (0.69)
2-3	13 (16.88)	35 (45.45)	10 (12.99)	19 (24.68)	—
3-5	11 (17.19)	4 (6.25)	6 (9.38)	43 (67.19)	—
5-10	4 (12.90)	4 (12.90)	4 (12.90)	13 (41.94)	6 (19.35)
Above 10	—	3 (27.27)	2 (18.18)	6 (54.55)	—
Chi-square = 114.365; df = 20; Significant at 1 per cent level					
Income (Rs.)					
<7500	2 (3.70)	20 (37.04)	14 (25.93)	14 (25.93)	4 (7.41)
7500-10000	30 (19.87)	56 (37.09)	9 (5.96)	53 (35.10)	3 (1.99)
10000-15000	13 (13.40)	48 (49.48)	4 (4.12)	30 (30.93)	2 (2.06)
15000-20000	19 (19.00)	6 (26.00)	15 (15.00)	39 (39.00)	1 (1.00)
20000+	14 (29.17)	16 (33.33)	2 (4.17)	12 (25.00)	4 (8.33)
Chi-square = 55.938; df = 16; Significant at 1 per cent level					
Training					
Got Training	38 (16.17)	105 (44.68)	13 (5.53)	71 (30.21)	8 (3.40)
No Training	40 (18.60)	61 (28.37)	31 (14.42)	77 (35.81)	6 (2.79)
Chi-square = 18.755; df = 4; Significant at 1 per cent level					
Sources of Finance					
Formal	7 (5.83)	38 (31.67)	7 (5.83)	58 (48.33)	10 (8.33)
Informal	71 (21.52)	128 (38.79)	37 (11.21)	90 (27.27)	4 (1.21)
Chi-square = 42.511; df = 4; Significant at 1 per cent level					
Age of Enterprise					
Below 10 years	60 (20.07)	106 (35.45)	31 (10.37)	90 (30.10)	12 (4.01)
Above 10 years	18 (11.92)	60 (39.74)	13 (8.61)	58 (38.41)	2 (1.32)
Chi-square = 9.096; df = 4; Insignificant					

significance. It shows that these two variables are positively associated. Women entrepreneurs hailing from rural areas face this problem slightly on higher side than their urban counterparts. It shows that social and cultural barriers act as obstacles for women entrepreneurs coming from rural and urban areas. The value of chi-square is statistically 'insignificant. 52 per cent women entrepreneurs hailing from joint families and 56 per cent from nuclear families face this problem. The value of chi-square is statistically insignificant. More than 52 per cent women entrepreneurs managing business under different forms of business organizations face this problem. The value of chi-square is statistically insignificant. Women entrepreneurs investing less money in business face this problem relatively more as compared to women entrepreneurs investing more money in business. The value of chi-square is statistically significant at 1 per cent level of significance. Women entrepreneurs earning even higher level of income also face this problem. The value of chi-square is statistically significant at 1 per cent level of significance. Trained women entrepreneurs (61 per cent) face this problem relatively more than untrained women entrepreneurs (47 per cent). The value of chi-square is statistically significant at 1 per cent level of significance. Women entrepreneurs using informal sources of finance face this problem relatively more as compared to women entrepreneurs using formal sources of finance. The value of chi-square is statistically significant at 1 per cent level of significance. Women entrepreneurs who have been managing business for last 10 years face this problem more than other women entrepreneurs. The value of chi-square is statistically insignificant.

Table 7.19 highlights that 62 per cent women entrepreneurs agree with the statement that being a women is boon for becoming entrepreneur. It shows the dexterity and skill possessed by women entrepreneurs. Education-wise information further shows that women entrepreneurs possessing lower level of education agree with this statement more than women entrepreneurs having higher level of education. It seems that women entrepreneurs after getting higher education may find it difficult to perform business related functions. On the other hand, women entrepreneurs possessing lower level of education due to inability to get job in formal sector may think business as a better alternative. The value of chi-square is statistically significant at 5 per cent level of significance. The almost same proportion of women entrepreneurs (55 per cent) in lower and middle age groups agree with this statement relatively less than women entrepreneurs in higher age groups (74 per cent). It seems that increase in age improves the skill to perform various functions of business. The value of chi-square is statistically significant at 1 per cent level of significance. It shows that these two variables vary significantly. Women entrepreneurs coming from rural areas (72 per cent) agree with this statement relatively more than women entrepreneurs coming from urban areas (59 per cent). It seems that women entrepreneurs in former case want to explore their hidden potential in business sector. The value of chi-square is statistically significant at 5 per cent level of significance. Women entrepreneurs hailing from joint families agree relatively more with this statement than women

TABLE 7.19

Being a Woman is Boon for Becoming Entrepreneur

Group	Strongly agree	Agree	Indifferent	Disagree	Strongly disagree
1	2	3	4	5	6
All Data	28 (6.22)	250 (55.56)	85 (18.89)	84 (18.67)	3 (0.67)
Education					
Primary	—	18 (75.00)	4 (16.67)	2 (8.33)	—
Matric	2 (2.50)	53 (66.25)	14 (17.50)	11 (13.75)	—
Graduate	13 (6.91)	88 (46.81)	45 (23.94)	39 (20.74)	3 (1 60)
Post Graduate	13 (8.23)	91 (57.59)	22 (13.92)	32 (20.25)	—
Chi-square = 22.408; df = 12; Significant at 5 per cent level					
Age (years)					
Below 30	10 (7.09)	67 (47.52)	26 (18.44)	36 (25.53)	2 (1.42)
30-40	10 (6.54)	75 (49.02)	37 (24.18)	31 (20.26)	—
Above 40	8 (5.13)	108 (69.23)	22 (14.10)	17 (10.90)	1 (0.64)
Chi-square = 23.770; df = 8; Significant at 1 per cent level					
Place of Origin					
Rural	10 (11.49)	53 (60.92)	9 (10.34)	15 (17.24)	—
Urban	18 (4.96)	197 (54.27)	76 (20.94)	69 (19.01)	3 (0.83)
Chi-square = 10.381; df = 4; Significant at 5 per cent level					

1	2	3	4	5	6
Type of Family					
Joint	11 (5.26)	124 (59.33)	40 (19.14)	32 (15.31)	2 (0.96)
Nuclear	17 (7.05)	126 (52.28)	45 (18.67)	52 (21.58)	1 (0.41)
Chi-square = 4.438; df = 4; Insignificant					
Form of Business Organization					
Sole	24 (7.77)	163 (52.75)	63 (20.39)	57 (18.45)	2 (0.65)
Others	4 (2.84)	87 (61.70)	22 (15.60)	27 (19.15)	1 (0.71)
Chi-square = 6.384; df = 4; Insignificant					
Investment (Lacs)					
<1	11 (8.94)	62 (50.41)	32 (26.02)	16 (13.01)	2 (1.63)
1-2	12 (8.33)	79 (54.86)	16 (11.11)	36 (25.00)	1 (0.69)
2-3	—	43 (55.84)	17 (22.08)	17 (22.08)	—
3-5	3 (4.69)	44 (68.75)	9 (14.06)	8 (12.50)	—
5-10	1 (3.23)	17 (54.84)	9 (29.03)	4 (12.90)	—
Above 10	1 (9.09)	5 (45.45)	2 (18.18)	3 (27.27)	—
Chi-square = 32.643; df = 20; Significant at 5 per cent level					
Income (Rs.)					
<7500	5 (9.266)	25 (46.30)	19 (35.19)	5 (9.26)	—
7500-10000	12 (7.95)	84 (55.63)	20 (13.25)	33 (21.85)	2 (1.32)
10000-15000	7 (7.22)	65 (67.01)	10 (10.31)	14 (14.43)	1 (1.03)
15000-20000	3 (3.00)	52 (52.00)	19 (19.00)	26 (26.00)	—
20000+	1 (2.08)	24 (50.00)	17 (35.42)	6 (12.500)	—
Chi-square = 39.838 ; df = 16; Significant at 1 per cent level					
Training					
Got Training	14 (5.96)	105 (44.68)	63 (26.81)	52 (22.13)	1 (0.43)
No Training	14 (6.51)	145 (67.44)	22 (10.23)	32 (14.88)	2 (0.93)
Chi-square = 30.443; df = 4; Significant at 1 per cent level					
Sources of Finance					
Formal	6 (5.00)	82 (68.33)	12 (10.00)	19 (15.83)	1 (0.83)
Informal	22 (6.67)	168 (50.91)	73 (22.12)	65 (19.70)	2 (0.61)
Chi-square = 12.819; df = 4; Significant at 1 per cent level					
Age of Enterprise					
Below 10 years	18 (6.02)	155 (51.84)	63 (21.07)	60 (20.07)	3 (1.00)
Above 10 years	10 (6.62)	95 (62.91)	22 (14.57)	24 (15.89)	—
Chi-square = 6.969; df = 4; Insignificant					

entrepreneurs coming from nuclear families. The value of chi-square is statistically insignificant. Women entrepreneurs managing business under other than individual forms of business organizations agree relatively more as compared to women entrepreneurs managing business on individual basis. It seems that women entrepreneurs in joint ventures feel more confident than women entrepreneurs doing business on individual basis. The value of chi-square is statistically insignificant. It shows that there is no association between these two variables. Women entrepreneurs investing less money in business agree relatively more with this statement than women entrepreneurs investing more money. It seems that women entrepreneurs investing more money needs extra care than other women entrepreneurs. The value of chi-square is statistically significant at 5 per cent level of significance. It shows that these two variables vary significantly. Women entrepreneurs earning moderate level of income agree with this statement more than women entrepreneurs earning lower and higher level of income. The value of chi-square is statistically significant at 1 per cent level of significance. Untrained women entrepreneurs agree more with this statement than trained women entrepreneurs. The reason being, untrained women entrepreneurs might be using their skill to increase their standard of living. The value of chi-square is statistically significant at 1 per cent level of significance. Women entrepreneurs using formal sources of finance agree with this statement relatively more as compared to women entrepreneurs using informal sources of finance. The reason being, the women entrepreneurs in former case might be able to overcome large number of problems with availability of money at low cost. The value of chi-square is statistically significant at 1 per cent level of significance. Women entrepreneurs having enterprises more than 10 years old agree with this statement relatively more than other women entrepreneurs. The reason being, these women entrepreneurs might be able to establish their business more effectively. The value of chi-square is statistically insignificant.

Table 7.20 shows that 70 per cent women entrepreneurs agree with the statement that women can compete with man. Education-wise information further shows that more than 60 per cent women entrepreneurs irrespective of their level of education agree with this statement. But this proportion is found to be more among educated women entrepreneurs. It shows that education enhances the knowledge and confidence. There is a need to formulate policies to strengthen the education system so that level of education may increase among females. The value of chi-square is statistically insignificant. Women entrepreneurs in lower age group agree with this statement relatively more as compared to women entrepreneurs in middle and higher age group. It seems that women entrepreneurs in lower age groups might be having more information and skill. On the other hand, women

TABLE 7.20

Women can Compete with Men

Group	Strongly agree	Agree	Indifferent	Disagree	Strongly disagree
1	2	3	4	5	6
All Data	47 (10.44)	266 (59.11)	56 (12.44)	65 (14.44)	16 (3.56)
Education					
Primary	2 (8.33)	13 (54.17)	5 (20.83)	4 (16.67)	—
Matric	7 (8.75)	50 (62.50)	9 (11.25)	14 (17.50)	—
Graduate	19 (10.11)	110 (58.51)	27 (14.36)	26 (13.83)	6 (3.19)
Post Graduate	19 (12.03)	93 (58.86)	15 (9.49)	21 (13.29)	10 (6.33)
Chi-square = 12.079; df = 12; Insignificant					
Age (years)					
Below 30	23 (16.31)	86 (60.99)	12 (8.51)	14 (9.93)	6 (4.26)
30-40	12 (7.84)	77 (50.33)	25 (16.34)	31 (20.26)	8 (5.23)
Above 40	12 (7.69)	103 (66.03)	19 (12.18)	20 (12.82)	2 (1.28)
Chi-square = 23.268; df = 8; Significant at 1 per cent level					
Place of Origin					
Rural	12 (13.79)	48 (55.17)	11 (12.64)	12 (13.79)	4 (4.60)
Urban	35 (9.64)	218 (60.06)	45 (12.40)	53 (14.60)	12 (3.31)
Chi-square = 1.806; df = 4; Insignificant					
Type of Family					
Joint	12 (5.74)	124 (59.33)	30 (14.35)	40 (19.14)	3 (1.44)
Nuclear	35 (14.52)	142 (58.92)	26 (10.79)	25 (10.37)	13 (5.39)
Chi-square = 20.298; df = 4; Significant at 1 per cent level					

(Contd.)

1	2	3	4	5	6
Form of Business Organization					
Sole	40 (12.94)	176 (56.96)	39 (12.62)	45 (14.56)	9 (2.91)
Others	7(4.96)	90 (63.83)	17(12.06)	20 (14.18)	7 (4.96)
Chi-square = 7.858; df = 4; Insignificant					
Investment (Lacs)					
<1	22 (17.89)	69 (56.10)	12 (.76)	14 (11.38)	6 (4.88)
1-2	17 (11.81)	79 (54.86)	10 (6.94)	32 (22.22)	6 (4.17)
2-3	8 (10.39)	35 (45.45)	17 (22.08)	16 (20.78)	1 (1.30)
3-5	—	53 (82.81)	7 (10.94)	2 (3.12)	2 (3.12)
5-10	—	19 (61.29)	10 (32.26)	1 (3.23)	1 (3.23)
Above 10	—	11 (100.0)	—	—	—
Chi-square = 72.576; df = 20; Significant at 1 per cent level					
Income (Rs.)					
<7500	12 (22.22)	27 (50.00)	1 (1.85)	10 (18.52)	4 (7.41)
7500-10000	15 (9.93)	97 (64.24)	24 (15.89)	15 (9.93)	—
10000-15000	8 (8.25)	53 (54.64)	6 (6.19)	23 (23.71)	7 (7.22)
15000-20000	8 (8.00)	60 (60.00)	14 (14.00)	13 (13.00)	5 (5.00)
20000+	4 (8.33)	29 (60.42)	11 (22.92)	4 (8.33)	—
Chi-square = 47.483; df = 16; Significant at 1 per cent level					
Training					
Got Training	43 (18.30)	112 (47.66)	30 (12.77)	36 (15.32)	14 (5.96)
No Training	4 (1.86)	154 (71.63)	26 (12.09)	29 (13.49)	2 (0.93)
Chi-square = 48.239; df = 4; Significant at 1 per cent level					
Sources of Finance					
Formal	19 (15.83)	79 (65.83)	10 (8.33)	9 (7.50)	3 (2.50)
Informal	28 (8.49)	187 (56.67)	46 (13.94)	56 (16.97)	13 (3.94)
Chi-square = 13.999; df = 4; Significant at 1 per cent level					
Age of Enterprise					
Below 10 years	45 (15.05)	156 (52.17)	39 (13.04)	45 (15.05)	14 (4.68)
Above 10 years	2 (1.32)	110 (72.85)	17 (11.26)	20 (13.25)	2 (1.32)
Chi-square = 29.017; df = 4; Significant at 1 per cent level					

entrepreneurs in higher age groups might have gained confidence over the period of time. The value of chi-square is statistically significant at 1 per cent level of significance. It shows that these two variables are positively associated. Almost same proportion of women entrepreneurs hailing from rural and urban areas agree with this statement. The value of chi-square is statistically in significant. Women entrepreneurs hailing from nuclear families agree with this statement relatively more as compared to their counterparts coming from joint families. It clearly reveals that nuclear families are providing more education to females and they are gaining more knowledge and confidence over the period of time. On the other hand, women entrepreneurs hailing from joint families due to stringent conditions fail to get adequate exposure. The value of chi-square is statistically significant at 1 per cent level of significance. It shows that these two variables are positively associated. Almost same proportion of women entrepreneurs managing business under individual and other forms of business organization agree with this statement. The value of chi-square is found to be statistically insignificant. Women entrepreneurs investing more money in business agree with this statement more than their counterparts investing less money in business. It shows that the level of investment enhances the confidence. The value of chi-square is statistically significant at 1 per cent level of significance. The level of income earned by women entrepreneurs shows that more than 60 per cent women entrepreneurs earning different levels of income agree with this statement. But this proportion is found to be more among women entrepreneurs earning income upto Rs. 10,000 per month. The value of chi-square is statistically significant at 1 per cent level of significance. It shows that there exist variations between these two variables. Untrained women entrepreneurs (73 per cent) agree more with this statement than trained women entrepreneurs (65 per cent). It seems that untrained women entrepreneurs possess more confidence than trained women entrepreneurs. The value of chi-square is statistically significant at 1 per cent level of significance. Women entrepreneurs using formal sources of finance agree with this statement relatively more than women entrepreneurs using informal sources of finance. The value of chi-square is statistically significant at 1 per cent level of significance. It seems that availability of finance at low cost enhances the confidence among women entrepreneurs. Women entrepreneurs who have been in business for longer period of time agree with this statement more than their counterparts who have been in business for less than

10 years. The reason being, experience enhances confidence. The value of chi-square is statistically significant at 1 per cent level of significance. It shows that these two variables are positively associated.

Table 7.21 shows that only 16 per cent women entrepreneurs agree with the statement that success in business results in neglect of family and children. It reveals that due to availability of servants and growth of childcare centers and nurseries, women do not face much problem related to neglect of children. Education-wise information further shows that women entrepreneurs possessing lower level of education agree with this statement more than women entrepreneurs possessing higher level of education. The value of chi-square is statistically significant at 1 per cent level of significance. It shows that these

TABLE 7.21

Success Results in Neglect of Children, Family and Home

Group	Strongly agree	Agree	Indifferent	Disagree	Strongly disagree
1	2	3	4	5	6
All Data	10 (2.22)	63 (14.00)	84 (18.67)	251 (55.78)	42 (9.33)
Education					
Primary	—	7 (29.17)	8 (33.33)	9 (37.50)	—
Matric	2 (2.50)	21 (26.25)	9 (11.25)	46 (57.50)	2 (2.50)
Graduate	2 (1.06)	15 (7.98)	48 (25.53)	97 (51.60)	26 (13.83)
Post Graduate	6 (3.80)	20 (12.66)	19 (12.03)	99 (62.66)	14 (8.86)
Chi-square = 48.417; df = 12; Significant at 1 per cent level					
Age (years)					
Below 30	—	5 (3.55)	35 (24.82)	83 (58.87)	18 (12.77)
30-40	4 (2.61)	15 (9.80)	31 (20.26)	88 (57.52)	15 (9.80)
Above 40	6 (3.85)	43 (27.56)	18 (11.54)	80 (51.28)	9 (5.77)
Chi-square = 50.668; df = 8; Significant at 1 per cent level					
Place of Origin					
Rural	2 (2.30)	10 (11.49)	17 (19.54)	50 (57.47)	8 (9.20)
Urban	8 (2.20)	53 (14.60)	67 (18.46)	201 (55.37)	34 (9.37)
Chi-square = 0.588; df = 4; Insignificant					

1	2	3	4	5	6
Type of Family					
Joint	5 (2.39)	33 (15.79)	39 (18.66)	119 (56.94)	13 (6.22)
Nuclear	5 (2.07)	30 (12.45)	45 (18.67)	132 (54.77)	29 (12.03)
Chi-square = 5.090; df = 4; Insignificant					
Form of Business Organization					
Sole	8 (2.59)	37 (11.97)	62 (20.66)	166 (53.72)	36 (11.65)
Others	2 (1.42)	26 (18.44)	22 (15.60)	85 (60.28)	6 (4.26)
Chi-square = 10.941; df = 4; Significant at 5 per cent level					
Investment (Lacs)					
<1	5 (4.07)	12 (9.76)	24 (19.51)	61 (49.59)	21 (17.07)
1-2	2 (1.39)	22 (15.28)	15 (10.42)	92 (63.89)	13 (9.03)
2-3	2 (2.60)	14 (18.18)	19 (24.68)	37 (48.05)	5 (6.49)
3-5	1 (1.56)	8 (12.50)	13 (20.31)	40 (62.50)	2 (3.12)
5-10	—	7 (22.58)	11 (35.48)	12 (38.71)	1 (3.23)
Above 10	—	—	2 (18.18)	9 (81.82)	—
Chi-square = 41.324; df = 20; Significant at 1 per cent level					
Income (Rs.)					
<7500	5 (9.26)	7 (12.96)	9 (16.67)	25 (46.30)	8 (14.81)
7500-10000	—	16 (10.60)	22 (14.57)	99 (65.56)	14 (9.27)
10000-15000	2 (2.06)	23 (23.71)	20 (20.62)	40 (41.24)	12 (12.37)
15000-20000	3 (3.00)	12 (12.00)	19 (19.00)	60 (60.00)	6 (6.00)
20000+	—	5 (10.42)	14 (29.17)	27 (56.25)	2 (4.17)
Chi-square = 42.525; df = 16; Significant at 1 per cent level					
Training					
Got Training	6 (2.55)	13 (5.53)	40 (17.02)	142 (60.43)	34 (14.47)
No Training	4 (1.86)	50 (23.26)	44 (20.47)	109 (50.70)	8 (3.72)
Chi-square = 41.948; df = 4; Significant at 1 per cent level					
Sources of Finance					
Formal	3 (2.50)	14 (11.67)	28 (23.33)	69 (57.50)	6 (5.00)
Informal	7 (2.12)	49 (14.85)	56 (16.97)	182 (55.15)	36 (10.91)
Chi-square = 5.981; df = 4; Insignificant					
Age of Enterprise					
Below 10 years	7 (2.34)	32 (10.70)	65 (21.74)	170 (56.86)	25 (8.36)
Above 10 years	3 (1.99)	31 (20.53)	19 (12.58)	81 (53.64)	17 (11.26)
Chi-square = 12.572; df = 4; Significant at 1 per cent level					

two variables are positively associated. Women entrepreneurs in higher age groups agree more with this statement. It may be due to involvement of career of young children at later stages. The value of chi-square is statistically significant at 1 per cent level of significance. Women entrepreneurs hailing from urban areas (17 per cent) face this problem slightly on higher side than their counterparts coming from rural areas (13 per cent). It may be due to joint family system prevailing in rural areas. The value of chi-square is statistically insignificant. Less than 17 per cent women entrepreneurs coming from joint and nuclear families agree with this statement. It shows that child care and family management are no longer a problem for women entrepreneurs. It may be due to easy availability of manpower to look after household work. The value of chi-square is statistically insignificant. Women entrepreneurs (20 per cent) managing business under other than individual forms of business organizations face this problem more than women entrepreneurs (14 per cent) managing business under individual forms of business organization. The value of chi-square is statistically significant at 5 per cent level of significance. It shows that these two variables vary significantly. Less than 22 per cent women entrepreneurs investing upto Rs. 10 lacs in business agree with this statement and none of women entrepreneurs investing more than Rs. 10 lacs in business agree with this statement. It shows that only small proportion of women entrepreneurs are facing the problem of management of time between household activities and business. The value of chi-square is statistically significant at 1 per cent level of significance. Women entrepreneurs (26 per cent) earning income in the range of Rs. 10,000-15,000 per month agree more with this statement than women entrepreneurs earning income in the other ranges. The value of chi-square is statistically significant at 1 per cent level of significance. It shows that these two variables vary significantly. Untrained women entrepreneurs (25 per cent) agree more with this statement as compared to trained women entrepreneurs (8 per cent). The value of chi-square is statistically significant at 1 per cent level of significance. Less than 17 per cent women entrepreneurs using formal and informal sources of finance agree with this statement. It shows that women entrepreneurs do not face much problem related to management of family, children and home. The value of chi-square is statistically insignificant. Women entrepreneurs (22 per cent) having enterprises more than 10 years old agree more with this statement as compared to women entrepreneurs having enterprises less than 10 years old (13 per cent). It may be due to difficulty in management of enterprises in the former case. The value of chi-square is statistically significant at 1 per cent level of significance.

Table 7.22 shows that 75 per cent women entrepreneurs agree with this statement that it is difficult to survive without the help of husband. It reveals that business process is so cumbersome and difficult that women have to take the help of their husbands in various business matters. Education-wise information further shows that women entrepreneurs possessing lower level of education agree with this statement more than women entrepreneurs having higher level of education. The reason to this may be assigned to more confidence and knowledge possessed by women entrepreneurs in latter case. The value of chi-square is statistically significant at 5 per cent level of significance.

TABLE 7.22

Difficult to Survive without Help of Husband

Group	Strongly agree	Agree	Indifferent	Disagree	Strongly disagree
1	2	3	4	5	6
All Data	63 (14.00)	276 (61.33)	27 (6.00)	74 (16.44)	10 (2.22)
Education					
Primary	6 (25.00)	18 (75.00)	—	—	—
Matric	12 (15.00)	53 (66.25)	3 (3.75)	12 (15.00)	—
Graduate	26 (13.83)	109 (57.98)	19 (10.11)	29 (15.43)	5 (2.66)
Post Graduate	19 (12.03)	96 (60.76)	5 (3.16)	33 (20.89)	5 (3.16)
Chi-square = 22.657; df = 12; Significant at 5 per cent level					
Age (years)					
Below 30	9 (6.38)	88 (62.41)	9 (6.38)	27 (19.15)	8 (5.67)
30-40	40 (26.14)	76 (49.67)	11 (7.19)	24 (15.69)	2 (1.31)
Above 40	14 (8.97)	112 (71.79)	7 (4.49)	23 (14.74)	—
Chi-square = 44.524; df = 8; Significant at 1 per cent level					

(Contd.)

1	2	3	4	5	6
Place of Origin					
Rural	13 (14.94)	50 (57.47)	2 (2.30)	20 (22.99)	2 (2.30)
Urban	50 (13.77)	226 (62.26)	25 (6.89)	54 (14.88)	8 (2.20)
Chi-square = 5.605; df = 4; Insignificant					
Type of Family					
Joint	29 (13.88)	122 (58.37)	16 (7.66)	36 (17.22)	6 (2.87)
Nuclear	34 (14.11)	154 (63.90)	11 (4.56)	38 (15.77)	4 (1.66)
Chi-square = 3.228; df = 4; Insignificant					
Form of Business Organization					
Sole	38 (12.30)	192 (62.14)	16 (5.18)	55 (17.80)	8 (2.59)
Others	25 (17.73)	84 (59.57)	11 (7.80)	19 (13.48)	2 (1.42)
Chi-square = 4.953; df = 4; Insignificant					
Investment (Lacs)					
<1	19 (15.45)	65 (52.85)	10 (8.3)	23 (18.70)	6 (4.88)
1-2	15 (10.42)	99 (68.75)	4 (2.78)	24 (16.67)	2 (1.39)
2-3	14 (18.18)	41 (53.25)	8 (10.39)	12 (15.58)	2 (2.60)
3-5	10 (15.62)	48 (75.00)	1 (1.56)	5 (7.81)	—
5-10	5 (16.13)	18 (58.00)	4 (12.90)	4 (12.90)	—
Above 10	—	5 (45.45)	—	6 (54.55)	—
Chi-square = 41.382; df = 20; Significant at 1 per cent level					
Income (Rs.)					
<7500	5 (9.26)	28 (51.85)	6 (11.11)	13 (24.07)	2 (3.70)
7500-10000	15 (9.93)	108 (71.52)	6 (3.97)	18 (11.92)	4 (2.65)
10000-15000	18 (18.56)	60 (61.86)	7 (7.22)	10 (10.31)	2 (2.06)
15000-20000	9 (9.00)	57 (57.00)	6 (6.00)	26 (26.00)	2 (2.00)
20000+	16 (33.33)	23 (47.92)	2 (4.17)	7 (14.58)	—
Chi-square = 41.072; df = 16; Significant at 1 per cent level					
Training					
Got Training	34 (14.47)	132 (46.17)	14 (5.96)	45 (19.15)	10 (4.26)
No Training	29 (13.49)	144 (66.98)	13 (6.05)	29 (13.49)	—
Chi-square = 13.553; df = 4; Significant at 1 per cent level					
Sources of Finance					
Formal	16 (13.33)	79 (65.83)	5 (4.17)	20 (16.67)	—
Informal	47 (14.24)	197 (59.70)	22 (6.67)	54 (16.36)	10 (3.03)
Chi-square = 5.150; df = 4; Insignificant					

1	2	3	4	5	6
Age of Enterprise					
Below 10 years	43 (14.38)	177 (59.20)	21 (7.02)	48 (16.05)	10 (3.34)
Above 10 years	20 (13.25)	99 (65.56)	6 (3.97)	26 (17.22)	—
Chi-square = 7.444; df = 4; Insignificant					

Women entrepreneurs in lower age groups agree with this statement less than their counterparts in higher age groups. The value of chi-square is statistically significant at 1 per cent level of significance. It shows that these two variables vary significantly. Women entrepreneurs in urban areas agree relatively more with this statement than women entrepreneurs coming from rural areas. The value of chi-square is statistically insignificant. Women entrepreneurs hailing from nuclear families agree with this statement relatively more than women entrepreneurs coming from joint families. It seems that dependence on family is found to be more in the former case. The value of chi-square is statistically insignificant. Women entrepreneurs managing business under other than individual forms of business organizations agree with this statement slightly on higher side than women entrepreneurs managing business on individual basis. It seems that joint forms of business organization need more help. The value of chi-square is statistically insignificant. Women entrepreneurs investing less money in business agree with this statement relatively more than their counterparts investing more money in business. It seems that availability of finance helps women entrepreneurs in hiring the services of various experts. On the other hand, women entrepreneurs investing less money have to seek assistance from their family to reduce the cost. The value of chi-square is statistically significant at 1 per cent level of significance. Women entrepreneurs earning higher level of income agree more with this statement than their counterparts earning lower and moderate level of income. The value of chi-square is statistically significant at 1 per cent level of significance. It shows that these two variables are positively associated. Untrained women entrepreneurs agree with this statement relatively more than trained women entrepreneurs. It seems that training increases the confidence and in this process women entrepreneurs disagree with this statement.

The value of chi-square is statistically significant at 1 per cent level of significance. Women entrepreneurs using formal sources of finance agree with this statement relatively more than women entrepreneurs using informal sources of finance. It shows that women entrepreneurs have to depend on their family to fulfil various requirements in former case. The value of chi-square is statistically insignificant. Women entrepreneurs having enterprises more than 10 years old agree with this statement relatively more than their counterparts having enterprises less than 10 years old. It may be due to difference in perception and confidence among women entrepreneurs who have been in business for a longer period of time. The value of chi-square is statistically insignificant.

Table 7.23 shows that 89 per cent women entrepreneurs agree with the statement that success stories of women entrepreneurs can act as motivator. Information vividly highlights that publication of success stories of women entrepreneurs can motivate other women to adopt self employment activities. Success stories should be published in newspapers commonly read by persons coming from different walks of life. Education-wise information further shows that more than 80 per cent women entrepreneurs possessing different levels of education agree with this statement. The value of chi-square is statistically insignificant. It shows that women entrepreneurs want to go through the various steps which successful women entrepreneurs have adopted in their business. Similar type of observations have been made by women entrepreneurs in different age groups. The value of chi-square is statistically significant at 5 per cent level of significance. Women entrepreneurs hailing from rural areas agree with this statement slightly on higher side than women entrepreneurs coming from urban areas. The value of chi-square is statistically insignificant. It seems that women entrepreneurs hailing from rural areas want to learn from experience of successful women entrepreneurs. More than 60 per cent women entrepreneurs coming from joint and nuclear families agree with this statement. The value of chi-square is statistically insignificant. More than 85 per cent women entrepreneurs managing business under different forms of business organizations agree with this statement. It shows that women entrepreneurs even managing business under joint ventures want experience of successful women entrepreneurs. The value of chi-square is statistically

TABLE 7.23

Success Stories of Women Entrepreneurs can Act as Motivator

Group	Strongly agree	Agree	Indifferent	Disagree	Strongly disagree
1	2	3	4	5	6
All Data	94 (20.89)	308 (68.44)	25 (5.56)	20 (4.44)	3 (0.67)
Education					
Primary	3 (12.50)	17 (70.83)	3 (12.50)	1 (4.17)	—
Matric	13 (16.25)	63 (78.75)	1 (1.25)	3 (3.75)	—
Graduate	39 (20.74)	123 (65.43)	13 (6.91)	10 (5.32)	3 (1.60)
Post Graduate	39 (24.68)	105 (66.46)	8 (5.06)	6 (3.80)	—
Chi-square = 15.534; df = 12; Insignificant					
Age (years)					
Below 30	33 (23.40)	90 (63.83)	11 (7.80)	6 (4.26)	1 (0.71)
30-40	29 (18.95)	116 (75.82)	4 (2.61)	2 (1.31)	2 (1.31)
Above 40	32 (20.51)	102 (65.38)	10 (6.41)	12 (7.69)	—
Chi-square = 15.534; df = 8; Significant at 5 per cent level					
Place of Origin					
Rural	19 (21.84)	61 (70.11)	6 (6.90)	1 (1.15)	—
Urban	75 (20.66)	247 (68.04)	19 (5.23)	19 (5.23)	3 (0.83)
Chi-square = 3.793; df = 4; Insignificant					
Type of Family					
Joint	38 (18.18)	147 (70.33)	16 (7.66)	8 (3.83)	—
Nuclear	56 (23.24)	161 (66.80)	9 (3.73)	12 (4.98)	3 (1.24)
Chi-square = 7.606; df = 4; Insignificant					
Form of Business Organization					
Sole	64 (20.71)	209 (67.64)	20 (6.47)	15 (4.85)	1 (0.32)
Others	30 (21.28)	99 (70.21)	5 (3.55)	5 (3.55)	2 (1.42)
Chi-square = 3.715; df = 4; Insignificant					
Investment (Lacs)					
<1	27 (21.95)	87 (70.73)	3 (2.44)	4 (3.25)	2 (1.63)
1-2	27 (18.75)	109 (75.69)	5 (3.47)	3 (2.08)	—
2-3	18 (23.38)	44 (57.14)	14 (18.18)	1 (1.30)	—
3-5	15 (23.44)	37 (57.81)	1 (1.56)	11 (17.19)	—

(Contd.)

1	2	3	4	5	6
5-10	4 (12.90)	23 (74.19)	2 (6.45)	1 (3.23)	1 (3.23)
Above 10	3 (27.27)	8 (72.73)	—	—	—

Chi-square = 68.314; df = 20; Significant at 1 per cent level

Income (Rs.)					
<7500	8 (14.81)	39 (72.22)	1 (1.85)	4 (7.41)	2 (3.70)
7500-10000	27 (17.88)	107 (70.86)	7 (4.64)	10 (6.62)	—
10000-15000	26 (26.80)	65 (67.01)	5 (5.15)	—	1 (1.03)
15000-20000	21 (21.00)	62 (62.00)	12 (12.00)	5 (5.00)	—
20000+	12 (25.00)	35 (72.92)	—	1 (2.08)	—

Chi-square = 33.691; df = 16; Significant at 1 per cent level

Training					
Got Training	47 (20.00)	173 (73.62)	12 (5.11)	2 (0.85)	1 (0.43)
No Training	47 (21.86)	135 (62.79)	13 (6.05)	18 (8.37)	2 (0.93)

Chi-square = 17.006; df = 4; Significant at 1 per cent level

Sources of Finance					
Formal	30 (25.00)	77 (64.17)	5 (4.17)	5 (4.17)	3 (2.50)
Informal	64 (19.39)	231 (70.00)	20 (6.06)	15 (4.55)	—

Chi-square = 10.608; df = 4; Significant at 5 per cent level

Age of Enterprise					
Below 10 years	68 (22.74)	202 (67.56)	17 (5.69)	9 (3.01)	3 (1.00)
Above 10 years	26 (17.22)	106 (70.20)	8 (5.30)	11 (7.28)	—

Chi-square = 7.235; df = 4; Insignificant

insignificant. All the women entrepreneurs investing more than Rs. 10 lacs in business agree with this statement. Similarly, more than 90 per cent women entrepreneurs investing upto Rs. 2 lacs and Rs. 5-10 lacs in business also agree with this statement. The value of chi-square is statistically significant at 1 per cent level of significance. 98 per cent women entrepreneurs earning more than Rs. 20,000 per month agree with this statement. It shows that these women entrepreneurs still want to earn more money by taking the help of success stories of women entrepreneurs. 94 per cent trained and 84 per cent untrained women entrepreneurs agree with this statement. The value of chi-square is statistically significant at 1 per cent level of significance. 90 per cent women entrepreneurs using formal and informal sources of finance also agree with this statement. The value of chi-square is statistically significant at 5 per cent level of significance. More than 85 per cent women entrepreneurs irrespective of their life of enterprises agree with this statement. The value of chi-square is statistically significant at 1 per cent level of significance.

Table 7.24 shows that only small proportion of women entrepreneurs agree with the statement that home is the right place for women. It shows that there has been shift in the attitude of women. 29 per cent of women entrepreneurs possessing lower level of education agree with this statement, whereas only small proportion of women entrepreneurs having higher level of education agree with this statement. It shows that educated women entrepreneurs want to utilize their skill and knowledge which they have acquired over the period of time. The value

TABLE 7.24

Home is Right Place for Women

Group	Strongly agree	Agree	Indifferent	Disagree	Strongly disagree
1	2	3	4	5	6
All Data	28 (6.22)	38 (8.44)	38 (8.44)	194 (43.11)	152 (33.78)
Education					
Primary	—	7 (29.17)	—	12 (50.00)	5 (2.83)
Matric	5 (6.25)	4 (5.00)	9 (11.25)	46 (57.50)	16 (20.00)
Graduate	16 (8.51)	18 (9.57)	17 (9.04)	67 (35.64)	70 (37.23)
Post Graduate	7 (4.43)	9 (5.70)	12 (7.59)	69 (43.67)	61 (38.61)
Chi-square = 35.899; df = 12; Significant at 1 per cent level					
Age (years)					
Below 30	7 (4.96)	7 (4.96)	11 (7.80)	40 (28.37)	76 (53.90)
30-40	7 (4.58)	8 (5.23)	7 (4.58)	76 (49.67)	55 (35.95)
Above 40	14 (8.97)	23 (14.74)	20 (12.82)	78 (50.00)	21 (13.46)
Chi-square = 67.002; df = 8; Significant at 1 per cent level					
Place of Origin					
Rural	2 (2.30)	11 (12.64)	5 (5.75)	41 (47.13)	28 (32.18)
Urban	26 (7.16)	27 (7.44)	33 (9.09)	153 (42.15)	124 (34.16)
Chi-square = 6.334; df = 4; Insignificant					

(*Contd.*)

1	2	3	4	5	6
Type of Family					
Joint	18 (8.61)	17 (8.13)	13 (6.22)	101 (48.33)	60 (28.71)
Nuclear	10 (4.15)	21 (8.71)	25 (10.37)	93 (38.59)	92 (38.17)

Chi-square = 11.345; df = 4; Significant at 5 per cent level

1	2	3	4	5	6
Form of Business Organization					
Sole	22 (7.12)	27 (8.74)	26 (8.41)	126 (40.78)	108 (34.95)
Others	6 (4.26)	11 (7.80)	12 (8.51)	68 (48.23)	44 (31.21)

Chi-square = 3.027; df = 4; Insignificant

1	2	3	4	5	6
Investment (Lacs)					
<1	5 (4.07)	5 (4.07)	10 (8.13)	49 (39.84)	54 (43.90)
1-2	8 (5.56)	17 (11.81)	7 (4.86)	75 (52.08)	37 (25.69)
2-3	7 (9.09)	10 (12.99)	2 (2.60)	26 (33.77)	32 (41.56)
3-5	7 (10.94)	5 (7.81)	12 (18.75)	23 (35.94)	17 (26.56)
5-10	1 (3.23)	1 (3.23)	7 (22.58)	13 (41.94)	9 (29.03)
Above 10	—	—	—	8 (72.73)	3 (27.27)

Chi-square = 52.451; df = 20; Significant at 1 per cent level

1	2	3	4	5	6
Income (Rs.)					
<7500	2 (3.70)	—	6 (11.11)	38 (70.37)	8 (14.81)
7500-10000	13 (8.61)	15 (9.93)	10 (6.62)	59 (39.07)	54 (35.76)
10000-15000	3 (3.09)	15 (15.46)	4 (4.12)	49 (50.52)	26 (26.80)
15000-20000	10 (10.00)	8 (8.00)	15 (15.00)	21 (21.00)	46 (46.00)
20000+	—	—	3 (6.25)	27 (56.25)	18 (37.50)

Chi-square = 68.305; df = 16; Significant at 1 per cent level

1	2	3	4	5	6
Training					
Got Training	11 (4.68)	14 (5.96)	11 (4.68)	87 (37.02)	112 (47.66)
No Training	17 (7.91)	24 (11.16)	27 (12.56)	107 (49.77)	40 (18.60)

Chi-square = 46.023; df = 4; Significant at 1 per cent level

1	2	3	4	5	6
Sources of Finance					
Formal	5 (4.17)	8 (6.67)	18 (15.00)	62 (51.67)	27 (22.50)
Informal	23 (6.97)	30 (9.09)	20 (6.06)	132 (40.00)	125 (37.88)

Chi-square = 18.991; df = 4; Significant at 1 per cent level

1	2	3	4	5	6
Age of Enterprise					
Below 10 years	15 (5.02)	11 (3.68)	25 (8.36)	123 (41.14)	125 (41.81)
Above 10 years	13 (8.61)	27 (17.88)	13 (8.61)	71 (47.02)	27 (17.88)

Chi-square = 43.860; df = 4; Significant at 1 per cent level of chi-square is statistically significant at 1 per cent level of significance. It shows that these two variables are positively associated. Age-wise information further shows that women entrepreneurs in higher age group feel that home is the right place for women. It may be due to the family compulsions which are compelling the women to do business. The value of chi-square is statistically significant at 1 per cent level of significance. Almost same proportion of women entrepreneurs coming from rural and urban areas fully agree with this statement. It shows that place of origin does not influence the attitude of women. It is only the socio-cultural environment that might have restricted their mobility. The value of chi-square is statistically insignificant. Women entrepreneurs coming from joint families agree with this statement slightly more than women entrepreneurs coming from joint families. It may be due to environmental factors which are compelling reasons for women to agree with this statement. The value of chi-square is statistically significant at 5 per cent level of significance. Similar type of results have been obtained in case of women entrepreneurs managing business under various forms of business organizations. The value of chi-square is statistically insignificant. Only small proportion of women entrepreneurs investing lower and moderate level of money in business strongly agree with this statement. On the other hand, one-fourth women entrepreneurs investing money in the range of Rs. 2-3 lacs in business agree with this statement. It reveals that these entrepreneurs might feel burden while doing business activities. The value of chi-square is statistically significant at 1 per cent level of significance. It shows that these variables vary positively. Women entrepreneurs earning middle level of income agree with this statement. The value of chi-square is statistically significant at 1 per cent level of significance. 19 per cent of women entrepreneurs who have not undergone training before start of business agree with this statement than trained women entrepreneurs (10 per cent). It may be due to various difficulties faced by untrained women entrepreneurs while doing business. The information also shows that business process needs intensive training. The value of chi-square is statistically significant at 1 per cent level of significance. Women entrepreneurs who have used informal sources of finance feel that home is the right place for women. It may be due to high-cost of loans available from informal sector. The value of chi-square is statistically significant at 1 per cent level of significance. Women entrepreneurs who have been in business for a longer period of time fully agree with this statement. Interaction with these women entrepreneurs reveal that over the period of time business process has become so cumbersome, complicated and less lucrative that women entrepreneurs prefer to leave their business. The value of chi-square is statistically significant at 1 per cent level of significance.

Table 7.25 shows that 64 per cent women entrepreneurs agree with the statement that women inspectors should deal with women. Women entrepreneurs possessing lower level of education agree more with this statement. It may be due to low level of education and difficulty in dealing with educated officials of the government department. The value of chi-square is statistically insignificant. It shows that these two variables are independent. Women entrepreneurs in lower age group agree less with this statement. It may be due to age difference. The value of chi-square is found to be statistically significant at 1 per cent level of significance. It shows that their exists variations between these two variables. Women entrepreneurs hailing from rural areas agree with this statement more than women entrepreneurs coming from urban areas. It may be due to difference in place of origin of women entrepreneurs. The value of chi-square is found to be statistically significant at 1 per cent level of significance. Women entrepreneurs coming from joint families agree more with this statement than women entrepreneurs hailing from nuclear families. The reason to this may be assigned to lack of exposure in the former case. The value of chi-square is statistically insignificant. It shows that these two variables are independent. Women entrepreneurs managing business under other than individual forms of business organizations agree more with this statement. The value of chi-square is found to be statistically significant at 1 per cent level of significance. Women entrepreneurs investing more money in business agree less with this statement than women entrepreneurs investing low and moderate level of money in business. It may be due to more capacity among women entrepreneurs in former case to hire experts to deal with government officials and in this process they do not face much problem. The value of chi-square is found to be statistically

TABLE 7.25

Women Inspectors should Deal with Women Entrepreneurs

Group	Strongly agree	Agree	Indifferent	Disagree	Strongly disagree
1	2	3	4	5	6
All Data	96 (21.33)	194 (43.11)	29 (6.44)	129 (28.67)	2 (0.44)
Education					
Primary	3 (12.50)	16 (66.67)	1 (4.17)	4 (16.67)	—
Matric	14 (17.50)	45 (56.25)	2 (2.50)	18 (22.50)	1 (1.25)
Graduate	47 (25.00)	72 (38.30)	12 (2.38)	57 (30.32)	—
Post Graduate	32 (20.25)	61 (38.61)	14 (8.86)	50 (31.65)	1 (0.63)
Chi-square = 19.475; df = 12; Insignificant					
Age (years)					
Below 30	28 (19.86)	40 (28.37)	15 (10.64)	57 (40.43)	1 (0.71)
30-40	40 (26.14)	70 (45.75)	6 (3.92)	37 (24.18)	—
Above 40	28 (17.95)	84 (53.85)	8 (5.13)	35 (22.44)	1 (0.64)
Chi-square = 30.970; df = 8; Significant at 1 per cent level					
Place of Origin					
Rural	19 (21.84)	43 (49.43)	3 (3.45)	20 (22.99)	2 (2.30)
Urban	77 (21.21)	151 (41.60)	26 (7.16)	109 (30.03)	—
Chi-square = 12.071; df = 4; Significant at 1 per cent level					
Type of Family					
Joint	43 (20.57)	97 (46.41)	15 (7.18)	53 (25.36)	1 (0.48)
Nuclear	53 (21.99)	97 (40.25)	14 (5.81)	76 (31.54)	1 (0.41)
Chi-square = 2.916; df = 4; Insignificant					
Form of Business Organization					
Sole	63 (20.39)	130 (42.07)	23 (7.44)	92 (29.77)	1 (0.32)
Others	33 (23.40)	64 (45.39)	6 (4.26)	37 (26.24)	1 (0.71)
Chi-square = 2.932; df = 4; Insignificant					
Investment (Lacs)					
<1	21 (17.07)	56 (45.53)	10 (8.13)	36 (29.27)	—
1-2	33 (22.92)	51 (35.42)	7 (4.86)	52 (36.11)	1 (0.69)
2-3	12 (15.58)	48 (62.34)	3 (3.90)	13 (16.88)	1 (1.30)
3-5	16 (25.00)	22 (34.38)	7 (10.94)	19 (29.69)	—

(Contd.)

1	2	3	4	5	6
5-10	12 (38.71)	13 (41.94)	2 (6.45)	4 (12.90)	—
Above 10	2 (18.18)	4 (36.36)	—	5 (45.45)	—

Chi-square = 34.654; df = 20; Significant at 5 per cent level

Income (Rs.)

<7500	2 (3.70)	22 (40.74)	5 (9.26)	25 (46.30)	—
7500-10000	34 (22.52)	59 (39.07)	10 (6.62)	47 (31.13)	1 (0.66)
10000-15000	23 (23.71)	49 (50.52)	2 (2.06)	23 (23.71)	—
15000-20000	22 (22.00)	45 (45.00)	10 (10.00)	22 (22.00)	1 (1.00)
20000+	15 (31.25)	19 (39.58)	2 (4.17)	12 (25.00)	—

Chi-square = 28.984; df = 16; Significant at 5 per cent level

Training

Got Training	43 (18.30)	97 (41.28)	19 (8.09)	75 (31.91)	1 (0.43)
No Training	53 (24.65)	97 (45.12)	10 (4.65)	54 (25.12)	1 (0.47)

Chi-square = 6.377; df = 4; Insignificant

Sources of Finance

Formal	28 (23.33)	38 (31.67)	7 (5.43)	46 (38.33)	1 (0.83)
Informal	68 (20.61)	156 (47.27)	22 (6.67)	83 (25.15)	1 (0.30)

Chi-square = 11.264; df = 4; Significant at 5 per cent level

Age of Enterprise

Below 10 years	69 (23.08)	111 (37.12)	23 (7.69)	95 (31.77)	1 (0.33)
Above 10 years	27 (17.88)	83 (54.97)	6 (3.97)	34 (22.52)	1 (0.66)

Chi-square = 14.073; df = 4; Significant at 1 per cent level

significant at 5 per cent level of significance. Women entrepreneurs earning moderate level of income agree with this statement more than women entrepreneurs earning low and higher level of income. The value of chi-square is found to be statistically significant at 5 per cent level of significance. Trained women entrepreneurs agree with this statement less than untrained women entrepreneurs. The reason being, training helps in increasing the knowledge and skill of women entrepreneurs. The value of chi-square is statistically insignificant. Women entrepreneurs using formal sources of finance agree relatively less with this statement as compared to women entrepreneurs using informal sources of finance. The reason to this may be assigned to more knowledge of business in the former case. The value of chi-square is found to be statistically significant at 5 per cent level of significance. Women entrepreneurs having enterprises less than 10 years old agree relatively less with this statement than other women entrepreneurs. The value of chi-square is found to be statistically significant at 1 per cent level of significance.

Table 7.26 shows that 42 per cent women entrepreneurs agree with this statement and 26 per cent disagree. Information vividly shows that women want to settle first in life than want to go for marriage. 42 per cent women entrepreneurs possessing graduate level of education agree with this statement and 47 per cent

TABLE 7.26

Ideal Stage to be an Entrepreneurs is before Marriage

Group	Strongly agree	Agree	Indifferent	Disagree	Strongly disagree
1	2	3	4	5	6
All Data	52 (11.56)	136 (30.22)	143 (31.78)	106 (23.56)	13 (2.89)
Education					
Primary	2 (8.33)	7 (29.17)	8 (33.33)	7 (29.17)	—
Matric	10 (12.50)	28 (35.00)	26 (32.50)	15 (18.75)	1 (1.25)
Graduate	19 (10.11)	60 (31.91)	67 (35.64)	35 (18.62)	7 (3.72)
Post Graduate	21 (13.29)	41 (25.95)	42 (26.58)	45 (31.01)	5 (3.16)
Chi-square = 13.745; df = 12; Insignificant					
Age (years)					
Below 30	17 (12.06)	29 (20.57)	45 (31.91)	43 (30.50)	7 (4.96)
30-40	14 (9.15)	45 (29.41)	43 (28.10)	47 (30.72)	4 (2.61)
Above 40	21 (13.46)	62 (39.74)	55 (35.26)	16 (10.26)	2 (1.28)
Chi-square = 33.060; df = 8; Significant at 1 per cent level					
Place of Origin					
Rural	9 (10.34)	33 (37.93)	27 (31.03)	18 (20.69)	—
Urban	43 (11.85)	103 (28.37)	116 (31.96)	88 (24.24)	13 (3.58)
Chi-square = 5.768; df = 4; Insignificant					
Type of Family					
Joint	28 (13.40)	64 (30.62)	67 (32.06)	41 (19.62)	9 (4.31)
Nuclear	24 (9.96)	72 (29.88)	76 (31.54)	65 (26.97)	4 (1.66)
Chi-square = 6.459; df = 4; Insignificant					

(Contd.)

1	2	3	4	5	6
Form of Business Organization					
Sole	37 (11.97)	49 (28.80)	102 (33.01)	74 (23.95)	7 (2.27)
Others	15 (10.64)	47 (33.33)	41 (29.08)	32 (22.70)	6 (4.26)
Chi-square = 2.670; df = 4; Insignificant					
Investment (Lacs)					
<1	15 (12.20)	41 (33.33)	28 (22.76)	36 (29.27)	3 (2.44)
1-2	27 (18.75)	47 (32.64)	34 (23.61)	36 (25.00)	—
2-3	5 (6.49)	21 (27.27)	30 (38.96)	16 (20.78)	5 (6.49)
3-5	5 (7.81)	14 (21.88)	35 (54.69)	9 (14.06)	1 (1.56)
5-10	—	9 (29.03)	12 (38.71)	6 (19.35)	4 (12.90)
Above 10	—	4 (36.36)	4 (36.36)	3 (27.27)	—
Chi-square = 58.888; df = 20; Significant at 1 per cent level					
Income (Rs.)					
<7500	3 (5.56)	20 (37.04)	12 (22.22)	17 (31.48)	2 (3.70)
7500-10000	21 (31.91)	41 (27.15)	52 (34.44)	36 (23.84)	1 (0.66)
10000-15000	14 (14.43)	42 (43.30)	19 (19.59)	20 (20.62)	2 (2.06)
15000-20000	14 (10.00)	28 (28.00)	40 (40.00)	17 (17.00)	5 (5.00)
20000+	4 (8.33)	5 (10.42)	20 (41.67)	16 (33.33)	3 (6.25)
Chi-square = 38.889; df = 16; Significant at 1 per cent level					
Training					
Got Training	23 (9.79)	63 (26.81)	74 (31.49)	72 (30.64)	3 (1.28)
No Training	29 (13.49)	73 (33.95)	69 (32.09)	34 (15.81)	10 (4.65)
Chi-square = 18.141; df = 4; Significant at 1 per cent level					
Sources of Finance					
Formal	8 (6.67)	34 (28.33)	46 (38.33)	27 (22.50)	5 (4.17)
Informal	44 (13.33)	102 (30.91)	97 (29.39)	79 (23.94)	8 (2.42)
Chi-square = 6.793; df = 4; Insignificant					
Age of Enterprise					
Below 10 years	31 (10.37)	85 (28.43)	81 (27.09)	89 (29.77)	13 (4.35)
Above 10 years	21 (13.91)	51 (33.77)	62 (41.06)	17 (11.26)	—
Chi-square = 29.353; df = 4; Significant at 1 per cent level					

women entrepreneurs possessing matric level of education agree with statement. On the other hand, almost same proportion of women entrepreneurs possessing lower and higher level of education agree with this statement. It reveals that women are giving more preference to their career than marriage. The value of chi-square is statistically insignificant. Women entrepreneurs in higher age group give more weightage to career choice. It may be due to difficulty in management of business at latter stage of life. Similarly, women entrepreneurs in lower age group are concerned with their career than marriage issue. The reason being, women want to utilize their skill and knowledge in better manner after attaining it immediately. 48 per cent women entrepreneurs hailing from rural areas also hold similar opinion on this issue. It seems that women entrepreneurs hailing from rural areas want to get rid of social and cultural barriers prevailing in rural areas. The value of chi-square is statistically insignificant. Women entrepreneurs (44 per cent) hailing from joint families agree relatively more with this statement than women entrepreneurs (39 per cent) hailing from nuclear families. It may be due to prevalence of rigid norms in joint families. The value of chi-square is statistically insignificant. Women entrepreneurs managing business under other than individual forms of business organizations agree with this statement more than other women entrepreneurs. It may be due to dual problems faced by them while managing business. The value of chi-square is found to be insignificant. Women entrepreneurs investing less money in business agree relatively more with this statement than women entrepreneurs investing more in business. It seems that women entrepreneurs investing more money in business might be able to manage their business in a better manner. The value of chi-square is statistically significant at 1 per cent level of significance. Similarly, women entrepreneurs earning moderate level of income agree relatively more with this issue than women entrepreneurs earning lower level of income. The reason being, availability of finance helps them in solving various issues relating to business and family. The value of chi-square is statistically significant at 1 per cent level of significance. Proportion of women entrepreneurs (36 per cent) having taken training before the start of business agree relatively less with statement than untrained women entrepreneurs (47 per cent). It may be due to lack of training these women entrepreneurs face various problems in business. The value of chi-square is statistically insignificant. 35 per cent women entrepreneurs who have availed financial assistance from financial institutions agree relatively less with this statement than women entrepreneurs (44 per cent) who have used informal sources of finance. The reason to this may be assigned to easy availability of finance. The value of chi-square is statistically insignificant. Women entrepreneurs who have been in business for more than 10 years agree relatively more with this statement than women entrepreneurs who have been in business for less than 10 years. It may be due to more problems faced by them under changed economic scenario. The value of chi-square is statistically significant at 1 per cent level of significance.

The perception of women entrepreneurs towards various entrepreneurship related issues have been subject to factor analysis technique. Varimax rotated matrix have been used for extracting the factors.

TABLE 7.27

KMO and Bartlett's Test

Kieser-Meyer-Olin Measure of Sampling Adequacy		0.660
Bartlett's Test of Sphericity	Approx. Chi-Square	3827.059
	df	325
	Sig.	0.000

Table 7.27 shows the Keiser-Meyer-Olin (KMO) and Bartlett's test of sphericity. The KMO test measure of sampling adequacy equal to 0.660 vividly reveals that data is fit for factor analysis. Bartlett's test of sphericity (3827.039) further collaborates our finding.

Table 7.28 shows the varimax rotated factor matrix results for all women entrepreneurs in our study. Two factors have been extracted which altogether account for 27.161 per cent of variance. It shows that 27.161 per cent of total variance is explained by information contained in varimax rotated matrix. The percentage of variance explained by factor 1 to 2 are 16.076 and 11.084. The communalities have been shown at the right side of the Table 7.27, which explains the amount of variance in the variable that is accounted by two factors taken together. Large communalities indicate that a large amount of variance in a variable has been extracted by factor solution. A factor loading represents the correlation between an original variable and its factors. Factor loading is nothing but coefficient of correlation. The varimax factors solution shows that some of the variable have low factor loading values. The factor loading below 0.30 have been left. The name of factors, statements labels and factor loading are summarized in Table 7.29.

TABLE 7.28

Varimax Rotated Matrix

Sl. No.	Label	Statement	Factor 1	Factor 2	Commu- nalities
1	2	3	4	5	6
1.	X_1	It is difficult to survive without help of husband	0.084	0.143	0.027
2.	X_2	Women can compete with men	-0.031	-0.199	0.040
3.	X_3	Success results in neglect of children, family and home	-0.054	0.080	0.095
4.	X_4	Availing financial assistance from support system is a problem	0.347	0.149	0.143
5.	X_5	Home is the right place for women	-0.211	0.028	0.045
6.	X_6	Women become entrepreneur out of compulsion	-0.447	-0.013	0.200
7.	X_7	Job is better than entrepreneurship	-0.017	0.116	0.013
8.	X_8	Being a women is boon for becoming entrepreneur	0.169	0.159	0.054
9.	X_9	Marketing of the product is a problem for women entrepreneurs	0.158	0.163	0.051
10.	X_{10}	Ideal stage to be an entrepreneur is before marriage	0.284	0.169	0.109
11.	X_{11}	Present policy provisions are sufficient for growth of women entrepreneurship	0.218	-0.150	0.069
12.	X_{12}	With reduction of public sector self-employment is the only way	0.409	-0.150	0.190
13.	X_{13}	Ignorance of law is an obstacle	0.556	-0.014	0.309

(Contd.)

1	2	3	4	5	6
14.	X_{14}	Management should be a compulsory subject at graduate level	0.712	0.031	0.507
15.	X_{15}	Social and cultural barriers act as hindrance in the growth of business	0.540	0.339	0.406
16.	X_{16}	Emerging areas have more scope than traditional ones	0.513	0.047	0.266
17.	X_{17}	EDPs can act as stimulator	0.601	-0.044	0.363
18.	X_{18}	Business family can act as motivator	0.702	0.015	0.493
19.	X_{19}	Success stories of women entrepreneurs can act as motivator	0.677	-0.018	0.458
20.	X_{20}	Product produced by women entrepreneurs should be given due publicity	0.635	0.243	0.462
21.	X_{21}	Business incubators should be set-up	0.392	0.342	0.271
22.	X_{22}	Women officials should deal with women	-0.047	0.869	0.758
23.	X_{23}	Women inspectors should deal with women	-0.039	0.882	0.780
24.	X_{24}	Acquiring technical know-how is a problem	-0.025	0.535	0.286
25.	X_{25}	Management training is must for women	0.097	0.438	0.202
26.	X_{26}	There should be separate support agencies for women entrepreneurs	-0.052	0.738	0.548
Eigen value			4.180	2.882	
Percentage of variance			16.076	11.084	
Cumulative percentage of variance			16.076	27.161	

TABLE 7.29

Naming of Factors

Factors	Name of Dimensions	Label	Statements	Factor Loadings
F_1	Business and family-related issues	X_4	Availing financial assistance from support system is a problem	0.347
		X_6	Women become entrepreneur out of compulsion	-0.447
		X_{12}	With reduction of public sector self-employment is the only way	0.409
		X_{13}	Ignorance of law is an obstacle	0.556
		X_{14}	Management should be a compulsory subject at graduate level	0.712
		X_{15}	Social and cultural barriers act as hindrance in the growth of business	0.540
		X_{16}	Emerging areas have more scope than traditional ones	0.513
		X_{17}	EDPs can act as stimulators	0.601
		X_{18}	Business family can act as motivator	0.702
		X_{19}	Success stories of women entrepreneurs can act as motivator	0.677
		X_{20}	Product produced by women entrepreneurs should be given due publicity	0.635
		X_{21}	Business incubators should be set-up	0.392
F_2	Institutional-related issues	X_{22}	Women officials should deal with women	0.869
		X_{23}	Women inspectors should deal with women	0.882
		X_{24}	Acquiring technical know-how is a problem	0.535
		X_{25}	Management training is must for women	0.438
		X_{26}	There should be separate support agencies for women entrepreneurs	0.738

The explanation of these two factors has been discussed below.

Business and Family-related Issues (F$_1$)

It is an important factor which accounts for maximum percentage of variance equal to 16.076. Twelve variables have been loaded on this factor. The loading of twelve variables indicates that business and family-related issues are the main important issues before women entrepreneurs. These twelve variables have eigen value 4.180. The eigen value more than 4 further shows that these variables are main obstacles for the growth of entrepreneurship among women. The women entrepreneurs face the problem of ignorance of law, problem of publicity, infrastructure and knowledge relating to general management of small enterprises.

Women entrepreneurs are also agree with statements relating to various family related issues. Chief among them are socio-cultural factors prevailing in the environment and family having business background. Problems relating to business can be tackled by increasing the awareness of various rules and regulations relating to business. This problem can further be solved by incorporating business-related subjects at graduate or +2 levels. Knowledge of various business opportunities in the market economies should be enhanced by organizing workshops and seminars at colleges and universities level. Training programmes relating to entrepreneurship development should be strengthened further. Problem-related to family issues can be solved by publishing various success stories of women entrepreneurs in local newspapers. It will encourage the people to motivate the families to participate in the business activities.

Institutional related issues (F$_2$)

The second factor, which accounts for 11.084 per cent of variance consist of five variables and has been designated as institutional-related issues. The eigen value for these five variables is 2.882. Eigen value more than two further highlights that these variables in this factor acts as obstacles in business. Women due to male dominance society require separate support agencies and women officials to deal with their cases and in this process they face the problem of acquiring latest technology. This problem should be solved by creating separate cells in the various departments headed by women officials. It will help the women entrepreneurs in presenting their cases better.

SUGGESTIONS AND POLICY IMPLICATIONS

The foregoing analysis reveals that women entrepreneurs agree with majority of the statements relating to business, institutional and family. Issues relating to business can be tackled by enhancing level of awareness in the field of management of small enterprises and imparting training in the field of business. Infrastructure and other facilities need to be strengthened. In case of government-related departments requirements of separate support agencies can be tackled by creating special cells under the charge of women officials within different departments. It will help women entrepreneurs in presenting their cases better. Analysis of data further highlights that attitude of women has undergone a sea change over the period of time due to spread of education and availability of various opportunities in the economy. Women are becoming more career-oriented and are not facing much problem in case of care of children and family. To overcome the problem of other family-related issues, success stories of women entrepreneurs should be published in local and national newspapers. It will help in changing the mindset of people and women can get more cooperation from their families. Factor analysis clubbed the various variables discussed earlier into two factors, i.e. business and family related issues and institutional-related one. Policy formulated keeping in view business and institutional-related issues can be more successful for the growth of entrepreneurship among women.

Extent of Fulfilment of Expectations of Women Entrepreneurs from Supporting Agencies

The development of entrepreneurship among women is a major step to increase women participation in economic development. It will enhance economic growth and provide employment opportunities for women entrepreneurs. Providing economic opportunities for women can also improve the social, educational and health status of women and their families. Post-reform period has observed increase in various institutes imparting various facilities in the field of entrepreneurship development. Private and public sector institutes have widened their area of operations. In this chapter, an attempt has been made to analyse the extent of fulfilment of expectations of women entrepreneurs towards various supporting agencies.

Table 8.1 highlights that 42 per cent women entrepreneurs have been able to fulfil their expectations from SFCs and 19 per cent to some extent. It reveals that SFCs are playing an important role to provide financial and other supporting measures to women entrepreneurs. Education-wise information further shows that more than 45 per cent of women entrepreneurs possessing higher level of education feel that SFCs have provided services upto their expectations. On the other hand, 23 per cent women entrepreneurs having matric level of education get services according to their expectations. It may be due to lack of mobility and inability to comply with requirements of SFCs. The value of chi-square is statistically significant at 1 per cent level of significance. Women entrepreneurs in middle age group (79 per cent) have been able to fulfil their expectations relatively more than women

TABLE 8.1

Extent of Fulfilment of Expectations from SFCs

Group	To great extent	To large extent	To some extent	To little extent	Not at all
1	2	3	4	5	6
All Data	16 (8.89)	61 (33.89)	34 (18.89)	25 (13.89)	44 (24.44)
Education					
Primary	—	2 (33.33)	—	—	—
Matric	3 (10.00)	4 (13.33)	3 (10.00)	1 (3.33)	4 (66.67)
Graduate	7 (10.29)	24 (35.29)	17 (25.00)	9 (13.24)	19 (63.33)
Post Graduate	6 (7.89)	31 (40.79)	14 (18.42)	15 (19.74)	11 (16.18)
10 (13.16)					
Chi-square = 43.331; df = 12; Significance at 1 per cent level					
Age (years)					
Below 30	6 (7.79)	19 (24.68)	27 (35.06)	19 (24.68)	6 (7.79)
30-40	8 (21.05)	22 (57.89)	3 (7.89)	1 (2.63)	4 (10.53)
Above 40	2 (3.08)	20 (30.77)	4 (6.15)	5 (7.69)	34 (52.31)
Chi-square = 80.261; df = 8; Significance at 1 per cent level					
Place of Origin					
Rural	2 (5.00)	10 (25.00)	8 (20.00)	6 (15.00)	14 (35.00)
Urban	14 (10.00)	51 (36.43)	26 (18.57)	19 (13.57)	30 (21.43)
Chi-square = 4.498; df = 4; Insignificant					
Type of Family					
Joint	6 (7.32)	25 (30.49)	9 (10.98)	14 (17.07)	28 (34.15)
Nuclear	10 (10.20)	36 (36.73)	25 (25.51)	11 (11.22)	16 (16.33)
Chi-square = 12.825; df = 4; Significance at 1 per cent level					

(Contd.)

1	2	3	4	5	6
Form of Business Organization					
Sole	11 (11.00)	31 (31.00)	18 (18.00)	19 (19.00)	21 (21.00)
Others	5 (6.25)	30 (37.50)	16 (20.00)	6 (7.50)	23 (28.75)
Chi-square = 7.100; df = 4; Insignificant					
Investment (Lacs)					
<1	7 (16.67)	2 (4.76)	17 (40.48)	9 (21.43)	7 (16.67)
1-2	3 (5.26)	20 (35.09)	9 (15.79)	10 (17.54)	15 (26.32)
2-3	1 (4.00)	7 (28.00)	4 (16.00)	1 (4.00)	12 (48.00)
3-5	3 (11.54)	10 (38.46)	2 (7.69)	4 (15.38)	1 (26.92)
5-10	2 (10.53)	13 (68.42)	2 (10.53)	1 (5.26)	1 (5.26)
Above 10	—	9 (81.82)	—	—	2 (18.18)
Chi-square = 62.492; df = 20; Significance at 1 per cent level					
Income (Rs.)					
<7500	2 (11.76)	9 (52.94)	1 (5.88)	4 (23.53)	1 (5.88)
7500-10000	9 (16.67)	4 (7.41)	13 (24.07)	9 (16.67)	19 (35.19)
10000-15000	1 (3.57)	5 (17.86)	4 (14.29)	5 (17.86)	13 (46.43)
15000-20000	1 (1.85)	25 (46.30)	14 (25.93)	5 (9.26)	9 (16.67)
20000+	3 (11.11)	18 (66.67)	2 (7.41)	2 (7.41)	2 (7.41)
Chi-square = 58.347; df = 16; Significance at 1 per cent level					
Training					
Got Training	12 (12.50)	35 (36.46)	25 (26.04)	9 (9.38)	15 (15.62)
No Training	4 (4.76)	26 (30.95)	9 (10.71)	16 (19.05)	29 (34.52)
Chi-square = 18.554; df = 4; Significance at 1 per cent level					
Sources of Finance					
Formal	11 (15.07)	50 (68.49)	10 (13.70)	1 (1.37)	1 (1.37)
Informal	5 (4.67)	11 (10.28)	24 (22.43)	24 (22.43)	43 (40.19)
Chi-square = 91.026; df = 4; Significance at 1 per cent level					
Age of Enterprise					
Below 10 years	16 (13.22)	34 (28.10)	32 (26.45)	19 (15.70)	20 (16.53)
Above 10 years	—	27 (45.76)	2 (3.39)	6 (10.17)	24 (40.68)
Chi-square = 32.951 ; df = 4; Significance at 1 per cent level					

entrepreneurs in lower and upper age groups. It seems that women entrepreneurs in middle age group might possess better skill and knowledge to get better facilities from this institution. The value of chi-square is statistically significant at 1 per cent level of significance. Women entrepreneurs hailing from urban areas have been able to fulfil their expectations from SFCs more than their counterparts from rural areas. It may be due to difference in knowledge and more mobility. The value of chi-square is statistically insignificant. Women entrepreneurs belonging to nuclear families (47 per cent) have been able to fulfil their expectations relatively more as compared to women entrepreneurs hailing from joint families (38 per cent). The value of chi-square is statistically significant at 1 per cent level of significance. Women entrepreneurs managing business under other than individual form of business organizations have been able to get services of SFCs more than women entrepreneurs managing business on individual basis. It may be due to difference in size of business organizations. The value of chi-square is statistically insignificant. Women entrepreneurs having made more investment have fulfiled their expectations from SFCs relatively more as compared to other women entrepreneurs. It seems that SFCs are reluctant to provide services to micro and small-scale units. There is need to provide more financial assistance on liberal terms and conditions to small and micro enterprises. Moreover, these enterprises have more potential to generate gainful employment opportunities. The value of chi-square is statistically significant at 1 per cent level of significance. Women entrepreneurs earning higher level of income have been able to fulfil their expectations from SFCs more than women entrepreneurs earning lower level of income. The value of chi-square is statistically significant at 1 per cent level of significance. Trained women entrepreneurs (49 per cent) have been able to fulfil their expectations from SFCs more than untrained women entrepreneurs. It seems that SFCs might be giving more preference to trained women entrepreneurs, while providing assistance. Another reason may be less risk involved in providing assistance to trained women entrepreneurs. The value of chi-square is statistically significant at 1 per cent level of significance. It seems logical that women entrepreneurs having availed assistance from formal sources of finance are relatively more satisfied from these institutions than other women entrepreneurs. The value of chi-square is statistically significant at 1 per cent level of significance. Women entrepreneurs having enterprises more than 10 years old are able to get their expectations fulfilled from SFCs more than other women entrepreneurs. It shows that new enterprises are facing more problems. It may be due to change in economic scenario and increase in failure rate among small enterprises, the SFCs might be giving loans selectively to new enterprises. The value of chi-square is statistically significant at 1 per cent level of significance.

Table 8.2 shows that 48 per cent women entrepreneurs have fulfiled their expectations to a large extent from EDPs. It shows that EDPs are playing a significant role in developing entrepreneurship among women by imparting suitable training. Only 20 per cent women entrepreneurs could not fulfil their expectations from EDPs. Education-wise information further shows that women entrepreneurs having higher level of education have been able to fulfil their expectations relatively more as compared to less educated women entrepreneurs. It may be due

TABLE 8.2

Extent of Fulfilment of Expectations from EDPs

Group	To great extent	To large extent	To some extent	To little extent	Not at all
1	2	3	4	5	6
All Data	14 (7.69)	74 (40.66)	40 (21.98)	17 (9.34)	37 (20.33)
Education					
Primary	—	2 (33.33)	—	—	4 (66.67)
Matric	2 (6.67)	5 (16.67)	3 (10.00)	3 (10.00)	17 (56.67)
Graduate	9 (13.24)	25 (36.76)	17 (25.00)	8 (11.76)	9 (13.24)
Post Graduate	3 (3.85)	42 (53.85)	20 (25.64)	6 (7.69)	7 (8.97)
Chi-square = 50.352; df = 12; Significance at 1 per cent level					
Age (years)					
Below 30	6 (7.59)	34 (43.04)	27 (34.18)	9 (11.39)	3 (3.80)
30-40	5 (13.16)	21 (55.26)	8 (21.05)	1 (2.63)	3 (7.89)
Above 40	3 (4.62)	19 (29.23)	5 (7.69)	7 (10.77)	31 (47.69)
Chi-square = 57.647; df = 8; Significance at 1 per cent level					
Place of Origin					
Rural	2 (5.00)	14 (35.00)	5 (12.50)	7 (17.50)	12 (30.00)
Urban	12 (8.45)	60 (42.25)	35 (24.65)	10 (7.04)	25 (17.61)
Chi-square = 8.995; df = 4; Insignificant					

1	2	3	4	5	6
Type of Family					
Joint	6 (7.32)	29 (35.37)	12 (14.63)	14 (17.07)	21 (25.61)
Nuclear	8 (8.00)	45 (45.00)	28 (28.00)	3 (3.00)	16 (16.00)
Chi-square = 16.318; df = 4; Significance at 1 per cent level					
Form of Business Organization					
Sole	7 (6.86)	42 (41.18)	27 (26.47)	9 (8.82)	17 (16.67)
Others	7 (8.75)	32 (40.00)	13 (16.25)	8 (10.00)	20 (25.00)
Chi-square = 3.952 ; df = 4; Insignificant					
Investment (Lacs)					
<1	2 (4.76)	11 (26.19)	18 (42.86)	7 (16.67)	4 (9.52)
1-2	6 (10.17)	28 (47.46)	9 (15.25)	5 (8.47)	11 (18.64)
2-3	—	2 (8.00)	9 (36.00)	2 (8.00)	12 (48.00)
3-5	2 (7.69)	13 (50.00)	1 (3.85)	3 (11.54)	7 (26.92)
5-10	4 (21.05)	11 (57.89)	3 (15.79)	—	1 (5.26)
Above 10	—	9 (81.82)	—	—	2 (18.18)
Chi-square = 62.515; df = 20; Significance at 1 per cent level					
Income (Rs.)					
<7500	5 (26.32)	9 (47.37)	4 (21.05)	1 (5.26)	—
7500-10000	4 (7.41)	10 (18.52)	17 (31.45)	8 (14.81)	15 (27.78)
10000-15000	—	10 (35.71)	5 (17.86)	2 (7.14)	11 (39.29)
15000-20000	—	25 (46.30)	14 (25.93)	6 (11.11)	9 (16.67)
20000+	5 (18.52)	20 (74.07)	—	—	2 (7.41)
Chi-square = 60.258; df = 16; Significance at 1 per cent level					
Training					
Got Training	10 (10.20)	47 (47.96)	21 (21.43)	10 (10.20)	10 (10.20)
No Training	4 (4.76)	27 (32.14)	19 (22.62)	7 (8.33)	27 (32.14)
Chi-square = 15.431 ; df = 4; Significance at 1 per cent level					
Sources of Finance					
Formal	10 (13.70)	51 (69.86)	9 (12.33)	2 (2.74)	1 (1.37)
Informal	4 (3.67)	23 (21.00)	31 (28.44)	15 (13.76)	36 (33.03)
Chi-square = 63.686; df = 4; Significance at 1 per cent level					
Age of Enterprise					
Below 10 years	13 (10.57)	46 (37.40)	37 (30.08)	11 (8.94)	16 (13.01)
Above 10 years	1 (1.69)	28 (47.46)	3 (5.08)	6 (10.17)	21 (35.59)
Chi-square = 26.479; df = 4; Significance at 1 per cent level					

to difference in education or difficulties in understanding new concept of business. The value of chi-square is statistically significant at 1 per cent level of significance. Women entrepreneurs in higher age group fail to get expected results from EDP than women entrepreneurs in lower age groups. It may be due to difference in age. The value of chi-square is statistically significant at 1 per cent level of significance. Women entrepreneurs hailing from urban areas have received guidance according to their expectations from EDPs as compared to their counterparts from rural areas. The value of chi-square is statistically insignificant. Similar type of inferences have been obtained in case of women entrepreneurs coming from nuclear families. The reason to this may be assigned to more mobility and less dependence on others as prevalent in joint families. The value of chi-square is statistically significant at 1 per cent level of significance. Almost same proportion of women entrepreneurs managing business under different form of business organizations have got their expectations fulfiled from EDPs. The value of chi-square is statistically insignificant. Women entrepreneurs having made higher level of investment in business feel that EDP have been more helpful to them as compared to other women entrepreneurs. The value of chi-square is statistically significant at 1 per cent level of significance. Women entrepreneurs earning moderate level of income have failed to receive assistance as per their expectations from EDP as compared to women entrepreneurs earning higher and lower level of income. It may be due to more expectations and difficulty to face free markets. Trained women entrepreneurs have fulfiled their expectations from EDP due to more experience as compared to untrained women entrepreneurs. Women entrepreneurs using formal sources of finance have been able to fulfil their expectations more than women entrepreneurs using informal sources of finance. It seems that EDP programmes might have helped these women entrepreneurs in getting finance from financial institutions. The value of chi-square is statistically significant at 1 per cent level of significance. Almost same proportion of women entrepreneurs irrespective of life of their enterprises have received better services from EDPs. It seems that over the period of time performance of EDPs have improved. It may also be due to rapid expansion of institutions providing training in the field of entrepreneurship during post-reform period. The value of chi-square is statistically significant at 1 per cent level of significance.

Table 8.3 shows that 49 per cent of women entrepreneurs got their expectations fulfiled from commercial banks. It shows that commercial banks are doing their best to fulfil the requirements

TABLE 8.3

Extent of Fulfilment of Expectations from Commercial Banks

Group	To great extent	To large extent	To some extent	To little extent	Not at all
1	2	3	4	5	6
All Data	13 (7.14)	77 (42.31)	28 (15.38)	25 (13.74)	39 (21.43)
Education					
Primary	—	2 (33.33)	—	—	4 (66.67)
Matric	2 (2.67)	6 (20.00)	2 (6.67)	3 (10.00)	17 (56.67)
Graduate	6 (8.82)	33 (48.53)	10 (14.71)	8 (11.76)	11 (16.18)
Post Graduate	5 (6.41)	36 (46.15)	16 (20.51)	14 (17.95)	7 (8.97)
Chi-square = 41.027; df = 12; Significance at 1 per cent level					
Age (years)					
Below 30	7 (8.86)	29 (36.71)	23 (29.11)	17 (21.52)	3 (3.80)
30-40	6 (15.79)	27 (71.05)	1 (2.63)	—	4 (10.53)
Above 40	—	21 (32.31)	4 (6.15)	8 (12.31)	32 (49.23)
Chi-square = 81.601; df = 8; Significance at 1 per cent level					
Place of Origin					
Rural	1 (2.50)	17 (42.50)	6 (15.00)	4 (10.00)	12 (30.00)
Urban	12 (8.45)	60 (42.25)	22 (15.49)	21 (14.79)	27 (19.01)
Chi-square = 3.831 ; df = 4; Insignificant					
Type of Family					
Joint	7 (8.54)	25 (30.49)	18 (21.95)	9 (10.98)	23 (28.05)
Nuclear	6 (6.00)	52 (52.00)	10 (10.00)	16 (16.00)	16 (16.00)
Chi-square = 13.397; df = 4; Significance at 1 per cent level					
Form of Business Organization					
Sole	9 (8.82)	34 (33.33)	22 (21.57)	19 (18.63)	18 (17.65)
Others	4 (5.00)	43 (53.75)	6 (7.50)	6 (7.50)	21 (26.25)
Chi-square = 16.693; df = 4; Significance at 1 per cent level					

(Contd.)

1 ·	2	3	4	5	6
Investment (Lacs)					
<1	—	17 (40.48)	12 (28.57)	7 (16.67)	6 (14.29)
1-2	4 (6.78)	26 (44.07)	5 (8.47)	13 (22.03)	11 (18.64)
2-3	2 (8.00)	4 (16.00)	6 (24.00)	1 (4.00)	12 (48.00)
3-5	4 (15.38)	9 (34.62)	3 (11.54)	3 (11.54)	7 (26.92)
5-10	1 (5.26)	14 (73.68)	2 (10.53)	1 (5.26)	1 (5.26)
Above 10	2 (18.18)	7 (63.64)	—	—	2 (18.18)
Chi-square = 47.361; df = 20; Significance at 1 per cent level					
Income (Rs.)					
<7500	—	11 (57.89)	1 (5.26)	7 (36.84)	—
7500-10000	4 (7.41)	18 (33.33)	9 (16.67)	6 (11.11)	17 (31.48)
10000-15000	—	5 (17.86)	6 (21.43)	6 (21.43)	11 (39.29)
15000-20000	5 (9.26)	26 (48.15)	8 (14.81)	6 (11.11)	9 (16.67)
20000+	4 (14.81)	17 (62.96)	4 (14.81)	—	2 (7.41)
Chi-square = 43.839; df = 16; Significance at 1 per cent level					
Training					
Got Training	10 (10.20)	51 (52.04)	20 (20.41)	5 (5.10)	12 (12.24)
No Training	3 (3.57)	26 (30.95)	8 (9.52)	20 (23.81)	27 (32.14)
Chi-square = 30.904; df = 4; Significance at 1 per cent level					
Sources of Finance					
Formal	6 (8.22)	58 (79.45)	7 (9.59)	1 (1.37)	1 (1.37)
Informal	7 (6.42)	19 (17.43)	21 (19.27)	24 (22.02)	38 (34.86)
Chi-square = 79.065; df = 4; Significance at 1 per cent level					
Age of Enterprise					
Below 10 years	10 (8.13)	54 (43.00)	25 (20.33)	17 (13.82)	17 (13.82)
Above 10 years	3 (5.08)	23 (38.98)	3 (5.08)	8 (13.56)	22 (37.29)
Chi-square = 17.015; df = 4; Significance at 1 per cent level					

of women entrepreneurs. It vividly shows that commercial banks have been following liberal policies after introduction of new economic reforms. Women entrepreneurs having higher level of education are able to fulfil their expectations more than less educated women entrepreneurs. It may be due to lack of awareness and difficulty faced in fulfiling various requirements by women entrepreneurs having low level of education. The value of chi-square is statistically significant at 1 per cent level of significance. Women entrepreneurs in middle age-groups have been able to fulfil their expectations more than women entrepreneurs in lower and middle age-groups. It seems that commercial banks prefer to give assistance to mature and skilled women entrepreneurs. The value of chi-square is statistically significant at 1 per cent level of significance. Women entrepreneurs hailing from urban areas (51 per cent) have been able to fulfil their expectations from commercial banks more than women entrepreneurs coming from rural areas (45 per cent). It may be due to lack of mobility and difficulty in approaching commercial banks. The value of chi-square is statistically significant at 1 per cent level of significance. Women entrepreneurs managing business under other than individual forms of business organizations have got their expectations fulfiled from commercial banks more than other women entrepreneurs. It shows that banks still prefer to provide more assistance to joint ventures. The value of chi-square is statistically significant at 1 per cent level of significance. Women entrepreneurs having made more investment received better help than women entrepreneurs investing less money. The reason to this may be assigned to more risk involved in small enterprises. The value of chi-square is statistically significant at 1 per cent level of significance. Similarly, women entrepreneurs earning higher level of income have received better assistance from commercial banks than women entrepreneurs earning other levels of income. The value of chi-square is statistically significant at 1 per cent level of significance. Trained women entrepreneurs have received better services than untrained women entrepreneurs. The reason to this may be attributed to more experience and skill. The value of chi-square is statistically significant at 1 per cent level of significance. Women entrepreneurs using formal sources of finance receive better help than other women entrepreneurs. The value of chi-square is statistically significant at 1 per cent level of significance. Women entrepreneurs having enterprises less than 10 years old assistance as per their expectations than women entrepreneurs possessing enterprises more than 10 years old. The value of chi-square is statistically insignificant.

Table 8.4 shows that 60 per cent women entrepreneurs have been able to fulfil their expectations from women organizations meant for growth of entrepreneurship among women. It shows

TABLE 8.4

Extent of Fulfilment of Expectations from Women Organizations

Group	To great extent	To large extent	To some extent	To little extent	Not at all
1	2	3	4	5	6
All Data	24 (13.19)	86 (47.25)	20 (10.99)	12 (6.59)	40 (21.98)
Education					
Primary	—	2 (33.33)	—	—	4 (66.67)
Matric	4 (13.33)	5 (16.67)	2 (6.67)	1 (3.33)	18 (60.00)
Graduate	8 (11.76)	33 (48.53)	12 (17.65)	4 (5.88)	11 (16.18)
Post Graduate	12 (15.38)	46 (58.97)	6 (7.69)	7 (8.97)	7 (8.97)
Chi-square = 48.172; df = 12; Significance at 1 per cent level					
Age (years)					
Below 30	17 (21.52)	40 (50.63)	13 (16.46)	4 (5.06)	5 (6.33)
30-40	5 (13.16)	26 (68.42)	2 (5.26)	2 (5.26)	3 (7.89)
Above 40	2 (3.08)	20 (30.77)	5 (7.69)	6 (9.23)	32 (49.23)
Chi-square = 55.920; df = 8; Significance at 1 per cent level					
Place of Origin					
Rural	5 (12.50)	12 (30.00)	4 (10.00)	4 (10.00)	15 (37.50)
Urban	19 (13.38)	74 (52.11)	16 (11.27)	8 (5.63)	25 (17.61)
Chi-square = 9.816; df = 4; Significance at 5 per cent level					
Type of Family					
Joint	9 (10.98)	30 (36.59)	14 (17.07)	8 (9.76)	21 (25.61)
Nuclear	15 (15.00)	56 (56.00)	6 (6.00)	4 (4.00)	19 (19.00)
Chi-square = 12.334; df = 4; Significance at 1 per cent level					
Form of Business Organization					
Sole	15 (14.71)	45 (44.12)	12 (11.76)	10 (9.80)	20 (19.61)
Others	9 (11.25)	41 (51.25)	8 (10.00)	2 (2.50)	20 (25.00)
Chi-square = 5.237; df = 4; Insignificant					
Investment (Lacs)					
<1	1 (2.38)	23 (54.76)	8 (19.05)	4 (9.52)	6 (14.29)
1-2	12 (20.34)	27 (45.76)	3 (5.08)	5 (8.47)	12 (20.34)
2-3	2 (8.00)	5 (20.00)	6 (24.00)	—	12 (48.00)
3-5	6 (23.08)	9 (34.62)	1 (3.85)	3 (11.54)	7 (26.92)

1	2	3	4	5	6
5-10	1 (5.26)	15 (78.95)	2 (10.53)	—	1 (5.26)
Above 10	2 (18.18)	7 (63.64)	—	—	2 (18.18)
Chi-square = 47.321; df = 20; Significance at 1 per cent level					

Income (Rs.)					
<7500	2 (10.53)	12 (63.16)	—	4 (21.05)	1 (5.26)
7500-10000	8 (14.81)	17 (31.48)	7 (12.96)	5 (9.26)	17 (31.48)
10000-15000	—	13 (46.43)	4 (14.29)	—	11 (39.29)
15000-20000	9 (16.67)	24 (44.44)	9 (16.67)	3 (5.56)	9 (16.67)
20000+	5 (18.52)	20 (74.07)	—	—	2 (7.41)
Chi-square = 42.226; df = 16; Significance at 1 per cent level					

Training					
Got Training	13 (13.27)	61 (62.24)	9 (9.18)	3 (3.06)	12 (12.24)
No Training	11 (13.10)	25 (29.76)	11 (13.10)	9 (10.71)	28 (33.33)
Chi-square = 23.901; df = 4; Significance at 1 per cent level					

Sources of Finance					
Formal	12 (16.44)	55 (75.34)	4 (5.48)	—	2 (2.74)
Informal	12 (11.01)	31 (28.44)	16 (14.68)	12 (11.01)	38 (34.86)
Chi-square = 53.261; df = 4; Significance at 1 per cent level					

Age of Enterprise					
Below 10 years	17 (13.82)	64 (52.03)	16 (13.01)	8 (6.50)	18 (14.63)
Above 10 years	7 (11.86)	22 (37.29)	4 (6.78)	4 (6.78)	22 (37.29)
Chi-square = 12.673; df = 4; Significance at 1 per cent level					

that women organizations are doing their best for the growth of women entrepreneurs. There is a need to formulate policies for the further growth of organization meant for women entrepreneurship by providing them suitable incentives. Information further shows that women entrepreneurs are preferring women organizations for their help. Highly educated women entrepreneurs have been able to get maximum benefits from women organizations as compared to less educated women entrepreneurs. It may be due to lack of awareness among these women entrepreneurs regarding these organizations. There is a need to increase awareness of these women organizations among less educated women entrepreneurs. The value of chi-square is statistically significant at 1 per cent level of significance. Women entrepreneurs in higher age group have not been able to fulfil their expectations from women organizations as compared to other women entrepreneurs. It may be due to difference in age and inability to approach these organizations. The value of chi-square is statistically significant at 1 per cent level of significance. Women entrepreneurs hailing from urban areas have received help as per their expectations than women entrepreneurs coming from rural areas. The value of chi-square is statistically significant at 1 per cent level of significance. Women entrepreneurs coming from nuclear families receive more help from these organizations as compared to other women entrepreneurs. It may be due to more mobility. The value of chi-square is statistically significant at 1 per cent level of significance. Women entrepreneurs managing business under other than individual forms of business organizations have received maximum benefits from these organizations. It may be due to involvement of more than one person in business and availability of more information. The value of chi-square is statistically insignificant. As high as 80 per cent of women entrepreneurs investing more than Rs. 5 lacs in business have received assistance upto large extent, whereas this ratio is more than 24 per cent in case of women entrepreneurs investing Rs. 2-3 lacs in business. It seems that women entrepreneurs investing money in various ranges have been able to explore this opportunity to seek maximum benefits. The value of chi-square is statistically significant at 1 per cent level of significance. Women entrepreneurs earning higher and lower level of income have fulfilled their expectations from these organizations upto a large extent than women entrepreneurs earning moderate level of income. The value of chi-square is statistically significant at 1 per cent level of significance. Trained women entrepreneurs have received assistance upto their expectations than untrained women entrepreneurs. It shows that training helps women entrepreneurs in enhancing their knowledge about these organizations. The value of chi-square is statistically significant at 1 per cent level of significance. Women entrepreneurs using formal sources of finance have received assistance as per their expectations than women entrepreneurs using informal sources of finance. The reason to this may be assigned to more awareness among women entrepreneurs in former case. The value of chi-square is statistically significant at 1 per cent level of significance. 66 per cent women entrepreneurs possessing enterprises less than 10 years old receive assistance from these organizations upto a large extent. On the other hand, 49 per cent women entrepreneurs having enterprises more than 10 years old have received assistance upto a large extent. The reason to this may be assigned to less growth of these organizations during pre-reform period. On the other hand, in recent years activities of these organizations have increased considerably. Moreover, spread of education, information and change in pattern of employment opportunities during post-reform period have increased the utility of these organizations. The value of chi-square is statistically significant at 1 per cent level of significance.

Table 8.5 shows that 57 per cent women entrepreneurs have received help from SISI upto a large extent and slightly less than one-fourth women entrepreneurs have not received assistance. It shows that these organizations have spread their areas of operation to provide assistance to women entrepreneurs. Education-wise information further shows that educated women entrepreneurs have received more assistance than less educated women entrepreneurs. It shows that education has affected the use of these organizations considerably. It seems that women entrepreneurs having higher level of education have explored the maximum opportunities to seek assistance in the business. The value of chi-square is statistically significant at 1 per cent level of significance. Women entrepreneurs in lower age groups have received assistance more than women entrepreneurs in higher age groups. It shows that women entrepreneurs in lower age group do not want to leave any stone unturned before entering in business line. The value of chi-square is statistically significant at 1 per cent level of significance. Women entrepreneurs hailing from urban areas have received guidance relatively more than their counterparts from rural areas. It may be due to locational advantage and availability of more information. The value of chi-square is statistically significant at 1 per cent level of significance. More than 49 per cent women entrepreneurs managing business under different forms of business organizations have received guidance from this organization upto a large extent. The value of chi-square is statistically insignificant. Women entrepreneurs investing more money in business have received more assistance than women entrepreneurs investing low and moderate level

TABLE 8.5

Extent of Fulfilment of Expectations from SISIs

Group	To great extent	To large extent	To some extent	To little extent	Not at all
1	2	3	4	5	6
All Data	32 (17.58)	72 (39.56)	24 (13.19)	12 (6.59)	42 (23.08)
Education					
Primary	—	2 (33.33)	—	—	4 (66.67)
Matric	5 (16.67)	2 (6.67)	4 (13.33)	1 (3.33)	18 (60.00)
Graduate	15 (22.06)	28 (41.18)	10 (14.71)	6 (8.82)	9 (13.24)
Post Graduate	12 (15.38)	40 (51.28)	10 (12.82)	5 (6.41)	11 (14.10)
Chi-square = 43.631; df = 12; Significance at 1 per cent level					
Age (years)					
Below 30	19 (24.05)	32 (40.51)	16 (20.25)	7 (8.86)	5 (6.33)
30-40	11 (28.95)	18 (47.37)	3 (7.89)	1 (2.63)	5 (13.16)
Above 40	2 (3.08)	22 (33.85)	5 (7.69)	4 (6.15)	32 (49.23)
Chi-square = 50.905; df = 8; Significance at 1 per cent level					
Place of Origin					
Rural	7 (17.50)	10 (25.00)	3 (7.50)	5 (12.50)	15 (37.50)
Urban	25 (17.61)	62 (43.66)	21 (14.79)	7 (4.93)	27 (19.01)
Chi-square = 11.339; df = 4; Significance at 1 per cent level					
Type of Family					
Joint	11 (13.41)	29 (35.37)	15 (18.29)	6 (7.32)	21 (25.61)
Nuclear	21 (21.00)	43 (43.00)	9 (9.00)	6 (6.00)	21 (21.00)
Chi-square = 5.622; df = 4; Insignificant					
Form of Business Organization					
Sole	25 (24.51)	36 (35.29)	14 (13.73)	5 (4.90)	22 (21.57)
Others	7 (8.75)	36 (45.00)	10 (12.50)	7 (8.75)	20 (25.00)
Chi-square = 8.688; df = 4; Insignificant					
Investment (Lacs)					
<1	5 (11.90)	17 (40.48)	11 (26.19)	3 (7.14)	6 (14.29)
1-2	15 (25.42)	25 (42.37)	2 (3.39)	5 (8.47)	12 (20.34)
2-3	—	2 (8.00)	8 (32.00)	1 (4.00)	14 (56.00)
3-5	7 (26.92)	8 (30.77)	1 (3.85)	3 (11.54)	7 (26.92)

1	2	3	4	5	6
5-10	3 (15.79)	13 (68.42)	2 (10.53)	—	1 (5.26)
Above 10	2 (18.18)	7 (63.64)	—	—	2 (18.18)

Chi-square = 60.528; df = 20; Significance at 1 per cent level

Income (Rs.)

<7500	2 (10.53)	15 (78.95)	1 (5.26)	—	1 (5.26)
7500-10000	15 (27.78)	7 (12.96)	7 (12.96)	8 (14.81)	17 (31.48)
10000-15000	1 (3.57)	12 (42.86)	4 (14.29)	—	11 (39.29)
15000-20000	7 (12.96)	20 (37.04)	12 (22.22)	4 (7.41)	11 (20.37)
20000+	7 (25.93)	18 (66.67)	—	—	2 (7.41)

Chi-square = 59.669; df = 16; Significance at 1 per cent level

Training

Got Training	21 (21.43)	41 (41.84)	14 (14.29)	8 (8.16)	14 (14.29)
No Training	11 (13.10)	31 (36.90)	10 (11.90)	4 (4.76)	28 (33.33)

Chi-square = 10.164; df = 4; Significance at 5 per cent level

Sources of Finance

Formal	18 (24.66)	47 (64.38)	6 (8.82)	—	2 (2.74)
Informal	14 (12.84)	25 (22.94)	18 (16.51)	12 (11.01)	40 (36.70)

Chi-square = 54.619; df = 4; Significance at 1 per cent level

Age of Enterprise

Below 10 years	25 (20.33)	49 (39.84)	20 (16.26)	9 (7.32)	20 (16.26)
Above 10 years	7 (11.86)	23 (38.98)	4 (6.78)	3 (5.08)	22 (37.29)

Chi-square = 12.290; df = 4; Significance at 1 per cent level

of money. The value of chi-square is statistically significant at 1 per cent level of significance. Women entrepreneurs earning higher and lower level of income have taken assistance upto large extent than women entrepreneurs earning other levels of income. 62 per cent trained women entrepreneurs have taken assistance from SISI upto a large extent, whereas this ratio is 50 per cent in case of untrained women entrepreneurs. It shows that even untrained women entrepreneurs have been able to explore these facilities due to lack of training facilities to fill the gap of knowledge in business. The value of chi-square is statistically significant at 5 per cent level of significance. Women entrepreneurs using formal sources of finance have received more help from SISI than women entrepreneurs using informal sources of finance. It may also be due to guidance received from various formal sources of finance. The value of chi-square is statistically significant at 1 per cent level of significance. Women entrepreneurs having younger enterprises use this source more than women entrepreneurs possessing older enterprises. It shows that younger generation of women entrepreneurs are more conscious and want to avail services wherever and whatever area these services are available. The value of chi-square is statistically significant at 1 per cent level of significance.

Table 8.6 shows that 45 per cent women entrepreneurs have been able to fulfil their expectations from DICs and 22 per cent could not fulfil their expectations. 66 per cent to 60 per cent women entrepreneurs possessing primary and matric level of education could not fulfil their expectations from DICs. On the

TABLE 8.6

Extent of Fulfilment of Expectations from DICs

Group	To great extent	To large extent	To some extent	To little extent	Not at all
1	2	3	4	5	6
All Data	16 (8.79)	66 (36.26)	28 (15.38)	32 (17.58)	40 (21.98)
Education					
Primary	—	2 (33.33)	—	—	4 (66.67)
Matric	4 (13.33)	3 (10.00)	2 (6.67)	3 (10.00)	18 (60.00)
Graduate	8 (11.76)	24 (35.29)	11 (16.18)	14 (20.59)	11 (16.18)
Post Graduate	4 (5.13)	37 (47.44)	15 (19.23)	15 (19.23)	7 (8.97)
Chi-square = 49.446; df = 12; Significance at 1 per cent level					
Age (years)					
Below 30	7 (8.86)	28 (35.44)	20 (25.32)	21 (26.58)	3 (3.80)
30-40	8 (21.05)	19 (50.00)	2 (5.26)	5 (13.16)	4 (10.53)
Above 40	1 (1.54)	19 (29.23)	6 (9.23)	6 (9.23)	33 (50.77)
Chi-square = 67.767; df = 8; Significance at 1 per cent level					
Place of Origin					
Rural	2 (5.00)	11 (27.50)	4 (10.00)	10 (25.00)	13 (32.50)
Urban	14 (9.86)	55 (38.73)	24 (16.90)	22 (15.49)	27 (19.01)
Chi-square = 7.077; df = 4; Insignificant					

1	2	3	4	5	6
Type of Family					
Joint	5 (6.10)	25 (30.49)	17 (20.73)	12 (14.63)	23 (28.05)
Nuclear	11 (11.00)	41 (41.00)	11 (11.00)	20 (20.00)	17 (17.00)
Chi-square = 8.619; df = 4; Insignificant					
Form of Business Organization					
Sole	7 (6.86)	34 (33.33)	19 (18.63)	23 (22.55)	19 (18.63)
Others	9 (11.25)	32 (40.00)	9 (11.25)	9 (11.25)	21 (26.25)
Chi-square = 7.558; df = 4; Insignificant					
Investment (Lacs)					
<1	2 (4.76)	13 (30.95)	12 (28.57)	9 (21.43)	6 (14.29)
1-2	8 (13.56)	18 (30.51)	7 (11.86)	14 (23.73)	12 (20.34)
2-3	—	2 (8.00)	6 (24.00)	5 (20.00)	12 (48.00)
3-5	5 (19.23)	10 (38.46)	1 (3.85)	3 (11.54)	7 (26.92)
5-10	1 (5.26)	14 (73.68)	2 (10.53)	1 (5.26)	1 (5.26)
Above 10	—	9 (81.82)	—	—	2 (18.18)
Chi-square = 57.160; df = 20; Significance at 1 per cent level					
Income (Rs.)					
<7500	5 (26.32)	5 (26.32)	6 (31.58)	2 (10.53)	1 (5.26)
7500-10000	4 (7.41)	12 (22.22)	5 (9.26)	16 (29.63)	17 (31.48)
10000-15000	—	9 (32.14)	4 (14.29)	4 (14.29)	11 (39.29)
15000-20000	5 (9.26)	19 (35.19)	11 (20.37)	10 (18.52)	9 (16.67)
20000+	2 (7.41)	21 (77.78)	2 (7.41)	—	2 (7.41)
Chi-square = 53.985; df = 16; Significance at 1 per cent level					
Training					
Got Training	13 (13.27)	40 (40.82)	12 (12.24)	21 (21.43)	12 (12.24)
No Training	3 (3.57)	26 (30.95)	16 (19.05)	11 (13.10)	28 (33.33)
Chi-square = 18.348; df = 4; Significance at 1 per cent level					
Sources of Finance					
Formal	10 (13.70)	44 (60.27)	12 (16.44)	5 (6.85)	2 (2.74)
Informal	6 (5.00)	22 (20.18)	16 (14.68)	27 (24.77)	38 (34.86)
Chi-square = 51.317; df = 4; Significance at 1 per cent level					
Age of Enterprise					
Below 10 years	14 (11.38)	41 (33.33)	24 (19.51)	27 (21.95)	17 (13.82)
Above 10 years	2 (3.39)	25 (42.37)	4 (6.78)	5 (8.47)	23 (38.98)
Chi-square = 23.603; df = 4; Significance at 1 per cent level					

other hand, 47 per cent to 53 per cent women entrepreneurs possessing higher level of education have received adequate help from DICs. The reason to this may be assigned to more awareness of these agencies among women entrepreneurs having higher level of education. The value of chi-square is statistically significant at 1 per cent level of significance. 71 per cent women entrepreneurs in middle age group have received help from DICs upto a large extent, whereas this ratio varies from 31 per cent to 44 per cent in case of women entrepreneurs in other age groups. The value of chi-square is statistically significant at 1 per cent level of significance. 48 per cent women entrepreneurs hailing from urban areas have received assistance from DICs upto a large extent, whereas this ratio is 33 per cent in case of women entrepreneurs coming from rural areas. The low level of utilization of the services of DIC in latter case may be attributed to lack of knowledge. The value of chi-square is statistically insignificant. Women entrepreneurs coming from nuclear families (52 per cent) have received help from DICs, whereas this ratio is 37 per cent in case of women entrepreneurs coming from joint families. The reason to this may be due to paucity of resources and in this process, these women entrepreneurs might have found DICs to seek their assistance. The value of chi-square is statistically insignificant. 51 per cent women entrepreneurs managing business under other than individual forms of business organization have received help from DICs to a large extent, whereas 40 per cent managing business on individual basis have also received same extent of ·help. It may be due to involvement of more persons in case of joint ventures. The value of chi-square is statistically insignificant. More than 79 per cent women entrepreneurs investing more than Rs. 5 lacs in business have received help from DICs as per their expectations. Analysis vividly shows that women entrepreneurs investing less money in business are not getting assistance upto their expectations from DICs. The reason to this may be assigned to more risk involved in micro-level enterprises. The value of chi-square is statistically significant at 1 per cent level of significance. Women entrepreneurs earning more than Rs. 20,000 per month have been able to fulfil their expectations from DICs upto a large extent. The value of chi-square is statistically significant at 1 per cent level of significance. Trained women entrepreneurs (54 per cent) have received more assistance from DIC as compared to their counterparts (34 per cent) having taken no training. It shows that training enhances the knowledge and procedure to get assistance from DICs. The value of chi-square is statistically significant at 1 per cent level of significance. 74 per cent women entrepreneurs using formal sources of finance have received help as per their expectations, whereas this ratio is 25 per cent in case of women entrepreneurs using informal sources of finance. The value of chi-square is statistically significant at 1 per cent level of significance. Almost same proportion of women entrepreneurs irrespective of the life of their enterprises have received assistance as per their expectations. The value of chi-square is statistically significant at 1 per cent level of significance.

Table 8.7 shows that 43 per cent women entrepreneurs have received help from NGOs as per their requirements and 25 per cent to some extent. Education-wise information further shows that only one-third women entrepreneurs possessing primary and less than one-fourth women entrepreneurs having matric level of education have received help from NGOs to a large extent. On the other hand, more than 47 per cent women entrepreneurs having higher level of education have received more help from NGOs. The value of chi-square is statistically significant at 1 per cent level of significance. The reason to this may be assigned to more information among educated women entrepreneurs about various NGOs. Women entrepreneurs in middle age groups have received more help from NGOs than women entrepreneurs in lower and higher age groups. It seems that women entrepreneurs in middle age groups are more enterprising and want to avail maximum assistance from various possible sources to reduce risk in business. The value of chi-square is statistically significant at 1 per cent level of significance. Women entrepreneurs (45 per cent) hailing from urban areas have received more assistance from NGOs than other women entrepreneurs (37 per cent). It may be to easy accessibility of services in case of women entrepreneurs in former case. The value of chi-square is statistically significant at 1 per cent level of significance. Nuclear families (50 per cent) have availed more services from NGOs than their counterparts coming from joint families (35 per cent). It may be due to less need felt by women entrepreneurs coming from joint families. The value of chi-square is statistically insignificant. Women entrepreneurs

TABLE 8.7

Extent of Fulfilmént of Expectations from NGOs

Group	To great extent	To large extent	To some extent	To little extent	Not at all
1	2	3	4	5	6
All Data	18 (9.84)	62 (33.88)	45 (24.59)	18 (9.84)	40 (21.86)
Education					
Primary	—	2 (33.33)	—	—	4 (66.67)
Matric	2 (6.67)	5 (16.67)	2 (6.67)	3 (10.00)	18 (60.00)
Graduate	7 (10.14)	27 (39.13)	19 (27.54)	7 (10.14)	9 (13.04)
Post Graduate	9 (11.54)	28 (35.90)	24 (30.77)	8 (10.26)	9 (11.54)
Chi-square = 43.605; df = 12; Significance at 1 per cent level					
Age (years)					
Below 30	10 (12.66)	17 (21.52)	35 (44.30)	12 (15.19)	5 (6.33)
30-40	8 (21.05)	22 (57.89)	5 (13.16)	—	3 (7.89)
Above 40	—	23 (34.85)	5 (7.58)	6 (9.09)	32 (48.48)
Chi-square = 83.907; df = 8; Significance at 1 per cent level					
Place of Origin					
Rural	3 (7.50)	12 (30.00)	3 (7.50)	7 (17.50)	15 (37.50)
Urban	15 (10.49)	50 (34.97)	42 (29.37)	11 (7.69)	25 (17.48)
Chi-square = 15.378; df = 4; Significance at 1 per cent level					
Type of Family					
Joint	5 (6.10)	24 (29.27)	20 (24.39)	10 (12.20)	23 (28.05)
Nuclear	13 (12.87)	38 (37.62)	25 (24.75)	8 (7.92)	17 (16.83)
Chi-square = 6.492; df = 4; Insignificant					
Form of Business Organization					
Sole	13 (12.62)	29 (28.16)	32 (31.07)	9 (8.74)	20 (19.82)
Others	5 (6.25)	33 (41.25)	13 (16.25)	9 (11.25)	20 (25.00)
Chi-square = 9.089; df = 4; Insignificant					
Investment (Lacs)					
<1	5 (11.90)	14 (33.33)	13 (30.95)	6 (14.29)	4 (9.52)
1-2	4 (6.78)	15 (25.42)	19 (32.20)	7 (11.86)	14 (23.73)
2-3	2 (8.00)	2 (8.00)	7 (28.00)	2 (8.00)	12 (48.00)
3-5	6 (22.22)	8 (29.63)	3 (11.11)	3 (11.11)	7 (25.93)

1	2	3	4	5	6
5-10	1 (5.26)	14 (73.68)	3 (15.79)	—	1 (5.26)
Above 10	—	9 (81.82)	—	—	2 (18.18)
Chi-square = 54.380; df = 20; Significance at 1 per cent level					
Income (Rs.)					
<7500	—	14 (73.68)	2 (10.53)	2 (10.53)	1 (5.26)
7500-10000	8 (14.55)	6 (10.91)	18 (32.73)	6 (10.91)	17 (30.91)
10000-15000	1 (3.57)	4 (14.29)	9 (32.14)	3 (10.71)	11 (39.29)
15000-20000	6 (11.11)	20 (37.04)	12 (22.22)	7 (12.96)	9 (16.67)
20000+	3 (11.11)	18 (66.67)	4 (14.81)	—	2 (7.41)
Chi-square = 53.420; df = 16; Significance at 1 per cent level					
Training					
Got Training	14 (14.29)	39 (39.80)	22 (22.45)	11 (11.22)	12 (12.24)
No Training	4 (4.71)	23 (27.06)	23 (27.06)	7 (8.24)	28 (32.94)
Chi-square = 16.154; df = 4; Significance at 1 per cent level					
Sources of Finance					
Formal	11 (15.07)	48 (56.75)	8 (10.96)	4 (5.48)	2 (2.74)
Informal	7 (6.36)	14 (12.73)	37 (33.64)	14 (12.73)'	38 (34.55)
Chi-square = 71.626; df = 4; Significance at 1 per cent level					
Age of Enterprise					
Below 10 years	17 (13.82)	36 (29.27)	39 (31.71)	13 (10.57)	18 (14.63)
Above 10 years	1 (1.67)	26 (43.33)	6 (10.00)	5 (8.33)	22 (36.67)
Chi-square = 25.301; df = 4; Significance at 1 per cent level					

managing business under individual forms of business organizations have been able to fulfil their expectations to a large extent from NGOs than their counterparts managing business on individual basis. It may be due to availability of more information in case of joint ventures. The value of chi-square is statistically insignificant. 79 per cent to 81 per cent women entrepreneurs having made more investment in business availed benefits from NGOs to a large extent, whereas this ratio is less than 45 per cent in case of women entrepreneurs investing less than Rs. 1 lac in business. The value of chi-square is statistically significant at 1 per cent level of significance. 78 per cent women entrepreneurs earning more than Rs. 20,000 per month and 73 per cent earning less than Rs. 7,500 per month have been able to fulfil their expectations from NGOs to a large extent. On the other hand less than one-fourth women entrepreneurs earning income in the range of Rs. 7500-15000 per month have been able to fulfil their expectations to a large extent. The value of chi-square is statistically significant at 1 per cent level of significance. Trained women entrepreneurs have availed more benefits from NGOs than untrained women entrepreneurs. The value of chi-square is statistically significant at 1 per cent level of significance. Women entrepreneurs using formal sources of finance have received more assistance from NGOs as compared to their counterparts using informal sources of finance. The value of chi-square is statistically significant at 1 per cent level of significance. Almost same proportion of women entrepreneurs irrespective of life of their enterprises have utilized the services of NGOs more than other women entrepreneurs. The value of chi-square is statistically significant at 1 per cent level of significance.

GENERAL QUESTIONS

Table 8.8 shows shows that 36 per cent women entrepreneurs are using customers as a means to advertise their products one-fourth and one-fifth women entrepreneurs are using hoardings and pamphlets. Only small proportion of women entrepreneurs (15 per cent) are using newspapers as a mode to advertise their products. Information vividly shows that women entrepreneurs are using various means to advertise their products. 41 per cent to 45 per cent women entrepreneurs having education upto matric level are using customer as a means to advertise their products. On the other hand, almost same proportion of women entrepreneurs (34 per cent each) possessing graduate and post graduate level of education are using customers to advertise their products. 37 per cent women entrepreneurs having matric level of education are using hoardings to advertise their products, whereas this ratio is one-fourth in case of women entrepreneurs having primary and graduate level of education. 16 per cent to 20 per cent women entrepreneurs having graduate and post-graduate level of education are using newspapers to advertise their products. It shows that education enhances the significance of women entrepreneurs to use the modern methods to advertise their products. Pamphlets as a means of advertisements has been

TABLE 8.8

Media used for Advertising the Product

Group	Customers	Newspaper	Hoardings	Pamphlets	Others
1	2	3	4	5	6
All Data	165 (36.67)	70 (15.56)	115 (25.56)	92 (20.44)	8 (1.78)
Education					
Primary	11 (45.83)	2 (8.3)	6 (25.00)	5 (20.83)	—
Matric	33 (41.25)	5 (6.25)	30 (37.50)	10 (12.50)	2 (2.50)
Graduate	66 (35.11)	31 (16.49)	49 (26.06)	38 (20.21)	4 (2.13)
Post Graduate	55 (34.81)	32 (20.25)	30 (18.99)	39 (24.68)	2 (1.27)
Chi-square = 20.931; df = 12; Insignificant					
Age (years)					
Below 30	48 (34.04)	27 (19.15)	23 (16.31)	40 (28.37)	3 (2.13)
30-40	66 (43.14)	23 (15.03)	35 (22.88)	26 (16.99)	3 (1.96)
Above 40	51 (32.69)	20 (12.83)	57 (36.54)	26 (16.67)	2 (1.28)
Chi-square = 23.791; df = 8; Significant at 1 per cent level					
Place of Origin					
Rural	39 (44.83)	11 (12.64)	24 (27.59)	38 (18.18)	4 (1.91)
Urban	126 (34.71)	59 (16.25)	65 (26.97)	54 (22.41)	4 (1.66)
Chi-square = 5.281; df = 4; Insignificant					
Type of Family					
Joint	88 (42.11)	29 (13.88)	50 (23.92)	38 (18.18)	4 (1.91)
Nuclear	77 (31.95)	41 (17.01)	65 (26.97)	54 (22.41)	4 (1.66)
Chi-square = 5.281; df = 4; Insignificant					
Form of Business Organization					
Sole	132 (42.72)	57 (18.45)	61 (19.74)	54 (17.48)	5 (1.62)
Others	33 (23.40)	13 (9.22)	54 (38.30)	38 (26.95)	3 (2.13)
Chi-square = 32.588; df = 4; Significant at 1 per cent level					
Investment (Lacs)					
<1	71 (57.72)	10 (8.13)	14 (11.38)	24 (19.51)	4 (3.25)
1-2	51 (35.42)	34 (23.61)	34 (23.61)	25 (17.36)	—
2-3	20 (25.97)	4 (5.19)	23 (29.87)	28 (36.36)	2 (2.60)
3-5	18 (28.12)	8 (12.50)	27 (42.19)	11 (17.19)	—
5-10	5 (16.13)	10 (32.26)	12 (38.17)	4 (12.90)	—
Above 10	—	4 (36.36)	5 (45.45)	—	2 (18.18)
Chi-square = 108.472; df = 20; Significant at 1 per cent level					

(Contd.)

1	2	3	4	5	6
Income (Rs.)					
<7500	25 (46.30)	8 (14.81)	8 (14.81)	10 (18.52)	3 (5.56)
7500-10000	75 (49.67)	23 (15.23)	24 (15.89)	29 (19.21)	—
10000-15000	30 (30.93)	8 (8.25)	37 (38.14)	20 (20.62)	2 (2.06)
15000-20000	30 (30.00)	20 (20.00)	23 (23.00)	26 (26.00)	1 (1.00)
20000+	5 (10.42)	11 (22.92)	23 (47.92)	7 (14.58)	2 (4.17)
Chi-square = 60.822; df = 16; Significant at 1 per cent level					
Training					
Got Training	92 (39.15)	39 (16.60)	45 (19.15)	53 (22.55)	6 (2.55)
No Training	73 (33.95)	31 (14.42)	70 (32.56)	39 (18.14)	2 (0.93)
Chi-square = 11.802; df = 4; Significant at 1 per cent level					
Sources of Finance					
Formal	28 (23.33)	25 (20.83)	36 (30.0^)	28 (23.33)	3 (2.50)
Informal	137 (41.52)	45 (13.64)	79 (23.94)	64 (19.39)	5 (1.52)
Chi-square = 13.277; df = 4; Significant at 1 per cent level					
Age of Enterprise					
Below 10 years	103 (34.45)	52 (17.39)	66 (22.07)	74 (24.75)	4 (1.34)
Above 10 years	62 (41.06)	18 (11.92)	49 (32.45)	18 (11.92)	4 (2.65)
Chi-square = 16.401; df = 4; Significant at 1 per cent level					

used more by women entrepreneurs having higher and even lower level of education. The value of chi-square is statistically insignificant. It shows that these two variables are independent. Women entrepreneurs in lower age group are using modern means of advertisements such as newspapers and pamphlets. On the other hand, women entrepreneurs in higher age group are using customers and hoardings to advertise their products. Women entrepreneurs in middle age group are using customers (43 per cent) and hoardings (22 per cent) for the publicity of their products. The value of chi-square is statistically significant at 1 per cent level of significance. It shows that these two variables vary significantly. Women entrepreneurs (44 per cent) hailing from rural areas are giving more weightage to customers to advertise their products. On the other hand, women entrepreneurs coming from urban areas are laying more emphasis on newspapers and pamphlets. Hoardings as a media have been used by almost same proportion of women entrepreneurs (26 per cent each) irrespective of their place of origin. The value of chi-square is statistically insignificant. It shows that there is a no association between these to variables. Women entrepreneurs (42 per cent) coming from joint families are giving more importance to customers as a means to advertise their products. The reason to this may be attributed to more links and desire to reduce cost of advertisements. On the other hand women entrepreneurs coming from nuclear families are giving, more weightage to modern means of communication. It shows that women entrepreneurs in nuclear families want to give more coverage to their products and they also want to manage their business in a professional manner. The value of chi-square is statistically insignificant. Women entrepreneurs managing business under other than individual forms of business organization are using hoardings and pamphlets to advertise their products than other women entrepreneurs. The reason to this may be assigned to availability of expertise and finance in joint ventures. 42 per cent women entrepreneurs managing business on individual basis are using customers as a means to reduce the cost of advertisements. It may be due to lack of capacity to incur expenditure on advertisement. The value of chi-square is statistically significant at 1 per cent level of significance. It shows that these two variables vary significantly. Women entrepreneurs investing more money in business are using newspapers and hoardings to advertise their products. On the other hand, women entrepreneurs investing less money in business are using customers to advertise their products. Women entrepreneurs investing moderate level of money are using hoardings and pamphlets to advertise their products. The value of chi-square is statistically significant at 1 per cent level of significance. 46 per cent to 49 per cent women entrepreneurs earning income upto Rs. 10,000 per month are dependent on customers to advertise their products. It shows that women entrepreneurs earning low level of income are not using costly means of advertisements. Slightly less than one-third women entrepreneurs earning income in the range of Rs. 10,000-20,000 per month are also using customers as a means to advertise their products. 20 per cent to 22 per cent women entrepreneurs earning more than Rs. 15,000 per month are using newspapers to increase the awareness of their products. 47 per cent women entrepreneurs earning more than Rs. 20,000 per month are using hoardings as a means to give publicity to their products. Almost same proportion of women entrepreneurs (20 per cent each) earning upto Rs. 15,000 per month are using pamphlets to increase the awareness of their products. The value of chi-square is statistically significant at 1 per cent level of significance. It shows that these two variables are positively associated. 16 per cent to 14 per cent trained and untrained women entrepreneurs are using newspapers as a means of advertisements for their product. Pamphlets as a means of advertisements have been used more by trained women entrepreneurs. On the other hand, untrained women entrepreneurs (33 per cent) are using hoardings more intensively than trained women entrepreneurs (19 per cent). Trained women entrepreneurs are using customer as a means to advertise their products more than their untrained counterparts. It shows that trained women entrepreneurs are utilizing various means to give publicity to their products. The value of chi-square is statistically significant at 1 per cent level of significance. It shows that training and various means of advertisement used by women .entrepreneurs vary significantly. Women entrepreneurs using formal sources of finance are using modern means of advertisement more than women entrepreneurs using informal sources of finance. It highlights that women entrepreneurs using formal sources of finance are using modern means due to availability of finance at low cost. On the other hand, women entrepreneurs using informal sources of finance are using customers for the publicity of their products due to paucity of resources. The value of chi-square is statistically significant at 1 per cent level of significance. Women entrepreneurs who have established their business recently are using newspapers and pamphlets to advertise their products. It shows that women entrepreneurs in this category of business are more concerned to increase awareness of their products and revenue and these entrepreneurs also understand the significance of marketing in the era of increase in competition in the market. On the other hand, women entrepreneurs who have enterprises more than 10 years old are using customers and hoardings to advertise their products. It shows that these women entrepreneurs are still using traditional methods to advertise their products. The value of chi-square is statistically significant at 1 per cent level of significance. It shows that these two variables vary significantly.

Table 8.9 shows that 96 per cent of women entrepreneurs do not want to shift to another business over the period of time. It shows that business process is not so easy and shift from one line to another one does not seems to be easy. More than 93 per cent women entrepreneurs possessing different levels of education do not want to shift to another business. Almost same proportion of women entrepreneurs in various age groups do not prefer to shift to another business. Similar type of conclusions have been observed in case of women entrepreneurs hailing from rural and urban areas. The values of chi-square are statistically insignificant in these cases. 98 per cent women entrepreneurs hailing from nuclear families do not want to shift to other business, whereas 94 per cent women entrepreneurs hailing from joint families also hold the similar opinion. The value of chi-square is statistically significant at 5 per cent level of significance. Almost same

TABLE 8.9

Want to Shift to Another Business

Group	Yes	No
All Data	15 (3.33)	435 (96.67)
Education		
Primary	1 (4.17)	23 (95.83)
Matric	5 (6.25)	75 (93.75)
Graduate	4 (2.13)	184 (97.87)
Post Graduate	5 (3.16)	153 (96.84)
Chi-square = 3.026; df = 3; Insignificant		
Age (years)		
Below 30	3 (2.13)	138 (37.87)
30-40	6 (3.92)	147 (96.08)
Above 40	6 (3.85)	150 (96.15)
Chi-square = 0.928; df = 2; Insignificant		
Place of Origin		
Rural	2 (2.30)	85 (97.70)
Urban	13 (3.58)	350 (96.42)
Chi-square = 0.358; df = 1; Insignificant		

(Contd.)

Group	Yes	No
Type of Family		
Joint	11 (5.26)	198 (94.74)
Nuclear	4 (1.66)	237 (98.34)
Chi-square = 4.510; df = 1; Significant at 5 per cent level		
Form of Business Organization		
Sole	9 (2.91)	300 (97.09)
Others	6 (4.26)	135 (95.74)
Chi-square = 0.542; df = 1; Insignificant		
Investment (Lacs)		
<1	11 (8.94)	112 (91.06)
1-2	—	144 (100.0)
2-3	3 (3.90)	74 (96.10)
3-5	1 (1.56)	63 (98.44)
5-10	—	31 (100.0)
Above 10	—	11 (100.0)
Chi-square = 19.125; df = 5; Significant at 1 per cent level		
Income (Rs.)		
<7500	3 (5.56)	51 (94.44)
7500-10000	5 (3.31)	146 (96.69)
10000-15000	3 (3.09)	94 (96.91)
15000-20000	2 (2.00)	98 (98.00)
20000+	2 (4.17)	46 (95.83)
Chi-square = 1.500; df = 4; Insignificant		
Training		
Got Training	5 (2.13)	230 (97.87)
No Training	10 (4.65)	205 (95.35)
Chi-square = 2.219; df = 1; Insignificant		
Sources of Finance		
Formal	4 (3.33)	116 (96.67)
Informal	11 (3.33)	319 (96.67)
Chi-square = 0.000; df = 1; Insignificant		
Age of Enterprise		
Below 10 years	13 (4.35)	286 (95.65)
Above 10 years	2 (1.32)	149 (98.68)
Chi-square = 2.846; df = 1; Insignificant		

proportion of women entrepreneurs managing business under various forms of business organizations do not want to shift to another business. It shows that management and establishment of business have become considerably cumbersome over the period of time and nobody wants to shift to some other business. The value of chi-square is statistically insignificant. More than 91 per cent women entrepreneurs investing different levels of income do not want to shift to some other business over the period of time. The value of chi-square is statistically significant at 1 per cent level of significance. More than 94 per cent women entrepreneurs earning different levels of income do not want to shift to other line of business. The value of chi-square is statistically insignificant. Similar type of observations have been made in case of women entrepreneurs irrespective of their level of training and various sources of finance used by them. The values of chi-square are statistically insignificant. More than 95 per cent women entrepreneurs having enterprises of different age prefer to remain in same business line over the period of time. The value of chi-square is statistically insignificant. It shows that under new economic regime shifting of business does not seems to be encouraging one. The value of chi-square is statistically insignificant.

Table 8.10 shows that only one-fourth women entrepreneurs want to diversify the existing business. It seems that diversification of business also no longer seems feasible. It may be dual role and difficulty in management of existing business. Education-wise information further shows that only 31 per cent women entrepreneurs having post-graduate level of education want to diversity their business and only 20 per cent women entrepreneurs possessing lower level of income want to diversify their business. The value of chi-square is statistically insignificant. Proportion of women entrepreneurs those who want to diversify their existing business is found to be more among lower age group women entrepreneurs. It shows that women entrepreneurs in lower age groups are more enterprising. The value of chi-square is statistically significant at 5 per cent level of significance. It shows that these two variables are positively associated. Only one-third and one-fourth women entrepreneurs hailing from rural and urban areas want to diversify their existing business. It shows that women entrepreneurs from rural areas want to diversify their

TABLE 8.10

Want to Diversify Existing Business

Group	Yes	No
All Data	123 (27.33)	327 (72.67)
Education		
Primary	5 (20.83)	19 (79.17)
Matric	25 (31.25)	55 (68.75)
Graduate	44 (23.40)	144 (76.60)
Post Graduate	49 (31.01)	109 (68.99)
Chi-square = 3.666; df = 3; Insignificant		
Age (years)		
Below 30	47 (33.33)	94 (66.67)
30-40	31 (20.26)	122 (79.74)
Above 40	45 (28.85)	111 (71.15)
Chi-square = 6.588; df = 2; Significant at 5 per cent level		
Place of Origin		
Rural	26 (29.89)	61 (70.11)
Urban	97 (26.72)	266 (73.28)
Chi-square = 0.354; df = 1; Insignificant		
Type of Family		
Joint	62 (29.67)	147 (70.33)
Nuclear	61 (25.31)	180 (74.69)
Chi-square = 1.068; df = 1; Insignificant		
Form of Business Organization		
Sole	61 (19.74)	248 (80.26)
Others	62 (43.97)	79 (56.03)
Chi-square = 28.620; df = 1; Significant at 1 per cent level		
Investment (Lacs)		
<1	34 (27.64)	89 (72.36)
1-2	35 (24.31)	109 (75.69)
2-3	25 (32.47)	52 (67.53)
3-5	11 (17.19)	53 (82.81)
5-10	15 (48.39)	16 (51.61)
Above 10	3 (27.27)	8 (72.73)
Chi-square = 11.928; df = 5; Significant at 5 per cent level		

Group	Yes	No
Income (Rs.)		
<7500	4 (7.41)	50 (92.59)
7500-10000	40 (26.49)	111 (73.51)
10000-15000	26 (26.80)	71 (73.20)
15000-20000	37 (37.00)	63 (63.00)
20000+	16 (33.33)	32 (66.67)
Chi-square = 16.437; df = 4; Significant at 1 per cent level		
Training		
Got Training	57 (24.26)	178 (75.74)
No Training	66 (30.70)	149 (69.30)
Chi-square = 2.346; df = 1; Insignificant		
Sources of Finance		
Formal	27 (22.50)	93 (77.50)
Informal	96 (29.09)	234 (70.91)
Chi-square = 1.925; df = 1; Insignificant		
Age of Enterprise		
Below 10 years	91 (30.43)	208 (69.57)
Above 10 years	32 (21.19)	119 (78.81)
Chi-square = 4.315 ; df = 1; Significant at 5 per cent level		

business. The value of chi-square is statistically insignificant. Women entrepreneurs coming from joint families want to diversify their business more than women entrepreneurs coming from nuclear families. It may be due to availability of more persons in the family. The value of chi-square is statistically insignificant. 44 per cent women entrepreneurs managing business on large scale want to go for diversification of their existing business, whereas only 20 per cent women entrepreneurs managing business under individual basis want to go for diversification. The value of chi-square vary significantly. 48 per cent women entrepreneurs investing Rs. 5-10 lacs and 32 per cent women entrepreneurs investing Rs. 2-3 lacs want to diversify their existing business. On the other hand, only one-fourth women entrepreneurs investing other ranges of money in business want to go for diversification. It shows that diversification of business also needs more finance and expertise. The value of chi-square is statistically significant at 5 per cent level of significance. It shows that these two variables vary significantly. Women entrepreneurs earning higher level of income want to go for diversification. It shows that availability of money also influences the decision to go for diversification of business. On the other hand, women entrepreneurs earning low level of income do not want to go for diversification due to paucity of resources. The value of chi-square is statistically significant at 1 per cent level of significance. Untrained women entrepreneurs want to go for diversification more than their trained counterparts. The value of chi-square is statistically insignificant. Women entrepreneurs using informal sources of finance want to go for diversification more than women entrepreneurs using formal sources of finance. It might be due to easy availability of finance from informal sources. The value of chi-square is statistically insignificant. Women entrepreneurs possessing less than 10 years old enterprise are more inclined to go for diversification than women entrepreneurs having enterprises more than 10 years old. It may be due to more risk taking capacity among women entrepreneurs having established business recently. The value of chi-square further shows that these two variables vary significantly.

Table 8.11 reveals that women entrepreneurs are choosing only those business lines which have better scope in future. It seems that women entrepreneurs are taking into consideration various aspects of business. 73 per cent women entrepreneurs reveal that over the period of time business is expanding in which they are doing work. Only 22 per cent women entrepreneurs feel that their business is stagnating over the period of time. It may be due to increase in competition and various difficulties faced by them. Education-wise information further shows that only small proportion of women entrepreneurs (12 per cent) possessing primary level of education feel that their business is shrinking over the period of time. More than 62 per cent women entrepreneurs possessing different levels of education feel that over the years business is expanding. It may also be due to increase in size of market and availability of various business opportunities in free market economies. Age-wise information further shows that more than 69 per cent women entrepreneurs in different age groups feel that business is expanding over the period of time. It shows that women entrepreneurs in different

TABLE 8.11

Status of Business over the Period of Time

Group	Shrinking	Stagnant	Expanding
All Data	21 (4.67)	103 (22.89)	326 (72.44)
Education			
Primary	3 (12.50)	6 (25.00)	15 (62.50)
Matric	5 (6.25)	18 (22.50)	57 (71.25)
Graduate	7 (3.72)	36 (19.15)	145 (77.13)
Post Graduate	6 (3.80)	43 (27.22)	109 (68.99)
Chi-square = 7.866; df = 6; Insignificant			
Age (years)			
Below 30	3 (2.13)	29 (20.57)	109 (77.30)
30-40	9 (5.88)	37 (24.18)	107 (69.93)
Above 40	9 (5.77)	37 (23.72)	110 (70.51)
Chi-square = 4.003; df = 4; Insignificant			
Place of Origin			
Rural	6 (6.90)	21 (24.14)	60 (68.97)
Urban	15 (4.13)	82 (22.59)	266 (73.28)
Chi-square = 1.403; df = 2; Insignificant			
Type of Family			
Joint	15 (7.18)	48 (22.97)	146 (69.86)
Nuclear	6 (2.49)	55 (22.82)	180 (74.69)
Chi-square = 5.632; df = 2; Insignificant			
Form of Business Organization			
Sole	17 (5.50)	78 (25.24)	214 (69.26)
Others	4 (2.84)	25 (17.73)	112 (79.43)
Chi-square = 5.245; df = 2; Insignificant			
Investment (Lacs)			
<1	7 (5.69)	35 (28.46)	81 (65.85)
1-2	10 (6.94)	34 (23.61)	100 (69.44)
2-3	3 (3.90)	25 (32.47)	49 (63.64)
3-5	1 (7.56)	7 (10.94)	56 (87.50)
5-10	—	—	31 (100.0)
Above 10	—	2 (18.18)	9 (81.82)
Chi-square = 28.363; df = 10; Significant at 1 per cent level			

(Contd.)

Group	Shrinking	Stagnant	Expanding
Income (Rs.)			
<7500	3 (5.56)	14 (25.93)	37 (68.52)
7500-10000	10 (6.62)	36 (23.84)	105 (69.54)
10000-15000	7 (7.22)	23 (23.71)	67 (69.07)
15000-20000	1 (1.00)	26 (26.00)	73 (73.00)
20000+	—	4 (8.33)	44 (91.67)
Chi-square = 15.869; df = 8; Significant at 5 per cent level			
Training			
Got Training	5 (2.13)	61 (25.96)	169 (71.91)
No Training	16 (7.44)	42 (19.53)	157 (73.02)
Chi-square = 8.837; df = 2; Significant at 1 per cent level			
Sources of Finance			
Formal	3 (2.50)	28 (23.33)	89 (74.17)
Informal	18 (5.45)	75 (22.73)	237 (71.82)
Chi-square = 1.727; df = 2; Insignificant			
Age of Enterprise			
Below 10 years	15 (5.02)	66 (22.07)	218 (72.91)
Above 10 years	6 (3.97)	37 (24.50)	108 (71.52)
Chi-square = 0.519; df = 2; Insignificant			

age-groups are managing business in an effective manner. The value of chi-square is statistically insignificant. Almost same proportion of women entrepreneurs hailing from rural and urban areas feel that business has become stagnant over the period of time. 73 per cent women entrepreneurs hailing from urban areas feel that their business is expanding over the period of time, whereas 69 per cent of women entrepreneurs coming from urban areas feel that their business is expanding. The value of chi-square is statistically insignificant. Almost same proportion of women entrepreneurs hailing from joint and nuclear families feel that their business is stagnating over the period of time. But more than 69 per cent women entrepreneurs coming from nuclear and joint families feel that their business is expanding over the period of time. The value of chi-square is statistically insignificant. Women entrepreneurs (79 per cent) managing business under other than individual forms of business organizations feel that their business is expanding, whereas this ratio is 69 per cent in case of women entrepreneurs managing business under individual forms of business organizations. It may be due to involvement of more than one person in former case. The value of chi-square is statistically insignificant. More than 81 per cent women entrepreneurs investing money in the range of Rs. 3-10 lacs feel that their business is expanding over the period of time. It shows that more investment opens vast opportunities for business over the longer period of time. It has also been observed that large business fetches more economies of scale and increases the scope of business over the period of time. The value of chi-square is statistically significant at 1 per cent level of significance. It shows that these two variables vary significantly. One-fourth women entrepreneurs earning upto Rs. 20,000 per month feel that their business is stagnating over the period of time. 91 per cent women entrepreneurs earning more than Rs. 20,000 per month feel that their business is expanding over the period of time. On the other hand, almost same proportion of women entrepreneurs (69 per cent) earning income upto Rs. 15,000 per month feel that their business is expanding over the period of time. The value of chi-square is statistically significant at 5 per cent level of significance. It shows that these two variables are positively associated. Almost same proportion of women entrepreneurs irrespective of their level of training feel that their business is expanding over the period of time. The value of chi-square is statistically significant at 1 per cent level of significance. More than 71 per cent women entrepreneurs using formal and informal sources of finance feel that their business is expanding over the period of time. Women entrepreneurs irrespective of their life of enterprises feel that their business is expanding over the period of time. The values of chi-square are statistically insignificant.

SUGGESTIONS AND POLICY IMPLICATIONS

More then 45 per cent of women entrepreneurs have been able to fulfil their expectations from various supporting agencies. Analysis vividly reveals that these agencies are doing its best to provide services to these women entrepreneurs who have approached them. Low utilization of their services have been attributed to low level of awareness of these agencies among women entrepreneurs. The low level of awareness has been attributed to lack of opportunity to get information and indifferent attitude of women entrepreneurs. These agencies should lay more emphasis towards the increase in awareness of their activities. Modern communication media should be utilized in an effective manner. These agencies should also organize workshops and conferences at colleges level so that potential entrepreneurs may be able to get first hand information relating to various services available from these agencies and type of business opportunity available to educated students. Compulsory paper relating to entrepreneurship development can go a long way in increasing the basic understanding of various business concepts among potential entrepreneurs.

Women entrepreneurs are dependent on traditional methods such as customers to advertise their products. Modern methods of advertisements available in the market have not been used by these entrepreneurs. Only small proportion of women entrepreneurs are using modern means of advertisements to increase the awareness of their products. It may be due to lack of finance and even ignorance on their part to use modern means of advertisements. Proper training in the field of advertisement of the products can go a long way in solving various problems relating to marketing and finance faced by women entrepreneurs. Overwhelming proportion of women entrepreneurs do not want to shift to other business. Women entrepreneurs also do not want to diversify the existing business and majority of them agree that their business is expanding over the period of time. Suitable policies for the growth of women entrepreneurs can encourage the women to incorporate diversification in their business.

Summary and Conclusions

Entrepreneurship development and economic development are considered as two sides of same coin. The scarcity of adequate number of entrepreneurs is one of the main factors responsible for economic backwardness, of the so called underdeveloped but resourceful regions of the country.

The economic development of advanced countries of the world to a large extent has been attributed to growth of entrepreneurship in small and medium enterprises. Economic policies pursued in west have further demonstrated that as economies move from command to market driven, gender inequalities are bound to abridge over a period of time. In advanced countries, majority of small enterprises has been managed by women. Women-owned firms represented nearly 40 per cent of all firms in the United States and employed approximately 27.5 million people. Further, women are starting businesses at faster rate than their male counterparts. It has been seen that women out number men by at least two times, particularly when it comes to starting business in China. There are over five million women entrepreneurs constituting one fourth of all entrepreneurs in China. In Japan too a similar trends has been noticed. The percentage of women entrepreneurs increased from 2.4 per cent in 1980 to 5.2 per cent in 1995.

Keeping the experience of western economies the Government of India followed the policy for development of entrepreneurship among human resources of the country in general and women in particular during post-liberalisation regime. Government has set-up large number of institutions to provide financial and other supportive measures for the growth of entrepreneurship among women. Post-reform period has seen the increase in participation of even NGOs for the growth of entrepreneurship among human resources of the country. Under new economic regime the women participation in business has shown considerable improvement. At present in India 9.5 per cent women entrepreneurs are engaged in small business. The major factors responsible for increase in participation of women in economic activities have been: spread of general and technical education, growth of IT sector and entrepreneurship as a career.

OBJECTIVES OF THE STUDY

The study has been pursued to achieve the following objectives:

1. To study the growth and profile of women entrepreneurs in the States of Northern India.

2. To analyze the entrepreneurial process among women entrepreneurs in Northern India.

3. To examine the financial structure of enterprises owned by women entrepreneurs.

4. To study the various issues relating to training.

5. To examine the obstacles faced by women entrepreneurs in Northern India.

6. To seek the opinion of women entrepreneurs regarding various issues related to women entrepreneurs.

7. To study the extent of fulfilment of expectations from various business organizations.

8. To give suggestions and recommendations for the growth of women entrepreneurs.

FINDINGS

The following are the findings and recommendations of the

studies:

- Almost same proportion of women entrepreneurs in the age group of 30-40 and 40+ are participating in the business.
- Educated women entrepreneurs have started participating in the business activities. 42 per cent women entrepreneurs are possessing graduate level of education and another 35 per cent post-graduate level of education.
- 81 per cent women entrepreneurs are hailing from urban areas and 19 per cent from rural areas.
- 54 per cent women entrepreneurs belong to nuclear families and 46 per cent from joint families.
- 69 per cent of women entrepreneurs are managing business on individual basis and 31 per cent under other than individual form of business organizations.
- 42 per cent women entrepreneurs are involved in manufacturing sector and one-third in service sector. Only 16 per cent women entrepreneurs are doing business in trading activities.
- Majority of women entrepreneurs have been in the business for the last ten years.
- 44 per cent women entrepreneurs are motivated by their husband, 30 per cent by their parents and only small proportion of women entrepreneurs motivated by their relatives (11 per cent) and friends (13 per cent).
- Only 16 per cent women entrepreneurs started business without taking assistance from other sources. 58 per cent women entrepreneurs took idea from family members, 13 per cent from friends and 8 per cent from relatives.
- 37 per cent women entrepreneurs have completed their projects in less than three months, 43 per cent in 3-6 months period and 20 per cent women entrepreneurs complete their projects in more than 6 months.
- 28 per cent women entrepreneurs are managing their business from their home and purchase shops and 34 per cent from rental premises.
- 56 per cent women entrepreneurs are doing business to

achieve something, whereas 25 per cent women entrepreneurs are entering in business line to make use of free time.

- Money and desire to be independent have been one of the main factors motivating the women entrepreneurs to be an entrepreneur.

- Majority of women entrepreneurs (80 per cent) take the help from family members in project formulations. Role of outside experts and other sources are found to be negligible.

- 48 per cent women entrepreneurs have used family wealth to finance their business, one-fifth used personal wealth and institutional finance and only small proportion of women entrepreneurs has taken assistance from relatives and private agencies.

- 49 per cent women entrepreneurs have good knowledge of various sources of finance available to women entrepreneurs, 26 per cent possess average level of awareness and another 24 per cent possess low level of awareness.

- Only 26 per cent women entrepreneurs avail the assistance from financial institutions.

- 59 per cent women entrepreneurs have invested upto Rs. 2 lacs in business, 17 per cent between Rs. 2-3 lacs and only 14 per cent invested between Rs. 3-5 lacs. Small proportion of women entrepreneurs (9 per cent) invest more than Rs. 5 lacs in business.

- 45 per cent of women entrepreneurs are earning income upto Rs. 10,000 per month and almost same proportion of women entrepreneurs (22 per cent each) are earning in the range of Rs. 10,000-15,000 and Rs. 15,000-20,000 per month. Only 10 per cent of women entrepreneurs are earning more than Rs. 20,000 per month in business.

- 52 per cent women entrepreneurs have undergone training before start of their business.

- 83 per cent women entrepreneurs have taken training from private institutes and only 17 per cent from government institutes.

- Majority of women entrepreneurs (56 per cent) have not incurred expenditure on training.

- Almost same proportion of women entrepreneurs take training for the period of six and more than six months before start of their business.

- Women entrepreneurs have sought training in the field of management of small enterprises, marketing and quality control aspect.

- 36 per cent women entrepreneurs reveal that they face problem upto a great extent to get information relating to product and other 34 per cent to some extent. 12 per cent women entrepreneurs do not face problem of getting information.

- 25 per cent women entrepreneurs feel that product or services rendered by them fetches low prices.

- 49 per cent of women entrepreneurs face the problem of availability of spurious products to a large extent and other 28 per cent to some extent. Only 8 per cent of women entrepreneurs do not face this problem.

- 35 per cent of women entrepreneurs agree that there is decline in profit margin to a large extent, another 35 per cent feel that profit margin has declined to some extent. On the other hand, 16 per cent of women entrepreneurs observe that profit margin has not declined at all.

- Only small proportion of women entrepreneurs (20 per cent) face the problem of getting training in business to a large extent and 26 per cent women entrepreneurs face this problem to some extent.

- Slightly less than one-fourth women entrepreneurs face the problem of indifferent attitude of customers.

- 20 per cent of women entrepreneurs face the problem of estimation of demand for their product to a large extent, 36 per cent to some extent and 15 per cent do not face this problem.

- Only small proportion of women entrepreneurs (18 per cent) face the problem of identification of customers and one-fourth face this problem to little extent.

- One-fifth women entrepreneurs face the problem of

getting work regularly, 34 per cent to some extent and 27 per cent face this problem to little extent.

- 45 per cent of women entrepreneurs face the problem of competition from big producers to a large extent.

- 40 per cent of women entrepreneurs face the problem of publicity of product to a large extent and another 38 per cent face this problem to some extent.

- Only one-fourth women entrepreneurs face the problem of frequently changing market conditions, 39 per cent to some extent and another 28 per cent to little extent.

- Only one-fourth women entrepreneurs face the problem of fixed capital in business upto a large extent, 22 per cent face this problem to some extent and more than 50 per cent women entrepreneurs have been able to solve this problem.

- Only one-fifth women entrepreneurs are facing the problem of working capital in business and another slightly more than one-fourth women entrepreneurs face this problem to some extent. 22 per cent of women entrepreneurs do not face this problem.

- Only 16 per cent women entrepreneurs face the problem of collateral security to a large extent and one-third to some extent.

- Only 18 per cent women entrepreneurs face the problem of too much paper formalities by financial institutions and another 23 per cent face this problem to some extent. 38 per cent women entrepreneurs do not face this problem at all.

- Slightly more than one-fourth women entrepreneurs face the problem of delay in release of payments upto a large extent and one-third to some extent.

- Only one-third women entrepreneurs feel that there is a lack of coordination among financial institutions.

- 26 per cent women entrepreneurs face the problem of high rate of interest to a large extent and another 23 per cent to some extent.

- Only one-fourth women entrepreneurs face the problem of labour absenteeism to a large extent and 49 per cent to some extent.

- 38 per cent women entrepreneurs face the problem of non-availability of skilled labour to a large extent and another 36 per cent to some extent.
- 21 per cent women entrepreneurs face the problem of labour turnover to a large extent and another 45 per cent to some extent.
- 23 per cent women entrepreneurs face the problem of negative attitude of labour to a large extent and 26 per cent to some extent.
- Only 10 per cent women entrepreneurs face the problem of record keeping to a large extent and another 20 per cent to some extent.
- Only one-fifth women entrepreneurs are facing the problem of inventory management to a large extent and another one-third to some extent.
- 28 per cent women entrepreneurs face the problem of infrastructure to a large extent and 42 per cent to some extent.
- 40 per cent of women entrepreneurs face the problem of high cost of land and 37 per cent to some extent.
- 42 per cent women entrepreneurs face the problem of better technology to a great extent and another 36 per cent to some extent.
- One-fourth women entrepreneurs face the problem of time management in business.
- 26 per cent women entrepreneurs face the problem of fulfilment of legal formalities in business and another one-third face this problem to some extent.
- 27 per cent women entrepreneurs feel that lack of higher education act as an obstacle in business. 29 per cent women entrepreneurs face this problem to some extent.
- 38 per cent women entrepreneurs face the problem of gender discrimination while doing business.
- 88 per cent women entrepreneurs fully agree with the statement of products produced by women entrepreneurs should be given due publicity.
- 65 per cent women entrepreneurs agree with this statement that women officials should deal with cases of women entrepreneurs.

- 70 per cent agree with this statement there should be separate support agencies for women entrepreneurs and only 15 per cent women entrepreneurs disagree with this statement.
- 92 per cent women entrepreneurs agree with this statement that emerging areas have more scope than traditional ones.
- 93 per cent women entrepreneurs agree with this statement that business incubators should be established.
- 63 per cent of women entrepreneurs agree with the statement that marketing of the product is a problem.
- Slightly less than one-third women entrepreneurs agree with the statement that availing financial assistance from support system is a problem and 47 per cent of women entrepreneurs disagree with this statement.
- 72 per cent women entrepreneurs feel that ignorance of law is a problem and only 17 per cent women entrepreneurs disagree with this statement.
- 72 per cent women entrepreneurs agree with the statement that acquiring technology is a problem for women entrepreneurs.
- 79 per cent women entrepreneurs agree with the statement that management training is must.
- Overwhelming proportion of women entrepreneurs agree with this statement that management should be compulsory subject at graduate level.
- 72 per cent of women entrepreneurs agree with this statement that with the reduction in size of public sector self-employment is the only way.
- Slightly less than one-third women entrepreneurs fully agree with this statement that present policy provisions are sufficient for the growth of entrepreneurship among women and another slightly more than one-third women entrepreneurs are indifferent.
- 90 per cent of women entrepreneurs fully agree with this statement that EDP programmes can act as stimulator.
- 22 per cent of women entrepreneurs agree with the statement that women become entrepreneurs out of

compulsion and 63 per cent of women entrepreneurs disagree with this statement.

- 47 per cent women entrepreneurs agree with this statement that job is better than business.

- 82 per cent of women entrepreneurs agree with this statement that business family can be a motivating factor and only small proportion of women entrepreneurs disagree with this statement.

- 54 per cent women entrepreneurs agree with the statement that social and cultural barriers come in the way while doing business and slightly more than one-third women entrepreneurs disagree with this statement.

- 62 per cent women entrepreneurs agree with the statement that being a women is boon for becoming entrepreneur.

- 70 per cent women entrepreneurs agree with the statement that women can compete with man.

- Only 16 per cent women entrepreneurs agree with the statement that success in business results in neglect of family and children.

- 75 per cent women entrepreneurs agree with this statement that it is difficult to survive without the help of husband.

- 89 per cent women entrepreneurs agree with the statement that success stories of women entrepreneurs can act as motivator.

- Only small proportion of women entrepreneurs agree with the statement that home is the right place for women.

- 64 per cent women entrepreneurs agree with the statement that women inspectors should deal with women.

- 42 per cent women entrepreneurs agree with this statement that ideal stage for women to be an entrepreneur is before marriage.

- 42 per cent women entrepreneurs have been able to fulfil their expectations from SFCs and 19 per cent to some extent.

- 48 per cent women entrepreneurs have fulfiled their expectations to a large extent from EDPs.
- 49 per cent of women entrepreneurs got their expectations fulfiled from commercial banks.
- 60 per cent women entrepreneurs have been able to fulfil their expectations from women organizations meant for growth of entrepreneurship among women.
- 57 per cent women entrepreneurs have received help from SISI upto a large extent and slightly less than one-fourth women entrepreneurs have not received assistance.
- 45 per cent women entrepreneurs have been able to fulfil their expectations from DICs and 22 per cent could not fulfil their expectations.
- 36 per cent women entrepreneurs are using customers as a means to advertise their products one-fourth and one-fifth women entrepreneurs are using hoardings and pamphlets. Only small proportion of women entrepreneurs (15 per cent) are using newspapers as a mode to advertise their products.
- 96 per cent of women entrepreneurs do not want to shift to another business over the period of time.
- Only one-fourth women entrepreneurs want to diversify the existing business.
- 73 per cent women entrepreneurs reveal that over the period of time business is expanding in which they are doing work. Only 22 per cent women entrepreneurs feel that their business is stagnating over the period of time.

RECOMMENDATIONS

Following are the recommendations given for the growth of entrepreneurship among women under study:

Overwhelming proportion of women entrepreneurs are possessing higher level of education. There is a need to introduce business related course curriculum at +2 or graduate level to improve their skill in business field. With the spread of technical education in Northern India, suitable incentives should be provided to technically and professionally qualified women. Entrepreneurship is found to be at very low ebb in rural areas. Existing policies for the growth of women entrepreneurship in rural areas need to be further strengthened. Institutions of higher learning should be established in rural areas so that, female participation in higher education may be increased. Spread of education in rural areas will help in changing the mindset of people and problem relating to women participation in business will be increased to a large extent. Women prefer to establish home-based enterprises. Efforts should be made to provide information on various business opportunities available to potential women entrepreneurs, which can be started at their home place.

There has been shift in structure of enterprises owned by women entrepreneurs. Under new economic regime, women entrepreneurs are entering in trading and service sector. It shows that service sector has made considerable progress during post-reform period. Overwhelming proportion of women entrepreneurs are using five workers and managing business on individual basis. Enterprises managed on joint basis can be more beneficial to women entrepreneurs. It will help them in solving the various problems faced by them and ultimately fetch more economies of scale in their businesses.

The role of different agencies in motivating women to enter in business line has been found to be negligible. Moreover, overwhelming proportion of women entrepreneurs in our study has higher level of education. Educational institutions should play an important role in this direction. EDPs should be organized at colleges and universities level so that mindset of students may be changed during their study time period. These efforts will be beneficial to generate gainful employment opportunities in the economy and dependence on formal sector of the economy for employment generation will also decline. Similarly, majority of women entrepreneurs are achievement oriented. Institutions should provide various types of assistance in a liberalized manner to these women entrepreneurs. Although majority of the projects have been completed by women entrepreneurs well in time. There is a need to provide consultancy and guidance through various agencies in this direction. NGOs and women organisations should play a vital role in this direction. Similarly, large number of women entrepreneurs are operating their business from their home and rental places. It seems that location of enterprise at home is not suitable for business. Provision of fixed capital can be useful to these small enterprises.

Individual and family wealth constitute major sources of finance among women entrepreneurs. The role of institutional finance in financing enterprises owned by women entrepreneurs has remained low. Awareness of various sources of finance has not been percolated down to paraxis level in the real sense. There is a need to intensify the efforts to increase the level of awareness of various sources of finance available to women entrepreneurs. Modern communication media should be utilized more effectively to enhance the level of awareness among women entrepreneurs. It will help them in reducing dependence on informal sources of finance and cost of credit will reduce further. Women entrepreneurs will be able to increase the level of investment in their business. EDP programmes should be conducted for existing and potential entrepreneurs to increase their knowledge and awareness of various sources of finance and business opportunities available to them.

Overwhelming proportion of women entrepreneurs have undergone training before establishing their enterprises. The analysis of data further highlights that majority of women entrepreneurs have taken training from informal sources. It may be due to lack of finances and awareness of various institutes providing training in the field of entrepreneurship development. Effort should be made to increase the awareness of various institutes imparting training to new and existing entrepreneurs. To survive in the free-markets women entrepreneurs must have comprehensive understanding of various concepts of business and recent trends prevailing in the market. This information can only be provided through training programmes. A major proportion of women entrepreneurs have desired to take training in the field of marketing and quality control. Institutes providing training in specialized areas should be further strengthened and short-term courses should be conducted for those desires of taking training in these areas.

Women entrepreneurs face one of the biggest problems in the field of marketing of their products. Problems relating to marketing of the product can be solved by formulating various strategies for micro and small enterprises. Problem relating to various marketing-related aspects can be solved by organizing various conferences for existing women entrepreneurs. Various NGOs and women organizations should conduct seminar periodically at different cities. Industrial organizations should conduct various market-related surveys on the future demand on the product of these enterprises and information should be provided to existing SMEs. Short-term courses relating to marketing of the product should be organized for existing women entrepreneurs. It will help them in understanding the trends and challenges faced by their enterprises. Institutes of higher learning should also provide help to SMEs. Workshops and seminars should be organized at college levels. Training in general and specific areas should be made compulsory for women entrepreneurs, who want to avail loans from financial institutions. It will also reduce the problem of industrial sickness, which seems to be more in case of small and micro-level enterprises. With the spread of technical and professional education in Northern India, course curriculum should be made more business/self-employment oriented so that students after completing higher education can go for business ventures without much problems.

Women entrepreneurs face the problem of fixed capital in business. Suitable policies need to be followed to allot plots/sheds for women entrepreneurs. It becomes more important due to sky rocketing prices of land. It becomes very difficult for the women entrepreneurs to purchase plot/building to start their business and consequently have to pay high rent. Due to dual role performed by women existing rules and regulation regarding the operation of business at home or near home should be liberalized. It will help them in performing dual functions effectively.

The problem relating to working capital can be solved by providing loans against different assets. The problem relating to high rate of interest can be solved by following liberal policies by financial institutions. Micro and small enterprises should be given top priority while advancing loans. Financial institutions should not insist more on collateral securities while advancing loans. It will be useful to SMEs to sort out the various problems of finance.

Small proportion of women entrepreneurs also faces problem of lack of coordination and problem relating to various other formalities. Financial institutions should increase the awareness of their schemes among small and micro-level enterprises. Increase in awareness of these schemes can be more useful to these enterprises to avail various benefits. Schemes of various financial institutions should be published in local newspapers. Women entrepreneurs face the problem of labour absenteeism and labour turnover. Women entrepreneurs should manage their enterprises in a scientific manner. Worker should be trained as per requirements of business. Progressive wage structure and better leadership styles can act as an effective tool to sort out these problems. These techniques will also solve the problem of negative attitude of the labour. Large business associations should also provide training to the existing and potential women entrepreneurs so that they may be able to utilize modern human resource management practices in an efficient manner. Women entrepreneurs also face the problem of lack of availability of skilled labour. Government should lay more emphasis on vocational education to improve the skill and human capital base of the population. It will help in increasing supply of better quality of labour in the market, which is need of the free market economies. Women entrepreneurs are facing the large number of production related problems. These problems can be solved by following liberal policies for SMEs. Infrastructure constraints are being faced by SMEs sector more intensively. Various infrastructural facilities should be provided to SMEs sector on liberal terms and conditions. Government should lay more emphasize for the development of infrastructure for SMEs sector. Availability of infrastructure will reduced the cost of product of SMEs. Latest technology should be made available to SMEs at low price. Availability of technology will improve competitiveness of SMEs. Productivity improvement through technological development will solve large number of problems faced by women entrepreneurs. Problem of time management can be solved by providing training in this field. Human capital base of female should be improved. Quality education should be provided at school level.

Women entrepreneurs agree with majority of the statements relating to business, institutional and family. Issues relating to business can be tackled by enhancing level of awareness in the field of management of small enterprises and imparting training in the field of business. Infrastructure and other facilities need to be strengthened. In case of government-related departments requirements of separate support agencies can be tackled by creating special cells under the charge of women officials within different departments. It will help women entrepreneurs in presenting their cases better. Analysis of data further highlights that attitude of women has undergone a sea change over the period of time due to spread of education and availability of various opportunities in the economy. Women are becoming more career-oriented and are not facing much problem in case of care of children and family. To overcome the problem of other family related issues, success stories of women entrepreneurs should be published in local and national newspapers. It will help in changing the mindset of people and women can get more cooperation from their families. Factor analysis clubbed the various variables discussed earlier into two factors, i.e. business and family-related issues and institutional-related one. Policy formulated keeping in view business and institutional-related issues can be more successful for the growth of entrepreneurship among women.

Women entrepreneurs have been able to fulfil their expectations from various supporting agencies. Analysis vividly reveals that these agencies are doing their best to provide services to these women entrepreneurs who have approached them. Low utilization of their services have been attributed to low level of awareness of these agencies among women entrepreneurs. The low level of awareness has been attributed to lack of opportunity to get information and indifferent attitude of women entrepreneurs. These agencies should lay more emphasis towards the increase in awareness of their activities. Modern communication media should be utilized in an effective manner. These agencies should also organize workshops and conferences at colleges level so that potential entrepreneurs may be able to receive first hand information relating to various services available from this agencies and type of business opportunity available to educated students. Compulsory paper relating to entrepreneurship development can go a long way in increasing the basic understanding of various business concepts among potential entrepreneurs. Women entrepreneurs are dependent on traditional methods such as customers to advertise their products. Modern methods of advertisements available in the market have not been used by these entrepreneurs. Only small proportion of women entrepreneurs are using modern means of advertisements to increase the awareness of their products. It may be due to lack of finance and even ignorance on their part to use modern means of advertisements. Proper training in the field of advertisement of the products can go a long way in solving various problems relating to marketing and finance faced by women entrepreneurs. Overwhelming proportion of women entrepreneurs do not want to shift to other business. Women entrepreneurs also do not want to diversify the existing business and majority of them agree that their business is expanding over the period of time. Suitable policies for the growth of women entrepreneurs can encourage the women to incorporate diversification in their business.

Bibliography

Books

Alexander, Robert J., *The Entrepreneur, The Manager and Economic Development*, MacMillan Company, New York, 1962.

Allen, L.L., *Starting and Succeeding in Your Own Business*, Grosset and Dunlop, New York, 1968.

Anderson, Robert Lee and Dunkelbert, John D., *Entrepreneurship*, Harper and Row Publishers, New York, 1990.

Ashmore, M. Catherine *et. al.*, *Programme for Acquiring Competence in Entrepreneurship*, National Centre for Research in Vocational Education, Ohio State University, Columbus, Ohio, 1983.

Banga, T.R., *Project Planning and Entrepreneurship Development*, C.B.S. Publishers and Distributors, Shahdara, Delhi, 1984.

Baty, Gordon B., *Entrepreneurship: Playing to Win*, D.B. Taraporevala Sons & Company, Bombay, 1979.

Baumback, Clifford M. and Mancuso, Joseph R., *Entrepreneurship and Venture Management*, D.B. Taraporevala Sons and Co. Pvt. Ltd., Bombay, 1981.

Bhanushali, S.G., *Entrepreneurship Development: An Interdisciplinary Approach*, Himalayan Publishing House, Bombay, 1987.

Bisht, N.S., Mishra, R.C. and Srivastava, A.K, *Entrepreneurship: Reflections and Investigations*, Chugh Publications, Allahabad, 1989.

Bisht, Narendra S. and Sharma, Pamila K., *Entrepreneurship: Expectations and Experiences*, Himalaya Publishing House, New Delhi, 1991.

Burns, Paul and Dewhurst (Eds.), *Small Business and Entrepreneurship*, MacMillan Education Limited, London, 1990.

Cannon, T. *et. al.*, *The Nature, the Role and the Impact of Small Business Research*, Glower, Alder Shot, 1989.

Carter, S. and Cannon, T., *Women as Entrepreneurs: A Study of Female Business Owners, Their Motivations, Experiences and Strategies for Success*, Academic Press, London, 1992.

Casson, Mark, *The Entrepreneur: An Economic Theory*, Martin Robertson, Oxford, 1982.

Chandra, Shanti Kohli, *Development of Women Entrepreneurship in India*, Mittal Publications, New Delhi, 1991, p. 70.

Cole, A.H., *Business Enterprise in its Social Setting*, Harward University Press, Cambridge, 1959, p. 44.

Curran J., Bolton, *Fifty years on: A Review and Analysis of Small Business Research in Britain*, 1971-86, Small Business Research Trust, London, 1986.

Deshpande, Manohar U., *Entrepreneurship Development of Small Scale Industries*, Deep & Deep Publications, New Delhi, 1984.

Desingu, Setty, E., *Developing New Entrepreneurs, Entrepreneurship Development Institute of India*, Ahmedabad, 1987.

Dhameja, S.K. and Sharma, D.D., *Opportunities and Challenges of Women Entrepreneurs*, TTTI, Chandigarh, 1995.

Dowling, Colette, *Cinderella Complex—Women's Hidden Fear of Independence*, Fontana Paperback, 1981.

Dracker, Peter F, *Innovations and Entrepreneurship: Practice and Principles*, Willian Heinemann Limited, London, 1985.

EDII Faculty and Experts, *A Handbook of New Entrepreneurs: With Special Reference to Science and Technology Target Groups*, Entrepreneurship Development Institute of India, Ahmedabad, 1986.

Finney, S. Ruth, *Towards a Typology of Women Entrepreneurs—Their Business Venture and Family*, East-West Centre, East-West Technology and Development Institute, Honololu, Hawaii (USA), 1977.

Gautam, Vinayshil, *Technical Entrepreneurship: Issues of Research and Application*, Global Business Press, New Delhi, 1992.

Gilder, George, *The Spirit of Enterprise*, Viking Publishers, London, 1985.

Gupta, M.C., *Entrepreneurship in Small Sector Industries*, Anmol Publications, New Delhi, 1987.

Gupta, K., *Industrial Entrepreneurship*, Printwell Publication, Jaipur, 1992.

Hakim, C., *Occupational Segregation*, Department of Employment, Research Paper No. 9, London, 1979.

Harbison, F. and Myers, Charles A., *Education, Manpower and Economic Growth: Strategies of Human Resources Development*, New York, McGraw Hill Service in International Development.

Harper, Malcolm, *Entrepreneurship for the Poor*, Intermediate Technology Publications, London, 1984.

Jain, Gautam Raj and Ansari, M. Akbar, *Self-made Impact Making Entrepreneurs*, Entrepreneurship Development Institute of India, Ahmedabad, 1988 .

Kilby, Peter (Ed.), *Entrepreneurship and Economic Development*, The Free Press, New York, 1971.

Kumar, S. Ashok, *Entrepreneurship in Small Industry*, Discovery Publishing House, New Delhi, 1990.

Lasser, J.K., *How to Run a Small Business*, McGraw Hill Book Co., New York, 1963.

Martin, J. and Roberts, C., *Women and Employment: A Life Time Perspective*, Report of the 1980 DE/OPCS Women and Employment Survey, HMSO, London, 1984.

McClelland, D.C., *The Achieving Society*, Princeton, New Jersey, D. Van Nostrand Co., 1961.

McClelland, D.C., et. al., *Motivating Economic Achievement*, The Free Press, New York, 1969.

Mehan, K.K., *Small Industry Entrepreneurs Handbook*, Productivity Services International, Bombay, 1973.

Meredith, Geoffrey G., Nelson, Robert E. and Neck, Philip A., *The Practice of Entrepreneurship*, International Labour Office, Geneva, 1982, p. 3.

Naisbutt, John, *The Future of Franchising: Looking 25 years ahead to the year 2010*, Washington, D.C., International Franchise Association, 1985.

Patel, V.G., *Women Entrepreneurship Development*, National Convention of Women Entrepreneurs, under the Aegis of Women's Wing of NAYE, Gujarat Chapter, Ahmedabad, February 6-8, 1986.

Patel, V.G., *Entrepreneurship Development Programmes in India and its Relevance to Developing Countries*, Entrepreneurship Development Institute of India, Ahmedabad, 1987.

Pathak, H.N, et. al., *Management of New and Small Enterprises*, IGNOU, New Delhi, 1991.

Paul, Burns and Jim, Dewhurst, *Small Business and Entrepreneurship*, Macmillan Education Ltd., London, 1990.

Rao, J.V. Prabhakara, *Entrepreneurship and Economic Development*, Kanishka Publishers, New Delhi, 2000.

Rao, P. Subba, *Entrepreneurial Challenges*, EDP Series, Kanishka, New Delhi, 1993.

Rao, T.V. and Pareek, Udai, *Developing Entrepreneurship: A Handbook*, New Delhi learning systems, 1978.

Rathore, B.S. and Saini, J.S., *A Handbook of Entrepreneurship*, Aapga Publishers, Panchkula, 1997.

Rathore, B.S. and Dhameja, S.K., *Entrepreneurship in the 21st Century*, Rawat Publications, Jaipur, 1999.

Saini, J.S., *Entrepreneurship Development*, Deep & Deep Publications, New Delhi, 1996.

Saini, J.S. and Dhameja, S.K. (Eds.), *Entrepreneurship and Small Business*, Rawat Publications, Jaipur, 1998.

Saini, J.S., Gurjar, B.R. and Rathore, B.S., *Facilities and Incentives to Entrepreneurs*, TITI, Chandigarh, 1998.

Schumpeter, J.A., *The Theory of Economic Development*, Cambridge, Massachusetts, Harvard University Press, 1949.

Sen, Amartya, *Gender and Co-operative Conflicts*, WIDER Working Paper No. 18, 1987.

Singh, Nagendra P., *Role of Financial Institutions in Entrepreneurship and Development*, Development Banking Centre, New Delhi, 1982.

Srivastava, S.B., *A Practical Guide to Industrial Entrepreneur*, Sultan Chand and Sons, New Delhi, 1981.

Stevenson, L., *An Investigation of the Entrepreneurship Experience of Women: Implications for Small Business Policy in Canada*, Acadia University, Wofville, Nova Scotia, November, 1983.

Stoner, James A.F., Freeman, R. Edward and Gilbert Jr., Daniel, R., *Management*, Prentice Hall of India Pvt. Ltd., New Delhi, 1996.

Srivastava, Vatsala, *Social and Economic Dimensions of Indian Population*, Serials Publications, New Delhi, 2003.

Narasimhan, Sakuntala, *Empowering Women: An Alternative Strategy for Rural India*, Sage Publications, New Delhi, 2001.

Murthy, Ranjani K., *Building Women's Capacity*, Sage Publication, New Delhi, 2001.

Singh, Sheobahal, *Entrepreneurship and Social Change*, Rawat Publications, Jaipur, 1985.

Saini, Jasmer Singh, *Entrepreneurship Development: Programmes and Practices*, Deep & Deep Publication Pvt. Ltd., New Delhi, 2003.

Uddan, Soni, *Entrepreneurship Development in India*, Mittal Publications, New Delhi, 1999.

John, *et. al.*, *Emerging Entrepreneurship*, Discovery Publishing House, New Delhi, 2004.

Arya, Sadhna, *Women Gender Equality and the State*, Deep & Deep Publications Pvt. Ltd., New Delhi, 2000.

Bakshi, S.R. and Balakiran, *Welfare and Development of Women*, Deep & Deep Publications Pvt. Ltd., New Delhi, 2000.

Chauhan, Poonam S., *Lengthening Shadows: Status of Women in India*, Manak Publications (P) Ltd., New Delhi, 1996.

Rai, Rita, *Gender Dimensions in Banking*, Manak Publications Pvt. Ltd., New Delhi, 2004.

Jharta, Bhawana, *Women and Policies in India*, Deep & Deep Publications Pvt. Ltd., New Delhi, 1998.

Bhuimali, Anil, *Education, Employment and Empowering Women*, Serials Publications, New Delhi, 2004.

John *et. al.*, *Rural Entrepreneurship*, Discovery Publishing House, New Delhi, 2004.

Sengupta, R. and Sinha, A.K., *Challenges of Sustainable Development*, Manak Publications Pvt. Ltd., New Delhi, 2003.

Wadhwa *et. al.*, *Entrepreneur and Enterprise Management*, Kanishka Publishers Distributors, New Delhi, 1998.

Bakshi, S.R. and Balakiran, *Social Status and Role of Women*, Deep & Deep Publication Pvt. Ltd., New Delhi, 2000.

Thakur, D. and Thakur, D.N., *Tribal Women*, Deep & Deep Publication Pvt. Ltd., New Delhi, 1996.

Soundarapandian, M., *Women Entrepreneurship: Issues and Strategies*, Kanishka Publishers and Distributors, New Delhi, 1999.

Patrick, Martin, *Self-employment and Successful Entrepreneurship*, Kanishka Publishers and Distributors, New Delhi, 1999.

Kulshrestha, Kalyani, *Successful Entrepreneurship*, Kanishka Publishers and Distributors, New Delhi, 1999.

Vinze, M.D., *Women Entrepreneurs in India*, Mittal Publications, New Delhi, 1987.

Prasad Janardan and Kanishk V.K., *Women Education and Development*, Kanishka Publishers and Distributors, New Delhi, 1995.

Niranjana, *Status of Women and Family Welfare*, Kanishka Publishers and Distributors, New Delhi, 2000.

Verma, S.B. and Singla, V.K., *Business Interest and Social Contribution of Entrepreneurs Organisations*, RBSA Publishers, Jaipur, 2004.

Dollinger, M.J., *Entrepreneurship Strategies and Resources*, Pearson Education Pvt. Ltd., Patparganj, Delhi, 2003.

Holt, D.H., *Entrepreneurship New Venture Creation*, Prentice Hall of India Private Limited, New Delhi, 2002.

Batra, G.S., *Development of Entrepreneurship*, Deep & Deep Publications Pvt. Ltd., New Delhi, 2002.

Hisrich, R.D. and Peters, M.P., *Entrepreneurship*, Tata McGraw-Hill Publishing Company Ltd., New Delhi, 2002.

Soundarapandian, M., *Rural Entrepreneurship: Growth and Potentials*, Kanishka Publishers and Distributors, New Delhi, 2001.

Rao, J.V.P., *Entrepreneurship and Economic Development*, Kanishka Publishers and Distributors, New Delhi, 2000.

Saini, J.S. and Gurjar, B.R., *Entrepreneurship and Education: Challenges and Strategies*, Rawat Publications, New Delhi, 2001.

Batra, G.S. and Dangwal, R.C., *Entrepreneurship and Small Scale Industries*, Deep & Deep Publications Pvt. Ltd., New Delhi, 2003.

Rathore, B.S. and Dhamija, S.K., *Entrepreneurship in the 21st Century*, Rawat Publications, New Delhi, 1999.

Narasaiah, M.L., *Small Scale Entrepreneurship*, Discovery Publishing House, New Delhi, 2001.

Bhatia, B.S. and Batra, G.S., *Entrepreneurship and Small Business Management*, Deep & Deep Publications, New Delhi, 2003.

Subbarao, P.S., *Entrepreneurship and Small Business Management*, Discovery Publishing House, New Delhi, 2001.

Sharma, D.D. and Dhamija, S.K., *Green Entrepreneurship*, Abhishek Publications, Chandigarh, 2005.

Journals and Reports

Azad, G.S., Development of Entrepreneurship Among Rural Women—An Overview, *Sedme Journal*, Vol. 15, No. 2, 1988, pp. 41-50.

Beegam, S. Resia and Sarngadharan M., Female Entrepreneurship in Kerala, *Yojana*, Vol. 38, 1994, pp. 29-30.

Bliss, R.T. and Garratt N.L. (2001), Supporting Women Entrepreneurs in Transitioning Economies, *Journal of Small Business Management*, Vol. 39 (4), pp. 336-44.

Breen *et. al.*, Female Entrepreneurs in Australia: An Investigation of Financial and Family Issues, *Journal of Enterprising Culture*, Vol. 3, No. 4, 1995, pp. 445-61.

Caputo R.K. and Dolinsky, Arthur (1998), Women's Choice of Pursue Self-Employment: The Role of Financial and Human Capital of Household Members, *Journal of Small Business Management*, Vol. 36 (2), pp. 8-18.

Carter, S. and Cannon, T., *Women as Entrepreneurs: A Study of Female Business Owners: Their Motivations, Experience and Strategies for Success*, Academic Press, 1991.

Casson, Mark, The Entrepreneur: An Economic Theory, *Martin Robertson*, Oxford, 1982, p. 23.

Choudary, K.V.R., Successful Characteristics of Rural Entrepreneurship, *Sedme Journal*, Vol. 7, No. 2, 1980, pp. 89-103.

Cunningham, J., Barton and Lischerssen, Joe, Defining Entrepreneurship, *The Journal of Small Business Management*, Vol. 29, No. 1, Jan. 1991, p. 49.

Dutta, Umin, Women Entrepreneurs in Assam, Problems and The Role of Promoting Organizations, *Indian Journal of Commerce*, Vol. 1, No. 193, 1997, pp. 225-28.

Government of India (2001-02), Third All Indian Census of SSI, DC(SSI), Ministry of SSI, New Delhi

Kamble, H.Y., A Study of the Socio-Economic Back-Ground of Women Entrepreneurs of Belgaum Taluka, *Indian Journal of Commerce*, Vol. 1, No. 193, 1997, pp. 229-42.

Kilby, Peter, Entrepreneurship and Economic Development, *The Free Press*, New York, 1971.

Klein, Uta, Returning to Work: A Challenge for Women, *World of Work*, ILO, No. 12, May/June 1995.

Kolvereid, Lars *et. al.*, Is it Equally Difficult for Female

Entrepreneurs to Start Business in All Countries? *Journal of Small Business Management*, October 1993.

Kumar, Anil, Obstacles Faced by Women in Business: A Factor Analytical Study, *Asian Economic Review*, Vol. 47 (3), Hyderabad, Dec. 2005, pp. 457-64.

——, Enterprise Location: Choice of Women entrepreneurs, *Sedme Journal*, Vol. 33, No. 3, Sept. 2004, Hyderabad, pp. 11-20.

——, Marketing Practices used by Women Entrepreneurs, *Indian Development Review*, Vol. 3, No. 1, Dec. 2004, pp. 113-25.

——, Women Entrepreneurs: An Investigation of Factors Affecting Business Choice, *Indian Development Review*, Vol. 3, No. 1, pp. 113-25, June 2005, New Delhi.

——, Women Entrepreneurs: Their Perception Towards Various Support Agencies, *Indian Management Studies Journal*, Vol. 9, No. 2, Oct. 2005, pp. 149-62, Vishakhapatnam.

——, Women Entrepreneurs: Their Profile and Factors Compelling Business Choice, *GITAM Journal of Management*, Vol. 3, No. 2, July-Dec. 2005, pp. 134-44, Vishakhapatnam.

——, Women Entrepreneurs in Northern India: An Investigation of Labour Related Problems, *Journal of Social and Economic Policy*, Vol. 3, No. 1, June 2006, New Delhi, pp. 135-46.

——, Women Entrepreneurs: Perception Towards Family Issues, *Indian Journal of Development Research and Social Action*, Vol. 1, No. 2, December 2005, New Delhi, pp. 165-77.

——, Women Entrepreneurs: Their Profile and Barriers in Business, *Indian Journal of Social Development*, Vol. 4, No. 2, Dec. 2004, pp. 297-311.

Mambula, Perceptions of SME Growth Constraints in Nigeria, *Journal of Small Business Management*, Vol. 40, No. 1, 2002, pp. 58-65.

Masters, R. and Meier, R. (1988), Sex Differences and Risk-taking Propensity of Entrepreneurs, *Journal of Small Business Management*, Vol. 26 (1), pp. 31-36.

Meredath *et. al.*, *The Practice of Entrepreneurship*, International Labour Office, Geneva, 1982, p. 3.

Mohanty, K. Malay and Patnaik, K. Sushil, Women Entrepreneurs in Orissa: A Case Study of Dhenkanal District, *Indian Journal of Commerce*, Vol. 1, No. 193, 1997, pp. 276-85.

Nair, Tara S., Entrepreneurship Training for Women in the Indian

Rural Sector: A Re iew of Approaches and Strategies, *The Journal of Entrepreneurship*, 5, 1996, p. 1.

Naisbutt, John, *The Future of Franchising: Looking 25 Years Ahead to the Year 2010*, Washington D.C., International Franchise Association, 1985.

National Foundation for Women Business Owners (NFWBO, 2001). Entrepreneurial Vision in Action: Exploring Growth Among Women and Men-owned Firms, Washington DC.

Natrajan, K. and Thenmozhy, A., Entrepreneurial Development Programme for Women—A Case Study, *Yojana*, Vol. 35 (8), May 15, 1991, pp. 6-8.

Nelson, Blossom O' Meally, Small Business Opportunities for Women in Jamaica, *Sedme Jounral*, 1991.

Poojary, M.C., Entrepreneurship: Push or Pull Effect, *Sedme Journal*, Vol. 24, No. 3, 1997, pp. 11-18.

Prasad, A.G. and Rao, T. Venkateswara, Socio-Economic Background of Women Entrepreneurs—A Case Study of Andhra Pradesh, *Indian Journal of Commerce*, Vol. 1, No. 193, 1997, pp. 261-69.

Prasiñ, G.P. and Devi Sancharita R.K., Women Traders in Manipur: A Case Study, *Indian Journal of Commerce*, Vol. 1, No. 193, 1997, pp. 213-17.

Punitha. M. Sangeetha, S. Padmavathi, Women Entrepreneurs: Their Problems and Constraints. *Indian Journal of Labour Economics*, Vol. 42, No. 4, Oct.-Dec., 1999, pp. 701-06.

Rani, S. Swarupa, Potential Women Entrepreneurs—A Study, *SEDME Journal*, Vol. 13, No. 3, 1986, pp. 13-22.

Rao, C., Harinarayana, Promotion of Women Entrepreneurs, *SEDME Journal*, Vol 18, No. 2, 1991, pp. 21-28.

Rathore, B.S. and Chabbra, Rama, Promotion of Women Entrepreneurship—Training Strategies, *SEDME Journal*, Vol. 18, No. 1, 1991.

Saxena, Deepti and Tripathi, Hema, Entrepreneurship Among Milk Producers in Women Dairy Cooperative Societies, *Productivity*, Vol. 38, No. 4, 1999, pp. 582-90.

Shigeko Mitusuhasi, Access to markets. OECD Conference on Women Entrepreneurs in SMEs 2000: A major force in innovation and job creation. Synthesis, OECD 29 November-1 December, Paris, France, 2000.

Srivastava, A.K. and Chaudhary, Sanjay, *Women Entrepreneurs:*

Problems, Perspective and Role Expectations from Banks, Punjab University, Chandigarh, 1991.

Stoner *et. al.* (1990). Work-Home Role Conflict in Female Owners of Small Businesses: An Exploratory Study, *Journal of Small Business Management,* Vol. 28 (1), pp. 30-38.

Sugumar, M., Entrepreneurial Competence Among Small Entrepreneurs, *Sedme Journal,* Vol. 23, No. 4, 1996, pp. 1-11.

Suri and Sarupria, Psychological Factors Affecting Women Entrepreneurs—Some Findings, *The Indian Journal of Social Work,* Vol. 44, No. 3, 1983, pp. 287-95.

Taylor and Brooksbank, Marketing Practices Among Small New Zealand Organizations, *Journal of Enterprising Culture,* Vol. 3, No. 2, 1995, pp. 149-60.

Thomas, M.E. and Khan, M.Z., Women and Development in Wayanad, *Social Change,* Vol. 20, No. 2, 1990, pp. 26-34.

Watson, J. (2003). Failure Rates for Female-Controlled Businesses: Are They Any Different? *Journal of Small Business Management,* Vol. 41 (3), pp. 262-77.

Workshop proceedings, 2000. Second OECD Conference on Women Entrepreneurs in SMEs: A major force in innovation and job relation, Synthesis, OECD, 29 November-1 December, Paris, France.

Index